Literary Modernism Series
Thomas F. Staley, Editor

Stoppard's Theatre

Stoppard's

Finding
Order
amid
Chaos

University of
Texas Press,
Austin

Theatre

by John Fleming

Requests for permission to reproduce material from this work
should be sent to Permissions, University of Texas Press, P.O.
Box 7819, Austin, TX 78713-7819.

∞ The paper used in this book meets the minimum requirements of ANSI/NISO Z39.48-1992 (R1997) (Permanence of Paper).

Library of Congress Cataloging-in-Publication Data

Fleming, John (John Patrick), 1965–
    Stoppard's theatre : finding order amid chaos / by John
Fleming. — 1st ed.
        p.   cm. — (Literary modernism series)
    Includes bibliographical references and index.
    ISBN 0-292-72533-7 (alk. paper)
    1. Stoppard, Tom—Criticism and interpretation.   I. Title.
II. Series.

PR6069.T6 Z648   2001
822'.914—dc21   2001027788

To my family,
with love and gratitude

CONTENTS

ACKNOWLEDGMENTS

Quotations from the published plays of Tom Stoppard are reprinted with the permission of Faber and Faber, Grove Press, and Samuel French. Quotations from unpublished material from the University of Texas's Harry Ransom Humanities Research Center are reprinted with the kind permission of Tom Stoppard. An earlier version of chapter 1 appeared in *The Library Chronicle,* published by the Harry Ransom Humanities Research Center. Excerpts from my interview with Stoppard previously appeared in *Theatre Insight.*

For support in writing this book I am grateful to my colleagues at Auburn University and Southwest Texas State University, as well as my mentors at the University of Texas. Oscar Brockett, John Brokaw, Charlotte Canning, David Mark Cohen, and Elizabeth Richmond-Garza read and critiqued an earlier draft of this manuscript. The University of Texas at Austin provided a travel grant for much of the London-based research. An Auburn travel grant aided work on the *Invention of Love* chapter. Michael Vanden Heuvel offered insights that greatly improved the *Arcadia* chapter. Besides Oscar Brockett, the other scholar to whom I am greatly indebted, is Paul Delaney. His two books (*Tom Stoppard: The Moral Vision of the Major Plays* and *Tom Stoppard in Conversation*) were invaluable guides, providing source material as well as issues and ideas to consider. More significantly, in the sometimes cutthroat world of academe, Paul was generous enough to share his research, pointing me to hard-to-find sources and providing the actual documents when I could not locate them myself.

For all their hard work, organization, promptness, and camaraderie I extend my thanks to Pat Fox, Katherine Mosley, Kathy Henderson, and the rest of the staff at the Harry Ransom Humanities Research Center. On the editorial side, I am grateful to Tom Staley, Jim Burr, Leslie Tingle, and Bob Fullilove for their careful attention to detail in the refining of the text. I also appreciate the efforts of Nancy Bryan, Heidi Haeuser, and everyone else at the University of Texas Press who were involved in the production of this book.

Friends and family were also instrumental to this project. Mark Litton offered critical feedback that sharpened chapter 12. Besides offering enthusiastic support, my brother Mark was an invaluable research assistant, gathering the newspaper clippings used in that chapter. Likewise, my brother Paul was always quick to provide a translation when I needed it. My mom and dad, along with my brothers and sisters and their families, have provided years of encouragement and support. More recently, Julie Jalil has enriched my life and helped show me "the real thing." My deep appreciation to all of you.

ANNOTATED CHRONOLOGY
OF STOPPARD'S CAREER

1960   Writes *A Walk on the Water* (revised as *Enter a Free Man*).

1961–62   Writes *The Gamblers*. Writes *The Stand-Ins* (a.k.a. *The Critics*, later
          revised as *The Real Inspector Hound*).

1963   *A Walk on the Water* televised. Writes *I Can't Give You Anything
          but Love, Baby* (unproduced television play). Writes *Funny Man*
          (unproduced television play).

1964   The 15-minute plays *The Dissolution of Dominic Boot* and *"M" is
          for Moon Among Other Things* air on radio. Faber and Faber pub-
          lishes three short stories ("Reunion," "Life, Times: Fragments,"
          and "The Story"). Writes five trial episodes of the BBC radio serial
          The Dales. Writes *This Way Out with Samuel Boot* (unproduced
          television play). While on a Ford Foundation grant in Berlin,
          writes *Rosencrantz and Guildenstern Meet King Lear* (one-act play,
          later revised and expanded into *Rosencrantz and Guildenstern Are
          Dead*). *A Walk on the Water* staged in Hamburg.

1965   *The Gamblers* (two-act version) and the curtain raiser *Higg and
          Cogg* staged at Bristol University. Writes *How Sir Dudley Lost the
          Empire* (unproduced television play). *A Paragraph for Mr. Blake*
          (adaptation of "The Story") airs on television.

1966   Writes about 70 episodes of radio drama *A Student's Diary: An Arab in London*. *If You're Glad I'll Be Frank* airs on radio. Revises script of Nicholas Bethell's translation of Slawomir Mrozek's *Tango* for Royal Shakespeare Company. *A Separate Peace* and a corresponding documentary, *Pursuit of Happiness* (cowritten with Christopher Martin), televised. *Rosencrantz and Guildenstern Are Dead* staged at the Edinburgh Festival Fringe. *Lord Malquist and Mr. Moon,* a novel, published. Cowrites, with Gordon M. Williams, the pilot for a radio serial *Doctor Masopust, I Presume* (probably unproduced).

1967   *Teeth* and *Another Moon Called Earth* televised. *Albert's Bridge* airs on radio and wins Prix Italia Award. London and New York premieres of *Rosencrantz and Guildenstern Are Dead*. *Rosencrantz* is the first National Theatre production to transfer to New York. In New York, *Rosencrantz* wins Tony Award and the Drama Critics' Circle Award for Best Play; in London, Stoppard wins (jointly with Wole Soyinka) the John Whiting Award (from the Arts Council of Great Britain), *Plays and Players* Best Play Award, and (jointly with David Storey) the *Evening Standard* Award for Most Promising Playwright.

1968   London premieres of *Enter a Free Man* and *The Real Inspector Hound*. *Neutral Ground* televised. Writes unproduced screenplays of *Rosencrantz* and *Lord Malquist and Mr. Moon*.

1969   First stage productions of *Albert's Bridge* and *If You're Glad I'll Be Frank*. Cowrites, with Anthony Smith, a screenplay of *Albert's Bridge* (unproduced).

1970   London premiere of *After Magritte*. *Where Are They Now?* airs on radio. *The Engagement* (45-minute film expanded from *Dominic Boot* radio play) on American TV and in British cinemas. In 1970 or 1971 writes *Galileo* (unproduced screenplay).

1971   London premiere of *Dogg's Our Pet*.

1972   London premiere of *Jumpers,* which wins Best Play Award from both *Evening Standard* and *Plays and Players*. First New York productions of *The Real Inspector Hound* and *After Magritte*. *Artist Descending a Staircase* airs on radio. Subject of BBC TV series *One Pair of Eyes;* his episode is entitled "Tom Stoppard Doesn't

Know." In 1972 or 1973 turns his unproduced *Galileo* screenplay into a stage play intended for production at the London Planetarium; production never materializes.

1973   Translation of Federico Garcia Lorca's *The House of Bernarda Alba* produced. Directs Lynn Redgrave in Garson Kanin's *Born Yesterday*.

1974   London premiere of *Travesties,* which wins *Evening Standard* Best Comedy Award. First New York productions of *Jumpers* and *Enter a Free Man*. During the end of 1974 and the beginning of 1975 writes the unproduced screenplay *Naked without a Gun,* a free adaptation of David Hare's *Knuckle*.

1975   Cowrites, with Clive Exton, half-hour TV play *The Boundary*. Writes TV film of Jerome K. Jerome's novel *Three Men in a Boat*. Cowrites, with Thomas Wiseman, a screenplay of Wiseman's novel *The Romantic Englishwoman*. First New York production of *Travesties,* which wins Tony Award and Drama Critics' Circle Award.

1976   London premiere of *Dirty Linen* and its interrelated play *New-Found-Land*. *Dirty Linen* becomes the first lunchtime play to transfer to the West End and runs for over four years and more than one thousand performances. To help inaugurate their new building, the National Theatre returns *Jumpers* to their repertoire. *The (15-Minute) Dogg's Troupe Hamlet* (written in 1972) performed on the terraces of the National Theatre. Writes teleplay of *The Frog Prince;* citing artistic differences, removes his name. Writes, with Willis Hall, Jack Rosenthal, and Keith Waterhouse, *Michael the First* (unproduced screenplay, based on stories by John Collier).

1977   As part of the Queen's Silver Jubilee, the London premiere of *Every Good Boy Deserves Favor,* one performance with the London Symphony Orchestra. *Professional Foul* televised; wins the British Television Critics' Award for Best Play of 1977. First New York staging of *Dirty Linen*. First stage production of radio play *"M" is for Moon Among Other Things*.

1978   *Every Good Boy* revived in London with a chamber orchestra and given first American production in Washington, D.C. London premiere of *Night and Day,* which wins *Evening Standard* Best Play Award. Writes screenplay of Vladimir Nabokov's novel *Despair.*

1979   London premieres of *Undiscovered Country,* an adaptation of Arthur Schnitzler's *Das Weite Land* (1911), and *Dogg's Hamlet, Cahoot's Macbeth.* Has four plays running simultaneously on the West End. First New York productions of *Every Good Boy Deserves Favor* and *Night and Day.* Awarded the Shakespeare Prize (Hamburg).

1980   Writes screenplay of Graham Greene's novel *The Human Factor.* Writes screenplay for *Night and Day* (unproduced).

1981   Writes screenplay of P. D. James's novel *Innocent Blood* (unproduced). London premiere of *On the Razzle,* an adaptation of Johann Nestroy's *Einen Jux will er sich machen* (1842).

1982   London premiere of *The Real Thing,* which wins *Evening Standard* and *Plays and Players* (with Pinter's *A Kind of Alaska*) Best Play Awards. *The Dog It Was That Died* airs on radio

1983   *The Love for Three Oranges* (translation of libretto for Prokofiev's 1921 opera) performed.

1984   First New York production of *The Real Thing,* which wins New York Drama Critics' Circle, Drama Desk, Outer Circle, and Tony Award for Best Play. *Squaring the Circle,* an innovative pseudo-documentary about Poland's Solidarity, televised. British version of *Squaring* wins the Gold Award for Drama at the International Film and Television Festival. London premiere of *Rough Crossing,* an adaptation of Ferenc Molnar's *Play at the Castle* (1924); later rewrites it for the Chester Gateway Theatre. That text is unpublished.

1985   Cowrites, with Terry Gilliam and Charles McKeown, screenplay for *Brazil,* which is nominated for an Academy Award. Revises *Jumpers* for West End revival. Directs *The Real Inspector Hound* at the National Theatre.

1986   London premiere of *Dalliance,* an adaptation of Arthur Schnitzler's *Liebelei* (1895). Translates Václav Havel's *Largo Desolato* (1985) for the Bristol Old Vic.

1987   Writes screenplay of J.G. Ballard's novel *Empire of the Sun.*

1988   London premiere of *Hapgood*. Writes screenplay of Laurens van der Post's novel *A Far-Off Place* (unproduced). First stage production of *Artist Descending a Staircase*.

1989   Revises *Hapgood* for first American production in Los Angeles. First New York production of *Artist Descending*. Televised version of *The Dog It Was That Died*. Does uncredited work on *Indiana Jones and the Last Crusade* and *Always* screenplays.

1990   Writes and directs film of *Rosencrantz and Guildenstern Are Dead*, which wins the Golden Lion at the Venice Film Festival. Writes screenplay of John Le Carré's novel *The Russia House*.

1991   *In the Native State* airs on radio; wins the Giles Cooper Award. Writes screenplay of E. L. Doctorow's novel *Billy Bathgate*. Does uncredited work on *Chaplin* screenplay.

1992   Writes screenplay, from the original screenplay by Marc Norman, for *Shakespeare in Love* (production canceled in Oct.). Writes screenplay of Raymond Chandler and Robert Parker's novel *Poodle Springs* (released in 1998). Broadway revival of *The Real Inspector Hound*.

1993   London premiere of *Arcadia*. Royal Shakespeare Company revives *Travesties*. Becomes the first living playwright to have simultaneous productions at the National Theatre and the RSC. Both plays transfer to the West End in 1994. *Arcadia* wins *Evening Standard* and Olivier Best Play Award. Writes new narration for Franz Lehár's opera *The Merry Widow*. Writes screenplay of Nicholas Moseley's novel *Hopeful Monsters* (unproduced).

1994   First New York production of *Hapgood*. Writes screenplay for animated film of Andrew Lloyd Webber's musical *Cats* (forthcoming).

1995   London premiere of *Indian Ink*. First New York production of *Arcadia*, which wins Drama Critics' Circle Award and is nominated for a Tony Award. While *Arcadia* is in previews, Stoppard becomes the first playwright to have plays running simultaneously on Lincoln Center's two stages. National Theatre revival of *Rosencrantz*.

1996   Writes screenplay of *Hapgood* (unproduced).

1997   London premiere of Stoppard's new version of Anton Chekhov's *The Seagull.* Radio play of *Three Men in a Boat* airs. Writes screenplay of Robert Harris's novel *Enigma* (forthcoming). London premiere of *The Invention of Love,* which wins *Evening Standard* Best Play Award. Knighthood is conferred upon Stoppard.

1998   *Shakespeare in Love* released. Wins, with Marc Norman, Golden Globe, Writers Guild of America, and Academy Award for Best Original Screenplay. *Arcadia* becomes the first work by a living foreign playwright to be done on the mainstage of the Comédie Française.

1999   Does uncredited work on *Sleepy Hollow* screenplay. In San Francisco, the American premiere of *Indian Ink.*

2000   Broadway revival of *The Real Thing* wins three Tony Awards. In San Francisco, the American premiere of *The Invention of Love.* Writes the English version screenplay of Jeanne Labrune's French script, *Vatel.* Queen Elizabeth II awards Stoppard the Order of Merit, the highest personal honor bestowed by the Queen.

2001   *Enigma* released. New York premier of *The Invention of Love.*

Stoppard's Theatre

Introduction

In 1977, ten years after Tom Stoppard's breakthrough success with *Rosencrantz and Guildenstern Are Dead,* Kenneth Tynan, prominent critic and longtime Literary Manager for England's National Theatre, asserted that in terms of international prestige, the standard of British playwriting was held by Harold Pinter, Peter Shaffer, and Stoppard (46).[1] Since that assessment Pinter has done limited writing for the stage, while Shaffer's post-1980 work has received a mixed reaction. In contrast, Stoppard has consistently continued to garner both critical acclaim and commercial success. Of his nine major plays—*Rosencrantz and Guildenstern Are Dead* (1967), *Jumpers* (1972), *Travesties* (1974), *Night and Day* (1978), *The Real Thing* (1982), *Hapgood* (1988), *Arcadia* (1993), *Indian Ink* (1995), and *The Invention of Love* (1997)—only *Hapgood* and *Indian Ink* have failed to win one of London's Best New Play Awards. Beyond their status as award-winners these plays merit study and production by virtue of their intelligence, theatricality, and linguistic mastery.

Stoppard's plays cover an eclectic array of themes and topics. From the world of science, he has tapped into the metaphoric potential of quantum physics and chaos theory. From philosophy, he has dramatized logical positivism, Wittgenstein's language games, and debates over whether morality is relative and socially constructed or grounded in metaphysical absolutes.

Questions about the social responsibilities of the artist, journalist, and politician appear in plays that examine the role and nature of art, the relative merits of a free press, and the injustices and human rights violations of pre-perestroika Eastern Bloc politics. He has explored the nature of love and the requirements of intimate human relationships. He has considered the effects of colonialism as seen through a conflict of cultures and aesthetics. Interwoven through many of these plays are the recurrent issues of the nature of personal identity as well as the unreliability or variability of human memory and perspective. Cumulatively, Stoppard's work has been concerned with the social, moral, metaphysical, and personal condition of being human in an uncertain world.

While comedy is always a central feature, Stoppard has consciously explored different narrative techniques. He once remarked that ultimately he would like "to have done a bit of absolutely everything" (Watts, "Tom Stoppard," 47). Indeed, eclecticism is one of the hallmarks of Stoppard's canon, and it is a trait that makes his work appear fresh, vital, and enduring. While he has treated a diversity of subjects, a constant in Stoppard's work has been his preoccupation with aesthetics, with the formal properties of play construction, and above all with style. For Stoppard, a writer's only obligation is "to write well" (Freedman), and plays are "good" or "important" if the writing is "of a very high order" and not because of its social content (Hudson, Itzin, and Trussler 68). While Stoppard champions style, it is not, as Thomas Whitaker asserts, an end in itself. Stoppard's stylistic bravura and theatricality are always yoked to, and in service of, some more substantial ideas, ideas often antithetical to Whitaker's interpretations.

Stoppard sometimes gets labeled a postmodernist, but to my mind, he is more accurately seen as continuing and extending high modernism's experimentation with aesthetic expression.[2] Like modernist writers he admires (e.g., Joyce, Eliot, and Wilde), Stoppard downplays the social function of art, rarely writing works that directly engage the social-historical moment. Instead he rigorously pursues aesthetic effect and innovation. Furthermore, the ideology that informs his work is decidedly conventional: Stoppard firmly believes in the values associated with Western, liberal humanism. In *Theory of the Avant-Garde* Peter Bürger argues that modernism's noninstrumental aestheticism makes modern art the institutional collaborator of modern bourgeois ideology. Indeed, Stoppard lives the life of the bourgeois intellectual, and his work revolves around the values, views, and ideology of that lifestyle. While Stoppard is indebted to the art that has gone before him, his artistry is not linked to any one particular school of playwriting, but instead Stoppard embodies the Romantic notion of the artistic genius; his artistic vision has followed a determined course of individualism. This idea of the artistic genius who cannot be neatly explained by the sociopolitical context of the historical moment may be at odds with contemporary literary theory, yet it seems to me the most accurate way to assess Stoppard's work. That said, each play will be considered in light of the personal, historical moment of Stoppard's life and career.

One of the most debated aspects of Stoppard's canon concerns the interpretation of *Rosencrantz and Guildenstern Are Dead* (henceforth *Rosguil*), *Jumpers,* and *Travesties.*[3] Some scholars read these plays as exhibiting the relativist values of absurdism, existentialism, and structure for structure's sake. In contrast, more traditional scholars dispute these readings as being blind to the internal evidence that upholds Stoppard's own professed support of "Western liberal democracy, favoring an intellectual elite and a progressive middle class and based on a moral order derived from Christian absolutes" ("But for the Middle Classes"). These scholars argue that beneath the originality of Stoppard's dramatic structures fairly traditional dramaturgy is not only at work but in service of the ideas articulated in the play's dialogue. In contrast, the postmodern and poststructuralist critics elevate form to the level of content and meaning as they valorize form in and of itself, thereby deprivileging the dialogue as they argue that Stoppard's plays accent the unknowability of the world, the elusiveness of true knowledge, the fallibility of human memory, and the relativity of almost all aspects of life. My own interpretations draw on both sets of scholars. Plays do not possess one clear meaning, but rather are open to a multitude of responses, albeit some interpretations may be considered more valid than others. Thus, at times both the traditional and the postmodern critics are accurate, but on particular points I argue that there are reasons for favoring one or the other and sometimes these seemingly polar readings can be mutually valid in a both/and paradigm. Kenneth Tynan suggests the paradoxical nature of Stoppard and his work when he speculates that Stoppard believes in "a universe in which everything is relative, yet in which moral absolutes exist" (56). Indeed, in the chapter on *Professional Foul* I use Robert Kane's philosophy to elucidate how I believe Stoppard melds relative and absolute perspectives into a consistent worldview. This both/and paradigm permeates much of Stoppard's canon and will be most clearly seen in the discussion of deterministic chaos and *Arcadia,* the play that weds the pre- and post-*Travesties* Stoppard.

When Stoppard writes a play he assumes an audience similar to himself. Likewise, I am writing this book assuming an audience that has an interest and affinity for Stoppard. I write from the perspective of a scholar, a teacher, an audience member (both viewing and reading), and a practitioner (a playwright and director). Coming from, and writing for, these multiple identities and perspectives requires a consideration of different types of information. Practitioners tend to be more pragmatic than theoretical, and thus there is some justification in John Stride's (the original Rosencrantz in London) statement on the relative irrelevancy of the philosophical content of *Rosguil* for an actor: "You tell me the philosophy that is expressed in the play and I'll tell you if I tried to cope with it. . . . I don't think it's much good to an actor in performing a role" (Faraone 39). On the other hand, I think that Faraone is also correct when she says: "Perhaps one of the reasons [John] Wood has become the quintessential Stoppardian actor is the incisive quality of his intelligence" (39–40). In other words, while the production team and actors need to present the more "concrete" elements of the play, an understanding of the abstract ideas that permeate Stoppard's work is information worth knowing, even if those abstractions are not directly translated to the stage. (Indeed, my brief overviews of quantum physics (for *Hapgood*) and chaos theory (for *Arcadia*) are nowhere near as in depth as the coverage that Stoppard supplied the original casts.) Likewise, the audience member experiences the play via the live presence of the actor and the mise-en-scène, the reader via the written text, and ideally they are, as Stoppard says, "moved to tears or to laughter" ("Playwrights and Professors"). They are also likely "moved to thought." Many of Stoppard's plays challenge the receiver to think, to grapple with intellectual ideas. For students, teachers, and practitioners, I hope that this work helps elucidate and illuminate these complex plays. For scholars already well versed in Stoppard's work, new insights may be found in the notes, as the nuances culled from Stoppard's papers have often been placed there. Overall, I hope that this book will provide not only some measure of explanation but also stimulation for further thought, and a desire to experience Stoppard on the stage and on the page.

While much has been written about Stoppard, this book is as much a work of theatre history as it is of literary criticism. It documents Stoppard's career, the development of individual plays, and it draws on existing scholarship so as to provide sound interpretations of the plays while also pointing the way toward alternative perspectives and further avenues of study. This book benefits from my being the first scholar to examine in depth Stoppard's personal papers, which are now housed at the University of Texas's Harry Ransom Humanities Research Center (HRHRC).

Stoppard's Theatre seeks to locate Stoppard in his plays. By emphasizing the centrality of Stoppard himself I do not mean to suggest that I am offering biographical readings of his plays or positing authorial intent as the definitive meaning. In contemporary literary theory authorial intention is often discredited, but if one repositions Stoppard as a reader of his work and views intention as simply one reading of the work rather than the definitive meaning, it can be a useful tool for opening up potential interpretations of the plays. Stoppard aptly argues: "It's always worth trying what the author had in mind, even if you decide not do it" (Watts, "Tom Stoppard," 48). Conversely, Stoppard is also wise enough to acknowledge: "There's no superior truth in my description of the play. The main trouble with the premise is that none of these thoughts is a consideration while writing a play. It's all kind of fake, and the interview makes you fake by allowing retrospective ideas to masquerade as some form of intention" (Buck 170). This work draws extensively on Stoppard's comments in his interviews and his correspondence, not so much to treat his views as "the superior truth," but rather as information that is relevant and worth knowing. On the other hand, I point out a number of moments where Stoppard's view does not seem to be the most accurate description of a given event, circumstance, attitude, or idea. Likewise, I note instances where his private correspondence contradicts his public pronouncements.

Stoppard has often described theatre as an event, not a text, meaning that his plays are designed to live and breathe on the stage and are meant to be experienced in the theatre. Likewise, Stoppard notes that for each given production there is an equation to be gotten right. However, the ephemeral nature of a stage production makes it difficult to provide a detailed analysis of the actual stagings. On the other hand, by researching prompt books and production photos and by viewing the major productions of the 1990s I have occasionally been able to add insights gained from the London and New York stagings. (Often that information appears in the notes.) While his eclectic themes are partially conveyed by dialogue and character, Stoppard, in conjunction with collaborators, often employs a controlling metaphor that illuminates the central ideas. The metaphor and ideas are theatricalized not only by the dramatic structure but also by the stage images. While I tread through the familiar ground of themes and structures, I have tried to include a theatrical, as opposed to a purely literary, perspective.

A further feature of Stoppard's theatricality is the mutability of his written texts. Stoppard views the play text as but one of many production elements, and he has sometimes altered his writing to fit a particular production consideration. This view of the text as a kinetic object has resulted in plays that have evolved over the years and through different productions. One of Stoppard's most revelatory statements comes in his author's note to the Samuel French acting edition of *Rosguil:* "There is no definitive text of *Rosencrantz and Guildenstern Are Dead.* . . . I doubt that the same text has been performed in two different places anywhere in the world. This seems to me only sensible" (3). While Stoppard is rightly hailed for his literary qualities, it is important to keep in mind that he is first and foremost a man of the theatre, an art form that is ephemeral. Thus, the theatricality of Stoppard's plays includes the fact that they are flexible objects that have been, and that can be, adapted to the individual circumstances of different productions.

The first chapter covers Stoppard's career from his decision to turn to playwriting in 1960 to the success of *Rosguil* in 1967. It provides description and analysis of nine unpublished scripts (most notably *Rosencrantz and Guildenstern Meet King Lear* and *The Gamblers*), works not previously examined by scholars. These early efforts show Stoppard's development as a writer, not only in terms of honing his style and skill, but also in thematic terms. This chapter also offers the revelations of Stoppard's correspondence with Anthony C. H. Smith, his best friend, mentor, and source of both financial and emotional support during the seven years of doubt and development. Through these letters, which Stoppard will not allow to be quoted, one gets glimpses of the private man who can be as much of a stylist in his personal writing as he is in his plays.[4] The presuccess letters hint at the mind-set and emotions, the alternations of self-doubt and self-confidence, that bubbled under the cool surface during the years of struggle and striving.

Through individual chapters, the remainder of this book emphasizes Stoppard's nine major plays (listed above). These major plays represent the times that Stoppard deliberately crafted a full-length play for the West End or for one of the subsidized, establishment theatres (Royal National Theatre and Royal Shakespeare Company).[5] A separate chapter is also devoted to *Galileo,* the only unproduced, unpublished stage work of Stoppard's post-*Rosguil* career. This previously unknown Stoppard work was intended for production at the London Planetarium, but the project was shelved, and the manuscript removed from circulation until it was delivered to the HRHRC.

One other chapter discusses two of Stoppard's plays on pre-perestroika East-ern Bloc politics (*Every Good Boy Deserves Favor* and *Professional Foul*). Due to considerations of length, fine stage comedies and radio works such as *The Real Inspector Hound, Dirty Linen, After Magritte, Albert's Bridge,* and *Artist Descending a Staircase* are only mentioned in passing. Finally, the conclusion looks at Stoppard within the context of related theatrical traditions, contem-porary British theatre, and the cyclic mode of aesthetic/thematic explora-tions that he has used to create his canon.

While there are thematic and stylistic interconnections between his plays, I do not yoke them to an overall thesis. An overarching thesis offers a certain clarity of focus, but often results in the manipulation and distortion of evidence to fit the preordained pattern. In contrast, I concur with Stop-pard's view of his canon: "I am not consciously playing this hand of cards at all. Every play seems a new start for me, and then somebody quite like you points out that there are all these cross references in them. But then that is what you would expect because there is one person there with a pen in his hand" (Fleming, "A Talk," 25). In this study I treat the plays in isolation and point to interconnections when I find them illuminating. Likewise, while there are connections between the chapters, each chapter stands on its own. Thus, I hope this book can meet the needs of those interested in individual plays as well as those seeking a fuller view of Stoppard.

The methodology in each chapter is not identical, but rather, depending on the availability of information and its relevancy, the following considera-tions may be included: point of origin or personal connection to Stoppard, explication of the central ideas addressed, evolution of the script through dif-ferent published or produced versions, and thematic analysis of the text and production. For my analysis I largely rely on "close readings" as I directly re-late my interpretation to the specific moment of text under study. For some of the cornerstones of Stoppard's canon (e.g., *Rosguil*) I have synthesized the extensive scholarship available with my own insights so as to provide a well-reasoned interpretation. For these older plays I often side with the dominant interpretation, but in the text and notes I also point toward alternative in-terpretations. In examining these plays, I foreground Stoppard's presence, as each chapter places the play in the context of the personal, historical moment of Stoppard's life and career. These chapters consider the questions: Where and how did the central ideas originate? Where does Stoppard personally stand on the issues addressed? How and why did Stoppard revise his texts?

This last question leads to one of the unique features of my coverage of Stoppard's canon, a more detailed consideration of the variant texts that exist for all his major plays.

Unlike many other studies, my approach and methodology foregrounds the fact that plays are like quantum objects in that they have a dual nature, both as events to be produced and experienced and as written texts to be read. Furthermore, the written texts exist in multiple states and the quantum jump from text to production can vary significantly depending on the particular production; thus, how one encounters the play will influence one's reaction and interpretation. Aware of this fact, my analyses of Stoppard's major plays do not treat the plays as completely stable objects. It is important to acknowledge that for many of Stoppard's plays there is no definitive text, but rather multiple variant texts. Since the reader and producer only have access to the published texts, my discussions of the plays are based on them. However, the HRHRC has prerehearsal drafts and alternate versions that have been produced but not published, and so, in the notes, I have included discussion of some of the more interesting and illuminating alterations and excisions. For example, when analyzing *Rosguil,* I have examined the 1966 Edinburgh text, 1967 National Theatre text, 1967 Broadway text, 1968 unproduced screenplay, and 1990 film, thus extending a consideration of this play into its different incarnations. Overall, I have tried to document the major distinctions between the different texts and have noted how the variances affect meaning. That information also points to the many options available to producers.

In addition to considering multiple variant texts, my discussions of Stoppard's major plays are the first to include the insights culled from his correspondence. While neither extensive nor comprehensive, the HRHRC does include exchanges with producers, directors, and translators. These letters and memos foreground Stoppard's personal views on his plays and their ideas, but I have also noted places where Stoppard's retrospective interpretation seems to be at odds with his written texts, or places where his professed statements in interviews are contradicted by his private correspondence.

The most recent single-authored, book-length study of Stoppard's work was published in 1992, but since that time his canon of major plays has been significantly transformed. Not only have *Arcadia, Indian Ink,* and *The Invention of Love* appeared, but also *Travesties* and *Hapgood* have been produced and published in substantially altered form. Thus, my discussion of Stoppard's canon is able to reexamine old texts via the fresh insights of Stoppard's personal papers while also extending the scope of the study into new texts not previously examined by scholars. By considering Stoppard's personal views and by examining his career from his earliest scripts through his most recent, I hope to provide all that is essential for understanding and appreciating the work of one of the most gifted and distinctive playwrights.

Chapter 1

Career before
Rosencrantz and
Guildenstern

WHEN THE RAVE REVIEWS CAME IN DURING THE OPENING
night party for the 1967 Broadway production of *Rosencrantz and Guildenstern Are Dead,* Tom Stoppard turned to his wife and carried out a mock interview with himself: "'Question: Mr. Stoppard, what is your play about?
Answer: It's about to make me rich'" (Hedgepeth 96).[1] Indeed, the success
of the play in many of the major theatre centers of the Western world altered
not only Stoppard's financial fortunes but also his literary reputation, as he
went from a one-time writer of propagandistic radio soap operas to being
hailed as one of the "finest English-speaking writers of our stage" (Barnes 53).
In the ensuing decades Stoppard's reputation as one of the premier playwrights of the latter half of the twentieth century has been solidified through
a string of critically and commercially successful works.

Since *Rosencrantz and Guildenstern Are Dead* (henceforth *Rosguil*) was
Stoppard's first stage play to be professionally produced in English, he is
sometimes seen as an "overnight" success story, but Stoppard's meteoric rise
to the upper echelon of the theatrical world was actually many years in the
making.

First Love: Journalism

Though Stoppard is considered one of the most intellectual of playwrights,
he never went to university, having left school at the age of seventeen after

completing his "O" levels.[2] From 1954 to 1960 he lived in Bristol, working as a newspaper reporter. He wrote for the *Western Daily Press* (1954–58) and then for the *Bristol Evening World* (1959–60). For the latter, one of his assignments was to write regularly, both reviews and articles, about theatre and film.[3] In the process of reviewing the arts, Stoppard became friends with members of the Bristol Old Vic, among the most prestigious of Britain's regional repertory companies. One of those new friends was the then relatively unknown Peter O'Toole, who in the 1957–58 season turned in stellar performances as the lead in both *Hamlet* and *Look Back in Anger*. Stoppard cites these performances by O'Toole as one of the experiences that excited his interest in theatre. Indeed, in 1958 Stoppard began writing a play for a competition sponsored by the London newspaper the *Observer,* "but that one petered out after a dozen pages that were not unlike *Look Back in Anger*" ("Definite Maybe" 18).

In July 1960, while vacationing in Capri for his twenty-third birthday, Stoppard decided to forsake journalism to pursue a career in playwriting. When he returned to Bristol, he quit his newspaper job, but contracted to write two columns per week to support himself while he wrote plays.

Stoppard turned to playwriting with a sense of urgency, feeling that he should have already accomplished much more in life and in writing. In three months he wrote his first full-length play, *A Walk on the Water,* a work so heavily influenced by Arthur Miller's *Death of a Salesman* and Robert Bolt's *Flowering Cherry* that years later Stoppard jokingly nicknamed it *Flowering Death of a Salesman.* Since he had contacts at the Bristol Old Vic, Stoppard sent them his play for an assessment, but the play was rejected in February 1961. In the ensuing months, he wrote what was then a one-act play entitled *The Gamblers.*[4] While neither play has done much for Stoppard's reputation, they both played a crucial role in the progress of his career.

When Stoppard sought an agent, his friends at the Old Vic suggested Kenneth Ewing, who handled the literary side of Fraser and Dunlop. In late 1961 Stoppard sent Ewing *The Gamblers,* but the agent wanted to see more work, and so "with misgivings and deprecating noises, I sent him *A Walk on the Water,* explaining that it was, of course, rather *passé* compared to the one-acter" ("Definite Maybe" 19). But Ewing liked the play and in January 1962 agreed to represent Stoppard. The £10 advance, the largest lump sum Stoppard had ever earned, within a few weeks became one hundred pounds when H. M. Tennents, a prestigious producing agency, optioned *A Walk on the Water.* While noteworthy actors such as Ralph Richardson and Alec Guinness were discussed for the play, ultimately its year-long option expired and was not renewed. However, the play would resurface in the ensuing years and again aid Stoppard's career at a time when he needed it.

While beginning his writing career Stoppard remained in Bristol from July 1960 through August 1962 and supported himself by journalistic free-lancing, including theatre reviews for his former employer the *Western Daily Press*. More importantly, he became friends with Anthony C. H. Smith, the arts editor at the *WDP*, a would-be novelist, and the man whom Stoppard relied on as a close friend and mentor during the years of uncertainty and poverty that preceded the success of *Rosguil*. During those years of struggle, Smith served as a steadying influence, a man whose critical opinion Stoppard sought, and a friend who provided emotional support as well as small loans that helped keep the writer afloat during times of pecuniary need.

London

By August 1962 Stoppard realized that as an aspiring playwright he needed to be in London. Facilitating his move was the acceptance of a job as the drama critic/theatre editor of the new arts magazine *Scene*. The position provided him a weekly wage, tickets to all the major plays, and enough time to pursue his own writing. Meanwhile, *A Walk on the Water* was making the rounds (during the Tennents option year). Ralph Richardson was interested in the lead role and sent the script to Peter Brook, a director Stoppard greatly admired. Richardson, however, felt the script was too short, and so Stoppard added another half hour's material, mostly by developing the daughter Linda's relationship to the family in regard to her biker boyfriend.[5] Though this project didn't work out, from the outset Stoppard's work was being considered by some of the top people in British theatre.

During his seven months at *Scene* Stoppard reviewed about 132 shows. He also wrote articles and features, often using the pseudonym William Boot, a name taken from the protagonist of Evelyn Waugh's novel *Scoop*. Stoppard liked the character because he was "a journalist who brought a kind of innocent incompetence and contempt to what he was doing. . . . I used it, and got quite fond of Boot as a name" (Hudson, Itzin, and Trussler 71). Indeed, Stoppard frequently populated his early TV and radio plays with characters named Boot.[6]

From Stoppard's work for *Scene* it is clear that he admired Brecht, Ibsen, Shakespeare, and Beckett and that he valued "tight construction and maximum density of language" (Kelly 16). Though Stoppard often casts a skeptical eye on academic critiques, his own newspaper writing shows some deft analytical skills, and in his review of James Saunders's *Next Time I'll Sing to You,* Stoppard laid out three fundamental artistic principles: (1) everything should count; nothing should be arbitrary; (2) plays should have artistic unity, with no unnecessary digressions; and (3) plays should have a point; presenting too many random bits or treating everything as having the same significance only diminishes the play's intended impact. For the most part, Stoppard's plays have adhered to these principles.

"Mainly Self-Unemployed"

Scene folded in April 1963, and Stoppard describes the ensuing four years as a period during which he was "mainly self-unemployed" (Lewis, "How Tom Went to Work"). Until the success of *Rosguil,* Stoppard did the occasional freelance review or article, while also starting to earn a minimal living from his writing, mostly for TV and radio. During this four-year period Stoppard produced a number of unpublished scripts, works now housed at the HRHRC.

By June 1963 Stoppard had three short stories accepted for publication, but his focus was now on writing for radio, television, and the stage.[7] He began rewriting *The Gamblers* and had plans to finish revising *The Critics* (the ur–*Real Inspector Hound,* which he had first written while living in Bristol).[8] Another Bristol connection, director John Boorman (later known for films such as *Deliverance* and *Emerald Forest*), commissioned Stoppard and Smith to write for a series that would employ a new form of documentary. Stoppard was assigned surrealism, and the excerpt included in a June 1963 letter suggests that the documentary functioned by illustrating surrealism via examples rather than by talking about it. While this script was probably not filmed, in early 1964 Stoppard did assist Smith and Boorman in a pseudo-documentary series entitled *The Newcomers.* The show featured the Smith family and was loosely based on the family's attempt to adapt to life in a country town. Stoppard was scheduled to appear in at least the first four episodes.

In the summer of 1963 *A Walk on the Water* was bought for television. Ralph Richardson was still interested and so the producers decided to wait to see if he would be free in the fall. Stoppard dreamed that Richardson's involvement would give him great publicity as well as increase the likelihood the production could be resold in the United States. But as would happen during the years of struggle, hoped-for breakthroughs did not occur. Filming was delayed until the fall, but without Richardson in the cast. Though the cast loved the play, the first rehearsal where the cast read the script was a harrowing experience for Stoppard, and the producers demanded further cuts; a total of forty-two minutes would be excised from the script originally accepted. Things only got worse with Stoppard's first production. The play was filmed in November and intended for a March broadcast. Instead, one morning in late November, Stoppard was informed by the producers that his play would air that evening in place of John Whiting's *Marching Song,* which was deemed inappropriate so soon after the assassination of President Kennedy. Stoppard viewed this last-minute change with mixed emotions. He lost all the usual prebroadcast publicity, but since he disagreed with how the production interpreted his script, he was depressed by the final product and sought to distance himself from it.

In the summer of 1963 Stoppard was in good financial shape, for he had just earned £350 for *Walk* as well as $50 for a *New York Post* feature on his friend Peter O'Toole. But after a ten-week holiday in the Mediterranean with his girlfriend, Stoppard was back in dire financial straits, and by the fall of 1963 was in a fit of despair over his life and his writing. In October, after failing to get a journalism job, he wrote a colorful letter to Smith laying out his woes as if he were dealing out cards: no job, no money, debt-ridden, rent overdue, starving, listless, writer's block, and out of cigarettes. Despondent, he wondered if he had missed his chance to make it as a writer and was worried that he would be haunted by all the books and plays left unwritten. He desperately desired to write a full-length stage play and a TV play during the upcoming winter. But despite prodding from his agent as well as a possible BBC commission, he had not had any new ideas for weeks and was so bogged down by his bleak finances that he felt incapable of thought.

Amidst the depths of his despair and self-doubt, Stoppard maintained his desire to make it as a writer, and his follow-up letter showed his resiliency. There Stoppard engages in some apt self-criticism, noting the difficulty he has always had with plots. Instead he works from a basic idea, allowing the plot to develop out of his exploration of the idea. Not being plot-centered, Stoppard had difficulty providing synopses for proposed projects. Nonetheless, he came up with two television play ideas.

The first idea involved a young man so prone to maudlin self-dramatization that he circulates a rumor that he has only six months left to live. He begins to enjoy the effect it has on his girlfriend, his boss, and his coworkers, but it cascades out of control. When the deception is exposed, the anguished young man is extremely embarrassed and kills himself in order to preserve and justify the emotional structure he has erected. Stoppard felt this idea might work better as a novel; most likely it was never developed as a script.

The second idea involved a gagwriter going through a comedic crisis. The synopsis garnered a commission and was developed into a sixty-minute television play entitled *Funny Man*. Working from 6 P.M. to 7 A.M. Stoppard wrote the play in a week, using himself and Smith as models for the main characters. At this point in time, Stoppard and Smith were not only the closest of friends (with Stoppard to be best man at Smith's November wedding), but Smith was also the writer whose critical opinion Stoppard valued most. Buoyed by Smith's approval, Stoppard was optimistic about *Funny Man,* but it was rejected by both television producer Arthur Rank (AR) and the BBC. A second draft done in early 1964 was rejected by Associated Television and AR. A copy of *Funny Man* is at the HRHRC, and while it is not clear whether this is the first or second version, the surviving text focuses more on love and fidelity in relationships—themes developed more fully in *The Real Thing* (1982)—than it does on a gagwriter in a comedic crisis.[9]

Funny Man

Funny Man revolves around the personal and professional problems of Martin Bush, a gagwriter, and his wife Angeline, an actress and would-be poet. The attractive, thirtyish couple struggle to pay their bills and are in the midst of marital strife. Martin writes "additional material" for Danny Diamond, a comedian with a hit TV show, "Diamonds Is Trumps." Martin explains: "The company spends a lot of money on scripts, and then Diamond has me around full time to put stuff in, take stuff out and fill in the gaps so that he can appear to be even funnier. He calls it watching his style" (sc. 3, p. 2). Longing to be a novelist, Martin is unhappy as a gagwriter and also contemplates an affair with Frances Blake, a chorus girl dancer in Diamond's show and one of Diamond's mistresses.

Meanwhile, Angie is having an affair with her agent, Peregrine Preston, a man who later admits that her poetry is not very good: "I invested your poetry with some of your own beauty" (sc. 11, p. 2). Angie is torn between the two men, and through her, Stoppard explores the themes of love and fidelity. Angie explains her feelings to Preston:

PRESTON: Did you come because you wanted to, or because you were
angry with him?

ANGIE: I wanted to because I was angry with him.

PRESTON: I should have known better.

ANGIE: No, I wanted to. I d'know, I miss you quite a bit when I'm at
home, and when I'm here I feel—I hate it.

PRESTON: Do you?

ANGIE: No, I don't. Not being here. I like it. I was going to ask
you what kind of wit you took to, and the answer is that it doesn't
matter—it's relaxing after Jokesville [Martin]. I like being here. I
just hate myself for liking it. (sc. 4, pp. 1–2)

The disenchantment within Angie and Martin's marriage is developed in the
next scene:

MARTIN: I liked to think we were originals. I don't know what I mean
either. But we were originals then, there was nobody like us, and
now we're like everybody else. "The magic has gone out of my marriage, Mr. Thurber!" I d'know. One of us has dodged behind a pane
of glass. Is it me?

ANGIE: The trouble is—when everything's jokey, when joking is one's
business, then the things that should be just fun aren't fun any more
because they're the same as the rest of it, even though they aren't.
They get lost. Martin, everything we do becomes a joke, you know,
except our jokes. I seem to have run out of fun—it's all been deval-
ued, the currency has been thumbed over and over. We hardly talk
any more, we just gag our giggly way towards the ultimate joke till
plain ordinary dull jokeless living begins to look like a holiday. Do
you know what I mean? (sc. 5, pp. 6–7)

But Martin does not yet understand, for he responds by making a joke of it
and by starting to develop one of Angie's ideas for a comic sketch. The scene
ends with "Angie watching [Martin], pained but affectionate" (sc. 5, p. 7).

As the play progresses, Angie is forced to make a decision, and she explains her dilemma to Preston:

PRESTON: Will you leave him?

ANGIE: We're more than husband and wife. We're a double-act. We
just got out of sync.

PRESTON: I want to marry you, Angeline.

ANGIE: That helps. Sometimes I want to marry you.

PRESTON: Angeline—

ANGIE: Not here. And not now. I'm sorry. There's a lot more to it than simple preference, and I don't even know what *that* is. But I've got to decide soon. I'm on borrowed time.

PRESTON: There's no hurry.

ANGIE: Yes, there is. I don't want to be caught cheating. If I go I want to go on the level, if you call that on the level. I want to tell him before he finds out. . . . [Martin's] stripped to the nerves. That can be trying, but it's also why I fell in love with him. I know I can have too much of that. What worries me is I'm not sure if I can be happy without any of it. (sc. 8, pp. 2–3)

Angie has a heightened sense of self-awareness as she realizes how the advantages and disadvantages of the men she has to choose between will affect her own life. Her character is unique in that she is the most fully developed female figure from the early part of Stoppard's career. Indeed, it would not be until *Night and Day* (1978) that Stoppard would again place a complex, emotionally developed female character at the center of a play.

While Angie agonizes over her situation, Martin, unaware of Angie's affair, decides to accept Frances's sexual advances. Ironically, Martin and Frances's postcoital conversation focuses on how they have been unfaithful to their employer Danny Diamond. Martin closes the scene: "One of the big empty things about [Danny] is his lack of self-esteem as a lover. When his gagwriter tops him there, he won't see the joke" (sc. 7, p. 3). In contrast to Angie, Martin comes across as a shallow person, a man who cannot deal with the emotions of a relationship. As their affair approaches the point of having to make a decision, Frances tells Martin: "Come out from behind those gags, you coward. . . . Please start trusting me, Martin. You don't give anything of yourself away, do you? Every time anything comes close your sirens go off and you skid away on gags" (sc. 10, pp. 3–4). Indeed, whether by choice or lack of ability, Stoppard keeps Martin as a man who is emotionally underdeveloped. When Martin accidentally learns of Angie's affair, "it's as bad as he's ever felt" (sc. 9, p. 1), but he never vocalizes those emotions, nor does he ever acknowledge his own infidelity.

Near the end, Martin is seen as a weak man with low self-esteem. Danny summons Martin to a meeting where two events occur: (1) Martin accepts a good-paying job writing for Danny's New York appearance; and (2) Martin gives up Frances without a fight, for she is seen as being Danny's girl. Martin avoids answering Frances' direct questions about whether or not Danny had asked about their relationship. Instead he replies: "Danny Diamond, the girls' best friend! Accompanied by—Marty, the talking dog! Every time Marty passes a lamppost, he makes a JOKE! . . . Danny Diamond, a dog's best friend, has instructed me to say, in my master's voice, at the world record fee of one thousand dollars, to say—My People!" (sc. 14, p. 3). By now, Martin seems to have no will of his own; instead it is up to Angie to save him.

In a prior scene, Angie meets with Preston in order to give him the start of her novel and to end their relationship. She explains why she stayed with Martin: "I'm sorry. I had the alternatives, but I never really had the choice. I don't know why I didn't see that. What it boils down to is that I know if I'd been married to you, or anyone, all this time, and I met him—I mean, if it was the other way round, I'd want something which I've already got now" (sc. 14, p. 3). Angie not only stays with Martin, but in the last scene she reveals that the novel she submitted to Preston, which Preston thinks he can sell, is actually Martin's novel, and so "the family honor is saved" (sc. 15, p. 1). By the end, Martin knows that Angie has ended her affair and sold his novel, but though the opportunity is there, he does not tell her about his own affair.

An intriguing subtlety to the theme of fidelity is Stoppard's uncharacteristic inclusion of a subtext of class division. When Martin learns that Angie has not told her agent about Martin's published, though poor-selling, novel, he asks her, "Whose side are you on nowadays, Angie?" (sc. 3, p. 6). Martin later explains that he does not like Preston, that he thinks Preston is a phony, and that Preston "isn't exactly our type" (sc. 5, p. 3). Ultimately, Angie agrees with this. In ending her relationship with the proper, gentlemanly Preston she explains:

> Going to bed isn't the kind of infidelity I mean, and it's not all hypocrisy. It's a side-picking thing—there's a big line-up of opposing factions—Them and Us, if you like—and everything that touches one goes to form a code of attitudes, and everyone chooses sides. You know who to count on. I can't explain it and I don't want to because you can talk these things away, and they're important. But everyone has to make a show of allegiance to a collective coat of arms, and I'm on Martin's

side. He had to ask me to make sure, but I'm still there. If I left him, that wouldn't be true any more. (sc. ii, pp. 3–4)

For its leftist sense of class consciousness and solidarity and for its use of a complex female character who explores the emotional terrain of love and infidelity, *Funny Man* is unique among Stoppard's presuccess writing. Though Stoppard viewed it as a comedy, it reads more as a drama, and since it is a very respectable script, it is surprising that it was rejected by would-be producers.

On the Radio

Meanwhile, Stoppard's struggling finances led to some bold, daring, and comical adventures. In the fall of 1963, Stoppard went to his bank wearing a false beard, eyed-up a naive young teller, and promptly wrote out a self-cash check for £10. By the time the teller discovered that the check would bounce, Stoppard was out the door and on his way to buy more cigarettes. Inspired by this success, Stoppard planned another incognito raid upon his bank, but this one went amiss. On the day of the intended bank adventure Stoppard, having stayed up till 8 A.M., slept through his alarm, and did not wake until 2:30 P.M. Since the bank closed at 3:00 P.M., he hurried out the door, waited for a bus, and then in desperation took a taxi. The taxi arrived at the bank at 3:01 P.M., and Stoppard did not have enough money to pay the cab fare. After a short altercation, Stoppard handed over all his money and a promissory note. He was forced to walk back home, with the day being saved by his finding of two shillings, thereby allowing for the purchase of some Woodbine cigarettes. Stoppard quickly realized that this personal misadventure had dramatic potential, and that evening he devised a scenario about a penniless man taking a taxi to the bank, arriving at 3:01 P.M., and staying in the taxi, going from place to place trying to borrow the money to pay the fare, and never quite catching up with the meter. With minor alterations this became his fifteen-minute radio play *The Dissolution of Dominic Boot.*

The BBC inaugurated their fifteen-minute play series in January 1964, and Stoppard viewed it as a potential windfall for himself and for Smith. Stoppard, always aware of his strengths and weaknesses as a writer, was drawn to the format because its brevity allowed for the plays to be approached in the same spirit one took for writing an article. In contrast, longer scripts took on the weight of a "project" that looms over the writer, often preventing the script from being written. The format also favored dialogue over plot, as the shortened time frame means one deals more with a situation as opposed to an extended story. Indeed, the *Dominic Boot* play is essentially an extended joke. It was bought by the BBC in November 1963, and since demand was heavy, Stoppard quickly went to work on another.

He recycled a rejected short story into *"M" is for Moon Among Other Things,* a work that Stoppard has referred to as his Marilyn Monroe play.[10] Again, Stoppard employs a situation rather than a plot as it intersperses dialogue with the internal monologues of a middle-aged, middle-class couple. While Constance browses through her monthly installment of the M–N volume of an encyclopedia, her husband, Alfred, fantasizes about what he reads in the newspaper and hears on the radio—with the lead story being the death of Marilyn Monroe. Alfred's fantasy of comforting the lonely and misunderstood Monroe is ironically counterpointed by the absence of love and true communication in his own marriage. Noteworthy about both plays is how Stoppard exploits the medium of radio to craft tightly constructed works that effectively use different character voices and sound effects that aurally enhance the experience in a way that distinguishes them from works for the stage.[11]

TV Projects

While Stoppard wrote these radio plays, he was also working on a number of other projects. By late 1963 he had finished a sixty-minute television play entitled *I Can't Give You Anything but Love, Baby.* This unpublished, unproduced script concerns two brothers, Arthur (aged 32) and Jamie (aged 30). Jamie is mentally deficient and sheltered from society by his brother who cares for him since both of their parents, including an abusive father, are dead. Jamie compulsively buys items on an installment plan from door-to-door salesmen and newspaper advertisers. He knows that the items will eventually be repossessed, but he does not care because temporarily the objects are his, and they are new, rather than the hand-me-downs he has received from Arthur through the years. Arthur tries to tell Jamie that he is being stupid and wasting his money on objects that will be repossessed. Their confrontation moves from an intellectual plane to an emotional one and ends with the likable simpleton Jamie passionately declaring: "You don't need things—you got *people!*" (sc. 1, p. 19). Jamie's desperate need for human contact is one of the most poignant moments in Stoppard's early writing.

Complicating the brothers' relationship is the fact that Arthur is prepared to marry his fiancée Gwen, who clings to her virginity because of what she describes as an idealistic and romantic notion that the first time should be important. Arthur decides that he must introduce his fiancée to the brother who will be sharing their house, but Gwen is frightened by Jamie and wants him to be committed to a lunatic asylum. When next Arthur and Gwen meet, Arthur is drunk and rants about what constitutes sanity in this crazy world, while also questioning: "Who are you judging? And on what divine standard are you judging him?" (sc. 5, p. 6). In one of the somewhat forced and inconsistent moments in the play, Arthur delivers some of this speech after entering Jamie's room of prized possessions and returning dressed in "One miner's helmet, one pair of snow glasses. An Anorak jacket. A rucksack on his back. On one foot a flying boot. The other a ski. He carries an underwater harpoon gun. Binoculars are over his neck. And he is doing his best to ride the Tour de France bike" (sc. 5, p. 4). While dressed in this bizarre and surrealistic fashion, the authorities arrive and assume he is Jamie; Arthur willingly goes, pretending to be Jamie, realizing that he can prove his sanity, and thus prevent Jamie from being taken away.

The plot twist is that while Arthur is away saving his brother, Gwen is back home seducing Jamie; she does it both for herself and for Jamie: "I'm new, Jamie. I'm unused. I never belonged to anyone—not to Arthur, not to anybody—I'm new. So touch me, don't touch me like a thing.—I'm people—I'm your first people—and you're mine—and I'm glad it's you because I like you, Jamie—I like the way you look—I like the way you're new—so you touch me, Jamie, you touch me so I stay touched" (sc. 5, p. 11). It is her way of socializing Jamie, of not treating him like a child, the way Arthur does. In the process she also makes her first sexual encounter meaningful to herself. When Arthur returns, he learns of the seduction and Gwen's decision to break off their engagement. Despite the seduction, Arthur reaffirms that he would never let the authorities take Jamie away. Then when Gwen leaves, a salesman arrives, but now Jamie is changed and resists the salesman's pitch. The final feeling of the play is of two brothers affirming their filial love and commitment to each other. While the play exhibits characteristic Stoppard devices such as mistaken identity and surrealistic images, it is unique not only in its use of an "idiot" character, but in its emphasis on the bonds between siblings.[12] As with *Funny Man,* but to a lesser extent, there are flashes of emotional depth that Stoppard would not achieve until much later in his writing career, but the script's fundamental flaw is that the characters' inconsistent behavior strains credulity.

While *I Can't Give You Anything but Love, Baby* was never produced, it was on the ride back from a meeting where the script was rejected that agent Kenneth Ewing planted the seed that Stoppard should write a play about Rosencrantz and Guildenstern, with Ewing's idea being that when the two courtiers arrive in England they meet the mad King Lear.[13] The idea was appealing to Stoppard, but while the play developed in his mind, he worked on other projects. In late 1963 he was commissioned by Arthur Rank to adapt his Faber short story "The Story" into a television play. At the same time, Collins Publishers approached Stoppard about writing a novel. With multiple projects in the works, Stoppard was looking for a breakthrough on any front, and so long as he was being productive as a writer, he remained upbeat.

This positive attitude carried over into the new year. Both radio plays were going into production, and BBC Radio Four had commissioned him to write (as a trial run) five fifteen-minute episodes of the daily family serial *The Dales,* an assignment that he accepted for purely mercenary reasons.[14] Early in January 1964 he vacationed in Scotland and read heavily, including *King Lear, Hamlet,* and criticism such as Dover Wilson's *What Happens in Hamlet*—all preparatory work for his Rosencrantz and Guildenstern play. Besides contemplating that script, he had many other projects in the works. He owed Armchair Theatre a script by the end of February, had *The Dales* run from 27 January to 3 February, was adapting *A Walk on the Water* for radio, was writing the TV adaptation of "The Story," was waiting on Boorman for involvement with *The Newcomers* show, and was hoping for commissions for one or two more fifteen-minute radio plays as well as for a novel for Faber and Faber or Anthony Blond. Stoppard was also hoping to start a full-length stage play.[15] As would become customary with Stoppard, commitments accumulated, and at this point in his career he possessed a mixture of confidence and uncertainty. Contemplating all these projects made him nervous; he desired Mona Lisa–like perfection, but was almost afraid to start. Stoppard has long had high standards, but has sometimes suffered bouts of writer's block. Throughout his career, he has always referred to the first page as the hardest page to write.

One of the scripts that Stoppard had trouble starting was the unproduced television play *This Way Out with Samuel Boot,* a work that was, in part, Stoppard's attempt to salvage some of the ideas and situations from *I Can't Give You Anything but Love, Baby.* The *Samuel Boot* play concerns two brothers. Samuel Boot preaches the total rejection of property, while Jonathan Boot compulsively buys objects on credit, only to have them repossessed for nonpayment (similar to Jamie in *ICGYABLB*).[16] Kenneth Tynan, the only previous Stoppard chronicler to have read the script, characterizes it as "patchily brilliant, an uneasy blend of absurdist comedy and radical melodrama" (69). He also argues that the play contains the leftist message that "property is theft" (69), but that interpretation is more indicative of Tynan's politics than Stoppard's intent. The character who preaches the evils of property is heavily satirized, and does not, I believe, represent Stoppard's own point of view. In his correspondence, Stoppard referred to the play as devoid of philosophical content, with it simply being about a man who buys things. As will be evident, Stoppard satirizes both the rejecter of property as well as the hoarder of property.

The opening scenes of the play establish Jonathan as a collector of mail-order bargains and door-to-door salesmen's offerings. When he "purchases" a third vacuum cleaner, it is clear that he has more objects than he needs. In contrast, Samuel is shown to be on a crusade against property and has finally gotten two followers, Agnes and Stripe. In the public park, Samuel preaches:

> Greed and envy, theft, bankruptcy, inflation, despair—yes, war itself, I tell you—the symptoms of moral and spiritual decline—And it's to amass property, and then to protect what you have amassed, that's what does it—whether you call it bombs or refrigerators—it's property, it's all property and we are in the power of property, chained by property, dictated by property—ladies and gentlemen, we have been brought low by property! (16)

Samuel has the energetic fervor of a proselytizer at Speaker's Corner, and variations of the above speech are heard throughout the play. In short, he is an ideologue, which makes him a Stoppardian antihero.

When Samuel and his followers take up his customary winter lodgings at Jonathan's house (which was both of theirs until Samuel gave his half to Jonathan), there is conflict over their respective views. When Jonathan buys an underwater harpoon gun, Samuel is angry at this unnecessary purchase:

SAMUEL: (*Banging table*) Possibly you want to commit suicide in
   the bath!
JONATHAN: (*Mildly*) I like to have things.
AGNES: You can't have everything you like.
JONATHAN: You can, you can have mostly anything you like. Some-
   times for weeks and weeks. (27)

Jonathan is someone who has beaten the system. When he was an air
force administrator, he bought a wooden leg and then manipulated the pa-
perwork to get himself a disability discharge and a pension. Similarly, he ma-
nipulates the system of buying on credit. At one point a man comes to re-
possess his television:

MAN: You only paid a very small deposit and even after repeated warn-
   ings you refused to pay even the first installment—that's not playing
   the game, you know. . . . Don't you realize—the company loses
   money on this—it's uneconomical.
JONATHAN: I can't afford installments, you see.
MAN: But didn't you know that?
JONATHAN: Oh yes—I'm not a fool. (38)

Then in a comic coup that illustrates Jonathan's cleverness, the man leaves
with the repossessed television only to encounter another delivery man arriving with a new television.

The brothers' opposing philosophies eventually come to a crisis. As he
would do in his later work, Stoppard uses a dialectical exchange to critique
Samuel's "Crusade" and its philosophy, in part because it lacks logic. Here
Jonathan seems to speak for Stoppard:

JONATHAN: I don't think you're right in the head. . . . All I can see
   is a scruffy layabout telling everyone to give away every comfort and
   convenience they've worked for. Who are they supposed to give it to?
SAMUEL: People.
JONATHAN: Then *they've* got to give it away again. I don't think I
   follow.
SAMUEL: It's a question of values.
JONATHAN: It's a question of where's it going to end? You can't have a
   human chain passing stuff along as if it was buckets of water.

SAMUEL: You've got a literal mind, that's your trouble.

JONATHAN: One to another. Finally you reach your last man, standing with his back to the sea. I suppose he chucks it in.

SAMUEL: It's a matter of setting an example.

JONATHAN: I should have thought your sincerity might be doubted.

SAMUEL: No one doubts my sincerity.

JONATHAN: It's all right for him to get all righteous, they'll say—what has *he* got to give away?

SAMUEL: I've given mine already. I've got the clothes I stand up in.

JONATHAN: That would be something. Do it properly or not at all.

SAMUEL: I've had tracts printed.

JONATHAN: Tracts. Some people give bungalows. You don't give anybody anything worth anything and you want them to give away everything worth everything. I'd say you were swimming against the current. In fact I'd say you were a bit of a joke. (34–36)

At this point, Jonathan kicks Samuel and his followers out of his home. But Jonathan's speech has struck a chord with Samuel. He returns to the park and proves the sincerity of his message by disrobing, an action that results in his arrest for indecent exposure and disturbing the peace. Stoppard treats Samuel's cause ironically and satirically by having Samuel respond to his fine with great pleasure: "Official recognition—it gives the Crusade a kind of dignity" (50).

Instead of a dignified idea, Samuel's idealistic Crusade is seen as a practical impossibility. When Samuel thinks he has found a way out of the commercial materialism of society, Jonathan responds: "There's no *out*. You're in it, so you might as well fit. It's the way it is. Economics. All this stuff I've got. People have been paid to make it, drive it to the warehouse, advertise it, sell it to me, write to me about it, and take it away again. They get paid. . . . That's the way of it and you're in it. There's no way out with Samuel Boot" (53). Though Samuel's ideology may be impracticable, there is still sympathy for him. Stripe defends Samuel: "Whatever sense he makes, he's good. He don't take nothing and you give nothing. His feelings are all right. He's not like everybody and he's got this idea, all right. But his feelings are good and you've got no feelings at all" (55). As in Stoppard's later work, characters can be respected for their integrity even when their ideas are not sound.

After Jonathan refuses to pay Samuel's fine and again kicks him out of the house, the play moves toward its climax. Jonathan has a large collection of trading stamps, which he hopes will win him a bungalow, but Stripe steals them and gives them to Samuel. Ironically, Samuel plans to give away these valuable stamps to lure a crowd to hear him speak about the evils of property, but in the process Samuel is trampled to death by the eager mob.

While Samuel's give-it-all-away philosophy is shown to be impractical, Jonathan's excessive materialism is also called into question. Jonathan's cleverness and adherence to logic suggest that he may be the hero of the play, but sympathy for Jonathan is undercut when he is upset over losing his stamps, but indifferent to Samuel's death. Stripe then returns to defend Samuel's honor:

> STRIPE: He died of people. They trod on him.
> JONATHAN: That's what it is about people. Turn round and they'll tread on you. Or steal your property. . . .
> STRIPE: You don't know anything. You don't know about him. He was a silly old man, and being dead doesn't change that. But for a minute, getting his, on the bandstand, all bloody, for a minute his daft old crusade, like he said, it had a kind of dignity, for a minute. He knew about that and you don't know nothing. You've got too much in the way. (68–69)

At this point, Stripe picks up Jonathan's new vacuum cleaner. Defending his property, Jonathan kills him with the harpoon gun. Stoppard then closes the play with a dark-humored satire on Jonathan's excessive materialism, which comes at the expense of human decency:

> JONATHAN: (*Chattering*) He can't do that. That's no way to act. At all. No respect, he's got no respect for real people's property—Vandal, yes, oh yes, murderer, thief, deserter, vandal—oh, it's a public service—they know that—commendation—
> AGNES: He's not moving.
> (JONATHAN *taut, breathing hard*)
> JONATHAN: Oh yes, well, he wouldn't, it's a very reliable machine, this, very handy. I might write to the makers, I think they'd like to know—
> AGNES: (*Crying drily*) He was only young. And so bad already.
> JONATHAN: He was. Yes, he was. He can't do that. It's anti-social. I've got a lot of stuff in here. [Proceeds to list out many items.] I've got

responsibilities. I've got commitments. Yes. Oh yes. He can't do that. (69–70)

Overall, neither Samuel nor Jonathan is shown to be correct, but rather each man's philosophy is satirized as being incomplete in itself. While Stoppard felt *Samuel Boot* was a good script, the head of Armchair Theatre wanted more comedy and a more upbeat ending. Stoppard withdrew the script and abandoned it.

Berlin: Carpets on the Wall

In the spring of 1964 publisher Anthony Blond contracted Stoppard to write a novel. At the time he had no idea what the novel would be about, and when he signed the contract, Stoppard listed the tentative title as *Jose,* after his future first wife. This project eventually became *Lord Malquist and Mr. Moon.* Also in the spring, on the recommendation of Charles Marowitz, he was awarded a Ford Foundation grant to spend five months in Berlin. The four British playwrights selected were Stoppard, Derek Marlowe, Piers Paul Read (son of Sir Herbert, an honored poet and critic), and James Saunders, the elder statesman of the group and author of *Next Time I'll Sing to You,* a play that Stoppard deeply admired and that influenced his writing of *Rosguil.*[17] From early May to mid-September, these four were joined by three filmmakers and about a dozen German writers, all of whom were housed in a large, luxurious mansion where their hosts pampered the artists. The luxury of the rambling mansion bedazzled Stoppard, and he was amused by the expectations of eccentric writers. He was told that he was free to rearrange his room so as to create a comfortable writing environment. Rather than admit that he was just a middle-class boy who didn't want a real job, Stoppard jokingly considered rolling up his carpet and hanging it on the wall lest they think he was not a real writer.

During his time in Berlin, Stoppard experienced the first staging of one of his plays. On 30 June 1964 *A Walk On the Water,* in a German translation, was performed by Hamburg's Thalia Theatre. It was an appropriate touch that one of the premier comic playwrights should have his first production in a theatre named for the comic muse, while also nicely ironic that the Czech-born writer known for his mastery of English should be first produced in German.

Stoppard traveled to Hamburg to work on the script. Using the theatre company's ideas and his own, he rewrote the play, cutting out a flashback, making it all chronological, with a new beginning, new first-act curtain, and a new title (which changed throughout the rehearsal period)—the play was eventually produced as *Old Riley geht über'n Ozean* (*Old Riley Walked the Water*).[18] Still unsure of himself, he was nervous and almost embarrassed by the enthusiasm the company felt for the play. Faced with a 1,000-seat theatre, a prominent lead actor, excellent designs, and all the respect a high-quality play deserves, Stoppard felt it was just a matter of time before they realized that neither he nor the play deserved all the attention. The production had a strange schedule, as the plan was to rehearse the play until the end of June, depart on holiday for six weeks, and come back for dress rehearsals before a 16 August opening; but in late June the schedule was revised so that the play officially opened on 30 June, then the cast and production team took a six-week holiday, and afterward the show's run resumed in mid-August. As his first stage production approached, Stoppard was dispirited, having only a limited sense of pride or identity with the play, and so his main hope was for good reviews, which could lead to other German productions and boost his sagging finances.

Old Riley, a work that Stoppard once described as being about a middle-aged failure who grasps at the illusion of self-esteem and success only to find it illusory, received a mixed reaction, with the middle-class adults in the stalls applauding the work, while the students in the gallery hissed the conservative, conventional domestic drama. Tynan, with Felicia Londré following him, reports the apocryphal tale that during the curtain call Stoppard strode on stage "with a cigarette between his lips—perhaps in emulation of Oscar Wilde, who used the same method of showing his indifference to audience reaction" (71). This image of cool self-confidence was not the case; if there was a cigarette in Stoppard's mouth, it was there because of nervous tension.

Soon after the opening performance Stoppard wrote to Smith, describing his first production as a harrowing experience that left him hollow and shell-shocked. While it was a respectable production with an enthusiastic cast who delivered good performances, albeit of characters Stoppard didn't write, he felt that his script was thin and repetitive. Nonetheless the audience was attentive and fairly amused by the play. Ultimately Stoppard was persuaded to partake in the German tradition and appear with the cast for the curtain call. The star and the director dragged him onstage, at which point the gallery erupted into a storm of gleeful abuse, while the stalls counterattacked with bravos. In the midst of the chaos Stoppard realized what was happening. The local papers had promoted him as being a combination of absurdist, Beatle, and Angry Young Man, while his play more closely resembled a traditional 1930s script. Faced with the boos, paralysis overtook Stoppard, but robotlike and blank he was dragged twice more onto the stage with the scene growing ever more comically riotous. As he stood in the line-up amidst the conflicting cascade of audience reaction, Stoppard only wished that Smith were there to witness the scene.

During this period of Stoppard's life his twin sources of reassurance and support were Smith and Ewing, and Stoppard was grateful that the latter was there to offer comfort after this unpleasant, unnerving first production. Still, Stoppard took the blame because he realized that the script was not up to the high standards he sought. He regretted allowing *Walk* to be his first stage production, and in hyperbolic fashion he warned Ewing that he would fire him if he ever sought a London production. He vowed that he would only return to the play if he were desperate for money and that otherwise it should only be performed posthumously as a historical curiosity. Part of Stoppard's dissatisfaction with himself and the play is that as he later realized *A Walk on the Water* has a ring of falseness "because it's a play written about other people's characters" (Hudson, Itzin, and Trussler 56). Imitative of Robert Bolt and Arthur Miller, the play lacks a stamp of originality and individuality. That subsequently it was done in London in 1968 (under the revised title *Enter a Free Man*) was indeed due to financial need as Stoppard sold the option on it during a monetary crisis just prior to the success of *Rosguil*.[19]

While in Berlin Stoppard also engaged in one of the few acting experiences of his career. Part of the Ford group was an international freelance film trio for whom Stoppard played a pseudoabsurdist cowboy in an avant-garde film. Wearing black trousers, pink shirt, black cowboy hat, gunbelt, six-guns, and spurs, Stoppard did a high-noon walk down the middle of the highway leading to the Brandenburg Gate. While Stoppard enjoyed the experience, he was highly skeptical about the artistic merit of these avant-garde films that featured one take, no script, no plot, pretentious action, all images, and outlandish cuts. In his later plays *Artist Descending a Staircase* and *Travesties,* Stoppard would openly declare his distrust and dislike of seemingly nonintentional or unfocused avant-garde art.

Rosencrantz and Guildenstern Meet King Lear

The lasting result of Stoppard's stay in Berlin was that he began what would eventually evolve into *Rosguil*. His first version has traditionally been known by the title *Rosencrantz and Guildenstern Meet King Lear,* but the popular

conception, perpetuated by Stoppard himself, that it was a one-act verse burlesque is not accurate. The text that survives at the HRHRC is a one-act play,
but it is neither in verse nor a burlesque. Indeed, right after completing the
play in June 1964, Stoppard wrote to Smith and described the work:

> Rosencrantz, Guildenstern, and Hamlet are joined on the boat by the
> Player, and since the Player represents the Hamlet-figure in *The Mur-
> der of Gonzago,* the Player is made up to look like Hamlet. On the
> boat, Hamlet and the Player change identities, and the Player is cap-
> tured by the pirates and goes off to fulfill Hamlet's role in the rest of
> Shakespeare's play. Meanwhile Hamlet goes to England, witnesses the
> execution of Rosencrantz and Guildenstern, and then returns to Elsi-
> nore in time for the final tableau of carnage, but too late to take over.
> He is a man stuck in space, a man caught out of the action. It is a bit
> screwy, but fun.

Stoppard's description corresponds to the text that survives at the HRHRC.
This earliest version focused on the boat voyage to England (what was to become the third act of *Rosguil*), and their contact with the mad King Lear is
limited to four of the forty-four pages.

Based on hearsay or faulty memory, most descriptions of *Rosencrantz and
Guildenstern Meet King Lear* are inaccurate.[20] While Stoppard has described
this *Lear* draft as unspeakably bad, in fact, a number of passages in the first
half of the play were later incorporated into *Rosguil.* By examining the similarities and differences, one can see which of Stoppard's initial thematic concerns survived in his first major work.

Rosencrantz and Guildenstern Meet King Lear begins slowly as the first
quarter of the play has the protagonists standing on the plain, waiting to
board the boat that will take them and Hamlet to England. Interspersed
with excerpts of Hamlet's soliloquies and Fortinbras's speech on the plain,
Rosencrantz and Guildenstern provide exposition of the events of *Hamlet*
while also wrangling, in what will be a running joke, over how much each
of them got paid by the king.[21] As in *Rosguil,* the protagonists incorrectly introduce themselves, and with the Captain's prodding proceed to discuss the
melancholy and madness of Hamlet that, in the later play, culminates in a
declaration that Hamlet is "stark raving sane" (*Rosguil* 52).[22] Soon the Player,
wearing a mask that resembles Hamlet's face, enters and explains that he's a
fugitive.[23]

One of Stoppard's key conceits is that the Player wears his mask throughout, and that Rosencrantz and Guildenstern associate him with his masked character, not as the person behind the mask. Upon further interrogation, the Player explains that he is fleeing for having performed in *The Murder of Gonzago,* at which point Rosencrantz finally catches on:

ROS: He's one of the *Players!*
PLAYER: I told you.
GUIL: Lucianus, nephew to the king. Well. Well. Well. (*He laughs.*)
PLAYER: Only in my mask.
ROS: Of course. As I said, I knew your mask. Lucianus, poisoner and lecher, nephew to the king.
PLAYER: I just came as I was. They were all after us. (10)

In Rosencrantz's and Guildenstern's eyes, the mask imparts identity, and throughout the play identity is perceived as mutable — sometimes the protagonists consider the Player to be an actor, while at other times they view him as Lucianus. Indeed, Hamlet also addresses the Player as Lucianus, pointing out that they are both nephews to a king.

The first scene closes with Guildenstern philosophically ruminating about how on a boat one is free "[t]o move, to speak, extemporise, and yet. We have not been cut loose" (12),[24] and with the characters going aboard the boat. The second scene concerns the voyage to England. Rosencrantz and Guildenstern continue trying to trick each other into revealing how much money the other received. They also hope that the letter from the Danish king, concerning their delivery of Hamlet to the English king, will bring them even greater rewards. This leads to the comic confusion over who has the letter, the security of knowing that the letter's instructions provide a temporary sense of control, and the hope that the letter will give them something to keep them going (14–16).[25] Meanwhile they engage the Player, and to break the monotony they want "a show of oral initiative" (20), with Rosencrantz commenting: "Do a monologue, a set piece. Anything for God's sake. Here we are with an actor at hand and we have to suffer a string of pregnant pauses each one terminated by an abortion" (20). This section concludes with Rosencrantz's plea: "Incidents. All we get is incidents. Promise without fulfillment. Dear me, is it too much to ask for a little sustained action?" (21).[26] Thus, even in the first draft, Stoppard incorporated self-reflexive lines that not only fit the characters' situation but that also acknowledge the hand of the author and the play's constructedness.

While a fair amount of the first half of *Rosencrantz and Guildenstern Meet King Lear* was later incorporated into *Rosguil*, the full-length play contains almost nothing from the second half of the one-acter. Whereas the full-length play focuses more fully on the existential situation of Rosencrantz and Guildenstern, the one-acter centers more on the theme of role-playing (one of the Player's thematic functions in *Rosguil*) and, by extension, mutable identities. The switch in emphasis necessitated the elimination of the significant plot points of the second half of the one-act play.

Originally, when Rosencrantz and Guildenstern fall asleep, Hamlet convinces the Player to switch roles, exchanging hats, boots, and cloaks, with the Player's mask providing the facial resemblance. The plan is for the Player to impersonate Hamlet and go to England, where Hamlet assures him the English king will give him honor and safety, while Hamlet returns to Denmark to get his revenge. While everyone is sleeping, the Player checks the contents of the letter and is horrified to discover that it calls for Hamlet's execution.[27] The Player confronts Hamlet, informing him of the letter's contents, and refusing to follow through with the role reversal. After Hamlet plants the letter ordering the execution of Rosencrantz and Guildenstern, he appeals to the Player once again to accept the planned role reversal. In *Rosguil* it is Rosencrantz and Guildenstern who must consider the morality of not acting on their knowledge that the original letter calls for Hamlet's death, but in this earlier draft Stoppard offers a consideration of the morality of Hamlet's action:

> PLAYER: Why, this is no game, my lord; are they guilty men? Did they know the king's intention to have you killed?
> HAMLET: Why, man, they are the king's men. Is the king guilty?
> PLAYER: Yes, my lord.
> HAMLET: That will serve. They are bought and sold to trickery; let them die by it. Now, my Prince—Hamlet is safe again.
> PLAYER: I would stay a player.
> HAMLET: And an outcast?
> PLAYER: My Lord?
> HAMLET: Be my other self. Give me your hat.
> (*The* PLAYER *demurs.*) When a purge is made of the throne of Den-

mark, those loyal to me will stand much to gain; those unloyal, they will play at corpses. How then? (*The* PLAYER *hands over his hat unwillingly.*) (31)

The Player's moral qualms give way to self-interest.

Soon after the role reversal is again agreed upon, the pirate attack occurs, and the main characters hide in the barrels until the battle is finished. Then, in another deviation from *Rosguil,* Rosencrantz, Guildenstern, and Hamlet emerge from the barrels, only now Hamlet is playing the role of the Player. The confusion over identity is further extended when, while mourning the loss of Hamlet, Rosencrantz and Guildenstern begin to treat the Player (i.e., Hamlet) as if he were the character represented by his mask. Realizing that both Hamlet and Lucianus are nephews to a king, they start to think that Lucianus may also be a prince, and so they begin to interrogate Hamlet (who they think to be the Player / Lucianus). This sometimes confusing section revolves around the notion that people are always acting, always playing roles in everyday life. They may not be able to know the exact identity of their traveling companion, but when the ship docks at Dover, Rosencrantz reassures himself that though the pirates have the prince, "we have the other [prince]" (39).

Arriving in Dover, Rosencrantz, Guildenstern, and Hamlet (taken to be the Player) are greeted by the sight of the mad King Lear, fantastically dressed in wild flowers and speaking his "When we are born" speech, which concludes "kill, kill, kill, kill, kill, kill!" (*King Lear* 4.6.184–89). The travelers comically comment:

HAMLET: Why, who is that, so fantastically garlanded with flowers?
GUIL: A madman.
ROS: They are all mad here. It is well known in Denmark.
HAMLET: That is why you were to bring the mad prince here?
GUIL: He would not be noticed among such loons. (40)

Lear announces he is king, but then emits a mad hunting cry and runs off. Continuing the theme that the world is a stage upon which humans act, Rosencrantz and Guildenstern respond:

ROS: I say they are all mad. I have seen players more royal than that lunatic.

GUIL: Come, we must find one who plays the king with more authority. For we have important business with him. (40)

Lear's running brings him down to the level of the travelers where Hamlet stops him, and Rosencrantz and Guildenstern laugh at him when he claims to be king:

ROS: If he's the King I'll be Guildenstern.
GUIL: And my name's Rosencrantz.
HAMLET: And I'll be Hamlet if he's the King. (41)

Hamlet uses the confusion to revert to his "true" identity, and since Lear knew his father, Hamlet is greeted warmly. More importantly, Lear is given the letter, but since he cannot read, Guildenstern does it for him, and so they learn of the execution orders against them. When Lear orders their seizure, Rosencrantz draws his sword, Hamlet tells the guards to "Go to it," and Lear utters his earlier cry: "Kill, kill, kill, kill" (43). Rosencrantz and Guildenstern are stabbed, and there is a blackout.

Unlike the full-length version, the emphasis here is not on the title characters, but rather on the theme of role-playing and identity, and thus from the blackout a spotlight rises on Hamlet as the voice of the English ambassador is heard. Hamlet is back at Elsinore amidst a tableau of corpses, but he is no longer recognized as Hamlet—the Player (taken to be Hamlet) had returned to Elsinore and played out the events that conclude *Hamlet*. After Horatio concludes his "So shall you hear" speech (which eventually became the closing speech of *Rosguil*), Hamlet responds: "Horatio . . . And the King dead, my mother, Laertes, and—why, poor player, this was no stage for him. And I? What of me now? There is no end for a man caught out of the action. And Fortinbras returns from Poland to take my throne" (43). Though he is the "true" Hamlet, his role has been played out, his identity erased.

Stoppard follows Hamlet's line with Fortinbras's closing speech, but instead of ordering the four captains to take Hamlet's body *to* the stage, Stoppard amends the line to: "Bear Hamlet like a soldier *from* the stage" (44, emphasis added), thereby underscoring the metaphor of the world as a stage upon which humans act out their roles. Then as the procession proceeds past Hamlet, Stoppard circles the play back to its opening—the play begins with Fortinbras's speech on the plain of Denmark (*Hamlet* 4.4), and Hamlet's first exchange with the Captain ("Good sir, whose powers are these?" [*Hamlet*

4.4; *Rosguil Lear* 3]) is repeated, only this time it ends with the Captain asking Hamlet where he will go now. To this Hamlet replies: "To walk the earth. To walk the earth. . . . I have time. The sun is going down. It will be night soon. Do you think so? I was just making conversation. I have a lot of time" (44). He whistles softly and the ordnance shots that close *Hamlet* are heard to end the play. Hamlet's character has been removed from the stage, with the death of his recognizable identity signified by the cannon blast. His remarks about the position of the sun echo three earlier exchanges between Rosencrantz and Guildenstern, only now Hamlet fills both Rosencrantz's and Guildenstern's roles, and caught out of the action, he can only walk the earth, like his dead father before him.

The Gamblers

When Stoppard returned to London, he roomed in a Westminster flat with his Ford fellows Derek Marlowe and Piers Read. His fellowship over, Stoppard was again in bleak financial straits as he turned *The Gamblers* into a full-length play, transformed *Rosencrantz and Guildenstern Meet King Lear* into *Rosguil,* tried to get a TV sale, and fretted over the novel that was due in May 1965. That same month *The Gamblers* was staged at Bristol University. With major successes such as *Jumpers* and *Travesties,* Stoppard had lesser-known works that preceded them and that engaged in similar thematic subject matter. Likewise, one might consider *The Gamblers* a dry run for *Rosguil,* for there are a number of stylistic and thematic connections.

Traditionally, *The Gamblers* is referred to as a one-act play, but the Bristol Drama Department produced a two-act version. Though unpublished, the play survives in a typescript at the HRHRC.[28] Stoppard has dismissed this early effort as "*Waiting for Godot* in the death cell—prisoner and jailer" (Tynan 60). However, Stoppard's retrospective assessment is misleading.

The Gamblers is a two-character play set in a small-town jail cell at an indeterminate time in the past. The Prisoner, an intellectual and articulate man, has been sentenced to death as a leader of an unsuccessful revolution against the state. The Jailer, a slower-witted man, clings to romantic notions about death and martyrdom. Ironically, the prisoner was the former jailer who joined the revolution, not out of conviction, but out of the pragmatic belief that the revolution would succeed; conversely the Jailer supported the revolution but refrained from joining because he thought it would fail. Each rationalizes his choice by saying: "You have to be on the winning side to survive, that's all" (Synopsis). Thus, though the conflict is ideological and political, the characters' actions are based on pragmatics, not convictions. The Prisoner remarks: "If the revolution had succeeded, I would be a live hero, against my principles, and you would be a dead traitor, against yours. It could have gone either way" (59). The Prisoner also argues, "A traitor and a hero are the same thing. Only the circumstances change" (57). As in other Stoppard works, recurring themes are the relativity of perspectives and the importance of context to determine meaning.

Rosencrantz and Guildenstern Meet King Lear, and to a lesser extent *Rosguil,* focus on issues of identity and the roles people play in life; similarly these themes are fundamental to *The Gamblers.* Role reversal is integral to both the plot and theme. The Prisoner was the local jailer until he joined the revolution, and thus the Jailer is simply filling the Prisoner's original role. Furthermore, the Prisoner's desire to avoid death is countered by the Jailer's envy of the Prisoner's coming martyrdom. The philosophical and social implications of the role of the martyr are debated:

JAILER: The only heroes left are the leaders and the martyrs. Either way there's glory, but a martyr's lasts longer.

PRISONER: His posterity does seem more secure. Once dead he is immortal. Well. It's ironic at least. . . . The winners look to their leaders, the losers to their martyrs. In defeat he is a necessity.

JAILER: An inspiration for the future!

PRISONER: And spiritual comfort for the present. He symbolizes the ultimate righteousness of the cause and if the cause is supposed to be worth dying for it is well to have someone die for it, simply to reassure the survivors. (17–18)

The Jailer's idealistic view of martyrdom is consistently undercut by the Prisoner's pragmatism.

Though the Jailer glorifies martyrdom, he argues that he cannot be a martyr because: "One does not choose. One is chosen" (18). This idea of fate and assigned roles is developed in the second act. There the Jailer says: "It's my job, isn't it? We're all given a part and this happens to be mine. That's all there is to say about it" (52). But the Prisoner would like to opt out of his role of martyr, and argues that morally their roles should be reversed. Ultimately, the Prisoner does convince the Jailer to exchange roles. The men are cloaked in hoods that mask their identity as the Prisoner leads the Jailer, who is now shouting the empty phrases of the revolution, to his execution. Then the pragmatic Prisoner ironically tells the idealistic Jailer to "Keep your chin up" (67), at which point he slips the noose around his neck. While the Jailer had expressed a belief in the inevitability of fate and assigned roles (themes more fully developed in *Rosguil*), here the Prisoner takes decisive action to alter his situation, a point that differentiates this play from *Rosguil,* where the protagonists remain passive even after they read the letter ordering their execution.

Stoppard was revising *The Gamblers* and writing *Rosguil* at the same time, and so understandably there are a number of similarities. Stylistically, both plays rely on a mixture of philosophical monologues and stichomythic wordplay exchanges. Thematically, both plays discuss fate, role-playing, identity, theological doubt, and the idea that life is a gamble. Besides the difference in an active versus passive response to perceived notions of fate, *The Gamblers* differs from *Rosguil,* as well as from its acknowledged progenitor, Samuel Beckett's *Waiting for Godot,* by having a social context as well as a political dimension. Stoppard stipulates that the setting be in a time of class division between peasants and despots. Likewise, the Prisoner ruminates on the life cycle of governments:

> Our beloved president who has just been so nearly deposed by one popular uprising achieved his position by a similar one seven years ago. That's the life cycle of government, from the popular to the unpopular. The wheel goes slowly round until you get back to the starting point and it's time for another—(*a brief humorless laugh*)—revolution. It just goes on repeating itself, round and round. You can't break out of the circle, least of all by idealism. Ideals are impracticable without discipline and universal integrity. We have neither. Pity isn't it? Nothing to do but ride along. The trick is to jump off and on again at the right moment. It's only a matter of timing, and recognizing the false alarms. I never had enough practice, did I? What a tragic misjudgment that was. (56)

The Prisoner's pragmatic view suggests the political indifference that was seen as characteristic of the young Stoppard, who seemed to have little affinity for the idealism of the political Left. However, the play also contains the seeds of Stoppard's political views on the necessity of free expression:

JAILER: Well, a man's entitled to an opinion in a free country.
PRISONER: Of course. However, owing to the failure of the revolution

this is still a country dedicated to the suppression of freedom. From the highest motives. Self-preservation. . . . It is the State's role to hold opinions. It is your privilege to share them. (26)

The closing lines prefigure the phrasing and ideas that undergird *Professional Foul* and *Every Good Boy Deserves Favor,* Stoppard's 1977 "political" plays that critique and condemn Soviet Bloc repression.

While Stoppard has dismissed *The Gamblers* as a mere imitation of *Godot* and has forbidden any further productions of it, the play is actually a respectable, albeit obviously early, work, which understandably would benefit from some revisions. *The Gamblers* contains what Stoppard would consider soft moments—jokes that do not work, speeches that fall flat—but there are also sustained passages of thought-provoking comedy. One hopes, but doubts, that some day he will allow productions of this work, which he once referred to as "the first play which I regard as *mine*" (Hudson, Itzin, and Trussler 55).

As a curtain raiser for the 1965 Bristol production of *The Gamblers,* Stoppard penned *Higg and Cogg,* about a man, Higg, who threatens to make a suicidal leap. Rather than try to talk him out of it, Cogg simply moves aside so he will not get hit. Two other characters also encourage Higg to jump, calling him a coward when he vows that he will jump tomorrow when he is more in the mood. When the disappointed crowd leaves, Higg sees someone on a higher ledge and starts yelling for him to jump, berating his cowardice as the lights fade. This slight, situational play about insensitive people's desire for the sensational has its lasting impact in serving as a prelude for an incident in *Albert's Bridge,* Stoppard's 1967 award-winning radio play.

A Rocky Prelude to Success

While Stoppard prepped for these first English-language stagings, he and Jose were married, had a brief honeymoon, and found themselves begrudgingly accepting Smith's offer for a short-term loan to tide them over while Stoppard churned out TV synopses in hopes of securing an advance to pay some of the bills.[29] Instead the debt was paid with money from the Royal Shakespeare Company's £150 optioning of *Rosguil* in May 1965.

At the time of the optioning, the third act had not yet been written, but Peter Hall and Jeremy Brooks were enthusiastic about the first two acts. At Brooks's encouragement Stoppard wrote the third act in two weeks, thereby making the play one of six candidates for a fall production. The RSC maintained a year-long option on the play, but once again an anticipated breakthrough did not occur as *Rosguil* was not selected.[30]

Despite the setback the ensuing year was an active period in Stoppard's career. By early August 1965 he had finished his first, and only, novel, *Lord Malquist and Mr. Moon*.[31] Stoppard also had a number of television and radio commitments. He was commissioned to write a forty-five-minute radio play, *Albert's Bridge*, which he delivered a year late, and a half-hour television play, *A Separate Peace* (1966), which included an accompanying half-hour documentary (*Pursuit of Happiness*, cowritten with Christopher Martin) on chess. Also, during the fall of 1965, BBC radio hired Stoppard for his most unusual assignment. He was asked "to write the diary of an imaginary Arab student in London, which was then translated into Arabic and broadcast on the Overseas Service. He alternated with another author, and every other week he was paid £40 for five episodes. As far as I know, he had never met an Arab in his life. But the job kept him going for about nine months" (Kenneth Ewing, quoted in Tynan 73).[32] Stoppard dubbed this mercenary project "Ali in Wonderland," and he ultimately wrote about seventy episodes of the series. The show was called *A Student's Diary,* and the income generated by these propagandistic soap opera episodes kept Stoppard afloat during the year he revised his breakthrough play.[33]

Throughout this year, he also followed his pattern of debt and doubts, punctuated by holidays. After a fall vacation in France, Stoppard returned in a state of anxiety and severe writer's block. It had been about two months since he had written anything, and he was afraid he had lost the knack. *Albert's Bridge* was due in a month, plus he owed a sixty-minute TV play and needed to rewrite *Rosguil*. On the plus side, he had received a commission to write a TV play about gluttony and had received official word that he was hired for the Arab work. These factors bolstered his finances and allowed him to pay back part of another Smith loan. Fortunately, Stoppard soon regained confidence in his writing, and gradually paid the rest of his loans back via his Arab work, the sale of his 1966 radio play *If You're Glad I'll be Frank* (Stoppard's meditation on the nature of time and how modern society is imprisoned by it), through a May 1966 script polish of Slawomir Mrozek's *Tango* for the Royal Shakespeare Company, and from advances for television projects.

The commission for the gluttony teleplay was for a series on the seven deadly sins. Stoppard's offering, *How Sir Dudley Lost the Empire*, went unproduced. Privately, Stoppard admitted that it was strictly work for hire, and his lack of interest is apparent, for *How Sir Dudley Lost the Empire* is probably his most unremarkable surviving script. The play takes place on the fictitious island of Baku in the middle of the Arabian Sea. It is the "last dreg of the British Empire, having survived by neglect" with the "air of a ramshackle outpost" that the British government has used "as a kind of punishment posting for the discredited and the malcontent" (1). The two main characters are Sir Evelyn Travers, a man who has an idealistic nostalgia for the passing of the empire, and Sir Dudley Colquhoun, the governor, who is incredibly overweight. As might be expected, Sir Dudley is always eating or talking about eating, often waxing poetic over the thought of food. His insatiable desire for food will, of course, be a key plot point.

The British government is planning on building up Baku as a military installation, and so Travers is sent to inspect its Britishness, to see if there is any threat of secession, foreign encroachments, or independence. Indeed, the natives, led by Ngkayyad, are planning to revolt. Sir Dudley's tactical error is in spurning dinner with the American ambassador in favor of a sumptuous dinner with a German merchant, Block, who turns out to be East German. Another character, Palfrey, explains why Ngkayyad arranges this meal: "To make the Americans think that we've made a deal with the East Germans. . . . The point being that the Americans won't help keep us in Baku if we're going to let the Communists in" (65–66). When the British officials learn that Block is East German they consider throwing him out of the country, but Sir Dudley is against it because Block runs the local grocery store. This leads to Stoppard's overt addressing of the selected theme and his play's title:

LADY: (*Furiously*) Food, food! That's all you are capable of grasping in your food-fatted head!
    You big glutton!
COL: (*Calmly*) I'm a hearty eater, I see nothing to be ashamed about. As a personality trait gluttony is unjustly and grotesquely stigmatized. In fact I can't imagine how it ever fell into disrepute let alone became a deadly sin. I can well imagine a chap being kicked into hell for lust or something like that—being a bit overproud, avaricious, envious, full of wrath or even, at a pinch, bone-idle—but for liking his dinner—quite absurd—Even Christ never had anything against the old loaves and fishes, did he—I must say, I won't be maligned for

what is nothing more than a healthy appetite and a love of good food
and plenty of it. . . .

LADY: In Cairo you snubbed an invitation it was your duty to accept. In
Kuala Lumpur you refused to issue an invitation it was your duty to
make. And in Baku you have accepted an invitation it was your duty
to decline. In the first two cases the result was a diplomatic gaffe of
the first water that put every map of the world instantly out of date.
The third will doubtless be no exception—even now the cartogra-
phers flounder about in the wake of your spectacular career. (62–63)

As expected, the natives do revolt. Then, in an uncharacteristic satire of British patriotism, Stoppard has Travers grab the Union Jack and declare: "Keep
calm, everyone, stay where you are—I'll remind them that they're British!"
(71). But Travers is captured by the mob, who ultimately gain their independence. At the ensuing feast that closes the play, Stoppard hints that Travers,
not a wild boar, may actually be the main ingredient in the stew. Overall, the
script is one of Stoppard's weakest efforts. While he uses customary techniques such as cross talk and mispronunciation of names, the jokes often fall
flat, the characters are thinly developed, and the plot is rather predictable.

Stoppard's letter from October 1965 also discusses his least-known produced script, the television play *A Paragraph for Mr. Blake,* a reworking of
his short story, "The Story." The latter focuses on a reporter who, after
promising not to, sells a story about a headmaster (Mr. Blake) who got fined
for fondling a seven-year-old girl. Intended as a filler piece, the story soon
swells in details and importance, at which point Blake commits suicide.
Stoppard expanded this brief piece of fiction into an hour-long teleplay entitled *The Explorers.* A drama with very few jokes, *The Explorers* focuses on
capturing the atmosphere and lifestyle of a provincial reporter. The protagonist, John Haydon, is a journalist who ekes out an existence and who derives his greatest pleasure from "fiddling his expenses" (2). He cynically as-
sesses his profession: "[Journalism's] street of adventure stuff . . . is true on
every level except reality. . . . In many ways it's such a dreary awful job that
you've got to retain a few illusions to go on liking it—that and vanity, the
vanity of seeing it in print" (19–20). While Haydon dreams of being an
explorer, he ultimately endures his profession's pitfalls because deep down he
likes being a reporter; thus he consistently refuses his father-in-law's offer of
a more lucrative job selling central heating units.

The main action of *The Explorers* involves an immersion into the world of a small-time reporter. A young woman, Madge, is on her first day of work as she joins Haydon to cover the court cases. Going through the roster of cases, Haydon is not interested in Blake's case, but rather thinks there is a story to be written about three young thugs involved in a "malicious wounding" incident (25). While Haydon is out trying to pry information from a local police inspector, Madge diligently observes and documents Blake's indecency case. Despite all her news gathering, Haydon still doesn't want to report the story, but only because he feels it lacks newsworthiness for their particular market. However, when they meet a reporter for a news agency who is looking for something to sell to the national papers, they decide that since Blake is a headmaster and not an ordinary teacher, "it's worth a line" (35). However, Madge had told Blake that they were not writing anything about him, and so when Blake sees the story in a number of newspapers, he is distraught and eventually commits suicide by jumping in front of a subway train. When Madge learns of his suicide, she is troubled by it, wondering if her story is to blame; Haydon is more nonchalant:

> HAYDON: That's too simple—Because he ruined himself, and after thinking about it all week he got desperate enough or brave enough or cowardly enough to jump in front of a train. I don't know. . . . If he had gone to Blackpool instead of Pevington; if he had gone to the pictures instead of the beach; or if the girl had; if his mother hadn't conceived. . .
>
> MADGE: It's awful though.
>
> HAYDON: Yes, of course it's awful. It's one of a million awful things which happened today.
>
> MADGE: If he hadn't been a headmaster, just an ordinary teacher, you wouldn't have bothered to—
>
> HAYDON: But he wasn't. Rules of the game. I didn't make them. . . . I don't know what the moral of that is. Except, maybe. . . . Never be anybody. (52)

Thus, Blake's downfall is a combination of a wrong choice, his profession, and an element of chance. Blake had asserted that his actions were "totally out of character" (26), and when Madge said they were not reporting it, he thought he had escaped and could go back to his normal life. However, a chain of fortuitous events altered his life for the worse. In Stoppard's script

Blake is virtually a silent character, and somewhat of a "Moon" figure, someone to whom things happen.

Stoppard's script emphasizes the reporter's life, but while he was on holiday in France the text was severely altered. The producer decided to focus almost exclusively on the character of Mr. Blake, a man he saw as a social problem. He added numerous scenes that Stoppard felt were laborious, gratuitous, and stereotyped. The additions came at the expense of material about Haydon's home life. Stoppard considered removing his name from the project, but the production was so far advanced and he had already done all the media PR work, that he decided the best thing to do was to say nothing. *A Paragraph for Mr. Blake* was broadcast on Independent Television in October 1965 as part of their "Knock on Any Door" series. Subsequently there was a German TV production, but it has never been published. Since the script was severely altered from his draft, it stands as more of a historical curiosity than an actual piece of the Stoppard canon.

The Circuitous Path to Success

The Royal Shakespeare Company's option on *Rosguil* expired in May 1966.[34] The script was sent to the Oxford Playhouse, which in turn passed it on to the Oxford Theatre Group. When this amateur company asked permission to stage a production on the Fringe at that summer's Edinburgh Festival, Ewing reluctantly agreed.[35] Janet Watts, who played Ophelia in the Edinburgh production, recalls that the production was in disarray when Stoppard arrived for the last few rehearsals. The director and leading lady had quit, the stage manager was directing, and the actors were "bewildered by the play, which seemed clogged with repetitions and had no proper ending" (47).[36] Stoppard calmly entered the fray, "revised the last two acts, laughed the repetitions off as a massive typing error, and set the directions to right" (47). One of the actors later remarked: "He seemed to me pretty desperate to get the thing through. We went through several sleepless nights with him, trying to get it to sound the way he heard it in his head" (Watts, "Stoppard's Halfcentury," 17). Stoppard stayed for the first few performances and recalls it being received "politely rather than with hilarity" (G. Gordon 17).

The initial reviews ranged from mixed to less than flattering. The *Glasgow Herald* called it "as off-putting a piece of non-theatre as has been presented at the Festival for many a year." Even Michael Codron, Stoppard's future West End producer, wryly remarked: "It was difficult to see beyond the wrinkled tights" (Watts, "Stoppard's Half-century," 17). However, on the train back to London Stoppard discovered the review that was to mark the pivotal turn in his career. Ronald Bryden, writing in the *Observer,* described the play as an "erudite comedy, punning, far-fetched, leaping from depth to dizziness. . . . It's the most brilliant debut by a young playwright since John Arden's." When Kenneth Tynan, then Literary Manager at the National Theatre, read the review, he cabled Stoppard for a copy of the script, and thus the wheels were set in motion for his professional breakthrough.

Regarding this life-turning amateur production, Stoppard said in 1973: "I was very light-hearted about the whole thing because I had a novel [*Lord Malquist and Mr. Moon*] published in the same week that the play opened, and there was no doubt in my mind whatsoever that the novel would make my reputation, and the play would be of little consequence either way" (Watts, "Tom Stoppard," 47). Again, one might wonder about the accuracy of this retrospective public posture. While the prospect of an amateur production was no cause for great excitement, Stoppard's letters do little to corroborate this professed belief that the novel would make his reputation, or that he even desired to be a novelist. He told Smith that his only interest in writing a second novel was for the advance.[37] Likewise, long before the novel was due out, Stoppard had learned that his publisher's response was much less enthusiastic than he had hoped.[38]

Anthony Blond confessed that while he admired Stoppard's book, people were not buying many novels, short novels even less, and funny novels even less than that. And the problem was that Stoppard had written a short, funny novel. Nonetheless Blond decided to publish the book, but with the proviso that he was delaying publication until June, or possibly September. Likewise, a number of overseas publishers rejected the novel, only publishing it after *Rosguil*'s success at the National.

While the novel was headed toward relative obscurity, the play was on its way to forever altering Stoppard's life. The National Theatre was reading *Rosguil,* and Stoppard endured a few weeks of uncertainty, wondering how long he should let them consider the work. The problem was that while the deciding body of Literary Manager Kenneth Tynan, Artistic Director Laurence Olivier, and Director John Dexter were all enthusiastic about *Rosguil,* their first possible opening was in May, provided they canceled a documentary about Cuba that had run into problems. If not, they would have to wait until October 1967, but assumed that Stoppard would not wait that long. They did not realize that thus far no other London producers had expressed any interest. Tynan assured Stoppard that it was the best play they had ever received and that they had pushed out other plays in order to fit in Stoppard's. Likewise, John Dexter said he wanted to direct it more than any other play they had received. On the other hand, Stoppard remained wary, fearing that in the interim they may receive a play they liked even more and thus simply let the option lapse. Stoppard even consulted Peter O'Toole, who advised against Stoppard's leaving the play with the National for an October production. O'Toole had known too many other plays that were initially greeted with enthusiasm only to be passed over once other new plays arrived. Citing his theory that plays go off, like fruit, Stoppard agreed not to wait that long. Feeling that the play was already not as good when he wrote it a year earlier, he feared that in another year's time, the deterioration of the perception of the play would be even worse. Despite these misgivings, Stoppard ultimately accepted the National's offer of £250 for a nine-month option.[39]

While Stoppard waited for the National's decision, negotiated with multiple publishers, and fielded inquiries from America, Canada, Israel, Holland, Germany, Switzerland, Sweden, and other countries, he was beset by his customary financial problems. *Rosguil* was generating interest, but had not yet yielded any hard money, and creditors were besieging him. He sought a loan from Ewing and was on the verge of committing himself to an African radio soap opera, similar to the Arab one, a work that was still Stoppard's primary means of income.[40]

While Stoppard never did write the African propagandistic radio soap opera, he continued writing the Arab serial until at least the end of the year. He also cowrote, with Gordon Williams, the pilot for a radio serial that was to be entitled *Doctor Masopust, I Presume.* The series was to be a campy send-up of the maniacal-doctor-trying-to-take-over-the-world genre. The pilot is filled with vaudeville-type gags and the kind of stream-of-consciousness writing where the dialogue is based on puns rather than logical developments and where the characters burst into song when "prompted" by a phrase. A weak script that seems to have been hastily written, it was optioned by the BBC in January 1967, but presumably never broadcast.

Fortunately Stoppard did not have to rely on his radio work. In December 1966, after a cancellation of *As You Like It,* the National slated *Rosguil* for an April production.[41] Though the National was pleased with his revisions, Stoppard was not, privately expressing his dissatisfaction with the play.[42] Presumably, Stoppard's assessment of *Rosguil* changed after it received international acclaim; and most definitely, his financial fortunes were thereafter forever altered. As important as the relief from monetary worries, in that spring of 1967, for the first time since he had committed himself to writing in 1960, Stoppard had achieved what he truly sought: recognition. In 1974, Stoppard remarked: "As soon as *Rosencrantz* was seen and recognized and I had succeeded in reaching audiences, I felt, 'My God, the pressure is off for the first time in eight or nine years'" (Amory 71). The relief from the self-imposed pressure would, of course, be temporary, as the desire to be more than a one-hit wonder meant creating a body of work that could stand up to the lofty expectations created by the success of *Rosguil.*

2

Rosencrantz and Guildenstern Are Dead

SPEAKING ABOUT HIS EARLY WRITING CAREER AND PROCESS, Stoppard remarked: "The reason why *that* idea appealed to me rather than another one is that it does have this under-structure to it. . . . The important thing about a successful work of art is not that it should communicate X to everybody but that it should run through the absolute alphabet for each 26 people" (Taylor 28). The Stoppard work that most embodies this idea of presenting a metaphoric situation that offers a range of multiple meanings rather than specific intent is his 1967 breakthrough play *Rosencrantz and Guildenstern Are Dead* (henceforth *Rosguil*).[1] Though hailed as "the most important event in the British professional theatre of the last nine years [since Harold Pinter's *The Birthday Party*]" (Hobson, "Fearful Summons"), the National Theatre's production of Stoppard's play almost did not occur.[2]

When *Rosguil* was optioned by the National Theatre in the fall of 1966, no immediate production was scheduled; as director Derek Goldby states: "It only really got put on because there was this sudden emergency [a cancellation of an all-male *As You Like It*], it might never have been done if there wasn't a gap in the season" (Faraone 32). The National Theatre was gambling on the young, unknown playwright, but they seemed to be hedging their bet. John Stride (Rosencrantz) states: "We started rehearsing as a sort of cheap production thrown on at the National Theatre . . . and we had a very inexperienced young director who hadn't done much at all before, but was an assistant, a trainee director with the National, then we had a relatively inexperienced actor [Edward Petherbridge] given the role of Guildenstern" (32). Furthermore, trying to keep expenses to a minimum, the production, like the written text, contained an intertextual element, as it used costumes pulled from storage—the elaborate, romantic, though now partially faded, Elizabethan outfits used in Peter O'Toole's 1963 *Hamlet.* In the end *Rosguil* proved to be one of the National's greatest successes as it stayed in their repertory for almost four years and was their first production to transfer to Broadway, where it ran for over a year. In 1967–68 *Rosguil* was staged in twenty-three countries, and within a decade it had more than 250 professional productions in twenty languages.

More than three decades after its debut, *Rosguil* probably remains the work for which Stoppard is most recognized. Yet in terms of its genesis and approach, it is the least characteristic of his major plays; for all of the other works began with a specific thematic idea or subject that Stoppard wanted to write about, and then it was a matter of discovering who the characters were and what the situation was. In contrast, for *Rosguil,* Stoppard began with the characters and situation of *Hamlet,* and then let his themes emerge out of his exploration of the concrete situation faced by the characters. He has stated: "The play had no substance beyond its own terms, beyond its apparent situation. It was about two courtiers in a Danish castle. Two nonentities surrounded by intrigue, given very little information and much of that false. It had nothing to do with the condition of modern man or the decline of metaphysics" (Bradshaw 95). Elsewhere, Stoppard elaborates:

> I was not in the least interested in doing any sort of pastiche, for a start, or in doing a criticism of *Hamlet*—that was simply one of the by-products. The chief interest and objective was to exploit a situation which seemed to me to have enormous dramatic and comic potential— of these two guys who in Shakespeare's context don't really know what they're doing. The little they are told is mainly lies, and there's no reason to suppose that they ever find out why they are killed. And, probably more in the early 1960s than at any other time, that would strike a young playwright as being a pretty good thing to explore. I mean, it has the right combination of specificity and vague generality which was interesting at that time to (it seemed) eight out of ten playwrights. That's why, when the play appeared, it got subjected to so many different

kinds of interpretation, all of them plausible, but none of them calculated. (Hudson, Itzin, and Trussler 57)

The result of Stoppard's nonintentionality, coupled with the play's "literariness" (echoing and referencing of other literary works), is that *Rosguil* is his most open-ended play, one that has spurred numerous, sometimes antithetical, interpretations.[3]

In an article that appeared in the National Theatre program, Irving Wardle cited the play's indebtedness to Samuel Beckett's *Waiting for Godot,* and claimed that Stoppard provides "his two heroes with an existential development." This view of the play as an "existential comedy" was shared by many critics of the 1967 London production. In his book on Stoppard, Michael Billington argues that "philosophically, [*Rosguil*] belongs to the tradition of Theatre of the Absurd" (35). Beckett scholar Ruby Cohn counters: "*Godot* was stylistically rather than philosophically seminal for Stoppard" (114).[4] Others see it as being postabsurdist and/or postmodern, with the latter tag deriving, in part, from its conscious intertextuality. The play's borrowings from or similarities to Shakespeare, Beckett, and Pirandello have been discussed by many scholars, including Felicia Londré, Victor Cahn, and Normand Berlin, of whom the latter labels the play "theatre of criticism."[5] For intertextual analysis Thomas Whitaker goes the furthest as he argues for the ways in which *Rosguil* "rewrites" other texts, and his list includes not only *Hamlet* and *Godot,* but also James Saunders's *Next Time I'll Sing to You* (1963),[6] W. S. Gilbert's 1874 verse burlesque *Rosencrantz and Guildenstern,* as well as *Six Characters in Search of an Author, The Importance of Being Earnest, No Exit,* and *The Balcony.* Furthermore, Tynan and Faraone see Kafka as an influence, while Rusinko and Brassell add T. S. Eliot to the list.

The multiplicities of echoing have led to disparagement, such as Robert Brustein's dismissal of the play as a "theatrical parasite" (25), while others see something unique in its recombinations: "despite its multiple sources, *Rosencrantz* is a genuine original, one of a kind" (Tynan 85). Stoppard's argument that plays are events to be experienced, not literary documents to be analyzed, leads him to deemphasize the intertextuality of his work: "Playwrights try to move people, to tears or laughter. To sit in the theatre and mutter, 'Ah, Pirandello!'—or 'Hm, Kafka . . .' would be curious indeed" ("Playwrights and Professors"). The continued frequent productions, including multiple major revivals in London, suggest that the work does indeed offer a perspective that is more than mere borrowing and recycling.[7]

In reply to critics such as Corballis ("[*Rosguil* presents life as] a 'mystery' which can neither be understood nor controlled; and that death, far from being imbued with romance and significance, is mere negation—the absence of existence" [40]), there has been a steady stream of readings that try to overturn the initial existential and absurdist interpretations of the play. Jim Hunter believes that if *Rosguil* is "allegorical of human life, then it is allegory not of existentialism, materialism, or chance, but of a fixed purpose, a logic beyond and outside of us which we cannot visualize" (170). Similarly William Gruber argues that despite the protagonists' inability to comprehend the world around them, the play as a whole suggests that there is a "knowable logic that shapes men's fortunes" (116) and thus is not absurdist. Indeed, a recurrent point of debate in discussions of *Rosguil*'s thematic significance is the extent to which it is or is not existential in its worldview, and there are viable arguments for both sides.[8] Indeed, as with many of Shakespeare's plays, in *Rosguil,* critics often find what they bring to it; their own values are reflected back. From an interpretative point of view, it is advisable to keep in mind Stoppard's own assessment: "I personally think that *anybody's* set of ideas which grows out of the play has its own validity" (Hudson, Itzin, and Trussler 58). Also, the use of labels and categories tends to distort and restrict rather than liberate; and above all, *Rosguil* is a text that is contradictory and expansive, one that raises as many questions as it offers tentative answers.

Textual History

As discussed in chapter 1, the text began as the one-act play *Rosencrantz and Guildenstern Meet King Lear* (1964). In the fall of 1964 and spring of 1965 Stoppard turned it into the three-act play *Rosencrantz and Guildenstern Are Dead,* a script optioned by the Royal Shakespeare Company.[9] This version languished at the RSC from May 1965 to May 1966, only to resurface, with a revised third act at the Edinburgh Fringe, debuting on 24 August 1966. When the play moved to the National Theatre, there were further changes, but not as many as one might expect. Stoppard refined some of the phrasing and made two content-related changes. At the suggestion of Laurence Olivier, then Artistic Director of the National Theatre, Stoppard added a scene derived from *Hamlet,* in which Claudius instructs Rosencrantz and Guildenstern to find Hamlet after he's killed Polonius. The bigger change concerned the play's ending—eight different denouements were rehearsed before settling on the protagonists' disappearance and the excerpt from the closing scene of *Hamlet* (Faraone 42).[10] A result is that the play's first published edition contains an absurdist-like circularity as the two English ambassadors are summoned much like Rosencrantz and Guildenstern were;[11] though the play was never performed with that ending, some critics argue that the logic that dictated such an ending persists in the text (Corballis 42).

When the play was brought to New York, Stoppard cut nearly forty-five minutes from the play's three-hour running time in London. The most important thing to note about the text of *Rosguil* is what Stoppard writes in his preface to the Samuel French acting edition:

> This play-text is perhaps unusual in that it incorporates a good many speeches and passages enclosed in square brackets, and the material thus bracketed consists of optional cuts. There is no definitive text of [*Rosguil*]. . . . I would like each director to control the length and complication of each production (as is usual), and, on the other hand, I would like to define the area in which he has a free hand with the text. . . . Whatever else [*Rosguil*] is, [it] is a comedy. . . . It is worth bearing in mind that among the productions staged all over the world, two were comparative failures, and both of these took the play very seriously indeed. (3–4)

The biggest optional cut is the Olivier-suggested scene, while many of the other optional cuts correspond to those made for the New York production. There are also passages that did not appear in either New York or London, with most of those having been part of the Edinburgh text.[12] The Samuel French text thus offers the most flexibility and guidance for producers and interpreters.

Finally, many people are familiar with yet another version of *Rosguil*— the 1990 film that Stoppard wrote and directed, a work that won the Golden Lion as Best Film at the Venice Film Festival. The change in medium, and a contract requiring that the film be only two hours long, resulted in Stoppard's decision to cut nearly half the play's dialogue.[13] But for Stoppard the changes were desirable:

> There are chunks of [the play]—mainly in the character of the Player— which I don't actually *want* in the film. And some of the shorter lines, the duologues, they're probably more repetitive than they need to be. It was really easy to cut. . . . Mainly I was interested in trying to add

things which I was now able to think of because I could now change the *frame*—which frankly is the only important difference between theatre and film for me." (S. Smith 236)

The additions include a running sight gag through which "virtually all the laws of physics are revealed" to the duo "who bemusedly ignore them" (Owen 24).[14] There are also more scenes with the Tragedians, including a stunning puppet show version of *The Murder of Gonzago*. The film version tells much more of the *Hamlet* story, not so much through Shakespearean lines, but through visuals and snippets of dialogue that overall give a better sense of the incidents and events that are happening at Elsinore.[15] Often, these Shakespearean plot points are given a comic twist, such as when Rosencrantz and Guildenstern accidentally contribute to Polonius's death.

The addition of more of the *Hamlet* story is related to a basic change in the condition of Rosencrantz and Guildenstern. In the play, the protagonists wait for people to come to them, whereas in the film they move around Elsinore looking for the action. When asked if that fundamentally altered the theme, Stoppard replied: "For some people it has. It hasn't for me because it's relativity, isn't it? . . . The effect is the same" (Scaffidi). Overall, the effect is still that of two men searching for answers and dying without receiving a sufficient explanation. On the other hand a detailed comparison of the play text versus the film would show numerous alterations that do affect nuances of interpretation. Thus, the film is a work that has its roots in the play, but that was deliberately created to be its own entity—it is a film and not a film version of a play. It is the play text that will be analyzed in the remainder of this chapter.

Thematic Analysis of Text and Production

The plot and basic idea of *Rosguil* is relatively simple. Stoppard takes two minor characters, Rosencrantz and Guildenstern, who are almost indistinguishable in Shakespeare's *Hamlet,* and thrusts them into the foreground. For a reason that they either do not know or cannot remember, they have been summoned to Elsinore. Along the way they meet the traveling troupe of Players who appear in *Hamlet*. At Elsinore, the protagonists participate in episodes of *Hamlet* and have more encounters with the Players. In the third act, they are on the boat taking Hamlet to England, meet the stowaway Players, and discover two letters—one announcing Hamlet's death warrant, the other their own. Throughout the play, they wait, talk, philosophize, play games, and spend much of the time trying to make sense of their situation and the events transpiring around them.[16]

While working on the play, Stoppard realized that a play about Shakespeare's minor characters could be more than just a joke-filled comedy. Stoppard remarked: "Something alerted me to the serious reverberations of the characters. Rosencrantz and Guildenstern, the most expendable people of all time. Their very facelessness makes them dramatic; the fact that they die without ever really understanding why they lived makes them somehow cosmic" (Sullivan 27). Recognizing the metaphoric opportunity their situation represented, Stoppard crafted a play that deals with significant philosophical issues: (1) the nature of truth, (2) role-playing versus identity, (3) human mortality, and (4) whether life and the universe are random or deterministic—does chance or logic rule the world? On many of the themes Stoppard offers multiple viewpoints without taking a definitive position. For example, while the protagonists' situation may be described as existential, answers beyond existentialism, such as the hope that there are rational explanations for the world and human experience, are posited as equally possible or plausible.

Before moving into specific analysis of the play, it is important to note the multiple levels on which the characters Rosencrantz and Guildenstern operate. They exist both inside and outside the text of *Hamlet* and at times they also acknowledge the presence of the theatre audience, thereby suggesting what film director John Boorman called "a present-day identity, as actors caught and trapped within the roles" (Letter to Stoppard). When Boorman suggested that the proposed 1968 movie might physically move among these several levels of identity and reality, Stoppard objected: "I know now though I didn't when I was writing it, that possibly the main reason for the play's effectiveness is that it doesn't attempt to break down or analyze or explain; it simply pitches you into these ambiguities. . . . I do think that an attempt to lay it out on a slab so that actuality, reality, dream, impersonation and whatever are all separated would be a mistake" (Letter to John Boorman). One reason not to break down the ambiguities is that it would reveal illogical inconsistencies in Stoppard's construction of the characters. The more compelling reason is my assumption that most audiences do not try to differentiate the levels of reality on which the protagonists exist. While Rosencrantz and Guildenstern are simultaneously Shakespeare's characters (they speak Elizabethan verse and participate in *Hamlet*), Stoppard's characters (who use contemporary English as they spectate, comment on, and ruminate about the implications of the events transpiring around them), and have a meta-theatrical existence (they espouse lines that indicate their awareness of the live audience), they are, I assume, fundamentally seen as characters whose experiences have some relevancy to those of the viewers. So for my analysis, I shall, for the most part, bracket off the distinctions as to which level of reality Rosencrantz and Guildenstern are operating within, but rather treat them as emblematic of "ordinary" people who play many roles in life and who try to discern meaning from the situations they face.

The play begins with what has become one of the most memorable opening scenes in twentieth-century theatre. Rosencrantz and Guildenstern are betting on the toss of coins, and the audience soon learns that an incredible seventy-six straight times it has come down "heads." While seemingly impossible, the streak is more accurately described as improbable, something that goes against normal expectations of human experience. Guildenstern, the more intellectual and inquisitive member of the pair,[17] notes: "A weaker man might be moved to re-examine his faith, if in nothing else at least the law of probability" (7). Guildenstern, ever the believer that events happen for a reason, wants an explanation, preferably one grounded in logic. Feeling that the streak indicates something more than the redistribution of wealth, Guildenstern theorizes possible explanations. Of his four theories only time stopping dead is considered "doubtful," and thus human willpower, divine intervention, and mathematical principles are all considered viable explanations, not only for this particular event, but on a more general level, for why earthly phenomena occur.

These suppositions are only possible explanations and not answers, so Guildenstern pursues it further, trying to apply the logical, reasoning process of syllogisms: "One, probability is a factor which operates within natural forces. Two, probability is not operating as a factor. Three, we are now within un-, sub- or supernatural forces" (12). Thus, Guildenstern postulates the possibility of a nonnatural, nonmaterial realm or state of existence. However, his next speech proceeds to use logic to cancel out everything he has logically assumed, with one possible implication being that belief in supernatural forces as the controlling mechanism of life does not depend on logic and reasoning. Guildenstern's statement "The scientific approach to the examination of phenomena is a defence against the pure emotion of fear" (12) indicates a major tension found in the play—the degree to which knowledge is based on intellect versus being based on emotion, and which of those factors should take precedence in the determination of whether or not something is held to be "true." This tension persists throughout much of Stoppard's canon as continually characters struggle with the variances between what they know via logic, via intellect, via emotion, via temperament, and via experience, all different ways of comprehending the world, each of whose primacy of truthfulness depends on the context of the given situation and what is at stake.

Guildenstern's speech proceeds: "The equanimity of your average tosser of coins depends on a law, or rather a tendency, or let us say a probability, or at any rate a mathematically calculable chance, which ensures that he will not upset himself by losing too much nor upset his opponent by winning too often. This made for a kind of harmony and a kind of confidence. It related the fortuitous and the ordained into a reassuring union which we recognized as nature" (12). With a continual refinement of the selected words, Guildenstern tries to use language to pin down exactly what he means, and in the process moves from the certainty of a law to the uncertainty of a chance, all the while hoping for something that will ensure him that the world is not too chaotic. The close of the quotation hints at what is the overall tone of the play—that life and the world are a combination of chance and determinism. Indeed, Stoppard's opening scene involves an intriguing phenomenon and the issuance of possible explanations, but there is no unequivocal answer, and the run of heads is an image that captures the ambiguity of the play. Traditionally, the streak is seen as suggesting "a chance-ridden world" (Jenkins, *Theatre of Tom Stoppard,* 39) in which the "normal rules of probability and expectation are simply not operating" (Brassell 40), but the other side of the coin is its eerily deterministic quality—when they meet the Players, and the coin is tossed, both the protagonists and the audience are almost certain it will land as "heads." [18]

The one time the coin is "tails," the protagonists are genuinely surprised, and it is at that moment that Rosencrantz and Guildenstern are transposed into the world of *Hamlet,* where Claudius immediately misidentifies the two courtiers. One of Stoppard's significant elaborations from the *Hamlet* text is to extend everyone else's inability to distinguish between Rosencrantz and Guildenstern to the characters themselves. When meeting the Players, Rosencrantz says: "My name is Guildenstern, and this is Rosencrantz. (GUIL *briefly confers with him. Without embarrassment.*) I'm sorry—*his* name's Guildenstern, and *I'm* Rosencrantz" (16–17). Some critics see this as a failing: "In [*Godot*], the characters can answer to any name because a crazy world has robbed them of a sense of identity, but from an empirical perspective, when ordinary people feel so threatened and lost they tend to cling to their individuality; one's name is the essence of that self" (Jenkins, *Theatre of Tom Stoppard*, 41). But Stoppard's use of Rosencrantz and Guildenstern is more metaphoric than realistic, and their inability to know their own names on a consistent basis highlights the degree to which they are alienated from and uncertain about their ontology. The climax to the question game is Guildenstern's anguished cry: "WHO DO YOU THINK YOU ARE?" (34). In part, through Rosencrantz and Guildenstern's plight, Stoppard raises fundamental philosophical questions about the nature of identity and what constitutes self. Is there an essential self? Is one defined by his or her interactions with others? Is identity merely a series of roles people play? These types of questions are posed, but not definitively answered.

The question game, where the object is to "answer" every question with another question, epitomizes the play itself—Rosencrantz and Guildenstern inhabit a world that is full of questions, but to which they can find no answers. At the game's conclusion, Rosencrantz can only make the statement, "It's all questions" (34); and their final questions here are: "What's the game? What are the rules?" (34)—metaphorical questions that accent their existential angst at their inability to comprehend the world in which they live and the rules by which it is governed. Their quest for meaning, for answers to their questions, is one of the main thematic throughlines of the play. At the outset, Guildenstern declares: "We have not been . . . picked out . . . simply to be abandoned . . . set loose to find our own way. . . . we are entitled to some direction. . . . I would have thought" (14, ellipses in original). They have the existential feeling of being cut adrift, and in lieu of specific answers, they will settle for a general direction in which to search for explanations. Subsequent attempts to determine geographic direction might be seen as emblematic of this quest for epistemological directionality. For example, when Guildenstern tries to determine the position of the sun, Rosencrantz suggests, "Why don't you go and have a look?" but Guildenstern responds: "Empiricism?!—is that all you have to offer?" (45). Reading Guildenstern's response metaphorically suggests a rejection of sensory experiences as the definitive source of knowledge.

Though eschewing the scientific approach of empirical observation, Guildenstern continually harks back to a belief that events happen for causal, not arbitrary, reasons: "Your smallest action sets off another somewhere else, and is set off by it. . . . Till events have played themselves out. There's a logic at work—it's all done for you, don't worry" (30–31). This statement begins with a sense of human agency but gives way to a feeling of an inexorable fate, which here is somewhat comforting as it removes the anxiety of having to choose. Indeed, at times, Guildenstern is comforted by the thought of a fixed course that offers limited freedom:

> I'm very fond of boats myself. I like the way they're—contained. You don't have to worry which way to go, or whether to go at all. . . . One is free on a boat. For a time. Relatively. . . . Free to move, speak, extemporise, and yet. We have not been cut loose. Our truancy is defined by one fixed star, and our drift represents merely a slight change of angle to it. (79)

The image is one of free will, but within constraints—of limited freedom within a larger, determined course. At other points, the belief in a preordained destiny contains a darker sentiment: "Wheels have been set in motion, and they have their own pace, to which we are . . . condemned" (46). Thus, the belief in an ordered world leads to both a feeling of security and one of condemnation. Likewise, they are continually faced with the prospect that any action they take that they might consider to be the exercise of free will may in fact be nothing more than fated action:

> ROS: I wish I was dead. (*Considers the drop.*) I could jump over the side. That would put a spoke in their wheel.
> GUIL: Unless they're counting on it.
> ROS: I shall remain on board. That'll put a spoke in their wheel. (*The futility of it, fury.*) All right! We don't question, we don't doubt. We perform. (84)

For Rosencrantz and Guildenstern, even if there is a grand design, they can never know for certain what is and is not part of that design, and their inability to find a meaningful course of action or to assert their independence leads to a sense of frustration and futility.

One of the play's central concerns is the nature of truth. Guildenstern starts with an assumption that truth is within reach, though not clearly defined: "All your life you live so close to the truth, it becomes a permanent blur in the corner of your eye, and when something nudges it into outline it is like being ambushed by a grotesque" (30). But for the present time, as they try to get their bearings at Elsinore, the only truths he can articulate are that "we came" and that "the only beginning is birth and the only end is death" (30). Existence, though not necessarily essence, and mortality are the only certainties—all else in life is a mystery, an unanswered question; or as Rosencrantz states in Stoppard's unproduced 1968 screenplay: "The Player [is right]. Every answer reveals two questions" (73).

Throughout the play, the protagonists feel like "we've got nothing to go on; we're out on our own" (81); that they are forced to "act on scraps of information" (80). Sometimes they feel like "words [are] all we have to go on" (32), while at other moments they declare: "If we can't learn by experience, what else have we got?" (71). Feeling that he is in an epistemological vacuum, the once optimistic Guildenstern is reduced to saying: "I've lost all capacity for disbelief. I'm not sure that I could even rise to a little gentle scepticism" (78). In the end, when faced with the crucial moral decision of how to respond to the letter that orders Hamlet's execution, they see how dependent they are on others for knowledge of the world:

ROS: We're his *friends*.
GUIL: How do you know? . . . You've only got their word for it.
ROS: But that's what we depend on. (86) [19]

For Rosencrantz and Guildenstern knowledge has no essence.

The anxiety over the uncertainty of their situation, the nature of existence, and another perspective on the nature of truth form the core of a pivotal passage in the second act. Meeting up again with the Tragedians, Rosencrantz and Guildenstern are accosted for having abandoned the Tragedians on the road to Elsinore. In a speech that Guildenstern characterizes as "strong on metaphor" (50), the Player states: "You don't understand the humiliation of it—to be tricked out of the single assumption which makes our existence viable—that somebody is *watching*" (49). Just as the performers require an audience to give themselves a sense of purpose, similarly "Rosencrantz and Guildenstern, representatives of humanity, require knowledge of an observer to support the meaning of their existence. This observer traditionally has been God, and when knowledge of his presence falters . . . then life loses its stability" (Cahn 53). Cut from their metaphysical roots and tired of "being left so much to our own devices" (51), Rosencrantz and Guildenstern hunger for company, stability, and the wisdom of someone who has "been here before" (51). The Player, the quintessential chameleon of identity but also the enactor of roles with fixed destinies, does not offer the reassuring comfort they seek. Rather he argues that their existential angst at their inability to comprehend their situation is to be expected, even ordinary:

> PLAYER: Uncertainty is the normal state. You're nobody special.
> GUILD: But for God's sake what are we supposed to *do?!*
> PLAYER: Relax. Respond. That's what people do. You can't go through life questioning your situation at every turn.
> GUILD: But we don't know what's going on, or what to do with ourselves. We don't know how to *act.*
> PLAYER: Act natural. You know why you're here at least.
> GUILD: We only know what we're told, and that's little enough. And for all we know it isn't even true.
> PLAYER: For all anyone knows, nothing is. Everything has to be taken on trust; truth is only that which is taken to be true. It's the currency of living. There may be nothing behind it, but it doesn't make any difference so long as it is honoured. One acts on assumptions. (51–52)

The Player argues that truth and knowledge have no essence, and thus this passage is the play's strongest articulation of the perspective that truth is relative, not absolute. Since life only offers assumptions, not certainties, the protagonists can never be sure about the relative truth of what they hear.

The Player's advice to "Relax. Respond" suggests a defensive posture, one of reaction not action. At Elsinore, whenever Rosencrantz and Guildenstern try to control the exits and entrances of others, the opposite occurs. Also, when Rosencrantz contemplates confronting Hamlet with "a direct informal approach," "his nerve fails" him (58). Given a direct order by Claudius to find Hamlet after he has slain Polonius, Rosencrantz and Guildenstern remain indecisive, and ultimately carry out their search by remaining still and hoping that Hamlet crosses their path. Continually afraid to take action, it is no wonder they feel "We have no control" (56). In the end, their passivity proves fatal.

Passivity and fate are the downfall of Rosencrantz and Guildenstern, and Stoppard's key additions, first at Elsinore and then on the boat, show an equivocating attitude toward whether the characters, and by extension humans, are bound to determinacy versus having the free will to choose their own course of action. At Elsinore, Rosencrantz and Guildenstern encounter the Tragedians as they are rehearsing, only now the text of the dumb show is that of *Hamlet.* The action includes a dramatization of Rosencrantz's and

Guildenstern's own deaths, yet they fail to understand what it is they are see-ing.[20] Beyond their own deaths, what the protagonists fail to recognize is that they are an integral part of the incomprehensible world around them; rather than mere spectators, they have a role to play in the preordained plot in the world of *Hamlet*. This fact does not escape the Player, who beyond being a coparticipant also has godlike omniscience.

> PLAYER: There's a design at work in all art—surely you know that?
> Events must play themselves out to aesthetic, moral, and logical con-clusion. . . . We aim at the point where everyone who is marked for death dies.
> GUIL: Marked? . . . Who decides?
> PLAYER: (*Switching off his smile*) Decides? It is *written*. (63)

Here is where Stoppard's mediation between art and life becomes tenu-ous. The Player's notion that artistic events must be resolved according to aesthetic, moral, and logical conclusions is, Felicia Londré argues, "surely a statement of Stoppard's own preoccupation as a playwright; it will be seen that he scrupulously satisfies all three requirements, in this, and in each of his other plays" (28). But to what degree can one apply that design to human life? On this point critics are divided:

> The ideas of rôle and fate . . . invoke the inability of all mankind to understand those forces ultimately in control of their lives and fate. Yet precisely because Rosencrantz and Guildenstern's fate is determined by *Hamlet,* and not by random forces, Stoppard further suggests that there is some method behind the seeming madness of their lives. . . . Like the players, the audience can see the design where Rosencrantz and Guildenstern cannot, and there is some reassurance to be gained from this over-view. At the same time, what tempers our recognition of the courtiers' amusingly ironic plight is a latent awareness that, like them, we cannot see the "design" behind our own lives. Our sympathies are thus directed towards these two men groping in an existential void which, to varying degrees, may mirror our own. . . . [We see Rosen-crantz and Guildenstern] as human beings trapped in a world which does not make sense, which refuses to follow the expected rules. (Bras-sell 53–54)

Paul Delaney refutes Brassell's interpretation:

> But if the courtiers' world mirrors our own then ours is not just an existential void. It may be a world which does not *seem* to make sense, which refuses to follow the rules *we* might expect. But to the extent that the world of Rosencrantz and Guildenstern mirrors our own it shows us the inability of all mankind to understand those forces ultimately in control of their lives and fates at the same time that it asserts that such forces beyond human control or understanding do exist. . . . Ultimately Stoppard's play leads us to recognise that whether we can comprehend it or not that there is "design at work" in life as well as art, that there is order and coherence beyond man's ability to grasp. (*Moral Vision*, 18–19)

The problem with Delaney's insistence that the play takes an unequivocal stance is that the assurance of order is nothing more than the text of *Hamlet*, a fictional creation. And if one pushes Delaney's interpretation to *its* logical conclusion, the message of the play becomes nothing more than human life being bound to predestination, individuals assigned to roles whose outcomes have been scripted from the time they enter the stage of the world.

Stoppard's addition of the Tragedians' performance of the dumb show suggests that the fate of Rosencrantz and Guildenstern will be bound to the *Hamlet* text. However, there is still the third-act boat trip to England, a section that relies mostly on Stoppard's invention as its only precedence in Shakespeare is Hamlet's brief account (V. ii) of changing the letters and being saved by pirates. Stoppard's construction of what transpires on the boat trip to England contains three major additions, actual plot points that have the potential to change the course of the dramatic action: (1) the protagonists' discovery that the original letter calls for Hamlet's execution, (2) their subsequent discovery that the letter commands their own, and (3) Guildenstern's "killing" of the Player.

The ambiguity of Stoppard's treatment of the protagonists is conveyed in the events of the third act. Stoppard has stated: "I see them much more clearly as a couple of bewildered innocents rather than a couple of henchmen, which is the usual way they are depicted in productions of *Hamlet*" (G. Gordon 18).[21] Brassell argues that in *Rosguil* Stoppard views the courtiers as innocent victims and toward that end, Stoppard excised all dialogue from

Hamlet that might suggest their complicity (43–47). But in *Rosguil* the protagonists' innocence at Elsinore is countered by their culpability aboard the ship. After reading the letter announcing Hamlet's death sentence, they are faced with the choice of how to act in response. Guildenstern argues:

> Let us keep things in proportion. Assume, if you like, that they're going to kill him. Well, he is a man, he is mortal, death comes to us all, et cetera, and consequently he would have died anyway, sooner or later. Or to look at it from the social point of view—he's just one man among many, the loss would be well within reason and convenience. And then again what is so terrible about death? As Socrates so philosophically put it, since we don't know what death is, it is illogical to fear it. It might be . . . very nice. Certainly it is a release from the burden of life, and, for the godly, a haven and a reward. Or to look at it another way—we are little men, we don't know the ins and outs of the matter, there are wheels within wheels, et cetera—it would be presumptuous of us to interfere with the designs of fate or even of kings. All in all, I think we'd be well advised to leave well alone. (86)

Thus Guildenstern rationalizes a course of inaction, one that would not only make them complicitous if Hamlet were to be killed, but that also provides a sort of poetic justice for their own eventual deaths.

Rosencrantz makes meek objections to applying logic or justice to their analysis of the situation, but ultimately opts to follow Guildenstern in the decision to let fate run its course.[22] Hamlet proceeds to switch the letters, and soon thereafter the pirate attack occurs. With Hamlet gone, the courtiers feel at a loss, with Guildenstern articulating their sense of hopelessness and dependency on someone else to give their lives meaning: "The whole thing's pointless without him. . . . Nothing will be resolved without him. . . . We need Hamlet for our release. . . . We've travelled too far, and our momentum has taken over; we move idly towards eternity, without possibility of reprieve or hope of explanation" (93–94). But Guildenstern's pessimism is countered by Rosencrantz's optimism: "Be happy—if you're not even *happy* what's so good about surviving? We'll be all right. I suppose we just go on" (94). Whereas usually it is Guildenstern who must revive Rosencrantz's spirits, here the situation is reversed. Rosencrantz's attitude of "just going on" is reminiscent of Beckett's tramps in *Godot,* but here the protagonists have the letter from the king to give them a sense of direction. However, when they open the letter that now orders their own execution, they are again immobilized:

> GUIL: (*Quietly*) Where we went wrong was getting on a boat. We can move, of course, change direction, rattle about, but our movement is contained within a larger one that carries us along as inexorably as the wind and current.
>
> ROS: They had it in for us, didn't they? Right from the beginning. Who'd have thought that we were so important?
>
> GUIL: But why? Was it all for this? Who are we that so much should converge on our little deaths? (*In anguish to the* PLAYER.) Who are *we?*
>
> PLAYER: You are Rosencrantz and Guildenstern. That's enough.
>
> GUIL: No—it is not enough. To be told so little—to such an end— and still finally, to be denied an explanation—
>
> PLAYER: In our experience, most things end in death. (95)

Rosencrantz and Guildenstern passively accept this death sentence as their fate, and their biggest concern is not their destiny, but the desire for an explanation, for an understanding of who they are, what has transpired, and why.

Instead of trying to alter their fate by destroying the letter, Guildenstern protests the lack of an explanation, and with "fear, vengeance, [and] scorn" (95), he attacks the Player, stabbing him with a dagger. As the Player dies a compelling death, an "almost hysterical" Guildenstern again rationalizes an immoral action by blaming it on fate: "If we have a destiny, then so had he— and if this is ours, then that was his—and if there are no explanations for us, then let there be none for him" (96).[23] Guildenstern's pronouncement that all is destiny is followed by a moment of silence, and then a burst of applause; the Player rises and accepts congratulations on his performance.

This enactment, so convincing to observers, leads to Guildenstern's final, heavily existential, meditation on the nature of death: "Dying is not romantic, and death is not a game which will soon be over . . . Death is not anything . . . death is not . . . It's the absence of presence, nothing more . . . the endless time of never coming back" (97; ellipses in original). From Rosencrantz's amusing "death in a box" speech to the Player's discussion of stage deaths, the play has many ruminations on death, but this final one by Guildenstern is the most forceful, the most chilling. Soon thereafter, Rosencrantz and Guildenstern, still unsure which is which, "disappear"; this action fulfills

Guildenstern's earlier definition of death: "It's just a man failing to reappear, that's all—now you see him, now you don't . . . an exit, unobtrusive and unannounced, a disappearance gathering weight as it goes on, until, finally, it is heavy with death" (66–67). At their passing, Rosencrantz is "relieved" while Guildenstern unconvincingly says, "We'll know better next time" (98). Instead, the audience sees only death, for the stage picture is the ending tableau from *Hamlet*—four visible deaths and knowledge that Rosencrantz and Guildenstern have made their final exit.

Since the English ambassador announces that "Rosencrantz and Guildenstern are dead" (98), one assumes that they resealed the letter, delivered it to the English king, and were executed. This action, like the play as a whole, has generated numerous interpretations. Charles Marowitz sees the discovery of the switched letter and acceptance of their fate as a "masterstroke" that helps make the play "a blinding metaphor about the absurdity of life" (*Confessions* 124–25). Felicia Londré views the delivery of the fateful letter as "an existential choice to follow through with their mission, knowing that it will end in death. . . . It does not make tragic heroes of them, for their deaths are still meaningless, but it does give them, at last, a kind of identity" (33). In contrast, June Schlueter argues that the ending shows "that there is no other life for Rosencrantz and Guildenstern outside of the Shakespeare play, outside of their roles. . . . [They] are indeed heroes, having fulfilled (though less than nobly) their obligation in life and in the play, which is to perform" (84). For Paul Delaney, though Rosencrantz and Guildenstern remain nonentities, the play conveys the feeling that their fear and their deaths *do* matter, and that through their plight, the play can "start the whisper in [our] skulls that says—'One day you are going to die'" (*Moral Vision* 32).

Indeed, the specter of death looms over the play, and therein lies part of its uniqueness. Typically, comedy ends happily, with harmony restored, couplings on the horizon, and the promise that life goes on; but here the protagonists are dead, a fact the audience knew from the time they entered the theatre. Characteristic of the play's ambiguity, their deaths, though reminiscent of tragedy, in a sense, actually fulfill comedy's typical function of reaffirmation, for the status quo is intact, and the audience leaves the theatre secure in the same knowledge they had as they entered it—Rosencrantz and Guildenstern are still dead.

This foreknowledge of their fate also points to part of the play's shortcomings. Since Stoppard has preordained that Rosencrantz and Guildenstern shall remain wedded to Shakespeare's text, a thematic reckoning of whether their final choice was a positive acceptance of death or a negative decision not to fight or flee is almost moot. Whereas they begin the play outside of *Hamlet,* and thus might be seen as representative of humanity, they, and the play, end completely in Shakespeare's world, and thus represent characters not people.[24] Though not identifying it as a problem, Stoppard himself has noted:

> Rosencrantz and Guildenstern are two people who have been written into a scheme of things and there's nothing they can do about it except follow through and meet the fate that has been ordained for them. . . . But what I am wary of is the supposition that anything which appears to be true of the characters in my play is a definite reflection of my own feelings about life in general. Actually, I haven't got any feelings that could be so neatly defined. . . . There was really nothing premeditated or conscious about it, and I certainly don't take a gloomy view of the world; not in the least. The point is, I'm writing about two characters in a play and what's true for *them.* But to extend it to me, I'd have to say I'm using Shakespeare as a symbol of God, which I'm not prepared to say. I have written about two people on whom Shakespeare imposed inevitability, but I haven't got a philosophy figured out for you. (Louis)

As likable characters whose bewildered attempts to understand their world gain our sympathies, Rosencrantz and Guildenstern are a major part of the play's appeal, but their "characterness" (inability to define themselves sufficiently outside of Shakespeare's world) is somewhat unsatisfying and prevents them from reaching "Everyman" status. Guildenstern's statement "We are presented with alternatives. . . .—But not choice" (30) aptly summarizes the way Stoppard has constructed them. On the other hand, their very human struggle for comprehension, coupled with frequent comedy, override the script's flaws, and thus the play is often highly successful in production.[25] Though Rosencrantz and Guildenstern remain "characters," audiences can look to the play to "glean what afflicts us." While one might hope that all is not predestination, audiences can share their bafflement and desire for an explanation, relying on the hope, the protagonists' intuition, that there is something to comprehend and that human lives, no matter how seemingly small and insignificant, do matter.

Chapter

3

Galileo

THE INTERNATIONAL SUCCESS OF *Rosencrantz and Guildenstern Are Dead* made Stoppard a writer in great demand. When West End producer Michael Codron requested a script, Stoppard revised an early play, *The Critics,* into the work now known as *The Real Inspector Hound.* Also, *Enter a Free Man* was near the end of its option, but now was moved quickly into production on the West End. Thus, in 1968, Stoppard was in the rare position of having three new plays being produced in prestigious London venues.

The film industry also sought Stoppard's talents; within a month of *Rosguil*'s opening, Stoppard had been offered, and had rejected, at least four film projects. However, by the end of the year, he had sold the film rights to both *Rosguil* (for $350,000) and his novel *Lord Malquist and Mr. Moon.* Privately, Stoppard was skeptical about the viability of either one as a film, but in 1968 he wrote screenplays of both works. Neither script was ever produced. Likewise, in 1969, Stoppard cowrote, with his friend Anthony Smith, a film script of Stoppard's award-winning radio play *Albert's Bridge,* but again the film was never made. A fourth unproduced screenplay, about Galileo, was to become the seed for Stoppard's only post-*Rosguil* stage play never to be produced.

Paramount Pictures hired Stoppard to write a screenplay loosely based on Brecht's play *Life of Galileo.*[1] At the outset Stoppard made it clear that his research indicated that "Brecht's play was nonsensical in certain historical respects" and that his version "would be essentially faithful to history" (Letter to Peter Bart).[2] Stoppard wrote two drafts, but the script was rejected, in part because the Paramount executive felt that "one doesn't feel a sense of growing jeopardy for Galileo, nor is one involved in his personal ordeal" (Letter to Peter Bart). Indeed, in diligently adhering to historical fact, Stoppard's script *does* deviate from the normative narrative of a mainstream Hollywood film. However, Stoppard still believed in the script's quality and struck upon the idea of reshaping it into a stage play that he intended for production at the London Planetarium.[3]

Early in 1973 London newspapers reported a forthcoming *Galileo* production, with Michael White as the producer. Eschewing any attempt at physically representing seventeenth-century Italy on stage, Stoppard deliberately crafted his script for the Planetarium because it had a projector that could create various sky effects appropriate to Galileo's story.[4] However, it soon became clear that from the Planetarium's perspective there were too many technical difficulties to make the project feasible. The Young Vic, the forthcoming National Theatre building, and the RSC were all proposed as possible venues, but for reasons unknown, none of them produced *Galileo*. Stoppard then removed the script from circulation, with most scholars unaware of its existence. This "lost" Stoppard play can be found in the HRHRC archives.[5]

In replying to Paramount's rejection, Stoppard commented on his screenplay. Those remarks also apply to his play version:

If growing jeopardy and personal ordeal were the keynotes of Galileo's story you would have every right to complain, and clearly your complaint springs from such an expectation, as though Galileo were a man who from the beginning put his life on the line (for Conscience, Truth, and so on) and who was in constant danger from the Inquisition until, finally, they got him. But the equally interesting truth is that Galileo was a brilliant man of wide scientific interest who, living in a time of transition between the medieval and modern ages, was a gregarious irritant to disputing scholars and clerics of older persuasions, but who was widely admired and celebrated for most of his life until he took a calculated risk in publication and was brought down (rather gently for that time) because political considerations triumphed over Reason. He was a man who knew that Reason would triumph in the end but he was careful to test the wind and indeed stayed safe in Venice [for a number of years] emerging to be applauded by the Church. He did not leave himself open to serious attack until [later], and the [initial] attack failed. Certainly there was opposition, as is widely indicated throughout the script, but Galileo was a man who took some care not to put himself in jeopardy, who "played the system", was attractive, witty, irreverent and proud, but who finally miscalculated. (Letter to Peter Bart)

The events Stoppard selects *do* create dramatic interest, but his overall goal is to present an accurate depiction of Galileo's scientific life and his conflict with the Catholic Church. Thus, in Stoppard's handling, documentary fact takes precedence over manipulating the material for narrative suspense.

Stoppard's *Galileo* involves twenty-seven speaking roles (fifteen of which can be doubled) and at least ten supernumeraries. Having no formal scene divisions, the play is somewhat cinematic as it flows freely among events and locations spanning from 1600 to Galileo's recantation in 1633. Besides Galileo, the main characters are Barberini, Bellarmine, Castelli, and Colombe. Barberini was a Florentine aristocrat who became a cardinal and eventually Pope Urban VIII. Barberini was sympathetic to science, but he ultimately ordered the trial and condemnation of Galileo. Cardinal Bellarmine was more strongly opposed to scientific progress and actively pursued heretics. Bellarmine administered the first official reprimand against Galileo, as his admonition in 1616 would later be used against Galileo in his trial. Castelli is a monk who learns to reconcile religion and scientific inquiry. In the course of the play he will become a disciple and supporter of Galileo. Stoppard's main use of poetic license is the creation of the character Father Colombe. The play's Narrator explains: "[Colombe] is a fictitious person for whom we borrow the name of the slightly ludicrous figure of Ludovico del Colombe, a real-life pursuer of Galileo who was not in fact a priest or even an academic. Little is known about this Colombe, but Galileo often referred to him, and we now give his name to this Jesuit to represent the various clerics and teachers who opposed the new astronomy" (19). Throughout the play, Stoppard's Narrator notes when and how the play deviates from historical fact, thereby serving as a subtle rebuttal to the way Brecht manipulated the story to fit his own ideological ends.

Stoppard's play begins with a Narrator who establishes the scene in 1600 on the day that the Copernican, and thus heretic, Giordano Bruno is executed. Throughout the play, Bruno will be used as the touchpoint for whenever someone wants to warn Galileo of the danger he faces in contradicting Church teaching. Also, throughout the play the Narrator provides exposition. While some might interpret the use of the Narrator as a form of Brechtian alienation, Stoppard uses the character more in the manner of a documentary, informing the audience about the background and significance of these historical figures, sometimes extending beyond the scope of Galileo's story.

Copernicus's theory that the earth moves around the sun and not vice versa was published in 1570, and within the opening execution scene Bellarmine explains how Copernicus still remained true to the Catholic Church: "The first virtue [of Copernicus's book] is that it is written in Latin and is thus intelligible only to those who have the education to appreciate its second virtue, which is that it insists on nothing. It is mere hypothesis" (1.3). Writing in Latin, as opposed to the vernacular, and presenting the views as hypothesis, as opposed to fact, will be central issues in Galileo's conflict with the Catholic Church. Indeed, Bellarmine closes the opening scene by noting the central conflict between Copernican theory and the Church: "[Copernicus's hypothesis] simplifies certain mathematical calculations concerning the movement of the heavenly bodies. It does not presume to be a description of the heavens. That would be heretical. In this way we can keep apart the truths of theology and the superstition of science, and a reasonable man need come to no harm" (1.4). Besides reducing science to a superstition, Stoppard's subtle wordplay revolves around the irony that throughout the play Galileo is the man of reason, but in the end, in the eyes of the Church, he will act unreasonably and thus will have to be censored.

The play cuts from Bellarmine to Galileo instructing the young Prince Cosimo on the features of the Copernican solar system as opposed to the crystal spheres of Aristotle and Ptolemy. In this scene and throughout the play Galileo champions reason, common sense, and the power of observation, central tenets of modern science. In contrast, Galileo critiques Aristotle for presenting as fact ideas that were never empirically tested. In a comic demonstration, Galileo proceeds to use Aristotle's *Meterologica* and *De Caelo*, two books of very different weight, to show that, contrary to Aristotle, objects of different weight fall at the same rate. Then to highlight how Italian neoclassical culture unquestioningly accepts Aristotle's authority, Cosimo's mother remarks: "An interesting illusion. If I had not read Aristotle I would have said they fell together" (1.8). Throughout the play Galileo faces opposition from those who refuse to trust their eyes, but who instead rely solely on the authority of the ancients, from Aristotle to Holy Scripture.

The debate between the Copernican and Aristotelian view of the universe is not just a scientific debate, it is political, philosophical, and religious. Aristotle's description of the celestial universe offers a sense of divine sublimity. As a Priest describes Aristotle's crystal spheres theory of the universe, the Planetarium's projection system was to show what was being described. In this view, the earth stands still at the center of the universe, thus making it the centerpiece and focus of God's creation and attention.

Another fundamental aspect of Aristotle's theory is that the heavens are changeless and unchangeable. In 1604, Galileo and other scientists independently discover and confirm the existence of a new star, an event impossible in the Aristotelian conception of the universe. This leads to the play's first conflict between Galileo and the Church. The Priest says that it must have already been there, or that it is a collection of vapors that lies below the moon. To call it a star would equal heresy. Believing that scientific proof will change the Church's mind, Galileo asserts: "Bruno burned because he could not prove what he asserted. But when the senses apprehend what reason demands, then no man need fear for the truth" (1.15). Embodying the traits of the modern scientific era, Galileo is convinced that truth and reason will prevail.

The teenage Prince Cosimo presses the issue of whether Galileo is willing to die for his beliefs, but Galileo responds: "I believe in reason. And it is not reasonable to die for that. That would be a defeat. It proves nothing. The reasonable act is to live for the victory of reason, for if God's hopes in us are to be justified it will be in the ultimate triumph of reason over prejudice" (1.16). Whereas Brecht positioned Galileo's eventual recantation as a betrayal of truth, science, and humankind, Stoppard's Galileo views events through a more pragmatic lens, arguing that there would be nothing to be gained from martyrdom. His death would not change anything, and he can better serve humanity by engaging in what scientific research he can. Thus, as a man of reason, it is more reasonable to go on living.

Stoppard's Galileo is a practical man with great survival skills. Thus, when he acquires scientific evidence that it is indeed a new star, Galileo leaves Florence. He goes to Padua, which is under the rule of the Venetian Republic, an area that allows the expression of scientific ideas and discoveries that the Church may view as heretical. When Galileo returns to Padua in 1605, he delivers a major public lecture about the new star. In this speech he champions reason and observation over blind faith in authority. He also asserts: "The philosophers have spoken. They have outlawed change from the heavens. But the laws of nature are not written in the language of philosophy, they are written in mathematics!" (1.18). This statement that mathematics is the language of the Creator and the key to humanity's understanding of the universe causes an uproar. The Narrator explains: "It was an idea which he did not dare publish for another twenty years: to churchmen it seemed to say that God was a mere mathematician, but to Galileo it said that mathematics was divine" (1.19). Galileo closes his speech: "I tell you it is a new star in the furthest reaches of the sky—I outlaw the unchangeable!" (1.19).

Colombe brings Galileo's pronouncements to the attention of Cardinal Bellarmine. But since other matters carry greater political ramifications, Bellarmine dismisses the issue saying: "Heaven can safeguard itself against the quarreling of star-gazers and mathematicians" (1.20). In a later scene, Bellarmine asks Colombe: "Why don't you prove the man wrong, *scientifically?*— That would do it, wouldn't it? (*pause*) I am grateful to be kept informed, but ecclesiastical disputes have a long fuse and I cannot smell any smoke yet" (1.30). Indeed, for Galileo himself, the discovery of the new star does not immediately become a matter of great importance, and he turns his attention to other areas of scientific inquiry. In particular Galileo tests, and disproves, assumptions that had been held since the time of Aristotle. Stoppard shows the ingenious methods Galileo devises to measure the rate at which objects fall, ultimately proving: "The first quarter of the fall takes half the time of the whole and so on, and each such proportion of space corresponds to the square of the proportion of time" (1.21). To Galileo's mind, the beauty of the proportion and its consistency for different objects and different degrees of inclination does not mean that religion and science are at odds, but rather it is merely "an unfamiliar side of God" (1.25). Dramatically, as well as historically, Galileo remains a devout member of the Church who continually believes that his scientific findings reaffirm the glory of God and his creation.

In this section of the play Galileo also delivers a thematic monologue about the beauty and value of change:

> I do not understand why perfection should be a state of rest rather
> than a state of change. I am very fond of this earth. It is not of course
> perfect, but that which I find noble and admirable in it is all to do with
> change. The change of a bud to a flower, of a deer feeding to a deer run-
> ning, the change of grape to wine, child to man, wood to flame; and
> the ash is thrown on the soil to help the buds change to flowers again.
> Alteration, novelty, decay, regeneration—these are not the *blemishes* of
> the world. Who would want a crystal globe? What use is *that* to man as
> created by God? (1.22)

The neoclassical era relished the order and stability offered by a fixed view of the universe, the comfort and control that comes from a rigid hierarchy. In contrast, Galileo validates change as not only the norm and essence of nature, but also as something to be cherished, that the beauty of life and humans *is* their very imperfection, the things that change. Though change is one aspect of nature, Galileo also likes that "Nature is consistent" (1.23), and he believes "the laws of nature to be—universal" (1.34). Stoppard's celebration of the natural world as something that changes yet is consistent prefigures *Arcadia's* thematic use of deterministic chaos, where it is shown that mathematics is indeed the language of the natural world, but in a way more complex than scientists had imagined.

This scene where Galileo tests the rate of falling objects also shows how these scientific and religious issues are political matters. Paolo Sarpi, chief Theologian to the Doge of Venice, visits Galileo in his home laboratory. On theological matters, Sarpi has been challenging the Church's authority, and in response the Pope is about to place Venice under an Interdict, thereby forbidding priests to say Mass or administer the sacraments. In response, Sarpi will persuade the Doge to order the priests to disregard the Interdict, and the Doge will expel the Jesuits from Venice. Furthermore, Sarpi reveals that the Vatican is keeping a file on Galileo because he is "discrediting the sacred dogma of the school texts. The Jesuits will not stand for that either" (1.27). Sarpi expounds on the influence of the Jesuits: "The Jesuit notion of blind obedience was ever unknown to the church until invented by Loyola; it removes the essential feature of virtue which comes from knowledge and choice" (1.28). Thematically, Sarpi's words problematize the nature of virtue and resonate to contemporary faiths that demand strict obedience to literal interpretations of the Bible. Dramatically, the Jesuits will prove to be some of the strongest pursuers of Galileo.

In the ensuing scene the Church will try to assassinate Sarpi, and so he speaks with firsthand knowledge when he advises Galileo on how to stay safe: "It is when you have your proofs that you will have cause to fear the Inquisition. Offer them theories. Leave them a corner to make their stand in. That way you will be tolerably safe. . . . Science and theology will always find a way to dance together to the music of the universe, because time, which will reveal all truth, is infinite. But politics are matters of the moment" (1.28).[6] Throughout Stoppard's canon science and religion are presented not as adversaries, but as corollaries, arguing that God has a scientific mind. Indeed, reconciling his scientific impulses with his religious calling, the monk

Castelli soon returns, saying: "It can be no disgrace to seek the truths of Nature" (1.33).

Castelli also brings news of a new discovery; an Amsterdam spectacle-maker has discovered the means of bringing objects closer to the observer. Unlike Brecht's play where Galileo steals the invention outright, in Stoppard's play, Castelli does not know all the details and so Galileo must deduce the scientific principles that could create such a device.[7] Utilizing his servant's spectacles and a magnifying glass, Galileo "discovers" the telescope. Amazed, yet fearful, Galileo closes the first act by quietly saying: "Now there's going to be trouble" (1.35). He knows that his thirst for the truth will lead him into realms that the Church does not want him to explore. The first act was then to end with the dome of the Planetarium showing the night sky as it appears to the naked eye and as it appears through a telescope, thereby breaking down some of the mysteries of the universe, showing things not possible in the Aristotelian conception of the heavens.

Galileo's discovery of the principle of the telescope ends the first scene of Brecht's play, but for Stoppard it is the end of the first act. Galileo's closing line foreshadows the way in which the second act will focus on the impact the telescope has on Galileo's findings and, by extension, on his conflict with the Church. Starting the second act, the Narrator states: "The telescope that Galileo made for himself in the spring of 1609 was the first capable of astronomical observations. Within a year he had established that there were many more stars in the sky than had been realized—that the Milky Way was composed of stars—that the moon had no light of its own and had mountains and valleys like the Earth" (2.1). The philosophical and theological impact of these discoveries was that "the Earth was no longer uniquely blessed" (2.1). But to Galileo it is "a birth of wonder" that shows that "God has been gravely under-estimated" (2.1).

Realizing that he needs more time to research, Galileo abandons his professorship and returns to Florence. There he receives patronage from his former pupil, Cosimo, and the Medici family. Indicative of how Galileo knows how to play the system, he names the moons of Jupiter, "the Medici stars." The Grand Duke Ferdinand soon dies, and though Cosimo assumes the leadership Cosimo's mother, Christina, and her faithful priest, Baccini, continue to exert much power and influence. They are strong advocates of the Church and the Aristotelian conception of the universe. Baccini even writes a book that argues against the existence of the Medici stars.

Believing that his scientific proof will persuade the Church, Galileo ventures to Rome, giving the Vatican's chief astronomer a telescope for his own use. In Rome, Colombe has continued to press his case against Galileo, but now Bellarmine's attitude is beginning to change. He realizes that the Church can no longer ignore Galileo's discoveries. In 1611 Bellarmine appoints the Clavius Commission, four priests led by the Vatican's astronomer, to investigate the matter. Similar to characters in Brecht's play, Colombe believes that the "astral novelties live inside the tube" (2.3). He also issues a stern warning:

> Your Reverence, he claims to see things that contradict scholarship, and he makes interpretations that contradict the Bible itself. Where there was faith he plants seeds of doubt, and calls it reason. The Church is not based on reason, your Reverence. Self-denial is not a reasonable act—and how, in reason alone, can one explain charity, humility, obedience . . . ? The wholly rational man, acting only rationally, would put his own desires above his ruler's, his master's, his neighbor's, his very family. The rational man asks—who were the wives of Cain and Abel?—how can bread and wine be the body and blood of our Lord?—why do the pious and the impious suffer alike from earthquakes and plagues?—why have faith?! That is why I call it heresy, and the Holy Office must save us from it. (2.4)

By its very nature, religious belief requires a leap of faith, the acceptance of articles that are not based on empirical reasoning. However, Colombe seems to fear reason itself. Whereas Galileo can reconcile faith and reason, Colombe epitomizes those in authority who fear questioning and challenging of their official positions.

To Colombe's horror, the Church's commission confirms Galileo's findings. Initially both Barberini and Bellarmine congratulate Galileo. From the Church's point of view there is a key qualification. Galileo asserts that the sunspots prove that the sun stands still, but Bellarmine interjects: "I would not have thought it proved, Signor. The Commission confirmed the phenomena. The interpretation is your own" (2.6). Bellarmine also cautions Galileo against publishing his findings on the sunspots in Italian. Nonetheless, in 1613, Galileo publishes his book in Italian, and he now takes a much bolder stance on the validity of Copernicus's theory. The Narrator reports: "Orthodox astronomy had no answer to it. The book was acclaimed, and behind his shield of empirical and rational argument Galileo seemed safe from serious danger" (2.7).

After a domestic scene in which his common-law wife Marina leaves Galileo, the play moves to a scene where Galileo commits his first error.[8] The Narrator sets the scene and acknowledges Stoppard's other major piece of poetic license:

> This scene combines two of Cosimo's dinner parties—one a year or two earlier attended by Galileo and Barberini, and another in December 1613 which Galileo missed through illness; Castelli was there in his stead, venting Galileo's opinions, and the resulting argument gave rise to Galileo's letters on the subject of biblical authority; in the perspective of history, it was the moment when Galileo made his first, an ultimately crucial, tactical error. (2.9)

The banquet scene involves a gradual move into the celestial debate. It begins with Christina asserting that the life-size ice sculpture of a swan would sink rather than float. Christina is relying on Aristotle's statement that ice is contracted water, and thus is heavier and will sink. Galileo calmly tells her, and all assembled, that it will float. Offstage, servants toss the swan into a lake, where indeed it floats. Neither Christina nor her guests like being shown up by Galileo, and they begin to mock his Copernican beliefs. This leads to the pivotal exchange:

> BACCINI: Yet it is written in the Bible, "The World also shall be stable, that it be not moved."
> GALILEO: But who wrote it?
> (*It is as though he had slapped them across the face. Everybody at the table reacts.* CHRISTINA *and* LORINI *exchange looks.* BARBERINI *is taken aback.*)
> NARRATOR: Here it is.
> BARBERINI: That was not prudent, Signor. Do not play the theologian.
> GALILEO: And let not the theologians play the scientist.
> CHRISTINA: Signor Galileo, can the scriptures be in error?
> GALILEO: The scriptures cannot be in error, your Serene Highness, but its expounders and interpreters can err in many ways, and the most frequent is to invest in the words of scripture a literal meaning which they may not always bear. . . . We cannot be certain that all previous interpreters have been divinely inspired—Lactantius, a most religious scholar, expounded that the Earth was flat. (*defiantly*)

> It would be prudent if men were forbidden to employ passages of scripture for the purpose of sustaining what demonstrable proof contradicts. (2.13–14)

Dramatically, as well as historically, Galileo believes that the Copernican system can be reconciled with belief in the Bible. Those who fear the ramifications of a Copernican view rely on a strict, literal interpretation, whereas Galileo believes that the demonstrable proofs of science simply showed the grandeur and beauty of God's creation. Gerhard Szczesny argues: "Galileo was not only the man whose appearance marked the beginnings of the age of science but also the first representative of the breed of naturalists who see nothing difficult in the reconciliation of their faith in eschatological truths with their keen sense for the natural truths in the world of realities" (69).

Galileo's comments at the banquet make it back to Church officials, but Bellarmine decides that directly confronting Galileo carries unnecessary risks. Instead, in 1616, Bellarmine persuades the Church to rule on Copernicus, officially censuring and prohibiting the expression of the Copernican worldview.[9] Pope Paul V considers making the resolution official dogma, but Barberini counsels against such action: "St. Augustine guards us against making propositions of natural science a matter of faith, for demonstrable truths will demonstrate themselves. . . . One must not put the authority of the Church into a position from which there is no escape but retreat" (2.17). Barberini, the man of science, recognizes the validity of Galileo's claims, yet also knows the theological and political danger of accepting them. The Pope opts for a less public means of dealing with Galileo. He orders Bellarmine to give Galileo a private admonition to abandon the Copernican propositions. In 1616 Bellarmine carries out the orders, but their exact execution remains a source of contention when Galileo is put on trial in 1633.

The result of Bellarmine's admonition is that from 1616 to 1623 Galileo remains silent on the matter, publishing no new works. Galileo longs for the truth to be revealed, but he decides to wait for the political winds to change, for a new Pope to take power. During the seven-year period, Stoppard's Galileo is disillusioned by the way in which reason is losing out to superstition, a struggle seen in people's response to three comets that appear in 1623.[10] The Narrator notes that one of these comets is still the most impressive ever recorded in human history, and that at the time "[t]he end of the world was confidently predicted" (2.20). Deaths are also attributed to the comet, and in a very short span of time, Grand Duke Cosimo, Bellarmine, and Pope Paul V die.

Onstage, their deaths are presented in a stylized manner. The funeral music then gives way to triumphant, joyous peals of bells that announce Barberini as the new Pope. Galileo, now sixty, is overjoyed and soon meets with Pope Urban VIII. The new Pope offers Galileo the position of Papal Mathematician, but Galileo declines and recommends Castelli. Urban has also written "a poem of adulation for your discourse on the comets" (2.24) and has gotten Copernicus removed from the Index. However, the decree condemning Copernicus's propositions remains in effect. Pope Urban is not willing to go as far as Galileo wants and declares his official position:

> [Copernicus] made hypotheses. In that he showed wisdom and a commendable humility. . . . To say that something is so is to deny possibilities that are open to an omnipotent God. It is to limit God to your own understanding! . . . Galileo, I do not forbid your work but I cannot lift the decree of Pope Paul. If you took your eyes off the sky you would know that for every action there is a reaction. . . . The Copernican system remains interesting as an idea and heretical as a fact. Between the two you have freedom. (2.24–25)

In the play, it is clear that Urban likes and admires Galileo, but he is not one to be crossed. Marking out the acceptable middle ground where conjecture and hypothesis are allowed, Urban tries to balance science and theology by arguing that any proposition that asserts it is unquestionably valid runs the risk of placing limitations on an omnipotent God.

Urban's refusal to face the truth in a direct and scientific manner is unacceptable to Galileo, and so he vows: "I will give them interesting ideas. I will give them hypotheses. And I shall deliver them with such proofs that they will shake the chimneys off the Vatican" (2.25). Castelli warns that the stronger the proofs, the greater the danger from the Inquisition. But Galileo asserts: "If proof means so little, then how little means my life. To endanger it is nothing. . . . God made the world but he has put it in man's keeping and given him the power of reason so that we may understand it. It is in our understanding, not in stubborn ignorance, that we will fulfill his hope in us" (2.26). Once again, Galileo argues that reason is a divine gift, that science does not undermine God's power, but rather affirms it.

Determined to publish his views and proofs of the Copernican system, Galileo devises a strategy that will prove to be his undoing: "I have written two books in one, giving equal voice first to the truth of Aristotle and second to the hypotheses of Copernicus and I shall have a third character Simplicio, a common man to speak for common men" (2.25). By acceding to two papal requests—to create a "Preface re-affirming the wisdom of the decree of 1616" (2.26) and to include the Pope's own argument that definitively asserting the truth of either system would limit God's omnipotence—Galileo and Castelli convince the Papal Censor that the book falls within acceptable boundaries of being a hypothetical discussion of the issues.

Colombe returns to persuade Pope Urban of the error of allowing the book to be published. Besides arguing that the "Copernican statements are put forward with the force of fact" (2.28), Colombe points out Galileo's strategic error: the Pope's argument is placed in the mouth of Simplicio, the Simpleton. Feeling that he has been mocked, the Pope turns against Galileo and seeks his prosecution. Colombe proceeds to get Urban's nephew (another Cardinal Barberini) to devise the means of getting around the fact the book was legally printed and given the imprimatur of the Papal Censor. Colombe produces the injunction of 1616 that forbade Galileo "to hold, defend, teach, or in any way discuss the Copernican system" (2.29–30). Though the document is not an original nor is it signed, they decide it can still serve their purposes.[11]

Galileo is brought in front of the Inquisitors, who read the admonition of 1616. Old and in frail health, Galileo is initially unsure and bewildered as to the exact content of the admonition. As he gathers strength, he asserts that there was no formal injunction and demands to see the "signed" document. The Inquisitors refuse to show it to him.

The action cuts to a jail-cell meeting between Galileo and Castelli, a scene that is silently observed by a cowled monk. Galileo still thinks he can win: "They have a piece of paper which they are ashamed to let me see. I have the arguments of a lifetime's disposition, and they have nothing" (2.32). Castelli rebuts: "They need nothing! You are already condemned, so confess and put yourself in the way of their mercy" (2.32). Galileo refuses to surrender because he believes that the Pope is still on his side: "My accusers take the Pope's name lightly if they look to his friend for a confession!—He would not ask it of me!" (2.32). This outburst is punctuated by Galileo striking Castelli across the face with the banned book. The incident shows the man of reason acting irrationally. Likewise, he has misjudged how his book has been a slap in the face of the Pope. After Castelli exits, the play moves to its climactic scene.

In a melodramatic flourish, the cowled monk reveals himself to be Pope Urban. He shows Galileo the Inquisition's mysterious document, and they have their requisite confrontation:

GALILEO: This is a *report* of a meeting not a record of one. Nor is it signed or witnessed. . . .

URBAN: As you surmise it is a wretched scrap, hardly worthy of consideration; and yet it is all that might save you. Because failing a confession of oversight and forgetfulness, a confession of heresy will suffice. We would have to examine your very thoughts, and God forbid that we find you an avowed Copernican.

GALILEO: Do no speak so hastily for God. He is a reasonable God, and I would not make avowals for an unmoved Sun if I lacked reason.

URBAN: My friend, the Inquisition would examine you into a confession that the Sun moved round the four corners of a square if the Inquisition had a mind to put squares above circles, and then by those same instruments of examination it would hear you recant. (*pause*) Oh yes, the Inquisition has its science, too. Galileo, we are doing you a service. *We*—Urban; God's appointed—Christ's Vicar on this Earth— . . . *I* am doing you a service!—Maffeo Barberini—You would have me Pope of a lump of accidental rock—one rock among millions—and I concern myself for your *thumbs!*

GALILEO: My lord, if the truth could be squeezed out of my thumbs like the juice out of a lemon, I would hold out my hands to the Grand Inquisitor. But you need have no concern for this well-used body—I am too fond of it, and too fond of reason, to allow it to suffer pain only that it might speak lies. For the Earth moves. I am already a prisoner of the truth. How can I escape it?

URBAN: Facts!—figures!—observation, phenomena!—not truth. You have made yourself the prisoner of a small number of facts whose meaning may be changed by the discovery of one more fact, and changed again so long as science continues. Do you suppose that truth is merely an arrangement of whatever facts you have to hand? There is a higher truth—higher than the stars—so think on it before you flourish your facts and your spyglass before the Holy Office! We are not Pope of an empire that has been flung like dice out of a cup into an emptiness of unimaginable space!

GALILEO: (*small pause*) And yet it moves.

URBAN: The Inquisition will hear you deny it.

GALILEO: My lord, I can prove what I assert, so if it is truth they want, they will affirm it!

URBAN: Oh Galileo . . . you know something of the Earth but you know nothing of the world. This is not a trial of your science, nor even of your faith unless you choose to make it so. It is a trial of your strength, and you are not strong enough. For it is written that God made the Heaven and the Earth, and he made the sun to rise and set—and in the service of God the Church will crack your thumbs like walnuts, it will have you stretched till your joints crack, and branded till your fat bubbles through your skin and your veins split like flower-stems, and if the Earth still moves the Church will tie you to the stake in Campo di Fiori and make a torch of you.

GALILEO: (*pause*) Then it does not move. (2.33–34)

Realizing that he would eventually recant under the pain of torture, Galileo rationalizes his confession as the reasonable course of action. Galileo's steadfast belief that truth and reason will triumph is forced to concede defeat to the harsh realities of political and religious power. Thematically, the moment shows how institutions of power are often more interested in what maintains their power than they are in the truth.[12]

The play's denouement involves an excerpt of Galileo's official recantation as well as Castelli's reassurance that capitulation was the right and reasonable course of action. In contrast to Brecht's play, where Galileo's disciple Andrea castigates him for recanting, in Stoppard's play Castelli says: "To persist would have been irrational . . . useless . . . unscientific" (2.35). In Brecht's play, Galileo is ultimately portrayed as an antihero who offers a stinging self-condemnation of his recantation. In contrast, Stoppard's Galileo realizes that he has taken the pragmatic course of action, but rather than assess his own actions, he reflects on the humanistic implications of the play's events. Whereas Galileo has been the champion of reason, in his closing monologue, he asserts the value of the irrational aspects of life:

Thirty years ago in this piazza they burned Giordano Bruno, that unreasonable man, and I think now that his irrational stubbornness and useless agony spoke more for our divinity than the divine order of mathematics. Why is that? The truth is that saints are not reasonable men. We do not love with reason, or pray with reason. We do not even pursue knowledge because reason drives us. There is something else that makes one man unreasonably stubborn and another unreasonably true to his word, and another . . . No, the only triumph is that I am alive, and I may fall off my mule before I get to Florence. If so, reason will have prevailed for nothing. If not, I shall continue with my studies of how things float, or fall, or break; or bend. (2.36)

The play closes with the Narrator's brief summary of what Galileo accomplished while under house arrest before his death in 1642.

An intriguing aspect of Galileo's final thematic monologue is that it bears a striking affinity to the views of the protagonist of *Jumpers*. There, the moral philosopher George affirms the irrational as the defining feature of humanity. Likewise, Galileo's "there is something else that makes one man [this] and another [that], and another . . ." is suggestive of George's "there is more to me than meets the microscope" (68). While Stoppard spends the majority of the play celebrating reason and scientific advances, the closing moment gives voice to the rest of the equation—the irrational and metaphysical dimensions of human existence. While science can offer many answers to the mysteries of life, in Stoppard's eyes there will always be an indefinable element that makes humanity what it is.

In this regard Stoppard's metaphysical position stands in stark contrast to Brecht's materialist view of life. This fundamental disparity in worldview— liberal humanist versus Marxist—helps account for the divergent presentations of Galileo. While Stoppard celebrates Galileo, Brecht condemns him. In his commentary Brecht argues that Galileo's recantation was a "crime [that] can be regarded as the 'original sin' of modern natural science," that it robbed "these sciences of a greater part of their social importance," and that never again would the sciences "come into such close contact with the people" (225). In contrast, Stoppard presents a Galileo who is to be respected. Overall, it is Galileo's humanness—his great intellect, his passionate search for the truth, his wit and love of wine, as well as his understandable recantation—that is presented for our admiration and reflection.

4

Jumpers

THE HUGE SUCCESS OF *Rosencrantz and Guildenstern Are Dead* ensured two things: first, that whatever Stoppard wrote next the National Theatre would be interested in staging it; and second, that critical eyes would be focused on this second major play to see whether Stoppard was just a one-hit wonder. Stoppard started *Jumpers* with a few pages in the summer of 1968: "Then I stopped, and I wrote 'After Magritte' and a radio play [*Where Are They Now?*], and I left Jose [his first wife] and I bought and sold houses and was divorced and was in and out of courts on the custody case and all this money going to lawyers" (Tallmer 15). The turmoil and expenses led to a temporary change of focus; during the five-year gap between *Rosguil* and *Jumpers* Stoppard wrote multiple drafts of four unproduced screenplays, three one-act plays, a radio play, and three works for television.[1] One of those television pieces, *Another Moon Called Earth,* the half-hour play that Stoppard wrote within two months of the National Theatre production of *Rosguil,* was to be the seed for *Jumpers.*[2]

Exemplifying the critical divide over *Jumpers* is the fact that it won *Plays and Players* Best Play Award as well as its Most-Over-Rated Play Award. The antithetical reactions may stem from the uniqueness of *Jumpers* as a piece of theatre. *Jumpers* is "a farce whose main purpose is to affirm the existence of God. [It is] a farcical defense of transcendent moral values [and] an attack on pragmatic materialism" (Tynan 93). Not only does it use a comic tone to treat a serious issue, but its modes of discourse include song and dance, acrobatics, striptease, philosophy lecture, murder-mystery detective story, and a dream sequence, all of which interact to engage fundamental philosophical questions about the existence of God and the nature of goodness.

The play is set in a fictitious, indeterminate time and deals with a moral philosophy professor named George Moore (thematically linked to the historical philosopher of the same name) and his wife Dotty, a former musical-comedy songstress who is in the midst of another nervous breakdown following the landing of the British on the moon. At the play's opening, a victory celebration for the newly elected Radical Liberal Party (a left-wing Neo-fascist organization) is in progress in the Moores' apartment. The festivities include a troupe of "jumpers," philosophy professors who perform gymnastic and acrobatic feats. In the midst of a human pyramid, one of the jumpers, later identified as Professor Duncan McFee, is shot and killed. The need to dispose of the corpse and the investigation of the murder by Inspector Bones form one of the main plot lines. Throughout much of this, George remains ignorant of most of the proceedings as he is immersed in the writing of his paper that attempts to prove the existence of God and of moral absolutes. George's attempt to compose this lecture for the symposium on "Man—good, bad or indifferent?" forms the other main plot line. In the course of the action, Archie—the ultimate pragmatist and relativist, leader of the jumpers, and possible lover of Dotty—successfully disposes of the corpse and drives away the Inspector, leaving the case unsolved; despite some critics' suspicion of Dotty, all signs more accurately point to Archie as the murderer. In the play's coda, presented in bizarre, dreamlike fashion, George and Archie debate their respective philosophical positions.

Jumpers, along with *Travesties,* epitomizes Stoppard's attempt to form "the perfect marriage between the play of ideas and farce or perhaps even high comedy" (Hudson, Itzin, and Trussler 59). Beneath its spectacular surface of glamorous women, songs, acrobatics, video screens, and rollicking laughter, the play is aimed at discussing a serious issue. Stoppard explains his intent with *Jumpers:*

> I wanted a device enabling me to set out arguments about whether social morality is simply a conditioned response to history and environment or whether moral sanctions obey an absolute intuitive God-given law. I've always felt that whether or not God-given means anything,

there has to be an ultimate external reference for our actions. Our view of good behaviour must not be relativist. . . . I think it's a dangerous idea that what constitutes 'good behaviour' depends on social conventions—dangerous and unacceptable. That led me to the conclusion, not reached all that willingly, that if our behaviour is open to absolute judgement, there must be an absolute judge. I felt that nobody was saying this and it tended to be assumed that nobody held such a view. So I wanted to write a theist play, to combat the arrogant view that anyone who believes in God is some kind of cripple, using God as a crutch. I wanted to suggest that atheists may be the cripples, lacking the strength to live with the idea of God. (Kerensky 86–87)

Near the time of the play's 1974 Broadway premiere, Stoppard told Mel Gussow that Archie is the villain (*Conversations* 5). He added:

I identify emotionally with the more sympathetic character [George] in the play who believes that one's mode of behaviour has to be judged by absolute standards. At the same time I don't have to get anyone else to write the other characters for me, because intellectually I can shoot my argument full of holes. This conflict between one's intellectual and emotional response to questions of morality produces the tension that makes the play. (14)

Later in the interview, Stoppard elaborated on this tension:

I wanted to write a play about this particular conflict between emotional and intellectual responses to the idea of God, because I've always thought the idea of God is absolutely preposterous but slightly more plausible than the alternative proposition that given enough time, some green slime could write Shakespeare's sonnets. (15–16)

While Stoppard's stated stance is clear and direct, the play's dazzling form has led to a wide variety of interpretations, some antithetical to Stoppard's professed values.[3]

Textual History

There are three different published texts of *Jumpers*. The first version (1972) came out in conjunction with the play's premiere at the National Theatre.

When *Jumpers* returned to the National's repertory in 1973, the text had changed and a second edition was published. In 1976, to help inaugurate its new home on the South Bank, the National Theatre revived *Jumpers* in the Lyttelton Theatre. Michael Hordern reprised his role as George, but the rest of the cast was new and Stoppard made further changes to the script, but no new edition was published. In 1985 *Jumpers* was revived on the West End, and a new edition came out in 1986. This latest text incorporates many of the minor alterations made for the 1976 revival, and more importantly, it includes a few significant changes made for the 1985 production. With the exception of the coda, the 1986 text is slightly tighter. The 1973 and the 1986 texts have become the two standard texts, and a discussion of the major differences between these versions will show the ways in which Stoppard has attempted to clarify the narrative and alter nuances of interpretation.

During the opening party scene, the 1986 text includes George's anonymous phone call to the police to complain "about a disturbance of the peace" (10). This addition clarifies that the jumble of songs and striptease are occurring at a late-night party, and it also hints at the thematic strands of the play because George, while trying to hide his identity, claims to be Wittgenstein, one of the philosophers whom George will try to refute during the course of the play. Also, after the opening murder, the 1986 text places Archie onstage (as opposed to just an offstage voice) in Dotty's bedroom and adds dialogue that identifies the victim as Duncan McFee and that accents Archie's unfeeling pragmatism: "There's no need to get it out of proportion. Death is always a great pity of course but it's not as though the alternative were immortality" (13). While logically consistent, Archie's philosophy lacks humanity.

Between the two versions, Stoppard made minor emendations that affected the presentation of Dotty. He cut Dotty's denigrating characterization of herself as "unreliable, neurotic" (1973, 17) and tried to make her a little more sympathetic. In the latter text she directly appeals to her husband for help: "George, you can't go . . . there's a corpse in the cupboard" (27).[4] When he does not take her seriously, she decides, "I think [the problem of the corpse] needs a radical liberal solution. You wouldn't be sympathetic" (27). Rebuffed in her attempt to communicate with George, she turns to Archie. She is also made less vindictive—for example, in the 1986 text she tells George that "it was only a joke" (69) when she suggested that she and Archie were eating his pet hare for lunch.

The largest section of dialogue added to the precoda part of the play involves the second act entrapment of Inspector Bones. In the 1973 version the trap is made to look like Bones has attempted to rape Dotty (70–71).[5] In the 1986 text, Bones has been persuaded to play charades, and he dons a frock, headdress, and blackface (61–62). Here the Inspector's "crime" is much less sinister and much more ambiguous.[6] Jenkins's assertion that this change in the type of trap "links her to George instead of to Archie" (*Critical Essays* 4) seems to ignore that in both cases she works with Archie to derail the Inspector's investigation of the murder. On the other hand, the use of charades rather than a false rape charge is a less ruthless means of entrapment, and thus is another small way Stoppard has softened her character. Overall, Stoppard's changes to Dotty's dialogue are few in number, but point the way to a performance style that might make her "personal anguish clearer and easier to sympathize with" (Jenkins, *Critical Essays,* 4).

The three published versions of *Jumpers* (as well as the unpublished 1976 production text) all have different codas, and the pertinent variances are noted later in the chapter.

Thematic Analysis of Text and Production

Jumpers begins with a favorite device of Stoppard's early career: a mélange of provocative and seemingly disconnected images that jolt the audience. The succeeding action then proceeds to dispel the initial confusion as logical reasons will be provided for the bizarre occurrences. The opening section of *Jumpers* is essentially a prologue, and it includes the return of a glamorous songstress who is unable to sing, a striptease act performed on a trapeze (an action accompanied by a vaudeville-like gag of a waiter unaware of the stripper's presence until he is knocked over by the swinging, naked lady), and a troupe of gymnasts who perform acrobatic tricks. When the gymnasts form a human pyramid, a gunshot is fired, a jumper is "blown out of the pyramid," and Dotty "walks through the gap" (21).[7] The final image of this prologue is Dotty in a sexy evening gown, now stained by the blood of the dead jumper who clings to her leg.[8]

The set forms around Dotty and the dead jumper. They occupy a bedroom while on another part of the stage George is in his study, with the two rooms divided by a hallway. Thus, on one side there is an image of the scholar in the ivory tower, ruminating over philosophy in an abstract, theoretical way, while on the other side there is a tangible embodiment of the ethical issues that form the core of George's philosophical quest.

In the bedroom, covering the entire back wall and dwarfing the performers, there is a large screen that projects for the audience what Dotty sees on the television. On the screen an event occurs that is pivotal to the characters and that reverberates throughout the play. Projected are images of the moon, astronauts, a moon vehicle, and a rocket. An announcer reports that due to a damaged space capsule only one of the astronauts could return: "Millions of viewers saw the two astronauts struggling at the foot of the ladder until Oates was knocked to the ground by his commanding officer. . . . [Captain Scott closed] the hatch with the remark, 'I am going up now. I may be gone for some time'" (22–23).[9] The use of the names Oates and Scott reverberate much more for a British audience as their historical counterparts were part of the first English expedition to the South Pole. On their return the group experienced great difficulties, and Captain Oates, who was severely ill and weakened, decided to sacrifice himself so that his companions might have a chance to live. As Faraone notes, "Traditionally, the members of the Scott expedition have been considered heroes and exemplar models of British stoicism and bravery" (55). But in the *Jumpers* parallel event, self-sacrifice has been replaced by self-interest and a pragmatic, survival-of-the-fittest fight to determine who would live and who would die. The use of the moon setting tries to strip the murder of sociological, economic, political, psychoanalytic, and cultural contexts so that the action can be judged, as much as possible, in isolation. But Stoppard's point is that moral actions and moral judgments are absolute, not circumstantial. Through the Scott-Oates parallel, Stoppard shows a world in which traditional, cherished values have been overturned, and he implicitly implicates the dominance of pragmatic, relativist values as the cause of moral decay and a threat to the stability of society.

The incident on the moon is one of the strands that feeds into the three main perspectives on morality offered in the play: (1) Archie, his fellow jumpers, and the Radical Liberal Party espouse pragmatism and moral relativity; (2) George, the only member of the philosophy faculty who is not a member of the acrobatic jumpers, preaches traditional values and a belief in moral absolutes; (3) Dotty embodies a visceral response to the changing world, voicing moral relativity but emoting a belief in moral absolutes. The worldviews of the jumpers, George, and Dotty involve a logical/intellectual component as well as an emotional and/or experiential dimension that complicates the presentation of the characters and their views.

Stoppard has identified the pragmatist Archie as the villain of the play. In the National Theatre productions Archie was perceived as "a formidable Satanic dandy" (Barber, "Comedy") and "a cold-blooded opportunist" (Wardle, "Intellectual Impotence") who "ooz[ed] lechery" (Barker).[10] Archie is the leader of the jumpers, a group who represent various twentieth-century philosophical schools of thought. George articulates their ideological backgrounds: "Logical Positivists, mainly, with a linguistic analyst or two, a couple of Benthamite utilitarians . . . lapsed Kantians and empiricists generally . . . and of course the usual Behaviourists" (50–51). All these philosophical positions are in opposition to George's belief in metaphysical absolutes, and the Radical Liberal Party they support has made the Archbishop of Canterbury a political appointment, one that has been filled with an agnostic.

Viewing contemporary philosophy as mental acrobatics, Stoppard literalizes the metaphor, making the philosophers into a troupe of gymnasts. Stoppard's main objects of scorn are the logical positivists (which he read with "fascinated revulsion" [Tynan 90]) and the behaviorists (*Jumpers* is "an anti-Skinner play" [Gussow, *Conversations,* 8]). Both schools of thought deny any metaphysical basis for human action. Behaviorism, espoused by people such as American psychologist B. F. Skinner, argues that human actions and motives are prompted by empirical considerations dictated by society or controlled and reinforced by social conditioning. Thus from the behaviorist point of view moral judgments do not have an absolute validity but rather are a means of avoiding or preventing socially undesirable types of behavior and action. Logical positivism, which was a major force in British philosophy from the mid-1920s until the mid-1960s, tried to rationalize philosophy into a scientific activity. One of its key concepts is the verification principle, which, though modified over the years, is essentially an argument that all knowledge that can be considered genuine must be observable, capable of being verified, whether in actuality or principle, by empirical means.[11] A result was that questions relating to metaphysics, ethics, and aesthetics were considered meaningless and outside the scope of philosophy, which was supposed to turn most of its attention to linguistic analysis. Logical positivism is a form of extreme empiricism that argues that all moral judgments are only expressions of personal feeling and thus are self-reflexive and without meaning. In *Language, Truth, and Logic* A. J. Ayer asserts: "Sentences which simply express moral judgements do not say anything. They are pure expressions of feelings and as such do not come under the category of truth and falsehood" (108).[12]

One of Stoppard's main goals in *Jumpers* is to discredit logical positivism and behaviorism, schools of thought that helped provide "the intellectual impetus behind the modern drift toward materialism, utilitarianism, and state socialism" (Crump 51). In the play, the characters who hold the relativist values rarely speak for themselves, but rather their ideas are conveyed by George (when he tries to express and debunk McFee's views), by Dotty (who parrots Archie), and only occasionally by Archie himself. The philosophical ideas are made theatrically effective by being woven into the story line and into jokes.

One of Stoppard's favorite comic devices is cross talk, and he uses a variation of it when Inspector Bones arrives. Although Bones is there to investigate the murder, George thinks he is there in response to his complaint about the party being too loud. In the process of Bones's questioning about McFee, George articulates McFee's relativist position on the nature of goodness:

> [McFee] thinks good and bad aren't actually *good* and *bad* in any absolute or metaphysical sense, he believes them to be categories of our own making, social and psychological conventions which we have evolved in order to make living in groups a practical possibility. . . . He believes that on the whole people should tell the truth all right, and keep their promises, and so on—but on the sole grounds that if everybody went around telling lies and breaking their word as a matter of course, normal life would be impossible. . . . The point is it allows him to conclude that telling lies is not *sinful* but simply anti-social. (48)

Likewise, McFee "*philosophically* doesn't think [murder is] actually, inherently wrong in itself" (48). George characterizes McFee's philosophical position as "Orthodox mainstream" (49). In the process of this conversation, Stoppard has given a summary of McFee's half of the symposium (which the audience will never actually hear) and has provided a brief encapsulation of the philosophical moral relativity the play seeks to refute.

The irony of George's exposition on McFee's position that murder is not inherently wrong is that McFee himself has been murdered. While the murderer is never officially identified, Archie is the likely doer of the dirty deed.[13] Archie disposes of the corpse, invents a preposterous suicide explanation, and calmly tells Bones that he had sufficient motive: "Perhaps McFee, my faithful protégé, had secretly turned against me, gone off the rails and decided that he was St. Paul to Moore's Messiah. . . . McFee was the guardian and figurehead of philosophical orthodoxy, and if he threatened to start calling on his masters to return to the true path, then I'm afraid it would certainly have been an ice-pick in the back of the skull" (63–64). As the audience later learns, Archie is speaking the truth. The night of the party, Archie and McFee had a "furious row" (68). Crouch reveals the reason: "It was the astronauts fighting on the Moon that finally turned [McFee]. Henry, he said to me, Henry, I am giving philosophical respectability to a new pragmatism in public life, of which there have been many disturbing examples both here and on the Moon. . . . But he kept harking back to the first Captain Oates, out there in the Antarctic wastes, sacrificing his life to give his companions a slim chance of survival. . . . If altruism is a possibility, he said, my argument is up a gum-tree" (80). This is one of the places where the intellectual argument does not make as much sense as the emotional response. Why altruism depends on absolute values or why altruism cannot exist within a relativist framework is not adequately argued, but rather McFee's change of heart seems to be based on a belief that some actions are inherently right or wrong.

McFee's death and conversion are pivotal because at the symposium it was McFee who was to offer the relativist counterargument to George's insistence on absolute values. The 1976 production text goes on to indicate that McFee "was going to announce his conversion at the symposium" (81). From the jumpers' perspective, the removal of McFee is a pragmatic, utilitarian action taken to insure their survival and well-being. Paul Delaney argues: "The moral relativism which McFee represents is the cornerstone for the positions of all the other jumpers. . . . If McFee defects, if the central premise that all value judgements are relative is removed, the entire intellectual house of cards of the faddish philosophers comes tumbling down" (*Moral Vision* 40). The murder of McFee and the murder on the moon dramatize the harsh ramifications of an extreme extrapolation of the tenets of logical positivism into the daily sphere. Michael Billington argues that *Jumpers* suggests "that a world that denies metaphysical absolutes of good and evil, . . . that subverts moral sanctions . . . will fall into chaos" (*Stoppard* 87).

The philosophical argument for the existence of metaphysical absolutes is provided by George, who has numerous lengthy speeches that grapple with the theories of language and existence as articulated by Zeno, Saint Thomas Aquinas, the historical George Moore, Bertrand Russell, Ludwig Wittgenstein, A. J. Ayer, and other philosophers from the Western tradition.[14] George, like his historical counterpart, is an intuitionist philosopher, but whereas the historical philosopher was a realist who did not believe in God, the play's George Moore is an idealist. His quest is to prove: "There is, first, the God of Creation to account for existence, and second, the God of Goodness to account for moral values" (26). The catalogue of philosophers cited and the seriousness of the quest may seem daunting, but Stoppard is more of an entertainer than he is a philosopher, and George's lengthy speeches are spiced with numerous jokes and comic mishaps.

To try to prove the God of Creation, George, like Thomas Aquinas, relies on the First Cause argument: "a supernatural or divine origin is the logical consequence of the assumption that one things leads to another" (27). One of the rebuttals to the First Cause argument is that there are "many series which have no first term" (27), and so to rebut the rebuttal, George pulls out a bow and arrow. He argues that applying the logic of Zeno's paradox shows "in every way but experience that an arrow could never reach its target" (29) and so "St. Sebastian died of fright" (28). In part, George's point is that logic, mathematical theorems, and other concepts that seem theoretically sound can sometimes fail the pivotal test of experience, and thus cannot sufficiently explain everything. Of course, George also works himself into logical traps. His reasoning on the issue of infinite series without a beginning leads him to say: "But the fact is, the first term of the series is not an infinite fraction but *zero*. It exists. God, so to speak, is nought. No, that can't be right" (1986, 20). Throughout the play George flounders through his lecture, adequately refuting logical positivism but never quite proving his own position. He also adds an intriguing thought: "There is presumably a calendar date—*a moment*—when the onus of proof passed from the atheist to the believer, when, quite suddenly, the noes had it" (25). The significance is that it is easy to find flaws in a given philosophy or theoretical position, but much more difficult to "prove" anything.

George's belief in God is that of the theistic humanist, not the convinced Christian: "If God exists, he certainly existed before religion. He is a philosopher's God, logically inferred from self-evident premises. That he should have been taken up by a glorified supporters' club is only a matter of psychological interest" (39–40). Later he adds: "I'm not at all sure that the God of religious observance is the object of my faith" (68). George's desire for a logical proof of God's existence would give him a degree of certainty he knows he can't have: "Copernicus cracked our confidence, and Einstein smashed it: for if one can no longer believe that a twelve-inch ruler is always a foot long, how can one be sure of relatively less certain propositions, such as that God made the Heaven and the Earth" (75).

Relativity and epistemological uncertainty can be the source of much anxiety. On the personal level George encounters the ambiguous relationship between Archie and Dotty, and in the 1985 production, Paul Eddington played George as "deeply distraught at the prospect of his wife's infidelity" (Billington, *Stoppard,* 87). The process of examining Dotty via the dermatograph machine produces sounds and images that can be interpreted as sensual or as legitimately diagnostic. George's inability to determine the specific nature of Dotty and Archie's relationship leads him to pose one of the play's fundamental questions: "How the hell does one know what to believe?" (71). The question then reverberates from daily epistemology to metaphysical epistemology:

> How does one know what it is one believes when it's so difficult to know what it is one knows. I don't claim to *know* that God exists, I only claim that he does without my knowing it, and while I claim as much I do not claim to know as much; indeed I cannot know and God knows I cannot. (*Pause.*) And yet I tell you that, now and again, not necessarily in the contemplation of rainbows or new-born babes, nor in extremities of pain or joy, but more probably ambushed by some quite trivial moment . . . then I tell you I *know.* (71)

Thus, George argues that on metaphysical matters one must rely on intuition, that in life one can claim to know things even though they can never be proven via empirical or intellectual means.

In one of the play's two brief philosophical encounters between Archie and George, the latter asserts the reasons for his intuition of God: "When I push *my* convictions to absurdity, I arrive at God—which is at least as embarrassing nowadays. (*Pause.*) All I know is that I think that I know that I know nothing can be created out of nothing, that my moral conscience is different from the rules of my tribe, and that there is more in me than meets the microscope—and because of *that* I'm lumbered with this incredible, indescribable and definitely shifty *God*" (67–68). Belief that there must be a Creator, that there are moral absolutes, and that humans possess a metaphysical dimension are the criteria George uses to arrive at a personal affirmation of God's existence. George's statement contains an element of uncertainty, yet that fact only bolsters his belief: "The ability to doubt, to question, to think, seems to be the curve itself. *Cogito ergo deus est* [I think, therefore God is]" (72).

On metaphysical matters and theistic affirmations, George speaks with Stoppard's voice. Speaking with Reverend Joseph McCulloch, Stoppard argued that when people think about God, "surely they do so in ways which are bringing up questions of logical possibility, rather than a sort of mystical instinctive conviction about a Supreme Being" (42). He goes on to argue that personally he finds a point where human evolution requires a leap to God: "There is a gap between an object becoming as complex, as prolific, as intelligent and as extraordinary as it can be, of itself, and actually *knowing* all these things about itself" (43). Like his professor character, Stoppard makes the jump to theism, but not necessarily to religion: "When I am asked whether I believe in God, my answer is that I don't know what the question means. I approve of belief in God and I try to behave as if there is one, but that hardly amounts to faith. I don't know what religious certainty would consist of, though many apparently have it. I am uneasy with religious ceremonials, because I think intellectually, and the case for God is not an intellectual one. However, militant humanism grates on me much more than evangelism" (Guppy 188). Stoppard's distaste for "militant humanism" is aimed at those who view life in strictly materialist terms without any sense of mysticism. Indeed, Archie, in a speech that paraphrases philosopher Bertrand Russell's views, articulates the close connection between traditional liberal humanist values and Christian values:

> Religious faith and atheism differ mainly about God; about Man they are in accord: Man is the highest form of life, he has duties he has rights, et cetera, and it is usually better to be kind than cruel. Even if there is some inscrutable divinity behind it all, our condition for good or ill is apparently determined by our choice of actions, and choosing seems to be a genuine human possibility. Indeed, it is surely religious zeal rather than atheism which is historically notorious in the fortunes of mankind. (68)

In the course of the play, George's ruminations alternate between trying to prove the God of Creation and trying to prove that moral absolutes, whether God-given or otherwise, do exist. In the climactic speech of the first act, George does not dispute the logical positivist position that "the word 'good' has meant different things to different people at different times" (54); instead he proceeds to show that the linguistic basis of logical positivism makes it hermetically sealed: "[The above] is not a statement which anyone would dispute, and on the other hand, nothing useful can be inferred from it. It is not in fact a statement about value at all; it is a statement about language and how it is used in a particular society" (54). In a similar vein, George tries to turn moral relativity in upon itself:

> Whence comes this sense of some actions being better than others?—not more useful, or more convenient, or more popular, but simply pointlessly *better?* What, in short, is so good about good? Professor McFee succeeds only in showing us that in different situations different actions will be deemed, rightly or wrongly, to be conducive to that good which is independent of time and place and which is knowable but not nameable. . . . The irreducible fact of goodness is not implicit in one kind of action any more than in its opposite, but in the existence of a relationship between the two. It is the sense of comparisons being in order. (55)

Stoppard elucidated this concept in a later interview: "The point is not to compare one ruthless regime against another—it is to set each one up against a moral standard, a consistent idea of what constitutes good and bad in the way human beings treat each other regardless of class, colour or ideology, and at least my poor professor in *Jumpers* got *that* right" (Hudson, Itzin, and Trussler 64).

George's speech concludes the dialogue of act 1, but to get a "sense of comparisons" Stoppard dramatizes the difference between George's view and that of the moral relativists. To close the first act, Archie and the other jumpers enter to dispose of McFee's corpse. Mixing a magic trick with a small dance number, the jumpers deposit McFee's body in a large plastic bag thereby fulfilling George's earlier claim that in the Rad-Lib philosophy, "No problem is insoluble given a big enough plastic bag" (40). While George's "proofs" may not always be convincing, the action suggests that George's view is still "simply pointlessly better" than the relativist "plastic bag" approach to ethics.

Along with his belief in God, George relies on intuition as the basis for his belief in moral absolutes: "But when we say the Good Samaritan acted well, we are surely expressing more than a circular prejudice about behaviour. We mean he acted kindly—selflessly—*well.* And what is our approval of kindness based on if not on the intuition that kindness is simply good in itself and cruelty is not" (66–67). While Stoppard firmly believes that humans have an intuitive sense of right and wrong, and while he bases his theism on an intuitive feeling that there must be a First Cause, he also recognizes that intuition is not an infallible guide. Near the end of the play George asserts: "There are many things I know which are not verifiable but nobody can tell me I don't know them, and I think that I know that something happened to poor Dotty and she somehow killed McFee, as sure as she killed my poor Thumper" (78). He is wrong about both murders, with the latter providing the poignant moment where George discovers that it was his stray arrow that killed Thumper, and in the process of discovery George steps on and kills his pet tortoise.

His accidental killing of his pets points to the complex portrayal of George. His quest to prove that there is a source of meaning and values in the universe is a noble endeavor that can rightly gain the audience's sympathy, but he never rises to the level of a hero. Though he speaks for Stoppard on metaphysical issues, George fails to put his philosophy into action. Stoppard himself has noted: "While George has the right ideas, he is also a culpable person; while he is defending his ideas and attacking the opposition, he is neglecting everyone around him and shutting out his wife who is in need, not to mention shooting his hare and stepping on his tortoise" (Guppy 188). While George is in his study trying to "invent God" or have God "typed out" (34), Dotty is in the bedroom having another nervous breakdown.

The stage picture helps accent this divide as George's study is placed in opposition to Dotty's bedroom. The hallway corridor is a further physical divide between the world of theorizing about moral absolutes and the world of actual experience where moral actions and their ramifications are embodied by the dead jumper and the fragile housewife. The 1976 production text accents the dichotomy between George's words and his actions. In addition to saying that he is sorry he can't fulfill Dotty's desperate plea of "*Please don't leave me!*" (1973, 41), George has the added line: "I've only got until this evening to sort out goodness and badness" (1976, 24). His sorting out is in theory not practice. Repeatedly Dotty appeals to George for love, support, and attention, but as Stoppard's stage direction indicates: "*He doesn't really know what to do*" (42).

The suggestion that the world of moral theorizing and the world of moral action need to be wed occurs early in the play. In the midst of George's first long speech, where he ruminates on "the overwhelming question" of God's existence, Dotty's offstage voice interrupts: "*Is anybody there?*" (26). George's painstaking search for a metaphysical source of moral absolutes is matched by Dotty's plaintive plea for moral action, for someone to give her the help she needs. Indeed, it is Dotty who offers the most human response to the play's philosophical debate on morality.

Dotty is the person most affected by the moon landing, and though she often espouses Archie's relativist values, as she watches the moon program, she laments: "Poor moon man, falling home like Lucifer" (38). Dotty became a star by singing about the romance and mystery of the moon, and she is the embodiment of Stoppard's notion that "You can't just land on the moon. It's much more than a location, it's a whole heritage of associations, poetic and religious. There are probably quite a few people around who'll go mad when the first man starts clumping around this symbol in size-ten boots" (Halton 112). Thus, for Dotty, the desecration of the moon and the murder on its surface are a fall from grace that racks her psychological state.

While there is a certain implausibility to Dotty's being shattered by the demythologizing of the moon, Paul Delaney aptly argues that as a musical comedy star Dotty believes in a musical comedy view of life: "She has accepted its saccharine romanticism with a mindless optimism. . . . People are not good or bad; they are eternally hopeful, full of limitless possibilities, occasionally naughty but usually kind" (*Moral Vision* 50). Thus, the moon is the symbol of her beliefs, and she is forced to acknowledge the shallowness of what she held dear. She has literally and figuratively been bloodied and bewildered by the dead jumper, and now she has witnessed a murder on the moon. When she had the moon to believe in *"things were in place then!"* (41), but now she is broken, feeling with visceral intensity the breakdown of society and all she believed in. In a speech that can be very moving in performance, Dotty laments:

> Well, it's all over now. Not only are we no longer the still centre of God's universe, we're not even uniquely graced by his footprint in man's image. . . . All our absolutes, the thou-shalts and the thou-shalt-nots that seemed to be the very condition of our existence, how did they look to two moonmen with a single neck to save between them? Like the local customs of another place. When that thought drips through to the bottom, people won't just carry on. There is going to be such . . . breakage. . . . Because the truths that have been taken on trust, they've never had edges before, there was no vantage point to stand on and see where they stopped. (75)

Though Dotty often cites Archie's relativist values, she cannot calmly dismiss death and murder the way Archie can. Indeed, as this speech causes her to break down, she appeals not to Archie but to George (and his values) for support; but George is still culpable, unable to respond. Paul Delaney argues:

"We should not see her plight as simply illustrating—in a general way—the sadness and emptiness of much of modern society. If the jumpers are reprehensible and George's well-meaning conclusion embarrassing, Dotty is coming to a visceral understanding of the moral issues which the jumpers deny and which George, while affirming, does not experience" (*Moral Vision* 49).

The Coda

The moral issues of the play are recapitulated in the coda, where the symposium is seen through the lens of George's bizarre dream.[15] Archie presents his views of morality and human nature in a short speech of Joycean density that is bewildering both to George and to the audience, which has no time to even try to decipher it.[16] After Archie's speech, the 1986 text includes the appearance of Captain Scott and Tarzan.[17] Scott's arrival gives Archie a chance to argue that the moon murder was a "natural response to a pure situation" (1986, 74). After Captain Scott exits via a jet-propelled space suit, Tarzan swings in, clad in tuxedo top and loincloth. Archie explains the reason for Tarzan's appearance: "I have called Lord Greystoke [Tarzan] because he is uniquely in a position to tell us whether moral values as we know them are the distinguishing marks of human nature or merely the products of civilization" (1986, 75). But before Tarzan can testify he is disqualified as a witness because he is only a "character of fiction" (86). Scott and Tarzan amplify the coda's surreality and enhance the spectacle, but they add little in terms of content. Though more theatrical, the 1986 coda seems unnecessarily opaque and drawn out. In contrast, the 1973 coda has a tighter dramatic construction and a clearer thematic focus.

When Tarzan swings out, the coda moves to the pivotal plot point, common to all the variant coda texts—the murder of Clegthorpe, the Archbishop of Canterbury. Archie orchestrates the deed, an act that mirrors the opening killing of McFee. Both men are shot when they are part of a human pyramid. More importantly, both Clegthorpe and McFee are lapsed jumpers, men who defected from the philosophy of the moral relativists. Clegthorpe can see some validity in the people's desire for the sacraments. He pleads to Archie: "Surely belief in man could find room for man's beliefs?" (84). Archie responds with the words of Shakespeare's *Richard III* and with those of the historical Henry II, tyrants who killed former friends. Archie's echo of Henry II—"Will no one rid me of this turbulent priest!" (85)[18]—is the call to kill Clegthorpe, who becomes a modern Thomas à Becket; both have been transformed from a secular political ally to a dissenting religious believer. This melding of fiction to history reinforces the idea that some actions are "simply pointlessly better," while others are inherently wrong.

The 1973 (but not the 1986) text proceeds to show George's culpability, his inability to act on his moral convictions. Clegthorpe pleads: "Professor— it's not right. George—help" (85), but George desists: "Well, this seems to be a political quarrel. . . . Surely only a proper respect for absolute values . . . universal truths—*philosophy*—" (1973, 85, ellipses in original). At this point Clegthorpe is shot and killed.[19] As Paul Delaney notes, Clegthorpe's final plea is an extremely succinct phrasing that appeals "to George both on the philosophic level of moral absolutes and on the personal level. . . . If the professor does believe in absolute values, he ought to respond to a situation that is not right; but in any event George ought to respond on the human level to a plea for help" (*Moral Vision* 56). To be well-meaning is not enough; action must be joined to word. Indeed, in *Professional Foul*, Stoppard's other foray into the world of moral philosophy and the debate between absolute and relative values, the protagonist Professor Anderson is, unlike George, transformed by experience and acts on his newfound moral convictions.

Finally, George and Archie each give a closing speech, providing the other brief moment where their philosophies come face-to-face. Since George's position rests on intuition and a belief that life and humans have a metaphysical dimension, his argument will never meet the scientific, verifiable criteria of logical positivism. So instead of arguing his views, George's closing speech points to the double standards inherent in logical positivism. Tim Brassell argues: "[George's speech] presents another cogent illustration of the limitations of merely logical [positives] and, with some dexterity, suggests that the Logical Positivist is in practice forced to maintain fundamentally contradictory attitudes toward ethical and aesthetic standards" (132). In the process, George's approach implicitly reiterates the difficulty of proving a philosophical position, but the ease of disproving one.

Characteristic of his slickness, Archie uses his last speech to present a pragmatically optimistic view of the world:

> Do not despair—many are happy much of the time; more eat than starve, more are healthy than sick, more curable than dying. Not so many dying as dead; and one of the thieves was saved. . . . Millions of children grow up without suffering deprivation, and millions, while deprived, grow up without suffering cruelties, and millions, while deprived and cruelly treated, none the less grow up. No laughter is sad

and many tears are joyful. At the graveside the undertaker doffs his top hat and impregnates the prettiest mourner. Wham bam, thank you Sam. (87)

Some critics saw Archie's speech as a positive message: "Archie's last speech is God looking down on his universe and finding it okay, if not as good as it could have been" (Hobson, "*Jumpers*"); "[George] keeps looking for answers and while, to be sure, there are none, it is up to . . . Archie to suggest Stoppard's assertion of faith" (Coe). While these interpretations are understandable, they, in a metatheatrical way, show the ease with which one can be swayed into believing Archie and what he professes. Such positive "spin" on the state of the world is refreshing and uplifting, but the actions of the speaker discredit his words. Archie, the likely murderer of McFee and (though it is admittedly in George's dream) of Clegthorpe, could just as honestly say, "More jumpers live than are murdered." Remak Ramsey, who played Archie in the Broadway production, argues: "Coe's interpretation [cited above] couldn't have been more off the beam, because they [the world problems enumerated] are terrible things to worry about. And this passive, amoral acceptance is becoming more acceptable" (Faraone 80). Following Ramsey, Faraone sees this metaphysical farce as Stoppard's reactionary warning: "Let [Archie's] form of thinking, this approach to life, continue to encroach upon the formerly accepted verities and there will remain little to be thankful for except the negative fact that we are not dead" (80). Indeed, whether one takes an absolute or relative view of morality, *Jumpers* affirms the need for people to take a moral stand.

Conclusion

One of the accomplishments of *Jumpers* is the dramatization of the very human conflict between what one believes or knows on an emotional/intuitive level versus what one can verify via intellect or logic. The play also elucidates the difficulty of using language to articulate basic "truths" about life. George laments: "Though my convictions are intact and my ideas coherent, I can't seem to find the words. . . . Or rather, the words betray the thoughts they are supposed to express. Even the most generalized truth begins to look like special pleading as soon as you trap it in language" (46).

This point is significant because even if one believes that *Jumpers* argues for the existence of moral absolutes, what does that mean when extrapolated into the real world? Talking with Mel Gussow, Stoppard asserted that "there

are certain universal, transcendent virtues which are good in themselves."
When asked if he could name three, Stoppard replied: "Not really. If you say,
being kind is good, the next person asks, what about being kind to Hitler?
What this man in [*Jumpers*] says is that you can't name it because it isn't another word for being something else, like being kind. The notion of com-
paring one action to another would be meaningless without the predicate
that there is some standard to refer to" (*Conversations* 16). Elsewhere, Stoppard has aptly argued: "As long as one understands what a man means by a
statement, what he really *means,* then his failure to put it into a precise capsule which has absolutely no ambiguity about it, in a sense, doesn't matter"
(McCulloch 40). While a skeptic might use this inability to articulate a transcendent virtue as a debunking of absolutes, I suspect that Stoppard's concept of moral absolutes is something along the lines of the United Nations
Universal Declaration of Human Rights, a profession of the appropriate ethical treatment of human beings with which, I would guess, most moral relativists would agree.

Overall, *Jumpers* shows that concepts such as moral absolutes and moral
relativity are more complex than might first appear, with the difficulty deriving from the fact that "[l]anguage is an approximation of meaning and not
a logical symbolism for it" (24). Faced with a world where much is relative,
Stoppard tends to latch on to the islands of stability amidst the sea of uncertainty; Stoppard and his character George may not be able to "prove" their
intuitive position, but they can still, on a personal level, claim to know, which
is about as much as anyone can do in an environment where the proffering
of viable solutions is always open to valid criticism. If that seems irrational,
it is well to keep in mind George's observation: "The National Gallery is a
monument to irrationality! Every concert hall is a monument to irrationality!—and so is a nicely kept garden, or a lover's favour. . . . If rationality were
the criterion for things being allowed to exist, the world would be one gigan-
tic field of soya beans! . . . . The irrational, the emotional, the whimsical . . .
these are the stamp of humanity which makes reason a civilizing force" (40).
Stoppard, the intellectual and lover of logic, also realizes that many of the
things that make life worth living fall outside the realm of the rational. Indeed, as a whole, *Jumpers* suggests that it is through the embracing of both
reason and irrationality, of both logic and intuition, of both science and
metaphysics, of both belief and action, that a fuller understanding and appreciation of life can be achieved.

Chapter 5

Travesties

Rosencrantz and Guildenstern Are Dead and *Jumpers* were both award-winning successes at the National Theatre, and through them Stoppard was recognized for his linguistic and theatrical virtuosity. His reputation was that of a flashy, entertaining, apolitical, intellectual artist. But what is an artist? What are the possible roles, functions, and aims of the artist? What is the position of the artist in society? These questions formed part of Stoppard's internal debate, and so he followed *Jumpers* with two meditations on the nature of art and the role of the artist. His 1972 radio play *Artist Descending a Staircase* was a precursor of his next stage play, *Travesties.*

Artist Descending engages in a debate between the relative merits of traditional versus avant-garde art, and Stoppard asserts: "Donner is me. I'm a very square, conservative and traditional sort of mind" (Mayne 37). In the play Donner devalues nonintentional avant-garde art: "Skill without imagination is craftsmanship and gives us many useful objects such as wickerwork picnic baskets. Imagination without skill gives us modern art" (19). These artistic debates, as well as some actual dialogue, are carried through into *Travesties,* where added to the mix is a consideration of the interplay between art and politics. Stoppard notes a personal connection: "One of the impulses in *Travesties* is to try to sort out what my answer would in the end be if I was given enough time to think every time I'm asked why my plays aren't political, or ought they to be?" (Hayman, *Tom Stoppard,* 7).

The genesis of *Travesties* goes back to 1960 when Stoppard was still a journalist in Bristol. A friend remarked: "In 1916 in Zurich living within a stone's throw of each other and using the same cafe were the Dadaist Tristan Tzara, and Lenin, and I think Freud, maybe. Look into it" (Gussow, *Conversations,* 8). This historical nugget initially spurred the idea of doing "a two-act thing, with one act a Dadaist play on Communist ideology and the other an ideological functional drama about Dadaists" (8). But as Stoppard looked into the history, he discovered that James Joyce was also living in Zurich during World War I, and by now Stoppard's interest had become to ask "whether the artist and the revolutionary can be the same person or whether the activities are mutually exclusive. . . . How would you justify *Ulysses* to Lenin? Or Lenin to Joyce?" (20–21). More personally, for Stoppard, *Travesties* asks "whether an artist has to justify himself in political terms *at all*" (Hudson, Itzin, and Trussler 69), and it is part of "an ongoing debate with myself over the importance of the artist" (Wetzsteon 82). The historical figures offer three legs of a stool: Lenin, the political revolutionary who advocated art as a vehicle for social change and who repressed dissident voices; Tzara, the artistic revolutionary who advocated anti-art and the destruction of traditional views of art; and Joyce, the artistic evolutionary, who advocated art for art's sake. Stoppard notes: "[I added Joyce] mainly because I didn't want Tzara and the Dadaists to carry the artistic banner in the play, and Joyce was an artist with whom I sympathize a great deal" (Weiner).

While the historical figures spark immediate recognition, the protagonist of *Travesties* is Henry Carr, a man pulled from the footnotes of history—like Rosencrantz and Guildenstern, he is a nonentity thrust into the limelight. While reading Richard Ellman's biography of Joyce, Stoppard discovered that while in Zurich Joyce had directed a production of Oscar Wilde's play *The Importance of Being Earnest.* An offshoot was that Carr, a minor British consular official who played Algernon, was rankled by what he considered Joyce's condescending attitude and sued Joyce for reimbursement of the expensive trousers and accessories he had bought for the production. The two men were in and out of court for nearly a year with Joyce winning his countersuit for the cost of five tickets, but losing on his claim of slander. Ultimately, Joyce exacted his revenge by creating the character of Private Carr, a foul-mouthed drunken soldier who assaults Stephen Dedalus in *Ulysses.* For Stoppard, this historical footnote solved a few major problems. He had the characters who could debate his chosen themes, but until he learned of the *Earnest* production he had no narrative; this sparked the idea of grafting his plot onto Wilde's. Also, Carr's addition provided the desired major role for John Wood and more importantly served as the base of the stool—all the events would be filtered through the unreliable memory of an old man, thereby relieving Stoppard of any concerns for fidelity to history. Also, Carr adds a fourth perspective to the debate, that of a British bourgeois.

Textual History and Construction

Travesties exists in two published versions. Produced in the summer of 1974 at the Royal Shakespeare Company (remounted in the summer of 1975), the first text was published in the spring of 1975. When the RSC revived the play in 1993, Stoppard made significant revisions that strengthen the play.[1] Both published texts are longer than the scripts actually performed.[2]

The structure of *Travesties* is similar to *Jumpers:* "You start with a prologue which is slightly strange. Then you have an interminable monologue which is rather funny. Then you have scenes. Then you end up with another monologue. And you have unexpected bits of music and dance, and at the same time people are playing ping-pong with various intellectual arguments" (Hayman, *Tom Stoppard,* 12). Stoppard's description applies to the first act, where after the deliberately confusing prologue, Old Carr has a lengthy, linguistically dense, and laugh-filled monologue that establishes the memory-frame of the play and that discusses the significance of the wartime activities of the three historical figures. When the monologue is finished, Carr is his younger self, back in wartime Zurich, and the first-act scenes then often correspond to plot points in *The Importance of Being Earnest* with the *Travesties* characters taking on the identities of Wilde's. Thus, Young Carr corresponds to Algernon, Tzara to Jack Worthing, Joyce to Lady Bracknell, Bennett to Lane, and Gwendolyn and Cecily to their namesakes. When Stoppard revised the text in 1993, he left the content of act 1 the same, but cut approximately sixty lines from within speeches, trimmed Joyce's version of "Mr. Dooley" to its first and last verses, and substantially reduced (from six pages to three and a half pages) Joyce's interrogation of Tzara on the nature and history of Dadaism. This streamlined 1993 text is more effective for production.

Radically different in style and tone, the second act is devoted to Lenin. There are significant differences between the two published versions. The 1975 text begins with Cecily's long monologue (a scene hard to justify as being part of Carr's memory), which provides an overview of Marxist economic theory and Lenin's political development until he arrived in Zurich. Stoppard's initial thinking was that the lengthy monologue would be like a sadistic joke on the audience who were expecting more laughs but instead got lectured. Structurally, the idea was that the first act closes with an exposition of Dadaism, and so the second act should begin with a corresponding history of how Lenin, in political terms, got to Zurich (Hayman, *Tom Stoppard,* 9). During previews Stoppard discovered that in going from a rollicking first act to a straight lecture, he had misjudged, and so the speech was gradually cut until, as in the revised text, the speech begins with the mention of Lenin and his wife, Nadya, at the start of World War I.[3]

Much of the second act focuses on Lenin's attempt to return to Russia to join the Revolution, and it contains his views on art. Virtually all of Lenin and Nadya's dialogue come from their own writings; thus, much of the second act is almost documentary in nature. In fact, in the original draft there was a moment where the lights snapped to bright white, "destroying the set and ambience" (71). The actors playing Tzara, Lenin, and Nadya were then to break character and directly address the audience.[4] In 1976 Stoppard commented: "I felt very strongly—and now I believe I was right—that one thing I could not do was to integrate the Lenins into the *Importance* scheme. . . . It would have been disastrous to Prismize and Chasublize the Lenins, and I believe that that section saves *Travesties* because I think one's just about *had* that particular Wilde joke at that point" (Hayman, *Tom Stoppard,* 10).

By 1993 Stoppard's attitude toward the treatment of the Lenins had changed.[5] They have fewer and shorter speeches, which have also been re-ordered. Furthermore, Stoppard adds some lighthearted moments. When they appear for their first plan of escape, Nadya wears "*a bonnet, severely dressed and carrying a book*" while Lenin wears "*a clerical collar, but otherwise dressed in black from parson's hat to parson's leggings. He and Nadya look at each other and despair — Chasuble and Prism*" (53). They remove these costumes and proceed in the documentary fashion, but they will be travestied again, via one of the other main changes. Besides not integrating the Lenins into *Earnest,* the other structural flaw of the 1975 text is that while the play is supposed to take place in Carr's memory, the Lenin section seems to exist outside of it. The 1993 text makes clear Stoppard's "private sub-text . . . that Old Carr, researching his memoirs in the Zurich Library, is thinking through bits of Lenin" (6 Nov. 1975). Thus, at points during act 2, the audience sees Carr paging through a book as they hear the Lenins speak, and this device is introduced by having the mise-en-scène mimic one of Lenin's public orations, but the words he speaks are a paraphrase of Algernon and Lady Bracknell: "Really, if the lower orders don't set us a good example what on earth is the use of them?! They seem as a class to have absolutely no sense of moral responsibility! To lose one revolution is unfortunate. To lose two would look like carelessness!" (58). The travestying is all the more ironic and comic in that Lenin's own sentiments on the lower classes are diametrically opposed to the words he seems to say. At this point Carr reemerges with the book he is examining, and he acknowledges that his memory has slipped off the rails again. Carr proceeds to note when he agrees with Lenin, sometimes speaking simultaneously with Lenin and ultimately concluding: "There was nothing wrong with Lenin except his politics" (60).

While the Lenin section is changed the most, Stoppard also reworked other aspects of the second act. He cut approximately fifty lines from Cecily and Carr's political debate on Marxist socialism, and he added a variation on the Algy-Jack muffin-eating scene from *Earnest.* The result is that the second act is integrated more into both the *Earnest* framework and the memory structure. Also, the tone of the second act, originally seen as stodgy and deadening, is lighter and more playful. While some of the details of the political argument have been trimmed (mostly at the expense of the socialist position), the revised *Travesties* still maintains the core essence of the different voices in the debate. Though a producer may wish to reinsert some of the cuts, as a whole, the 1993 version is a more focused, more comedic, and more effective text for performance.

Plot summaries and descriptions of textual changes cannot do justice to the joie de vivre with which the play is written. Stoppard has said that he did not want to "write an inconsequential Dadaist play" (Kerensky 86), but rather he intended the play to include "a minor anthology of styles-of-play, styles-of-language" (Marowitz, "Tom Stoppard," 5). These styles include Wildean pastiche, political history lecture, documentary personal letters, Shavian dialectics, limericks, puns, parody, song, epigrams, and other wordplay. All the linguistic fireworks feed into the play's debate on the nature and function of art. While Thomas Whitaker argues that the play's style "sympathetically len[ds] itself to Tzara's own explosive spontaneity" (122), the overall style is actually Joycean. Joyce and Tzara represent two antithetical strains of modernism. From Tzara "descends the subversive tradition of 'anti-art' that has emphasized the spontaneous, absurd, and often socially provocative gesture, howl, or happening. From Joyce . . . descends the formalist tradition of 'art' that has emphasized the long-meditated, comprehensive, seemingly apolitical, and labyrinthine artifice" (Whitaker 120). It is not Dadaist chance but rather Joycean formalism that epitomizes the conscious craftsmanship and verbal virtuosity of *Travesties*. Indeed, Stoppard's attempt to create a minor anthology of styles is reminiscent of Joyce's "Oxen in the Sun" chapter of *Ulysses,* a chapter that provides a compressed history of English prose. In turn, Stoppard uses excerpts of the "Oxen in the Sun" chapter as part of the prologue to *Travesties*. Also, Stoppard's insertion of his characters into the framework of Wilde's *Earnest* is loosely analogous to Joyce's placement of his characters within the structure of Homer's *Odyssey*. Thus, the overall structure and style of *Travesties* evokes Joyce's artistic legacy, and reinforces Stoppard's repeated statement that in the play's artistic debate, he is on Joyce's side.

An intriguing feature of the script's construction is Stoppard's "time slip" device by which scenes are replayed with new dialogue. Stoppard's stage directions say that a result of the play being "under the erratic control of Old Carr's memory . . . is that the story (like a toy train perhaps) occasionally jumps the rails and has to be restarted at the point where it goes wild" (11).[6] On one hand the device allows the author to get himself out of any situation—the conversations do not need to have a logical conclusion but rather can be stopped whenever Stoppard has said what he wants about the topic. On the other hand, it epitomizes Clive James's notion that Stoppard abandons fixed viewpoints in order to clarify and be precise over a greater range of events (29–30). Director Peter Wood sees the device as feeding into the play's commentary on the difficulty of writing history: "[*Travesties* is] a view of history seen prismatically through the view of Henry Carr. At one point Tom was thinking of calling it *Prism*" (Hayman, "Peter Wood"). The proposed title alludes both to Wilde's character Miss Prism and to the play's prismatic treatment of history, art, and revolution through the "triangular prism of Joyce-Tzara-and-Lenin" who themselves are refracted "through Carr's memory, and again through Stoppard's multifaceted parody. It therefore becomes a model of the indirections by which we must move toward the white light of a truth beyond our full perception or expression" (Whitaker 114). The "time slip" device is also integral to the thematic emphasis on the artist. Michelene Wandor argues that in addition to providing narrative information the device "show[s] us that at each and every point a writer makes choices about what to say and how to say it. Stoppard's license in his version of 'history' is a salutary reminder to look closely at other apparently truthful glimpses into the past via personal reminiscence" (42). The "time slips" allow for multiple debates and multiple perspectives, but as will be argued,

Stoppard and the play do offer a point of view, and it is overall aligned with Joyce and Carr.

Thematic Analysis of Text and Production

Travesties begins with a prologue that is deliberately confusing in its conjunction of linguistic elements as it mixes a Dadaist "chance" poem, Joyce's dictation of the "Oxen in the Sun" chapter of *Ulysses* and the Lenins having a conversation in Russian. However, the seeming absurdist beginning in which there are few readily intelligible words masks a complex Joycean linguistic web. Tzara's opening chance poem is, as Stoppard informs would-be translators, also a bilingual pun as the sound of the words creates the approximation of a limerick in French. Translated back into English, the "nonsense" poem reads:

> There is a man called Tzara
> Who of riches had an embarrassment.
> He stays in Switzerland
> Because he's an artist.
> "We have nowhere else," he declared.
> ("Notes for Translators" 1)

This elaborate wordplay is presumably missed by most audiences and so on one hand, Stoppard's inside joke merely demonstrates his linguistic dexterity but is, from a pragmatic point of view, virtually empty of meaning. Paul Delaney's assertion that "the speech makes sense" (*Moral Vision* 64) is more true in theory than in reception. On the other hand, Delaney justifiably asserts that, in an inverse of Tzara's sentiments, "*Travesties* more nearly leads us to the conclusion that everything is design, including chance. . . . None of *Travesties*' intricacy bodies forth a vision of the cosmos as random, incoherent, chaotic" (64). Throughout the play Stoppard's controlling hand is that of the Joycean craftsman who plays with words in a manner that, if not always readily intelligible, is deliberate and thought-out. It is definitely not the anarchic, random hand of a Dadaist.

The prologue ends with Joyce delivering a limerick and strolling offstage singing "Galway Bay." The image of Joyce is a caricature, a stage Irishman; and indeed, it is at this point that Old Carr (perhaps onstage from the start) takes over and establishes the fact that the characters are creations of his imagination, of his fantasized past. Old Carr has a nearly fifteen-minute monologue that mixes a parody of the titles and style of Edwardian memoirs with a verbal Joycean flair of puns, alliteration, internal rhyme, phonetic echoing, and double entendres. Even Carr's self-described senile digression may be seen as Joycean stream-of-consciousness. As a piece of writing the speech exhibits superior artistry, and even the play's detractors find its performance "sublimely funny" (Tynan 108). Structurally, the monologue sets the scene, establishes the principal characters, and alerts the audience to Carr's unreliability as a reporter of history: "Carr of the Consulate!—first name Henry, that much is beyond dispute, I'm mentioned in the books. For the rest I'd be willing to enter into discussion but not if you don't mind correspondence, into matters of detail and chronology—I stand open to correction on all points" (9). The monologue, unlike George's in *Jumpers,* is a direct address to the audience and establishes Carr as a fallible narrator who is full of biases and delusions.

By the end of the monologue, Old Carr transforms into Young Carr and the play moves into its analogue of the first scene of *Earnest* as Carr (Algy) talks with his butler Bennett (Lane). Via the "time slip" device the scene is played five times. The first two focus on the war as Bennett reports that two different newspapers "announce, respectively, an important Allied and German victory, each side gaining ground after inflicting heavy casualties on the other with little loss to itself" (10). Such propaganda points to the unreliability of printed documents as objective pieces of evidence. Furthermore, the comment leads to Carr's description of both the romance and the horrors of war, again pointing to the role perspective plays in shaping reality and the telling of history. The third version is filled with Wildean epigrams of inversion, and has moved into a discussion of the Russian Revolution. Here Carr interprets a social revolution as "unaccompanied women smoking at the opera" (12). When told that it is class warfare, Carr, in Wildean fashion, inverts the scenario saying it is not surprising that the exploited upper class should turn upon their insolent servants. The fourth and fifth versions proceed with Bennett providing historical information on the progress of the Russian Revolution and Marxist theory, exposition that forms the backdrop to the events of the play's second act. Throughout this Wildean section, Stoppard uses comedy of inversion as the consular official Carr knows relatively nothing about politics, while the servant Bennett speaks eloquently on politics and political theory.[7]

After a virtuosic, style-for-style's-sake "nonsense scene" in which all the dialogue forms limericks, Tzara reenters (as Jack Worthing) and he and Carr, amidst moments from *Earnest,* engage in the first of the play's debates on art. Tzara's anti-art is pitted against Carr's bourgeois sensibilities. Though Carr is a bit of a buffoon figure, Stoppard's self-description as "an English middle-class bourgeois" (Hudson, Itzin, and Trussler 75) suggests that the playwright shares, on artistic matters, many of Carr's values. For example, Carr's view that "it is the duty of the artist to beautify existence" (20) is much closer to Stoppard's view than is Tzara's vision of that duty as being "to jeer and howl and belch" (20). One of Stoppard's main critiques of the Dadaists is their extreme relativity. The Dadaist notion of anti-art involves a reconfiguring of language and concepts so that, merely by asserting so, anyone can be an "artist" and anything can be called "art." In contrast, Carr, repeating Donner in *Artist Descending* and speaking for Stoppard, defines an artist as "someone who is gifted in some way that enables him to do something more or less well which can only be done badly or not at all by someone who is thus not gifted" (21). The speech proceeds to a defense of the objective meaning of language:

> If there is any point in using language at all it is that a word is taken
> to stand for a particular fact or idea and not for other facts or ideas.
> I might be able to claim to be able to fly . . . Lo, I say I am flying. But
> you are not propelling yourself about while suspended in the air, some-
> one may point out. Ah no, I reply, that is no longer considered the
> proper concern of people who can fly. . . . Don't you see my dear Tris-
> tan you are simply asking me to accept that the word Art means what-
> ever you wish it to mean; but I do not accept it. (21)

While Carr's comic demonstration serves as a compelling refutation of Tzara's extreme linguistic relativity, the notion of language having an absolute, objective meaning is also called into question. Even if words are "innocent, neutral, [and] precise" (as Stoppard will argue in *The Real Thing* [54]), Tzara offers a sufficient argument that their use is neither innocent nor neutral. Language lives in a web of associations, and meaning can be manipulated; though a word's definition can be relatively precise there can be a large gap between denotation and connotation. Indeed, Tzara argues that "words like patriotism, duty, love, freedom . . . [are] the traditional sophistries for waging wars of expansion and self-interest" (21). It is this section of the play, where Carr and Tzara argue over the politics of war, that Stoppard is at his dialectical best:

CARR: Wars are fought to make the world safe for artists. It is never quite put in those terms but it is a useful way of grasping what civilized ideals are all about. The easiest way of knowing whether good has triumphed over evil is to examine the freedom of the artist. . . .

TZARA: Wars are fought for oil wells and coaling stations; for control of the Dardanelles or the Suez Canal; for colonial pickings to buy cheap in and conquered markets to sell dear in. War is capitalism with the gloves off. . . .

CARR: I'll tell you what's *really* going on: I went to war because it was my *duty,* because my country needed me, and that's *patriotism.* I went to war because I believed that those boring little Belgians and incompetent Frogs had the right to be defended from German militarism, and that's *love of freedom.* . . .

TZARA: You ended up in the trenches, because on the 28th of June 1900 the heir to the throne of Austro-Hungary married beneath him and found that the wife he loved was never allowed to sit next to him on royal occasions, except! when he was acting in his military capacity as Inspector General of the Austro-Hungarian army—in which capacity he therefore decided to inspect the army in Bosnia, so that *at least on their wedding anniversary,* the 28th of June 1914, they might ride side by side in an open carriage through the streets of Sarajevo! (22–23)

Both the middle-class defender-of-traditional-ideals Carr, and the capitalist-critiquing, class-conscious Tzara (who in history did become a dedicated Communist) are given valid arguments. That these opposing ideologies can both be "right" points to the need to see historical events as being the result of many causes, and that even seemingly contradictory explanations of history may be needed to gain a fuller understanding.

Within this scene, Stoppard, as he will later do in his presentation of Lenin, subtly shows the ways in which Tzara contradicts himself. Tzara asserts that "causality is no longer fashionable owing to the war" (19) and thus Dadaism emphasizes chance. Carr responds: "How illogical, since the war itself had causes" (19). Indeed, Tzara himself will posit causal reasons for the war. Likewise Tzara's assertion that words are conscripted for waging wars of expansion and self-interest does not suggest the need for anti-art and turning everything on its head, but rather points to a need to minimize the manipulation of language so that events can be seen as clearly as possible. Language can be used to reveal as well as to conceal, and so logical reasoning and coherent arguments may be a more effective means of showing when patriotic rhetoric is a mask for profiteering.

After a "time slip" the Carr-Tzara scene is repeated, this time more closely following the plot points and style of *Earnest*. Ultimately it leads to another debate on art with Carr asserting: "Artists are members of a privileged class. Art is absurdly overrated by artists, which is understandable, but what is strange is that it is absurdly overrated by everyone else" (28). Carr, repeating a sentiment from *Artist Descending*, proceeds with one of the play's most memorable lines: "For every thousand people there's nine hundred doing the work, ninety doing well, nine doing good, and one lucky bastard who's the artist" (28). Surprisingly, Carr is speaking with Stoppard's voice: "I've always felt that the artist is the lucky man. I get deeply embarrassed by the statements and postures of 'committed' theatre. . . . I've never felt this—that art is important. That's been my secret guilt" (Watts, "Tom Stoppard," 50). Eventually, Stoppard's guilt was assuaged: "When I tried to visualize a completely technological world without culture, I realized that one does not have to apologize for being an artist. It took me many years to reach that understanding" (Kerensky 86). This latter sentiment suggests art's ability to transcend the material, and in a moment of seeming inconsistency, Tzara briefly champions the artist as "the priest-guardian of the magic" (29). More characteristically, Tzara proceeds to denounce art's corruption via patronage. Tzara ends his speech chanting "dada" at least fourteen times (29). However, Stoppard's emphasis on Dadaist anarchy and seeming nonsense does not show the whole picture. Hans Richter quotes prominent Dadaist Hans Arp: "We were seeking an art based on fundamentals, to cure the madness of the age, and a new order of things that would restore the balance between heaven and hell" (25). Dadaists wanted to use irrationality and chance to arrive at a freedom from constraints and what they perceived to be a more authentic reality. While Dadaism's manic, anarchic energy contained the seeds of its own demise, in its historical moment, the movement offered an acute response to the horrors of World War I. As in *Jumpers* where logical positivism was essentially dead when Stoppard attacked it, Tzara's Dadaism, in terms of "products" is a straw figure. It is Dada's spirit of challenging established institutions, and not the poems Tzara pulled out of a hat, that has had enduring value.

After another "time slip" Joyce and Gwendolyn (paralleling Lady Bracknell and Gwendolyn) arrive. As in history, Joyce requests the Consul's support of the *Earnest* production and asks Carr to play Algy. Out of the historical trial of Carr's suing for the cost of the trousers, Stoppard weaves an image of Carr as the quintessential dandy obsessed with sartorial splendor, and here it leads to a comic plot summary of *Earnest* based on Algernon's costume changes. Joyce also includes the apt observation that "culture is the continuation of war by other means" (32). While the armies battle, the exiled artists, in conjunction with their consulates, seek to establish their countries' dominance in different artistic endeavors.

The battle for artistic dominance and the debate between Dadaist anti-art and traditional art is then dramatized onstage as the dialectic moves from rational argument to contrasting works of art. Tzara has cut up Shakespeare's eighteenth sonnet and intends to transform it into a chance poem, but first Gwendolyn recites the entire poem. Not only does the audience hear the grandeur and beauty of the original, but Tzara and Gwendolyn proceed with a conversation that is composed entirely of excerpts from Shakespeare.[8] Here Stoppard's anthology of styles strives to show the superiority of conscious craftsmanship and linguistic mastery over the random and unstructured avant-garde. One assumes that an RSC audience would be more sympathetic and appreciative of Shakespeare's poetry and poetic dialogue than they would of Dadaist anarchy. The ensuing chance poem version of Shakespeare's sonnet is, like the prologue's opening bilingual limerick, under the careful control of Stoppard's guiding hand. Appropriate to the plot point of marriage proposal, Stoppard's manipulation of the "random" pull of words has been interpreted as "a free-verse poem of unmistakably phallic excitement" (Whitaker 116) that is "libidinously sensual" (Delaney, *Moral Vision*, 64). The poem climaxes with Gwendolyn's shriek of "heaven!" (36), and then the text relaxes back into the Wildean style and plot point analogues.

When Joyce reenters the room, he speaks with the voice of Lady Bracknell: "Rise, sir, from that semi-recumbent posture!" (37). The ensuing scene between Joyce and Tzara operates on three levels. Stoppard explains: "On one it's Lady Bracknell quizzing Jack. Secondly, the whole thing is actually structured on [the eighth] chapter in *Ulysses*,[9] and thirdly, it's telling the audience what Dada is, and where it comes from" (Tynan 109). While the multi-layered pastiche is ingenious, it has also led to charges of self-indulgence, such as Tynan's assertion that "the scene resembles a triple-decker bus that isn't going anywhere" (109). The interrogation begins with Tzara's nihilistic assertion: "It has no meaning. It is without meaning as Nature is. It is Dada" (38). Throughout the questioning, Tzara's account of Dadaism is contrasted with the visual image of Joyce conjuring, producing a carnation, a string of flags, and ultimately a rabbit. The action tells more than words. While Tzara is made to say that Dada's only original contribution to the world of art is "the word Dada" (40), Joyce is able to take Tzara's scraps of paper, his trash, and transform them into the beauty of a carnation. The image ties Joyce and his type of art to the subsequent definition of the artist as the magician among humanity. The interrogation scene ends with each man offering their clearest statement on art. Tzara castigates Joyce and traditional art:

> Your art has failed. You've turned literature into a religion and it's as dead as all the rest, it's an overripe corpse and you're cutting fancy figures at the wake. It's too late for geniuses! Now we need vandals and desecrators, simple-minded demolition men to smash centuries of baroque subtlety, to bring down the temple, and thus finally, to reconcile the shame and the necessity of being an artist! Dada! *Dada! Dada!! (He starts to smash whatever crockery is to hand; which done, he strikes a satisfied pose.)* (41)

While this Dadaist outburst against traditional art accents Tzara as perhaps the most dynamic and captivating character, the end product of his artistic views is broken crockery, a stage image that seems to be missed by critics who view the play as championing Tzara's point of view. It is another moment where actions speak louder than words, a theatricalization of the long-term weakness of the Dadaist approach to art.

Tzara's critique is met by Joyce's defense. It is one of the few moments where Joyce breaks out of his underwritten, stagy persona and speaks with the style and authority of his historical counterpart:

> You are an over-excited little man, with a need for self-expression far beyond the scope of your natural gifts. This is not discreditable. Neither does it make you an artist. An artist is the magician put among men to gratify—capriciously—their urge for immortality. The temples are built and brought down around him, continuously and contiguously, from Troy to the fields of Flanders. If there is any meaning in any of it, it is in what survives as art, yes even in the celebration of tyrants, yes even in the celebration of nonentities. What now of the Trojan War if it had been passed over by the artist's touch? Dust. . . . But it is we who stand enriched, by a tale of heroes, . . . of Ulysses, the

wanderer, the most human, the most complete of all heroes—husband, father, son, lover, farmer, soldier, pacifist, politician, inventor
and adventurer. . . . It is a theme so overwhelming that I am almost
afraid to treat it. And yet I with my Dublin Odyssey will double that
immortality, yes, by God *there's* a corpse that will dance for some time
yet and *leave the world precisely as it finds it.* (41–42)

This speech in which Joyce defends his style of art was not in the original rehearsal script, but rather was added on the advice of director Peter Wood.
Stoppard "now think[s] it's the most important speech in the play" (Hayman, *Tom Stoppard,* 9).[10] The opening of the speech asserts Stoppard's own
view of unstructured avant-garde "art" as being the handicraft of talentless
people who are not truly artists. The speech's ensuing emphasis on the immortality of art, on its ability to survive and speak through the ages is akin
to the historical Joyce's reverent view of art: "I am trying . . . to give people
some kind of intellectual pleasure or spiritual enjoyment by converting the
bread of everyday life into something that has a permanent artistic life of its
own . . . for their mental, moral, and spiritual uplift" (Ellman 169). The most
controversial part of the speech is the phrase that "*[art] leave[s] the world precisely as it finds it,*" a line that caused Kenneth Tynan to remark: "So much
for any pretensions that art might have to change, challenge, or criticize the
world, or to modify, however marginally, our view of it" (112). Michael Billington adds: "How can *Ulysses* be said to have left the world as it found it?
Is changing people's consciousness and extending the range of the novel not
as much a way of affecting the world as passing a piece of legislation? . . .
Joyce enlarged our vision; and that seems to me a legitimate way of changing
the world" (*Stoppard* 102). These critics have valid points, and I suspect what
Stoppard intended was a sense of art not having an immediate efficacious impact on society. In an interview that appeared while *Travesties* was in rehearsals Stoppard stated his oft-repeated stance that journalism is more effective
for short-term change whereas art works over the long term and "is important because it provides the moral matrix, the moral sensibility, from which
we make our judgements about the world" (Hudson, Itzin, and Trussler 66).

In interviews, Stoppard has clearly stated which side he takes in the artistic debate: "I empathize with Joyce, though I don't necessarily give him the
last word. The play is a dialectic; it just happens that I'm on his side. The
side of logic and rationality. And craftsmanship. . . . Craftsmanship is what
crystallizes art" (Maves 101). A couple of days later, Stoppard remarked: "Le-

nin had no use for the kind of art represented by Dada, which is one of the few things Lenin and I agree on. Joyce, on the other hand, is an artist I can respect and sympathize with, which is why I've given Joyce the last word. Consciously or not, I loaded the play for him" (Eichelbaum 103). Like Carr, Stoppard's personal biases color his retrospection; Joyce does indeed have the last word, but it is due to Peter Wood, not Stoppard. Artistically and temperamentally, Stoppard subscribes to Joyce's views, but *overtly* the play is *not* loaded for Joyce. Of the historical figures, Stoppard's construction of Joyce is the least engaging. Within *Travesties*, Joyce composes limericks, scrounges for money, accompanies Gwendolyn, and interrogates Tzara (an action that helps define Tzara but not Joyce). Missing is a viable demonstration of Joyce's artistry and the personal inner drive from which sprang *Ulysses*.[11] Instead there is a caricatured stage Irishman, accented in the original production via Joyce's wearing a jacket adorned with shamrocks. John Weightman argued: "The character of Joyce is a failure, a sort of blank, because it is easier to show how non-art is silly and political dogmatism limited than it is to explain how good art comes to be good" (59). Tim Brassell adds: "Largely because of the restrictions imposed on him by the ill-matched parallel with Aunt Augusta and the distortions of Carr's bias, Stoppard's Joyce never begins to suggest [the historical Joyce's] level of seriousness and commitment" (148). Despite these valid critiques of Joyce's stage character, Stoppard *does* load the play, but it is not for the stage Joyce, but rather for the Joycean view of art. The whole of *Travesties*, from its linguistic vitality to its switching of styles in midnarrative, is an embodiment of the Joycean aesthetic.

Act 2

Act 2 focuses on Lenin and his views on art and politics. When considering the stage presentation of Lenin, Stoppard's personal views are pertinent: "All political acts must be judged in moral terms, in terms of their consequences. . . . The repression which for better or worse turned out to be Leninism in action after 1917 was very much worse than anything which had gone on in Tsarist Russia" (Hudson, Itzin, and Trussler 64). The political and personal realities that resulted from Lenin's views and actions make him a rather serious and solemn figure. In consequence, Stoppard decided that virtually all of the dialogue spoken by Lenin and his wife Nadya should come from their historical writings. For many critics, the Lenin section (at least in the 1974–75 production) brought the play to a grinding halt. In a letter to the actors playing the Lenins in the 1975 Broadway production, Stoppard said that he felt that the length and number of authentic quotations was necessary and correct and that the Lenin part of the play "attempts to remind an audience (which is unwilling to be reminded) that in experiencing the real world we don't have the luxury of a Henry Carr to filter and make it fun" (6 Nov. 1975). Likewise, Tim Brassell sees this halting of the comic momentum and *Earnest* pastiche as serving a valuable thematic purpose: "This [is] a risk which Stoppard deliberately takes, for one of his major concerns is precisely to suggest how art can be overshadowed and even controlled by the currents of political activity" (158–59). Furthermore, the perception that the Lenin section, the play's most didactic, should be considered the weak link of *Travesties* might even be considered an ironic affirmation of Stoppard's own distrust of overtly political art.

While the Lenins rarely interact with the other characters, Stoppard integrates Leninist-Marxist ideology into the dialectic by making Cecily a disciple of Lenin. In the midst of the *Earnest* intrigue where Carr/Algy tries to woo Cecily under false pretenses, they engage in a debate on art, with Cecily offering the Leninist view: "The sole duty and justification of art is social criticism. . . . Art is a critique of society or it is nothing" (49–50). Carr counters that art "gratifies a hunger that is common to princes and peasants" (50) and that "art doesn't change society, it is merely changed by it" (50). Here Carr is aligned with Joyce (and Stoppard) in an affirmation of art for art's sake and in opposition to utilitarian, sociopolitical art.

After a "time slip" Carr and Cecily debate politics. Carr, speaking for Stoppard (Hudson, Itzin, and Trussler 65), critiques Marxism: "Marx got it wrong. He got it wrong for good reasons but he got it wrong just the same. By bad luck he encountered the capitalist system at its most deceptive period. The industrial revolution had crowded people into slums and enslaved them in factories, but it had not yet begun to bring them the benefits of an industrialized society" (51). However, Stoppard's argument ignores a consideration of global capitalism, of the Third World sweatshop laborers whose living and working conditions can be as bad or worse than those that informed Marx's writings. The 1975 text did include the Leninist view that "the European Worker is benefitting from the exploitation of his colonial brother" (76), but that has been cut from the 1993 text, as has Cecily's most impassioned definition of her views: "Socialism is about *ownership*—the natural right of the people to the common ownership of their country and its resources, the *land*, and what is *under* the land and what *grows* on the land, and all the profits and the benefits!" (1975, 77). She continues: "In England the rich own the poor and the men own the women. Five per cent of the people own eighty per cent of the property" (78). These and other cuts in the revision severely weaken the socialist pole of the dialectic.

What does remain is the brutal side of Lenin, the man who often took a coldhearted, ends-justifies-the-means approach. During a famine Lenin did nothing because "he understood that the famine was a force for the revolution" (52). Lenin's allowing of individual suffering for a sense of the greater good would later extend to his repression of artists and intellectuals who did not share the views of the party. In one of the moments where the *Earnest* plot line comments on the Lenin plot line, Tzara states his belief that "artists and intellectuals will be the conscience of the revolution" (57). However, the audience knows that Carr is nearer the mark when he transforms Tzara's desire "to urinate in different colours" (41) into a statement about Leninist repression: "And multi-coloured micturition is no trick to these boys, they'll have you pissing blood" (57).

The main plot connection between the Lenin material and Carr's reminiscences concerns Carr's role as a British official assigned to keep an eye on Lenin. Characteristic of Carr's political bunglings, it is only as Lenin's train leaves [12] that Carr decisively declares: "No, it is perfectly clear in my mind. He must be stopped. . . . All in all [Russia has] a promising foundation for a liberal democracy on the Western model" (57). Old Carr soon reemerges and reflects on this situation:

> I'd got pretty close to [Lenin], had a stroke of luck with a certain little lady and I'd got a pretty good idea of his intentions, in fact I might have stopped the whole Bolshevik thing in its tracks, but—here's the point. I was *torn*. On the one hand, the future of the civilized world. On the other hand, my feelings for Cecily.[13] And don't forget, *he wasn't Lenin then!* I mean, *who was he?*, as it were. There I was, the lives of millions of people hanging on which way I'd move or whether I'd move at all, another man might have cracked—sorry about that muffin business, incidentally. (58)

While this fantasy recollection earnestly overstates Carr's potential importance (the play's closing section clarifies that Carr was not in a position to stop Lenin), the speech does raise the question of whether or not the British and German governments recognized the potential ramifications of Lenin's return. In fact, desiring a peace agreement with Russia, the German government secured Lenin's return to Russia via a sealed train. As the play's ensuing speeches from Lenin indicate, "the lives of millions" did indeed hinge upon Lenin's fate, and thus looming over Carr's comic reminiscences is the shadow of history and the very real consequences of action, inaction, and ideology. The speech also suggests the importance of the individual (Lenin in actuality, Carr in potentiality) and thus rebuts the Marxist-Socialist devaluing of the individual. As Carr comically states: "Mind you, according to Marx, the dialectic of history will get you to much the same place with or without Lenin. If Lenin did not exist, it would be unnecessary to invent him" (56).

In reading Lenin's writings, Stoppard felt that "there's a sense in which Lenin keeps convicting himself out of his own mouth. It's absurd. It's full of incredible syllogisms" (Hayman, *Tom Stoppard*, 10). In particular Stoppard is referring to Lenin's 1905 essay on the need for art and literature to be aligned with the party:

> Publishing and distributing centres, bookshops and reading rooms, libraries and similar establishments must all be under party control. We want to establish and we shall establish a free press, free not simply from the police, but also from capital, from careerism, and what is more, free *from bourgeois anarchist individualism!* Everyone is free to write and say whatever he likes without restrictions. But every voluntary association, including the party, is also free to expel members who use the name of the party to advocate anti-party views. (59)

Such a contradictory and skewed view of a free press and free expression needs no rebuttal, and so Stoppard's portrait of Lenin proceeds to show the conflict between Lenin's personal and political responses to art. Lenin did not understand avant-garde art, but rather admired traditional art, which he ultimately rejected on political grounds. In *Travesties* Lenin's final speech concerns this internal contradiction between his personal response and his political actions:

> I don't know of anything greater than [Beethoven's] Appassionata. Amazing, superhuman music. It always makes me feel, perhaps naively, it makes me feel proud of the miracles that human beings can perform. But I can't listen to music often. It affects my nerves, makes me want to say nice stupid things and pat the heads of those people who while living in this vile hell can create such beauty. Nowadays we can't pat heads

or we'll get our hands bitten off. We've got to *hit* heads, hit them without mercy, though ideally we're against doing violence to people. . . One's duty is infernally hard. (62)

Stoppard, the artist and the humanitarian, who soon after *Travesties* was to become personally and artistically involved in condemning Eastern Bloc repression, makes sure that the audience does not forget the violently repressive nature of Lenin's views in action. Ironically, the speech also suggests that traditional "apolitical" art has the potential to be a "counter-revolutionary force, uniting or at least emasculating those who should consider themselves enemies" (Brassell 160). In production, throughout this speech the Appassionata is heard; it is another moment where the beauty of traditional art asserts itself above any intellectual argument. The power of the music that could reduce Lenin to tears washes over the audience, scoring another point for the view that art does not need to justify itself in political terms.

From the seriousness of Lenin and the power of Beethoven, the play changes tone and tune as the Appassionata degenerates absurdly into the vaudeville song "Mr. Gallagher and Mr. Shean." In a letter, Stoppard explains his intent: "I always wanted the Lenin scene to say 'Life is too serious for frivolous plays like *Travesties*' and for Gallagher and Shean to say 'You thought that was frivolous? You ain't seen nothing yet'" (6 Nov. 1975). While this idea may not come through in performance, it is another moment where Stoppard shows off his cleverness while also reasserting the validity of art for art's sake.

After the "Mr. Gallagher and Mr. Shean" scene, which parallels the *Earnest* tea scene between Gwendolyn and Cecily, *Travesties* moves to a quick close that mimics the lovers' coupling that ends Wilde's play. The quick, formal climax ends in a traditional closing device of comedy—a dance sequence (apparently added by Peter Wood) with the newly joined lovers. The final theatrical flourish occurs when Carr and Cecily dance offstage as young lovers and dance back on as octogenarians. Then Old Cecily reveals the truth—Carr's reminiscences have little or no basis in history. In part, it is Stoppard's acknowledgment that he has compressed and intermingled four years of events for dramatic convenience. It is also a fitting reminder of the fallibility of memory and the tendency for self-aggrandizement—the audience learns that Carr's would-be servant Bennett was, in history, Carr's superior at the consulate.

Finally, Carr closes the play: "I learned three things in Zurich during the war. I wrote them down. Firstly, you're either a revolutionary or you're not, and if you're not you might as well be an artist as anything else. Secondly, if you can't be an artist, you might as well be a revolutionary. . . I forget the third thing" (71). This speech is more than just another comic reiteration of the unreliability of Carr's memory; rather, the words return the play to one of the central questions Stoppard sought to answer: Can the revolutionary and the artist be the same person? Paul Delaney asserts: "Quite clearly the final words of *Travesties* answer in the negative" (*Moral Vision* 81). Even if one interprets Carr's speech that way, the spectator, armed with history, should realize that in some cases they can be. Artists such as Mayakovsky and Václav Havel *were* instrumental figures in their countries' political revolutions. Delaney's more telling observation is that the third thing "is to be Henry Carr, to be an ordinary human being" (81). Though *Travesties* is populated with notable figures of history, the play's central figure is Henry Carr. Though even he forgets it, the thing to keep in mind is that even the seemingly insignificant individual is important.

Ultimately, *Travesties* is a mixed bag whose uniqueness has led to equally impassioned support and detraction. The play has wit, erudition, artistic and political history, debate, song and dance, and a host of other theatrically and linguistically compelling attributes. As Stoppard prepared for the 1993 revival, he remarked: "I've always thought *Travesties* contained things that were actually better than I can write" (Spencer). Similarly, in 1977, he told Ronald Hayman: "Most of *Travesties*—not as a structure and a play but speech by speech—still seems to me as good as I can ever get" (*Tom Stoppard* 138). Stoppard's crucial qualification concerns the distinction between individual passages versus the cohesion of the play as a whole. Kenneth Tynan has offered a valid critique: "What [*Travesties*] lacks is the *sine qua non* of theatre; namely a narrative thrust that impels the characters, whether farcically or tragically or in any intermediate mode, toward a credible state of crisis, anxiety, or desperation" (109).[14] The play lacks narrative momentum and any sense of pain or pathos, attributes that *are* present in the structurally similar *Jumpers*. On the other hand, the writing embodies the notion of style for style's sake, which in turn affirms Stoppard's view that the artist does *not* need to justify him/herself in political terms. Ironically, after asserting this view, Stoppard proceeded to pen plays (*Every Good Boy Deserves Favor* and *Professional Foul*) that *were* overtly political, plays that dealt with the long-term ramifications of Lenin's ideology in action.

6

Examining Eastern Bloc Repression

BETWEEN MAJOR STAGE PLAYS STOPPARD TYPICALLY REMAINS busy by writing for other media, by composing adaptations, and by penning works for nonmainstream theatre venues. These "minor" works include some of Stoppard's most innovative and effective writing. In particular, in 1977, Stoppard's personal concern for human rights abuses in Czechoslovakia and the Soviet Union manifested itself in *Every Good Boy Deserves Favor* (henceforth *EGBDF*) and *Professional Foul*.[1] Since these plays directly confront social issues, critics initially hailed them as marking a new, more mature Stoppard, a playwright who would be serious and politically engaged. Stoppard quickly distanced himself from such claims: "I was always morally if not politically involved. . . . I haven't the faintest idea what my main preoccupation will be this time next year" (Shulman 108).[2]

Every Good Boy Deserves Favor

In 1974 André Previn, conductor of the London Symphony Orchestra, invited Stoppard to write a piece that utilized a live full-size orchestra. Since it was a rare opportunity, Stoppard accepted and then spent the next eighteen months searching for an appropriate topic. In October 1974 Stoppard began making notes for a play about a millionaire who made his money selling fruit and who played the triangle in an orchestra he owned. By January 1975 Stoppard had decided that the orchestra only existed in the imagination of the millionaire, who was now a lunatic in a padded cell. When Stoppard returned to the project in August 1975, he sent Previn a note saying the work would involve an old millionaire, a school teacher, and questions about Lenin and the Appassionata. By the time Stoppard began writing the following spring, he realized that since the orchestra was in the mind of a lunatic, there was no need for the madman to be a millionaire. Meanwhile he had been reading about Soviet dissidents whose political activities resulted in their imprisonment in insane asylums. Furthermore, in April 1976 Stoppard befriended Victor Fainberg, a dissident whom the Soviet authorities could neither break nor silence and whom they thus exiled. Suddenly the subject matter and the form coalesced: "the dissident is a discordant note in a highly orchestrated society" (Stoppard, quoted in Gussow, *Conversations,* 34).

In a span of 4–6 weeks during May and June 1976, Stoppard wrote the first draft of *EGBDF.* Fainberg read the completed play and offered enthusiastic praise: "You found the only key this topic could be dealt with—the music. . . . Then naturally a very delicate mixture of tragic and comic elements was balanced wonderfully with the comic one prevailing which *must be*—to depict a mad world" (Letter).[3] Fainberg was also pleased that Stoppard avoided treating the issue as a "heroic melodrama." Furthermore, the exiled dissident noted a few minor inaccuracies, but felt that there was no need to emend them; however, ever fastidious to factual fidelity, Stoppard promptly corrected them.

EGBDF is subtitled "A Play for Actors and Orchestra," and to be truly appreciated the work must be experienced and not merely read. Stoppard aptly notes that the "effectiveness of the whole depends on the music composed by André Previn" (5). The show runs approximately seventy-five minutes and includes some beautiful original compositions by Previn as well as a number of musical jokes where the music quotes Russian composers such as Prokofiev and Tchaikovsky.[4] Epitomizing its "event quality" is the fact that top theatre talent, including director Trevor Nunn and actors Ian McKellen, John Wood, and Patrick Stewart, worked on the project knowing that it initially would be staged for only one performance, as a portion of the Queen's Silver Jubilee at the Royal Festival Hall. Due to the nature of the piece, Stoppard conceived the show as being performed with severe physical limitations: three small platforms that limited the scenery and the actors' movement. However, Stoppard says: "On stage the action is surrounded by music and takes place on these little islands in the middle of the orchestra, which is very important to the aesthetics of the thing" (Kuurman 54). The artistic success of the show led Previn to rescore the piece for a chamber orchestra for a 1978 three-month run at the Mermaid Theatre.

EGBDF involves two inmates who share a cell in a Soviet insane asylum. Both are named Alexander Ivanov. One (Ivanov) is genuinely insane, thinking he has an orchestra, while the other (Alexander) is there for agitating against Soviet repression. Both men are treated by a Doctor who plays in a real orchestra. The other characters are the dissident's son (Sacha), the boy's school teacher who toes the party line, and a Soviet Bureaucrat, the Colonel who ultimately orchestrates the prisoners' release.

Ivanov and his imaginary orchestra provide much of the comedy. The madman also ironically comments on the social themes as Ivanov's critique of the orchestra ("the Jew's harp has applied for a visa" [17]) and cross-examination of Alexander's musical inclinations ("If I beat you to a pulp would you try to protect your face or your hands?" [17]) carry political overtones and intimations of violent repression. Also, it is Ivanov who extracts the exposition from Alexander as to how he ended up in this asylum for political agitation. Alexander's "crime" was writing letters to the Communist Party, to newspapers, and to foreigners informing them "that sane people were being put in mental hospitals for their political opinions" (23). Stoppard's ironic pun is that Alexander refers to his activism as doing "something really crazy" (24), and this process of telling the truth lands him in an insane asylum. Stoppard draws from real life when he offers the following exchange:

ALEXANDER: I have no symptoms, I have opinions.

DOCTOR: Your opinions are your symptoms. Your disease is dissent. (32)

Alexander started his incarceration in the Leningrad Special Psychiatric Hospital on Arsenal'naya Street, but like Fainberg, he could not be broken. Instead, he continued his resistance by going on a hunger strike: "They don't like you to die unless you can die anonymously. If your name is known in the West, it is an embarrassment. . . . Russia is a civilized country . . . and it is confusing if people starve themselves to death" (24). Making the international media aware of the dissidents' plight was crucial to their survival. Likewise, Stoppard had been personally involved in the cause of Czech playwright Václav Havel, who had refused to accept an exit visa. In an article for the *New York Times,* Stoppard wrote: "The Czechoslovaks are now stuck between two opposite embarrassments: to pursue the logic of repression, or to climb down" ("Dirty Linen"). In the play, Alexander puts the Soviet regime in a similar position.

A hunger strike brings media scrutiny, and so the Soviet authorities decide that the best pressure they can apply is for Alexander's son, Sacha, to try to talk him out of it. When he persists in his hunger strike, the authorities back down. The play's ending—where the Colonel seemingly mistakes the two identically named prisoners, thereby allowing for their respective release—is actually just the culmination of a carefully orchestrated plan to set Alexander free while still saving face. Alexander reveals that when they couldn't talk him out of the hunger strike: "They gave in. And when I was well enough they brought me here. This means they have decided to let me go. It is much harder to get from Arsenal'naya to a civil hospital than from a civil hospital to the street. But it has to be done right. They don't want to lose ground. They need a formula. It will take a little time but that's all right. I shall read *War and Peace*. Everything is going to be all right" (25).[5] Alexander, like the dissidents Stoppard knew and had read about, knows the formula the authorities use when they plan on releasing dissidents who cause more embarrassment than their incarceration is worth.

The second clear indication that Alexander's release is being orchestrated is the revelation that: "Colonel—or rather Doctor—Rozinsky, who has taken over your case, chose your cell- or rather ward-mate personally" (27). Rozinsky chose the pair of prisoners precisely because they share the same name (32). He is not a psychiatrist but rather is a Doctor of Philology, specializing in Semantics. This section explaining Colonel Rozinsky was added to the second draft (July 1976) and clarifies that the Soviet authorities are playing a game—that they will not openly acknowledge defeat, but rather will use a semantic confusion over prisoners with identical names. The Doctor refers to the Colonel as a genius who is "proud to serve the State in any capacity" (27). His genius lies in making Alexander's release appear to be accidental, thereby precluding any need for a public admission of the error of locking him up in the first place.

Furthermore, the Doctor reveals that despite Alexander's "delusions, that sane people are put in mental hospitals" (27), they are ready to release him: "It seems to me that the best answer is for you to go home. Would Thursday suit you? . . . There is an Examining Commission on Wednesday. We shall aim at curing your schizophrenia by Tuesday night" (28). The Doctor's casualness adds to the play's comedy, but it is balanced by his hope that Alexander will at least partially cooperate. The Doctor supplies him with the answers that the Commission wants to hear.

> DOCTOR: The sort of thing I'd stick to is "Yes", if they ask you whether you agree you were mad; "No", if they ask you whether you intend to persist in your slanders; "Definitely", if they ask you whether your treatment has been satisfactory, and "Sorry", if they ask you how you feel about it all. . . .
>
> ALEXANDER: I was never mad, and my treatment was barbaric.
>
> DOCTOR: Stupidity is one thing I can't cure. I have to show that I have treated you. You have to recant and show gratitude for the treatment. We have to act together.
>
> ALEXANDER: The KGB broke my door and frightened my son and my mother-in-law. My madness consisted of writing to various people about a friend of mine who is in prison. This friend was twice put in mental hospitals for political reasons, and then they arrested him for saying that sane people were put in mental hospitals, and then they put him in prison because he was sane when he said this; and I said so, and they put me in a mental hospital. . . . (28–29)

Alexander's monologue, based on Fainberg's real-life experiences, proceeds to give an account of the inhumane treatment that a prisoner receives in a hospital such as the Arsenal'naya. As well as other means of torture, the "treatment" includes the injection of various drugs that cause severe physical discomfort. Despite this harsh treatment, and the possibility that he could face it again, Alexander adheres to the moral course he has chosen.

Alexander is the most unambiguous Stoppard protagonist. He starts the play having made a firm decision to denounce Soviet repression, and he never wavers from that course. Paul Delaney writes:

> [Alexander's] actions spring neither from non-conformist self-indulgence nor from a pragmatic sense of what is feasible but from a firm sense of moral right and wrong. . . . Stoppard explicitly voices his concern that moral values must be incarnated in moral action. . . . [EGBDF] celebrat[es] an individual who adheres to a standard of values higher than that of his society and who has the courage to act upon those values. (Moral Vision 97)

Whether dealing with the Doctor or with his son, Alexander adheres to his values. Sacha is summoned to the Psychiatric Hospital to persuade his father to eat and to comply with the answers the authorities want to hear before they release him. Sacha pleads with his father: "Papa, don't be rigid! Be brave and tell them lies!" (35). If Alexander will do that, "Everything can be all right!" (35). The son's understandably pragmatic and very human desire for his father to capitulate so that they can be reunited is countered by Alexander's explanation of why he must remain rigid and adhere to his values and principles: "Dear Sacha, try to see/what they call their liberty/is just the freedom to agree/that one and one is sometimes three" (34–35).[6] To acquiesce to the terms of his release means disavowing the barbarity and inhumanity of his treatment. Alexander asserts that lying or recanting "helps them to go on being wicked. It helps people to think that perhaps they're not so wicked after all" (35). Though he loves his son and understands his son's desire for him to be home, he sacrifices personal well-being: "What about all the other fathers? And mothers?" (35).[7] The system can only be toppled when individuals sacrifice their own self-interest for what is the proper, moral thing to do. Alexander says: "To thine own self be true/one and one is always two" (36). He refuses to conform to Soviet doublethink and is willing to die to show the injustice of the repressive system. Throughout the play, Alexander acts on a consistent belief that the injustice and immorality of the Soviet system must be resisted regardless of personal consequences or political expediency. Sacha's school lessons about mathematical principles merge with the political and moral lesson that Alexander is teaching—that some actions are simply better than others, that the United Nations' Declaration of Universal Human Rights must be practiced.

Sacha's inability to change his father's mind puts the authorities in a bind. They cannot let Alexander die, but nor can they release him until he admits he is cured. Sacha now tells the Doctor, "*you* must not be so rigid" (36). The Doctor does not have a solution to this dilemma. The situation appears to be at an insolvable impasse. Then the Colonel sweeps onstage in a grand entrance, and his subsequent actions have been widely misunderstood by audiences as well as critics. The Colonel asks Ivanov a question appropriate for Alexander and Alexander a question appropriate for Ivanov. Each can thus answer truthfully and still satisfy the Colonel, who releases both men. Many critics and audiences interpreted this confusion as emblematic of bureaucratic bungling, that the prisoners were released by mistake. Since there was initially only one performance, there was no opportunity to correct the misperception. However, when the show was remounted a year later at the Mermaid Theatre, the text remained identical but the final scene was restaged, trying to indicate that the Colonel knew exactly what he was doing. Paul Delaney reports that by the end of the run "the doctor was frantically gesticulating to call the attention of the colonel to the correct identities of the prisoners while the colonel was suavely—and quite deliberately—ignoring him" (*Moral Vision* 99). Despite this change, audiences and critics have sometimes persisted in their misunderstanding of Stoppard's intent.

Those who perceived the release as accidental interpreted the ending as a farcical comment on the bungling bureaucracy, a comic suggestion that the Soviet regime could fall through its own ineptitude. However, Stoppard's intent carries more serious and sobering overtones. The Soviet authorities know exactly what they are doing; though they tacitly concede defeat, Alexander cannot claim victory. They have not overtly acknowledged any wrongdoing, and thus the thousands of other political prisoners, the other mothers and fathers Alexander referred to, remain incarcerated. Though Alexander is released, it is not on his own terms because what he is fighting—the State system of repression—remains. Stoppard notes: "It's not a particularly optimistic ending" (Kuurman 53). Martin Huckerby adds: "The final anguish is caused by the dissident having to decide whether to go along with the ploy in order to gain his freedom" (114). Thus, *EGBDF* offers a mixed message. Alexander is free to go, but Sacha's closing line "Everything can be all right" (37) is not equivalent to "everything *is* all right." The harsh reality is that thousands of other dissidents remain imprisoned. The audience can revel in Alexander's release, but they should realize that it is a partial and limited victory over the repressive Soviet regime.

Finally, one moment might serve as a microcosm for the political protest that undergirds both *EGBDF* and *Professional Foul.* These plays were inspired by dissidents who opposed their respective regimes in the Soviet Union and Czechoslovakia. In both cases, the "subversives" were essentially simply seeking that their countries' constitutional freedoms be enforced. In *EGBDF* Sacha's teacher reports: "The [Soviet] Constitution guarantees freedom of conscience, freedom of the press, freedom of speech, of assembly, of worship, and many other freedoms" (29). Sacha wonders if they can appeal to the man who wrote that Constitution for assistance, but the teacher reveals that Nikolai Bukharin was shot soon after he wrote it (30). This fact makes clear that these "guaranteed" freedoms—the basic human rights that underlie most modern free and democratic societies—are principles that exist on paper but not in practice. It is the allowance of these freedoms that Stoppard champions as being universal human rights, rights that people must actively promote, protect, and preserve, both at home and in other countries.

Professional Foul

EGBDF was performed on 1 July 1977 and was soon followed by *Professional Foul*, which was broadcast on 24 September 1977. Their close proximity played into the perception of a "politicized" Tom Stoppard. However, the playwright dissented:

> There was no sudden conversion on the road to Damascus. . . . It was really only a coincidence that both of these plays about human rights should have been written about the same time. For some time I had been involved with Amnesty International, the worldwide human rights organization. The BBC had been asking me to write a TV play for them. . . . [And when Amnesty made] 1977 Prisoner of Conscience year, I thought a play on TV might help their cause. . . . On a subject like this a TV play would have more impact than a play for the stage. After all, on TV you would get a large audience on a single night. In a theater, the impact would be spread over weeks and months. (Shulman 109)

In the summer of 1976 Stoppard promised the BBC "a play about persecution behind the Iron Curtain to be delivered at the end of the year. But when the deadline came I had written nothing and had nothing in mind" (109).

In February 1977 Stoppard joined Peter Luff, a friend and Amnesty official, on a quasi Cook's Tour to Moscow and Leningrad. While they occasionally partook of the tour's sight-seeing events, they also went off on their own to meet with Russian dissidents and add signatures to an Amnesty petition. That trip, including Stoppard's own brushes with Soviet intimidation and repression, helped spark an idea for *Professional Foul*.[8] Near the same time Stoppard heard about some Czechoslovakian artists who were arrested "because they attempted to deliver to the Czech Government a document asking it to implement for the Czech people the human rights that had been called Charter 77. . . . One of the men arrested was Václav Havel" (Shulman 110). Like many of Stoppard's major plays, *Professional Foul* came into focus when different threads wove themselves together. Stoppard sums up: "So you can see that with my desire to write something about human rights, the combination of my [Czech] birth, my trip to Russia, my interest in Havel and his arrest, the appearance of Charter 77, [those] were the linking threads that gave me the idea for *Professional Foul*" (110–11). Elsewhere, Stoppard has stated:

> I wanted to write about somebody coming from England to a totalitarian society, brushing up against it, and getting a little soiled and a little wiser. I spent a long time wondering what to do, and I thought: a ballroom dancing team, with those wonderful ladies in tangerine tulle. . . . But I was really interested in the moral implications, and the equation just simplified itself until the formation dancers became moral philosophers. (Gollob and Roper 156)

Once Stoppard figured out the play's basic premise, he wrote it in approximately three weeks. *Professional Foul* went on to win the British Television Critics' Award as Best Play and had an unprecedented three transmissions in its first year. Though a television play, *Professional Foul* ranks with the best of Stoppard's stage plays. His characteristic comedy, including copious amounts of cross talk, is joined with serious ideas, engaging characters, a compelling story, and moments of genuine emotion.

Professional Foul concerns Anderson, a distinguished Cambridge professor of ethics, who attends an academic colloquium in Prague, but who goes there with the ulterior motive of attending the England-Czechoslovakia World Cup soccer qualifying match.[9] In Prague, Anderson encounters Pavel Hollar, a former student, who asks Anderson to smuggle his doctoral thesis out of Czechoslovakia. Initially Anderson declines, but after seeing the repressive practices of the state police, he alters his views. He changes his conference paper to a passionate declaration about the moral nature of human rights, and he smuggles the thesis out in the luggage of a fellow philosopher.

The principal characters of the play are philosophers, and they offer different perspectives on the nature of morality.[10] Chetwyn is a moral absolutist who believes that moral principles are God-given absolutes. Though a minor character, he expresses Stoppard's own notion that on moral matters, one can often count on the wisdom of a child to ascertain the difference between right and wrong. McKendrick is a Marxist moral relativist who champions catastrophe theory (discussed later), and who denies the existence of fixed moral principles or any transcendent basis for moral values. Anderson's view lies between these two. He believes that moral principles are fictions, but that people should treat them as if they were truths because it helps people behave properly. The arc of the play shows Anderson moving from a disengaged moral philosopher to one who acts upon moral values. Paradoxically, he uses a variation of McKendrick's catastrophe model to arrive at a position similar to Chetwyn's. Finally, there is Pavel Hollar, the catalyst for the play's illumination of the difference between moral theory and moral practice, how moral actions must be judged in real-world terms. Through his encounter with Hollar, Anderson loses his intellectual detachment and is put in a moral dilemma that parallels the moral issues that the philosophers are there to discuss.

Hollar, Anderson's student ten years ago at Cambridge, pays a surprise visit to his former mentor. Though possessing an advanced degree from Cambridge, Hollar, like other Czech intellectuals, has worked at a series of manual labor positions and is currently a janitor. Hollar has recently written a philosophical treatise on the nature of correct behavior and asks Anderson to smuggle the thesis to England. This situation raises the first philosophical debate. On the personal level, Anderson is worried that he could get into trouble, while on the ethical level, he fears that since he is a guest of the Czech government, it would be bad manners: "I know it sounds rather lame. But ethics and manners are interestingly related. The history of human calumny is largely a series of breaches of good manners. (*Pause.*) Perhaps if I said correct behaviour it wouldn't sound so ridiculous" (54). The initial impression of Anderson is as a likable but ineffectual man who does not wish to get involved; he can speak about moral and ethical issues, but he does not wish to engage them in practice and action.

In contrast, Hollar's writing of his thesis is itself a putting into practice of his belief that individuals have inalienable rights that cannot be abridged by the state. In this case, the act of writing puts Hollar and his family in danger. The thesis is considered dangerous because it contradicts the practice of the Czech political system. Hollar's thesis argues: "The ethics of the State must be judged against the fundamental ethic of the individual. The human being, not the citizen. I conclude there is an obligation, a human responsibility, to fight against the State correctness. . . . To me the idea of an inherent right is intelligible. I believe that we have such rights, and they are paramount" (55). At this point in time, Anderson is not, from a philosophical point of view, willing to accept that certain individual rights can be said to be inherent and inalienable. Anderson concludes that to smuggle the thesis would be unethical.

Anderson's ethical position is based on a theoretical proposition. The remainder of his time in Prague shall add an experiential component that shall alter his position. The next day when Anderson goes to return Hollar's manuscript, he walks into an unexpected situation. Hollar has been arrested, and the Czech secret police are searching the apartment for evidence; however, they are using a trumped-up charge of trafficking in illegal currency. With much of the dialogue in Czech, Mrs. Hollar screaming, faces cautiously peering out between cracked doorways, and numerous plainclothes policemen scouring the small apartment, a climate of fear is created. The intimidation tactics unnerve Anderson who simply wants to get to his soccer game. His impulse is to save himself and not get involved. After being detained an hour he asserts: "I assure you that unless I am allowed to leave this building immediately there is going to be a major incident about the way my liberty has been impeded by your men. I do not know what they are doing here, I do not care what they are doing here" (69). Dominated by fear and self-preservation, Anderson does not yet extend his view of the infringement of personal liberty to the Hollar family. Anderson passes the police interrogation, but he refuses Mrs. Hollar's request for him to stay while they finish searching her apartment. When the police produce the planted money, the Hollars appeal to Anderson for help, but "out of his depth and afraid, [he] decides abruptly to leave" (73). Overwhelmed by this firsthand experience with state repression, Anderson only thinks of saving himself.

After Anderson has had some time to think about the situation, but before he has an opportunity to act, Stoppard introduces the second philosophical discussion. As the philosophers finish dining McKendrick explains catastrophe theory. This theory is not Stoppard's invention, but rather the brainchild of René Thom, a Parisian professor of mathematics. McKendrick's "audacious application" is in taking this mathematical/scientific theory into the realm of moral philosophy.[11] McKendrick states his application of the theory:

> It's like a reverse gear—no—it's like a breaking point. The mistake
> that people make is, they think a moral principle is indefinitely extend-
> ible, that it holds good for any situation, a straight line cutting across
> the graph of our actual situation. . . . "Morality" down there; running
> parallel to "Immorality" up here—and never the twain shall meet.
> They think that is what a principle means. [But] the two lines are
> on the same plane. They're the edges of the same plane—it's in three

dimensions, you see—and if you twist the plane in a certain way, into what we call the catastrophe curve, you get a model of the sort of behaviour we find in the real world. There's a point where your progress along one line of behaviour jumps you into the opposite line; the principle reverses itself at the point where a rational man would abandon it. (77–78)

McKendrick concludes that there aren't any principles in Chetwyn's absolutist sense: "There are only a lot of principled people trying to behave as if there were" (78). While Anderson will not reach that conclusion, he will, consciously or not, use McKendrick's catastrophe model.[12]

Anderson is the character placed in the moral dilemma. His quandary might be stated as: If he takes the thesis, he violates his conviction that foreign guests should abide by the civil laws of the host nation; if he doesn't take the thesis, he acts against a natural or humanitarian instinct to help a victim of political oppression. Anderson's initial refusal to smuggle the thesis corresponds to McKendrick's statement: "So you end up using a moral principle as your excuse for acting against a moral interest" (78). Anderson initially rejects McKendrick's line of thought, arguing: "What need have you of moral courage when your principles reverse themselves so conveniently?" (79). The key word here is "courage," the trait Anderson lacked earlier in the day when the police were searching the Hollars' apartment. There is also the (unfounded) assumption that the principles reverse themselves "conveniently," that it is a model used to rationalize pragmatic, expedient behavior. However, Anderson soon concedes: "You're right up to a point. There would be no moral dilemmas if moral principles worked in straight lines and never crossed each other. One meets test situations which have troubled much cleverer men than us" (79).

So how does one bridge the moral relativism of McKendrick and the moral absolutism of Chetwyn? How does Anderson use the catastrophe model to act on behalf of universal human rights? How does one resolve the seeming paradox of Kenneth Tynan's assertion that Stoppard believes in "a universe in which everything is relative, yet in which moral absolutes exist" (56)? To understand Stoppard's both/and view of the world and how it applies to *Professional Foul,* it is instructive to look at the work of contemporary philosopher Robert Kane.

One of the difficulties of discussing moral relativism versus moral absolutism is that the terms have different connotations for different people, and rarely does one stop to define them. Kane, however, offers a perspective on moral values that I think is consistent with Stoppard's view, and it is a perspective that utilizes situational ethics to arrive at universal values.[13] Kane starts with the scientific principles of "openness" and "objectivity." Traditional, conservative minds such as Allan Bloom (*The Closing of the American Mind*) argue that openness (tolerance toward other points of view) leads to relativism (the belief that no point of view is better than any other) and hence to an indifference to objective truth and absolute right. However, Kane believes that Bloom is incorrect about the consequences of openness: "Properly conceived, it does not lead to relativism or indifference, but (quite the contrary) to a belief in some universal values" (22). Kane views openness as a way of searching for the objective truth about values, not a denial of that objective truth. In real life, people encounter situations where "you *cannot* open your mind to every point of view in the sense of respecting *every* way of life" (22).

Among the hypothetical test cases he offers, Kane discusses a situation where a woman is assaulted by a mugger. In that situation it is impossible to respect both the view of the assailant and the view of the victim. Kane writes: "When such situations occur, I say that the 'moral sphere' has 'broken down'—the moral sphere being the sphere in which every way of life can be respected. When the moral sphere breaks down, we must treat some ways of life as *less worthy* of respect than others" (22). The criteria for deciding which way of life to respect is to determine which course of action will "restore and preserve conditions in which *the ideal of respect for all can be followed once again.* In other words . . . stop those who have broken it and made it impossible for others to follow the ideal" (22). Thus, Kane concludes that openness is impossible in practice and thus leads not to relativism, but rather to the conclusion that some ways of life are less worthy of respect than others.

Kane applies his paradigmatic process to absolutism as well as to relativism:

In addition to showing that relativism fails in practice, this line of reasoning shows something else of enormous importance to ethics. It shows why there are exceptions to many traditional moral commandments— thou shalt not kill, lie, steal, cheat, etc. (e.g., self-defense and just wars are commonly recognized exceptions to the rule against killing). The existence of exceptions to traditional moral commandments (recognized even in the religious traditions) is another source of confusion about values in the modern world, along with relativism. The thought is that if moral commandments have exceptions they cannot be universal or absolute. But the above line of reasoning shows that exceptions to moral rules can be dealt with in the same way that relativism is dealt with. For the exceptions to rules arise at just that point where relativism fails—where the moral sphere breaks down. (24)

Kane offers a standard ethics test case of a situation where Nazis are searching for a Jewish family who is hiding on your property. If you are asked if you know where they are, should you lie or not? Again, you cannot respect both the Jewish view and the Nazi view, and thus one view must be treated as less worthy of respect. Thus, in this situation, the moral principle of not lying is reversed, and lying is deemed the moral course of action. The key condition is that the moral sphere has broken down. Kane is careful to note: "the exceptions are not *ad hoc;* they follow naturally from the principles themselves" (24). Kane concludes that provided the moral sphere is not broken, his line of reasoning, beginning with "openness" and "objectivity" toward all points of view and ways of life, does not lead to relativism and indifference but rather to ethical principles such as the Golden Rule and the idea of universal human rights. Thus, the attitude of openness sometimes means that one must "stand up and affirm that some ways of acting really are right and others wrong, and some ways of life really are better than others, more worthy of respect, and some less worthy" (24). Kane's ideas sound similar to the conclusions that Stoppard has reached, and they show that the idea that situational ethics can lead to universal values is not a contradiction in terms.

Kane insists that when dealing with views and values "the burden of proof [is] on everyone equally to prove themselves right or wrong by their actions" (24). Likewise, in *Professional Foul* it is specific actions that lead Anderson to change both his views and his actions. After the postdinner debate on catastrophe theory, Anderson again meets with Mrs. Hollar and her son. Learning that Pavel will likely be sent to prison, and encountering the family's grief, Anderson now vows: "I will do everything I can for [Pavel]" (82). In Kane's terms, the Czech regime has broken the moral sphere, and Anderson sees Pavel's view as more worthy of respect. In catastrophe terms, his initial moral principle of respecting local civil law has been reversed. He must now act for a greater moral interest, that of universal human rights.

Anderson decides to change his planned paper. He revisits the issue of the rights of the individual versus the rights of the community, but now he puts forth Hollar's view that there are inalienable human rights that the state cannot abridge. Anderson cites both the American and Czech constitutions and proceeds to argue: "What strikes us is the consensus about an individual's rights put forward by both those who invoke God's authority and by those who invoke no authority at all other than their own idea of what is fair and sensible" (88). Whether or not these moral standards are God-given or not is immaterial both to Anderson and to Stoppard's argument as the issue is the morality of human rights, rights that should hold for both theists and nontheists. Ultimately, Anderson argues for an intuitive sense of natural justice, that "there is a sense of right and wrong which precedes utterance" (90). This three-page speech, along with Anderson's earlier statement—"The important truths are simple and monolithic. The essentials of a given situation speak for themselves, and language is as capable of obscuring the truth as of revealing it" (63)—sum up the thematic thrust of the play and Stoppard's protest against Eastern Bloc repression as being an immoral infringement upon universal human rights.

The play dramatizes the validity of Anderson's position by having Anderson's speech get censored by the Czech officials. A false fire alarm causes an evacuation of the lecture hall. In the radio play version, an amused Chetwyn articulates the irony of the situation: "Falsely shouting fire in a crowded theatre. [It's] the classic abuse of free speech, to prevent speech" (72). While Anderson's ideas can be repressed in Prague, he has decided on a second way to put his moral views into action.

In the final scene, the audience learns that Anderson is smuggling Hollar's thesis out of the country. Aware that he will be searched at the airport, he has put the document in McKendrick's briefcase.[14] Thus Anderson has reversed his earlier moral position against violating the host country's laws. Furthermore, Anderson also violates his earlier statement to McKendrick: "Ethically I should give you the opportunity of choosing to be [a coconspirator] or not" (47). That line was delivered on the plane ride to Prague and referred to his innocuous action of skipping part of the conference to attend the soccer game. Now as they sit in the airplane waiting to leave Prague, Anderson reveals what he has done. McKendrick is outraged at the potential danger he has been put in, but Anderson glibly says: "I'm afraid I reversed a principle. . . . I thought you would approve" (93). Again, Anderson applies McKendrick's catastrophe theory. He violates a moral principle (that of consent) to act on a moral interest (freedom of speech and the abridgment of

Hollar's individual right). This calculated gamble, Anderson's "professional foul," raises its own moral ambiguities and suggests the difficulty of narrowly reducing ethics to being simply either morally relativistic or morally absolute. Furthermore, it is not only the play's final joke but also a reiteration of the thematic view that moral theories devoid of moral action are ineffectual and incomplete. Moral theories—whether they be McKendrick's, Anderson's, or anyone else's—must ultimately be tested in the cauldron of experience. Stoppard summarizes:

> What happens is that [Anderson has] got a perfectly respectable philosophical thesis and he encounters a mother and a child who are victims of this society, and it cuts through all the theory. It's as though there are two moralities: one to do with systems of government and an alternative morality to do with relationships between individuals. The latter is governed by instinctive feelings about what good and bad behaviour consists of and an instant and instinctive recognition of each when they occur. The pay-off really is that when Anderson puts his friend at risk by hiding the essay which he is smuggling in his colleague's briefcase, he says something like, "I thought you would approve!" This is the man's public stance. And of course his colleague makes the same discovery that it's all very well in the bloody textbooks, but this is *me,* I could be in jail, this is *my* briefcase, you bastard! So it's more to do with a man being educated by experience beyond the education he's received from thinking. (Gollob and Roper 155)

This idea of being educated by experience and not just by thinking, reading, or theorizing marks one of the major distinctions between *Professional Foul* and *Jumpers.* While one is naturalistic television drama and the other audacious theatrical showmanship, both plays, according to Stoppard, "are about the way human beings are supposed to behave towards each other" (Hebert 127).[15] At their core, each play is about "a moral philosopher preoccupied with the true nature of absolute morality, trying to separate absolute values from local ones and local situations" (Stoppard in Gollob and Roper 154). Unlike George in *Jumpers,* Anderson learns by experience and then takes action.[16] He finds the moral courage to do what he believes is the right thing to do.

7

Night and Day

In a 1976 interview, Stoppard remarked: "A lot of things in *Travesties* and *Jumpers* seem to me to be the terminus of the particular kind of writing which I can do. I don't see much point in trying to do it again" (Hayman, *Tom Stoppard,* 138). Indeed, when *Night and Day,* Stoppard's next major play, debuted at the Phoenix Theatre in November 1978, audiences encountered a work that Stoppard sheepishly described as "one of those beginning, middle and end plays with one set and eight characters, including a woman who's falling for somebody" (Berkvist 135). The change in style from the flashy showmanship of *Jumpers* and *Travesties* to the modified realism of *Night and Day* was "not the consequence of any act of principle" (Bragg 116), but rather derived from the practical concerns of writing for the West End and as a response to a personal artistic challenge:

> There is also a side of me which makes me want to prove I can do things which nobody is really asking me to prove at all. . . . I'd also been told repeatedly, by actresses and others, that I hadn't ever written a really good part for a woman. Quite separately, I had decided I'd like to write a play about journalism, and I felt I owed a play to Michael Codron, a West End producer. . . . I knew quite clearly I couldn't write a West End play which required 14 acrobats. . . . I was also thinking that

> I wanted to demonstrate I could actually write a story-telling number.
> (Berkvist 136)

Critics responded to the resulting realist, and mildly political, play with cries of both delight and despair. Those who were delighted viewed Stoppard as having matured into a serious artist while the despairing felt he had betrayed his unique theatrical gifts and descended into the norms of naturalism.[1]

Stoppard's desire to write about journalism stemmed from personal connections. A former journalist, Stoppard says that he reads "three newspapers a day as a minimum, five on Sunday" (Gussow, *Conversations,* 99). He also claims that he once dreamed of being a great journalist: "My first ambition was to be lying on the floor of an African airport while machine-gun bullets zoomed over my typewriter" (Bradshaw 91). Stoppard notes that "very few people think of journalism on the level of social philosophy, or examine it for its importance" (Berkvist 137), and so *Night and Day* addresses these thematic issues as it weds Stoppard's personal passion for journalism with his desire to write a love story.

Night and Day is set in the fictional African country of Kambawe, a former British colony on the cusp of a secessionist civil war between the right-wing, dictatorial, London-educated President Mageeba and the Marxist, Soviet-supplied rebels led by Colonel Shimbu. The play's action occurs in the household of Geoffrey Carson, a wealthy British colonial who runs copper mines, and his sexy, sarcastic second wife, Ruth, who was raked through the British tabloids during her divorce. Lured by Carson's telex machine, three newsmen use the home as a base for their press coverage. Guthrie is a seasoned photographer of world trouble spots who has been teamed with Wagner, an Australian-born "fireman" (reporter of hotspots) who is a staunch union man. Both men work for the reputable London paper *The Sunday Globe.* The third man is Jacob Milne, a young, idealistic freelancer whose antiunion stance led to his leaving a provincial paper. Wagner and Milne become professional, ethical, and sexual rivals. They compete for the latest scoop, clash over their union stances, and vie for Ruth's attention. A main plot point occurs when Wagner cunningly lets Milne return to cover the rebels while he remains at Carson's home, having secretly learned that the President and the Colonel are due for a clandestine negotiating session. While driving through the war zone, Milne is killed. Meanwhile, Wagner gets a precious interview with the President only to be hoist with his own petard. Having earlier protested the *Globe's* publishing of the nonunion Milne's material, Wagner's scoop is for naught as a union protest over Milne's story has shut down the paper for the weekend. At the very end, Ruth and Wagner seek solace in a brief affair.

Textual History and Construction

Resembling a Shavian drawing-room comedy, *Night and Day* is a more narrative-based play, but it is far from pure naturalism. Stoppard modifies the tenets of realism as his narrative includes a dream sequence, an expressionistic fantasy, melodramatic plot points, dialectical debates, and an aside-like "inner voice" for Ruth. Stoppard writes: "When Ruth's thoughts are audible she is simply called 'RUTH' in quotes, and treated as a separate character. Thus, RUTH can be interrupted by 'RUTH'" (viii). The Ruth/"Ruth" device gives her character two roles and intertwined identities. While Ruth is lively, combative, and independent and actively involves herself in the play's activities, "Ruth" is primarily a self-reflecting commentary role, revealing a bruised and lonely person, a woman who was physically abused by her first husband. This device probes the conflicts and divisions within Ruth's complex personality as the voiced thoughts mingle Freudian "id" with "superego." The device also helps accent the way in which Ruth is continually performing, living a role.

Unlike *Travesties* and *Jumpers,* where the two main variant texts correspond to different productions, the two main published editions of *Night and Day* (1978 and 1979) are related to the same production.[2] The 1978 text, published in conjunction with the play's London opening, does not include changes Stoppard made during the play's preview performances in Wimbledon. Furthermore, during the first few months of its West End run, Stoppard discovered some narrative problems, which were addressed for the remainder of that production. These alterations appear in the more authoritative 1979 version. The most significant emendations are discussed in the ensuing analysis.[3]

Thematic Analysis of Text and Production

While the main focus of *Night and Day* is journalism, the play, to varying degrees, engages with three different struggles for freedom. The central debate on the freedom of the press argues over the best way to operate newspapers; the bored housewife Ruth, though married to a decent and well-providing man, yearns for sexual and personal freedom, something to give her life meaning and vitality; and finally, the action is set amidst the backdrop of Kambawe, a country in the midst of political turmoil. Though Kambawe is independent and emergent, it is "neither free from strife nor from the vested economic interests of the big powers" (Billington, *Stoppard,* 124). While the plots are not entirely intertwined, the different plot lines' characters do contribute to the play's perspectives on the press.

In *Night and Day* Stoppard provides five perspectives on journalism, through five characters with different relationships to the press, and at alternate moments different characters speak with Stoppard's voice. Wagner is a seasoned veteran who places the union above the news, while the youthful, antiunion Milne has idealistic views toward the importance of journalism.[4] Guthrie possesses Wagner's experience and Milne's idealism, but tempers his idealism with a strong sense of pragmatism as he is neither prounion nor antiunion, but rather places top priority on delivering the news. Guthrie is the most laconic of the three, but his actions speak louder than his words as he is willing to work with the nonunion Milne, and he is genuinely surprised that Wagner tries to prevent Milne from publishing his story. Ruth provides the cynical perspective of someone who has been pursued by the tabloid press, and she offers counterarguments to both Guthrie's idealism and Wagner's unionism. While there is some justification to reviewers' charges that Ruth does not fit into the rest of the play, she *is* involved in a significant debate with each of the three journalists. The fifth perspective is that of Mageeba, the dictator opposed to the scrutiny of a free press.

Though much of *Night and Day* is realistic drawing-room comedy, the play has a theatricalized opening. In Peter Wood's production, fog wafts over the stage while a beautiful African sunset is projected on a cyclorama, quickly passing into darkness and moonlight as the sound of a helicopter approaches, and then: "*Helicopter very loud. Shadow of blades whirling on the floor of the stage. Violent shaking of foliage. A spotlight from the helicopter traverses the stage. It disappears. A jeep drives onto the stage with its headlights on*" (1). The sound of machine-gun fire joins the din, and Guthrie emerges from the jeep shouting "Press! Press! You stupid fuckers!" (2), but he is soon caught in the spotlight and shot. The highly energized opening, at odds with the conventions of realism, is indeed not reality. It is Guthrie's dream sequence, a dramatization of the nightmare of journalists who thrive on the danger of covering a war, but who also risk their lives in the process. Indeed, the dream sequence prefigures Milne's death while also providing a structural parallel for Ruth's fantasy that opens act 2.

Most of Stoppard's major plays have a distinctive first scene, but whereas the engaging opening images of *Rosguil, Jumpers,* and *Travesties* figure prominently into the thematic ordering of those plays, *Night and Day*'s opening mostly serves to order the plot, to establish the personal risks involved. Anthony Jenkins argues: "No metaphor governs the ideas of *Night and Day* . . . which might account for a disappointing flatness" (*Theatre of Tom Stoppard* 144). On the other hand, the opening sequence is linked to the "Ruth" device, as the dream gives us access to Guthrie's mind. Indeed, one of the genre-bending aspects of Stoppard's modified realism is to give greater theatrical agency to interior thoughts.

The play's first journalism debate is not until midway through the first act; up until that point Stoppard is concerned with exposition and with providing a realistic image of reporters covering a foreign war. Throughout most of the play, Guthrie is disheveled, catching naps wherever he can, showing the unglamorous side of the romantic job of the globe-trotting war correspondent. Guthrie and Wagner also often show their competitive side, the ego that drives them to risk their lives. Wagner sums it up: "Our own telex and a helicopter, and the competition writing post cards. If this war starts on a Saturday morning you and I are going to be famous" (16). Throughout the play they name-drop the cities and events they have covered, and while they are out to impress other reporters, Wagner comments on Milne's article: "It's somebody who wants to impress the world and doesn't know the world isn't impressed by reporters" (21). But, for the reporters, to scoop the competition and gain the respect of their colleagues is recognition enough.

During the expositional scene between Guthrie and Wagner, Stoppard utilizes one of his trademarks—parody—as a means of commenting on the way in which news is reported, and thus the way in which readers receive their knowledge of world events. Stoppard accurately apes the style and tone of the *Sunday Times,* with Wagner assessing the writing as "All facts and no news" (20). In contrast, *Newsweek*'s colorful account of the unfolding civil unrest is viewed as "All writing and no facts" (21). Unfortunately, in the 1979 text Stoppard eliminates his parodies of the *Observer* and the *Sunday Telegraph.* The *Observer*'s sources report "that the peasant army of the ALF has the tacit support of the indigenous population of the interior," whereas the *Sunday Telegraph*'s version of events is that the "civilian population . . . has been intimidated into supporting the Russian-equipped rural guerrillas of the ALF" (1978, 31). The excised passage accents the way in which editorial bias colors the presentation of "objective" news. Indeed, when asked whether Mageeba or Shimbu is in the wrong, Carson answers: "Depends on which paper you read, doesn't it?" (44). Even the Kambawe press officer wants to know whether Wagner's paper is "objective-for or objective-against?" (18). While Wagner views this as an intelligent, legitimate question, the idealistic Guthrie believes in an unbiased press: "We're not here to be on somebody's side, Geoffrey. That was World War Two. We try to show what happened, and what it was like. That's all we do, and sometimes people bitch about which side we're supposed to be on" (108). This issue of "objectivity" is one of many in the play where there is tension between the ideal and the actual practice of the press.

The first extended press discussion revolves around how much control unions should have; in part this scene was sparked by the historical moment in which Stoppard was writing. In 1977 Britain's National Union of Journalists (NUJ) sought a "closed shop"—only union members could work for a newspaper. Stoppard told Melvyn Bragg: "When the NUJ closed shop controversy blew up, I was passionately interested in it. I felt and thought all sorts of things which bore upon that question and they sort of pop up in the play" (122). On the personal level, Stoppard wrote to the *Times* arguing that an "unclosed shop" means that anyone can try to publish a paper and that is "called freedom of expression. A closed shop is a state of affairs where if, for example, I want to work for a newspaper, all I need is to avoid offending some person or group in a position to withdraw my right to do so, on that paper or any other. This is called absence of freedom of expression" (11 Aug. 1977). In *Night and Day* the antiunion Milne offers Stoppard's libertarian critique of unionist, leftist sympathizers. Called a scab, Milne replies: "I don't keep an abusive vocabulary ready for anyone who acts on different principles" (31), with the implication being that the journalist union is dictatorial and oppressive to dissenters. Milne proceeds to ridicule the catchphrases of the political Left:

> On any other subject . . . they spoke ordinary English, but as soon as they started trying to get me to join the strike it was as if their brains had been taken out and replaced by one of those little golf ball things you get in electric typewriters . . . "Betrayal!" . . . "Confrontation" . . . "Management" . . . My God, you'd need a more supple language than that to describe an argument between two amoebas. (31–32)

While Stoppard's own writing could be more supple on this point, the speech does suggest the danger and tendency for political views to be expressed in clichéd phrases that elicit knee-jerk responses instead of informed debate. Indeed, the scene's shortcoming is that Stoppard's own antiunion stance loads the debate for Milne; Stoppard does not supply Wagner any prounion arguments beyond: "We're working to keep richer men than us richer than us, and nothing's going to change that without worker solidarity" (34). The curious result is that the one debate that involves two journalists is much weaker than the discussions of journalism in scenes involving Ruth.

The issue of a journalists' closed shop is taken up again later in the act when Ruth meets Milne for the first time. It is here that the idealism of Milne, whom Stoppard acknowledges "has my prejudice" (Gollob and Roper 163), is seen in full force. Milne's antiunionism is partly based on his belief that journalism is "special"—that "a free press, free expression [is] the last line of defense for all the other freedoms" (63). Believing in the sanctity of the press, Milne opposes any constraints, which he feels a closed shop incurs. Partly it is a conflict between the ideal and the real; part of the idea of a closed shop is to establish professional standards such as exist in other fields where one needs a license to practice. However, Milne argues that Wagner's unionism is not concerned with standards: "Nothing could be further from Dick's mind. The fact is nobody's going to be drummed out of the NUJ for illiteracy or getting drunk at the Lord Mayor's table. On the contrary it's the union which is going to keep them in their jobs. No, what Dick wants is a *right-thinking press*—one that thinks like him" (64). Milne's argument, as well as his desire to avoid blacklisting, is compelling, but it is also mitigated by the fact that Milne claims to know Wagner's position and thus can defeat the argument without any opposition. As with *Jumpers,* the characters who hold views in opposition to Stoppard's rarely speak for themselves, but rather have their views summarized and rebutted by Stoppard's ideological surrogate.

As the scene progresses, Milne and Ruth discuss the discrepancy between the ideal of a free press and the way journalism is actually practiced:

MILNE: No matter how imperfect things are, if you've got a free press everything is correctable, and without it everything is concealable.
RUTH: I'm with you on the free press. It's the newspapers I can't stand.
MILNE: . . . The celebration of inanity, and the way real tragedy is paraphrased into an inflationary spiral of hackneyed melodramas. . . . It's the price you pay for the part that matters. (66)

At the time *Night and Day* was written, Stoppard was actively involved in protesting Eastern Bloc repression, including the suppression of free speech, and it is this type of totalitarian control that is most identifiable as objectionable. However, Milne's argument exists in the ideal; specific terms and details are not defined. Michael Billington argues:

> Stoppard ignores the pressures on press freedom that come from interventionist proprietors, strong-minded print unions (who refuse to set copy they find politically objectionable), the Official Secrets Act, lacklustre editors, government secrecy, the stringent libel laws. Obviously press freedom is a sacred ideal; obviously the British press is freer than most, but there are daily, visible pressures on that freedom (of the kind David Hare and Howard Brenton subsequently dealt with in *Pravda*) that neither Milne nor Stoppard acknowledges. (*Stoppard* 127)

Milne's sanctified view leads to a more detailed defense of tabloid journalism, a beat he once worked:

> I felt part of a privileged group, inside society and yet outside it, with a license to scourge it and a duty to defend it, night and day, the street of adventure, the fourth estate. And the thing is—I was dead right. That's what it was, and I *was* part of it because it's indivisible. Junk journalism is the evidence of a society that has got at least one thing right, that there should be nobody with the power to dictate where responsible journalism begins. (67)

Again, Milne's view that there should be no limits on the press, while strong in theory, ignores the practical application; "the public's right to know" is often an economically fueled rationalization for sensationalized muckraking and personal scandal exposés. While Stoppard shortchanges the debate aspect of the first Ruth-Milne scene, his writing effectively shows how Milne's idealistic fervor serves as a source of sexual attraction for Ruth. This sexual desire sets up the second-act fantasy scene as well as Ruth's sense of loss at Milne's death, which sparks her eventual critique of the press as based on product not principle.

Act 2 includes the play's liveliest discussion of journalism as it presents the divergent views of Wagner, Ruth, Mageeba, and Guthrie. Whereas the idealists Milne and Guthrie remain firm in their stands, Wagner, Stoppard's ideological antithesis, is subjected to satirical skewering. Intent on interviewing Mageeba, the leftist Wagner expresses conservative views as he kowtows to the Kambawean president, telling him: "Your determined stand against Russian imperialism in Africa has won the admiration of the British people" who "are watching with intense and sympathetic interest your courageous stand against the communist menace" (87–88). Here, Wagner sacrifices his notion of worker solidarity in favor of getting the scoop he craves. Furthermore, Wagner now justifies the previous publishing of Milne's piece (an interview with the rebel leader, Colonel Shimbu), saying the *Globe* was "bound to use it, because—well, all the news that's fit to print, as they say" (91).

While Wagner could laugh at Milne's naiveté and inexperience in how to cover a foreign war, Wagner's desire to placate Mageeba blinds him to the degree to which Mageeba is infuriated by the Shimbu interview. Behind Mageeba's cool, polite exterior rages a powerful, menacing man who does not welcome the critique a free press offers. At the outset, Mageeba toys with Wagner:

MAGEEBA: You would give me equal space?
WAGNER: Oh—absolutely—
MAGEEBA: That's very fair. Isn't it, Geoffrey? Mr. Wagner says I can have equal space.
WAGNER: And some space is more equal than others. I think, sir, I could more or less guarantee that an interview with you at this juncture of the war would be treated as the main news story of the day. . . .
MAGEEBA: What war, Mr. Wagner? . . . Kambawe is not at war. We have a devolution problem. . . .
WAGNER: A devolution problem? Yes . . . I see. [Starts taking notes.]
MAGEEBA: If it is a war, it is not of my waging. I am a man of peace . . . (*He waits for* WAGNER *and repeats as he writes*) man of peace. When a man strikes me without cause or warning, I invite him to breakfast. (91–92)

Mageeba puts his own "spin" on the events, and the eager-for-the-scoop Wagner seems to accept it uncritically, epitomizing how a reporter's ego can mediate how the news will be reported.

While the particular political problems of Kambawe are largely left in the background, the dictator's views on the press are foregrounded, with emphasis given to the role journalism plays in influencing the views and politics of a society. Mageeba argues that a newspaper is a unique enterprise because "it is the voice of the people, and [at the time of independence] the Kambawe paper was the voice of an English millionaire" (96). Like Milne, Mageeba views journalism as special, but for Mageeba its specialness means that it is especially important that it be controlled. Mageeba proceeds to note that initially the newspaper was "free to select the news it thought fit to print, to make much of it or little, and free to make room for more and more girls wearing less and less underwear. You may smile, but does freedom of the press mean freedom to choose its own standards?" (100). Mageeba then moves into political doublespeak:

> I did not believe a newspaper should be part of the apparatus of the state; we are not a totalitarian society. But neither could I afford a return to the whims of private enterprise. I had the immense and delicate task of restoring confidence in Kambawe. I could afford the naked women but not the naked scepticism. . . . Freedom with responsibility, that was the elusive formula. (100–101)

Mageeba closes his speech by defining a relatively free press as "a free press which is edited by one of my relatives" (101). His ensuing laughter crescendos into a violent outburst as he unleashes his fury on Wagner (the representative of the *Globe,* the paper that published Shimbu's secessionist views), striking him down with his walking stick and cursing a press that allows dissenters to voice their critiques. In an even tone, Mageeba concludes: "I'll give [Shimbu] equal space. Six foot long and six foot deep, just like any other traitor and communist jackal" (101–2). Though at the opposite end of the political spectrum from Lenin, who in *Travesties* had an equally skewed doublespeak definition of a free press, Mageeba embodies Stoppard's concern that media control is a vital weapon of government repression and that prohibition of free speech is often accompanied by violent enforcement. As Stoppard told Melvyn Bragg: "I am passionate about [free expression]. It's the one thing that makes a free society different from an unfree one" (123). Stoppard's political plays of the late 1970s show his denunciation of totalitarianism whether it be of the Left or the Right.

In the midst of the Mageeba scene, Ruth and Wagner argue over the relative power held by the unions and by the wealthy owners. Wagner's view is that "a newspaper is too important to be merely a rich man's property" (96). Ruth counters: "I had no idea it was the millionaires who were threatening your freedom to report, Dick. I thought it was a millionaire who was picking up the *bill* for your very freedom to report" (98). Ruth proceeds to argue: "[England] is littered with papers pushing every political line from Hitler to St. Francis" and "it's the very free-for-all which guarantees the freedom of each. . . . You don't have to be a millionaire to contradict one. It isn't the millionaires who are going to stop you, it's the Wagners who don't trust the public to choose the marked card" (98). Michael Billington argues that Ruth's notion of a diverse press pushing every available view is fallacious when applied to English society where at the time of *Night and Day*'s debut "the national press was dominated by a Conservative political viewpoint" (*Stoppard* 127). In the 1978 text Ruth directly stated her argument, whereas in the 1979 text the argument is presented in the context of a sarcastic, contrived conversation between Ruth and her eight-year-old son. While Billington sees this change as an improvement, more plausibly the alteration only further skewers Wagner's views as now the suggestion is that even a child can see the "fallacy" of Wagner's leftist, union line.

Pursuing the role money plays in the operation of the press, Ruth, via the imaginary conversation with her son, argues that "people don't buy rich men's papers because the men are rich: the men are rich because people buy their papers" and thus concludes: "Freedom is neutral. Free expression includes a state of affairs where *any* millionaire can have a national newspaper, if that's what it costs. A state of affairs, Allie says, where only a particular approved, licensed, and supervised non-millionaire can have a newspaper is called, for example, Russia" (99). The problem with the debate is that it not only is rigged for Ruth but also sets up a false binary, suggesting that the choice is only between a capitalist model and a totalitarian one. In his review of the play, Billington notes that Stoppard "never grapples with the question as to whether profitability should determine the right to publish opinion or the common-sense fact that the bulk of English national press supports one particular party." Likewise, Neil Sammells argues that Stoppard ignores the ramifications of wealthy individuals and corporations buying out the competition: "The problem is Stoppard's unwillingness to take a critical look at his initial premise: that a free-*market* society is the necessary index of a free one" (133; emphasis added). While Stoppard rightly views the press as a vital aspect of a free society, his libertarian position often results in an oversimplification that ignores nuances that would offer a more stimulating debate.

While Ruth champions the free-market system, she also offers the most stinging critique of the divide between the ideal and the real, between the stated principles and the actual practice. After she has learned of Milne's death, she lashes into Guthrie:

I'm not going to let you think he died for free speech and the guttering candle of democracy—crap! You're all doing it to impress each other and be top dog. . . . It's all bloody ego. And the winner isn't democracy, it's just business. As far as I'm concerned, Jake died for the product. . . . Somewhere at the end of a long list I suppose he died for the leading article too, but it's never worth *that.* (109)

Ruth's salvo offers a temporary deflation of Guthrie and Milne's idealistic view of journalism, an acknowledgment that ego and product are fundamental forces affecting a free press. It also suggests Stoppard's interest "in the idea of people risking their lives for what was, in the real world, a commercial enterprise" (quoted in Hebert 127). On the other hand, Stoppard believes that the journalist is different than other corporate workers, and so he gives Guthrie the final word. For Guthrie, gathering the news is almost a moral duty. In a speech that Stoppard moved for the 1979 text so that it became Guthrie's exit line, he offers the play's climactic speech on the value of news/journalism: "People do awful things to each other. But it's worse in places where everybody is kept in the dark. It really is. Information is light. Information, in itself, about anything, is light. That's all you can say really" (110). Stoppard notes that Guthrie's final statement "does speak for me" and that though it is somewhat of a simple statement it "nevertheless expresses a reality" (127).

While the characters say many things about journalism, their actions are also integral to the play's debate. The two events that carry the most consequences are (1) the entry into the war zone that results in Milne's death and (2) Wagner's union protest that backfires and blocks his own scoop. The latter is Stoppard's way of "proving" his argument that a closed shop is an unhealthy state of affairs that curtails the free flow of information, and it suggests that Stoppard views the unions as more threatening to press freedom than the proprietors.[5]

On the other hand, Milne's death has generated divergent responses. Benedict Nightingale writes: "I do not know if Stoppard expects us to wince when we hear that Milne has been killed by unruly troops, but I suspect he does. Alas, the moment passes with a massive shrug—because he is more a set of principles, a series of excited and enthusiastic arguments than a young man cut down in his prime" (671). Nightingale seems nearer the mark than Stoppard's own assessment. Stoppard has noted that the play cannot bear too much profundity, yet in the same interview Stoppard himself seems to attach too much weight to Milne's death. In Stoppard's eyes Milne speaks the truth and so his death has grand significance: "That's what happens in myth. That in a sense confirms—not directly, but in some psychological way—the truth to which he becomes a martyr" (Gollob and Roper 163). Here, Stoppard the retrospective interpreter seems to be at odds with Stoppard the playwright, for within the play Milne's death is the result of inexperience, not ideals or bravery. Guthrie holds the same ideals, but Guthrie's views have been gained through experience. It is Guthrie who knows that the jeep and Milne's camouflage outfit make them more of a target, and at the pivotal moment Milne lacks Guthrie's wisdom. Caught in a cross fire, Milne panics and ignores Guthrie's advice. Milne could have maintained his ideals and stayed alive; therefore, this is not the death of a martyr but that of an inexperienced idealist.

The other aspect to note about Milne's death is Guthrie's response. Both men knew the risk of going into the war zone after dark, but they did it because they had a press deadline: "The *Globe* is a Sunday paper. If you miss it by an hour you've missed it by a week. Story could be dead as a—" (105). Despite Milne's death and despite the fact that his cursing of Mageeba has put his own life in danger, Guthrie is eager to return to the front. Guthrie's sense of a moral duty to provide news is counterweighted by his lack of personal feeling for Milne's death. He has even capitalized on Milne's death by taking photographs of the corpse, a powerful image sure to be splashed across many newspapers. Depending on one's views, Guthrie is either a cool, seasoned professional doing the job to the best of his ability or a callous professional who values the abstract concept of the news over the humanity of those it purports to cover. Indeed, *Night and Day* might even suggest that the best news, that which sheds light on the world, is gained by those who can close their eyes to the human aspect of what they cover, thus allowing them to strive for Stoppard's ideal of objective truth.[6]

The Ruth/"Ruth" Love Line

While Ruth plays an active role in the play's journalism debate, her more prominent role is to carry the love plot. Stoppard has remarked that while he wanted to write a journalism play: "I *also* wanted to write a play . . . about a woman, not exactly falling in love, but having an instant love reaction to somebody just-like-that. It didn't stay like that, but *Night and Day* is also a play about this woman and a young reporter. . . . I discovered pretty shortly after starting rehearsal that this play wished to be more about that woman and that young man than I had realised" (Bragg 123). The connection between the journalism plot and the love plot is tenuous as they are bound through the characters but their interlacing sheds little light on the respective themes.

While the journalism plot focuses on the nature and ethics of a free press, the love plot's central theme revolves around issues of fidelity. On a recent trip to London Ruth had an affair with Wagner, but she has not told her husband. Ruth's caustic jabs at Wagner and journalists in general make her husband question her behavior, at which point her inner voice takes over, expressing her guilty conscience. The audience hears her try out different ways of breaking the news, but she cannot get herself to admit the affair out loud. After the first failed attempt, the audience is privy to Ruth's internal debate as "Ruth" says: "Yes, I wouldn't mind a change, actually, Geoffrey darling. Just a thought you know. I had this cowardly idea—delusion, I mean—that I might change everything in one go by the pointless confession of an unimportant adultery" (52). The meaninglessness of the affair and the desire for any kind of change point to the emptiness and despair of Ruth's present life.

Ruth's guilty conscience makes her think Wagner has come to her home to resume the affair. Near the end of the first act Ruth and Wagner have a brief moment alone onstage, and Ruth tries to distance herself from Wagner and defend her sense of self:

> If I had fancied you *at all* when you chatted me up in the visa office
> I would have run a mile. That's what we honorable ladies with decent
> husbands do. . . . I let you take me to dinner because there was no danger of going to bed with you. And then because there was no danger of
> going to bed with you a second time I went to bed with you. A lady, if
> surprised by melancholy, might go to bed with a chap, once; or a thousand times if consumed by passion. But twice, Wagner, *twice* . . . a lady
> might think she'd be taken for a tart. (55–56)

In explaining the thought process of a married woman faced with temptation, Ruth rationalizes the affair, trying to maintain her self-respect. In a speech added at Peter Wood's suggestion, Wagner pulls Ruth off her pedestal and asserts his own sense of self, his pride in being a good, professional journalist, and his knowledge that their affair was purely a physical escape for a bored and lonely housewife "on her fifth drink in a hotel room three thousand miles from home" (57).[7] Wagner adds:

All I can see is a fairly interesting woman with a very boring problem: you don't know what you're doing here, and the days go very slowly. But I didn't come here to brighten up your day. . . . [I am a good reporter.] It's not much to be proud about, and if I fail nothing happens—not to Kambawe, not to the paper—but such as it is it's my pride, and what I want to know is, what are *you* so proud of that you can look at your life and sneer at mine. (57)

Ruth's response is to exhibit her tough outer shell, the part of her that denies her emotional problems. While "Ruth" expresses a variety of feelings, Ruth is seen to have no deep emotional ties with anyone else, and she admits that she does not love her husband, but rather likes him a great deal more than others (57).

Act 2 opens with a ten-minute scene that bends the boundaries of the realist genre. Stoppard continues the Ruth/"Ruth" device, and so the audience is led to believe they are witnessing a seduction scene between Ruth and Milne. But perception and objective observation are undercut as ultimately the scene is revealed as a fantasy, an imaginary encounter between Ruth and the object of her desire.[8] In essence the fantasy is the materialization of the subjective interior self, and thus the scene is really between "Ruth" and her construction of Milne as she wants him to be. In a sense, the scene exists on two levels: a "real-time" level, and a retrospective level. The initial audience response is to accept everything at face value, to read the dialogue as real and representative of Ruth and Milne. The second response and interpretation comes from the retrospective understanding that the scene is essentially an interior duologue, as all that is said emanates from Ruth's mind. Thus, any interpretation of this scene must mediate this tension as to what "reality" the audience is responding to and interpreting. In the theatre, the audience presumably does not have the time or wherewithal to go back and reinterpret the scene beyond the level of noting that Ruth fantasizes about seducing Milne. In contrast, the scholar or reader can retrospectively read the scene to interpret what a given line of Milne's means when reread as being a projection of Ruth's own inner psyche.

Within the fantasy scene, Stoppard pursues the ramifications of infidelity. The fantasized Milne states: "But if I indulged my desire for you I would be numbering you among [Carson's possessions]" (75). On the "real-time" level, this "enlightened thought" is in character with the principled Milne, while on the retrospective level, this statement may be indicative of Ruth's desire for personal autonomy, to be more than the wife of a rich husband, to act upon her belated knowledge that she is brighter than most of the people she meets. This fantasized Milne proceeds to speak of an imagined affair with Ruth that occurred in "a parallel world. No day or night, no responsibilities, no friction, almost no gravity" (76). But this world where actions do not carry consequences does not exist, and so Ruth is left rationalizing her affair with Wagner: "Hotel rooms shouldn't count as infidelity. They constitute a separate moral universe" (77). Ruth admits that she felt "post-coital remorse" over her affair with Wagner, but she continues the rationalizing process: "I mean, it's a bit metaphysical to feel guilt about the idea of Geoffrey being hurt if Geoffrey is in a blissful state of ignorance—don't you think?" (77). But Milne (both as a representative idealist and as a projection of Ruth's) concludes the opposite: "You shouldn't try to make it sound like a free ride. 'Geoffrey will never know and I'm not his chattel so there's nothing to pay.' There are no free rides. You always pay" (78). On the "real-time" level, Milne rejects the idea of consequence-less adultery, while on the retrospective level, Ruth's guilty conscience also prevents her from dismissing it.

Accepting Milne's judgment that there are no free rides, Ruth's imagined seduction occurs via acknowledgment of how wrong it is rather than by rationalizing it as acceptable. Ruth recognizes that her actions may not be moral, but she settles for being honest about it. Her adultery, whether imagined with Milne or later in reality with Wagner again, is entered into with knowledge that it involves betrayal and corruption and will mess up her life, and yet, knowing better, still her response is "to hell with that" (79). The reason she can acknowledge the potential negative repercussions of an affair and still go through with it becomes clear at the end when the audience learns just how near collapse she is. She tells Wagner: "I want to be hammered out, disjointed, folded up and put away like linen in a drawer" (113). Ruth is at the depths of despair, numb beyond caring. Her earlier insistence that she was a lady, not a tart, gives way to her self-identification that "Lady Is a Tramp."

In regard to Ruth/"Ruth," Tim Brassell offers the compelling argument that Stoppard establishes an emotional alliance between Ruth and Wagner and between "Ruth" and Milne. In the fantasy scene, Stoppard allows the double ("Ruth") to materialize and pursue "an illusory love affair which is more impossible than even she knows, since, with heavy irony, Milne is by this time already dead" (Brassell 218). In contrast Ruth, though not strongly attracted to Wagner, can nonetheless identify with him. Their verbal sparring and sometimes tense encounters make it believable that after the stressful night, and on the edge of despair and exhaustion, Ruth would turn to

Wagner for solace. As Brassell argues: "Wagner is an opportunist, an entirely unromantic man whose career—and the egotism it embodies—is far more important to him than any woman could be. He thus draws out the cynical, pragmatic side of Ruth's nature" (217). Her second fling with Wagner parallels the journalistic debate in that there is a discrepancy between the ideal and the real, as principle sometimes gives way to pragmatism, compromise, and expediency. Indeed, one of the recurring features of *Night and Day* is the continual tension between the ideal and the real and the way in which the ideal can be invoked as a mask for the real or the way in which the two are intertwined.

While *Night and Day* is typically not ranked in the upper echelon of Stoppard's canon, the play enjoyed a successful fifteen-month West End run followed by a British national tour and earned Stoppard the *Evening Standard* Best New Play Award. Though not as artistically or intellectually challenging as his earlier plays, it is an entertaining and thought-provoking work whose intelligence is above that of most West End fare. While *Night and Day* does not always cohere as a whole, its foray into the realm of modified realism and the probing of infidelity served as a trial run for *The Real Thing,* where Stoppard would more effectively utilize realism to get at the emotional dynamics of love relationships.

Altered Views

With most of Stoppard's major plays, there are sections that he no longer likes, places where he no longer cares for the artistic expression, but for the most part he still agrees with the central views expressed. In the case of *Night and Day,* Stoppard's views toward journalism have changed some since he wrote the play. Stoppard is fond of having characters educated by experience and thus changing the perspectives they had arrived at intellectually. Likewise, I suspect that Stoppard's altered views toward journalism are related to his own affairs being dragged through the tabloid press; his divorce from his second wife Miriam and his relationship with actress Felicity Kendal were top tabloid fodder for more than two years.

In December 1994, Stoppard spoke at length with Mel Gussow about how his views had changed over time: "*Night and Day* contains statements which are still flourished. I read one last week by people who want to leave the press completely untrammelled. I don't know what I want now. I've arrived at a kind of defensive position, which is not entirely where I stand intellectually" (*Conversations* 97). While Stoppard still believes that journalism is an important line of defense, that "people would be getting away with much more, were it not for the newspapers blowing the whistle, or just being there to observe" (97–98), he goes on to note:

> The tabloids purport to be looking after the public's interest, but if you ever see the face of a news editor when somebody comes in with a story of a politician's sexual escapade, there's no sense of saving the country from anything or of informing the public of anything important. It's a saturnalia. It's vicious, vindictive, unprincipled and should be beneath the dignity of the profession. It's an ancient, honourable profession, which has fought for its rights, and I don't think it's fought for the right to trade in domestic tribulation. But privacy laws are pretty sinister. (98)

Stoppard lays part of the blame on "tacky journalism" (100) and part of the blame on the readership who do not seem to mind that they are being treated like morons (97).

Ever the debater, Stoppard still struggles with his views on the press, and his continued interest may feed back into his playwriting career: "I'm very unfocused and incoherent on the subject because I'm in the middle of it. For the last year or two I've thought if I can get this properly in focus, I really would like to write another play about journalism. I've shifted to the right here. It's partly because the newspapers are that much worse, partly that I'm that much older and more conservative" (98–99). While Stoppard has not yet written another journalism play, his treatment in *The Invention of Love* (59–65) of how publishers responded to Oscar Wilde may serve as a miniversion of the type of commentary he would likely make.

8

The Real Thing

WHILE *Night and Day* WAS A FAIRLY SUCCESSFUL FORAY INTO the realm of modified realism with a narrative throughline and three-dimensional characters, it was with *The Real Thing* (1982) that Stoppard more fully answered the critics who said he could not write truthfully about the depths of basic human emotions. A witty, intelligent romantic comedy focusing on the joys, pains, and emotional dynamics of adult love relationships, *The Real Thing* is Stoppard's most realistic, most personal, and most accessible play, the one in which audiences can most identify with the characters and their situations. Not surprisingly, it ranks with *Rosencrantz and Guildenstern Are Dead* as Stoppard's most commercially successful play. Through four cast changes, the play ran for more than two years on the West End. In the United States its lengthy Broadway run garnered five Tony Awards and was followed by a national tour.

Stoppard has often described the genesis of his plays as the joining together of different threads, and for *The Real Thing* there were at least four threads that came together. In addition to wanting to write about love and sexual attraction, "he'd had an idea about a play in which the same situation is repeated twice, three times and each time the reaction is different; he wanted to do a play where the first scene is the work of the person in the second scene, which means the hero has to be a playwright; he wanted to ex-

plore 'public postures having the configuration of private derangement'"
(Buck 169). While Stoppard did not want to write about a playwright and
actresses, his structural idea necessitated it:

> Once you're stuck with him being a playwright who wrote the first
> scene, whatever narrative you invent would be about his life. [Like-
> wise, in my scheme] where it turns out a woman is married to the man
> who wrote the first scene. If the writer's wife has got to be in both situ-
> ations, she's got to be an actress. It's determined by the playful idea
> of having people repeat their situation in fiction. [Similarly, for Annie]
> there's a love scene with a person who becomes her lover except in fact
> they're in 'Tis Pity She's a Whore. As soon as you decide that's what's go-
> ing to happen, the woman in the rail scene has got to be an actress be-
> cause she ends up acting in 'Tis Pity She's a Whore. (Gussow, Conversa-
> tions, 41–42)

While not strictly autobiographical, the result is, according to Stoppard, that
"a lot of it is auto something. Henry sounds off on the subject of writing in
exactly the same way the reporters in *Night and Day* said what I wanted to
say about journalism" (41).

The parallels between Stoppard and his protagonist, Henry, are numerous. Both are successful, middle-aged playwrights known for erudite comedies but not for heartfelt emotion. Stoppard notes that Henry's inability to
write about love mirrored himself prior to *The Real Thing*: "Henry says when
he tries to write a play about love, it comes out 'embarrassing, childish or
rude.' The love story, as I wrote it, tries to avoid banality while suggesting it.
Henry says in the same scene, 'It makes me nervous to see three-quarters of
a page and no *writing* on it. I *talk* better than this.' That's self-reference" (62).
Both playwright and character have a reverential view of language. Both are
serious artists who are also for hire, in part writing films to pay alimony and
so as to enjoy a particular lifestyle. Both get moody when their playwriting
does not get done. Both "steal" another man's wife and find happiness in
their second marriage.[1] Both are lovers of pop music and neither, despite frequent exposure through their second wives' love of opera, can distinguish between one opera and another. Both encourage their wives to be active even
if it means being separated. Both enjoy cricket and fly-fishing, and in the
original London production, the scene 3 excerpt from *Desert Island Discs*
revealed that Henry, like Stoppard, was a journalist before becoming a playwright. Both have relatively close relationships with their children. Both are

conservative, outspoken critics of the political Left, particularly Marxism. While not all the details of Henry can be aligned with Stoppard, for the most part Henry's views are also Stoppard's.

The title *The Real Thing* refers both to a love affair that is destined to last and to the discrepancy between reality and appearance; thus, it is appropriate that Stoppard's play begins with an illusion. The play opens with what looks like reality as the audience encounters a husband (played by Max) confronting a wife (played by Charlotte) over possible infidelity. However, in the second scene the audience discovers that the first scene was actually part of Henry's play *House of Cards* and that Charlotte is actually Henry's wife, while Max is married to Annie. But the fictional infidelity is mirrored by actual infidelity as Henry and Annie are having an affair, which leads to the dissolution of both marriages. Act 1 closes with Henry and Annie in the midst of the excitement of new love. Throughout the play Annie tries to free the imprisoned Private Brodie, who as part of an antimissile demonstration burned the wreath of the Unknown Soldier. To help his cause Brodie writes a play about his story, and Annie gradually persuades Henry to rewrite the script. Brodie is Henry's political and artistic antithesis. Through their contrast the play broaches Stoppard's perception of the real thing not only in love but also in art, politics, and writing. Meanwhile, Annie's acting career brings her in contact with Billy, an actor who is Brodie's alter ego (playing him in a televised play), and who has an affair with Annie. In the end, Brodie is discovered to be an ungrateful lout whose motivation for political protest sprung not from moral convictions but from a lustful desire to impress Annie. Near the same time that Brodie is exposed, Annie stops her affair and reaffirms her commitment to Henry. Thus, the play ends optimistically as Henry and Annie have survived the painful affair and gained self-knowledge in the process.

Textual History

The text of *The Real Thing* exists in many versions with editions coming out in 1982, 1983, and 1984;[2] even within copyrighted years (1983, 1984) there are multiple editions. Furthermore, some material was added to the London production that has never made it into print.[3] The 1982 text came out near the play's London opening, whereas the various 1983 and 1984 versions incorporate changes made in response to the production's reception. It is worth examining the differences between the way in which the play was first produced in London (1982) and then on Broadway (1984) fourteen months later.[4]

As usual, many of the emendations are aimed at clarifying the narrative with the first major change occurring in the second scene as Stoppard grudgingly took pains to spell out that the first scene was part of a play written by Henry and that Charlotte is Henry's wife. In part the added dialogue reads:

CHARLOTTE: I've decided it's a mistake appearing in Henry's play.
MAX: Not for me it isn't.
CHARLOTTE: Well, of course, not for you, you idiot, you're not his wife. (1984, 20)[5]

Stoppard also tightens the text by cutting some of the bickering between Charlotte and Henry (1982, 21; 1984, cf. 22) and trims back the Brodie story (1982, 32–35; 1984, cf. 36–39).[6] The post-1982 texts also cut Annie's solo reading of *Miss Julie,* where she demonstrates the subtext's steaming lust (1982, 41). The rest of act 1 contains only minor alterations.

Act 2 is the more revised portion of the play, and again some of the additions clarify the narrative; in scene 5, the post-1982 texts have dialogue that clearly indicates that just over two years have passed between the acts. Other individual line changes within speeches within the scene vary with the edition and again are not consistent within years.

The largest change is that Stoppard combines 1982's scenes 7 and 9 into one scene. In the 1982 text Henry and Charlotte's daughter Debbie has left home and is living in a communal squat in London. Thus the parents first meet to discuss her situation and then Henry visits her in the sparsely furnished squat. While the core of the scenes remains the same, the revision combines the scenes, puts Henry, Charlotte, and Debbie onstage together, and has Debbie going on tour with a fairground worker rather than living in a squat. The change makes Debbie a more "normal" teenager rather than a runaway.[7] In the rewrite Stoppard makes Charlotte, who in the first act is a seemingly uncaring mother, into a more conscientious parent; in the former Charlotte hoped that the Council would cut off the squat's water supply, whereas in the later version Charlotte insists that Debbie write to her every week. Charlotte is still the least likable of the four married adults, and so the rewrite at least adds some redeeming qualities to her character. Other changes, discussed later, include the elimination of some of Debbie's views on fidelity and the addition of Henry's response to Charlotte's position that there are no commitments, only bargains.

The last few scenes also have significant revisions. In scene 9 (1982, sc. 10; cf. 74–75) when Henry is suspicious of Annie, who has not yet started the affair, there is added tension at the prospect of Annie continuing to see Billy:

HENRY: It's all right to come with you, is it?

ANNIE: Why not? Don't let me out of your sight, eh, Hen? (1984, 87; 1983, 72)

The added dialogue clarifies that both parties are aware that an affair is imminent. The ensuing excerpt (1982, sc. 11; sc. 10 in other editions) from Brodie's play is entirely rewritten in the post-1982 texts as Stoppard makes the dramatization the same as the script Henry quoted in scene 5. The revelation that the excerpt is from the old script indicates that Henry, despite all his objections, has indeed rewritten the script, a point also made by the later added acknowledgment that he is "the ghost writer" (1984, 92).[8] Finally, in the second to last scene where Henry and Annie deal more directly with Annie's continued affair, Billy's phone call is handled differently in each of the three main versions; and more importantly, in each version Stoppard alters Annie's explanation for the affair and her difficulty in trying to get out of it—a point discussed later.

Thematic Analysis of Text and Production

The Real Thing was a hit both in London and on Broadway, but whereas Stoppard often has the same director for both the London and New York productions of his major plays, this time it was not the case.[9] In part, the play explores the tension between appearance and "the real thing," and Peter Wood's London production emphasized the artifice, the way in which reality is mediated by representation, while Mike Nichols's production was much more naturalistic. In London, Carl Toms's stylized set had no walls surrounding the furniture for each indoor location, only gray, translucent panels that indicated where walls might be. The front of the stage had seven panels facing out front and a varying number of screens rose to frame the action. Thus the scenery mixed a sense of realism with abstraction. More notably: "The screens were arranged to create different apertures for viewing the action at the beginnings and ends of scenes before they were flown out as a scene proper began. This had the effect of framing each scene so that the 'life' which the actors were portraying was at the same time perceived by the audience as though it were a work of art" (R. Gordon 94–95).

In terms of scene design, in Henry and Charlotte's living room there was a painting of the couple on their sofa. In the second act, there was a portrait of Henry "which exactly reproduced the characteristically stooped-shouldered stance of Roger Rees so that, when he stood in front of it, there was an actor whose own mannerisms inscribed Henry, who was then re-flected in the picture behind him" (Jenkins, *Theatre of Tom Stoppard*, 159). Like the written text, the stage design utilized a "Chinese boxes" type of self-referentiality, showing different levels of representation that have their own level of reality and that affect the perception of "reality." The overall visual recursion might be seen as a statement that even what passes for reality involves mediated representation, or alternatively one might construe it as positing that ultimately one can recognize the difference between "the real thing" and "appearances." In contrast to the London production's frequent use of framing, Mike Nichols's Broadway production emphasized realistic detail and Tony Walton's design utilized "a revolving stage of handsome, nat-uralistic sets that looked very much lived in" (Corliss 69). The production proved that Stoppard's writing can accommodate a high degree of natural-ism and emotional depth, something not always evident in a written text that some critics felt was Cowardesque and "more artificial than the excerpt from Henry's play" (Jenkins, *Theatre of Tom Stoppard*, 160).

The contrast in design between cool artifice and more gritty realism carried over into much of the acting. In terms of the portrayal of Henry, Holly Hill notes that most critics preferred Jeremy Irons (New York) over Roger Rees (London) "because Irons is more vulnerable and because there is more sexual chemistry in his relationship with Annie."[10] Richard Corliss felt that while Rees played Henry as a "manic depressive child," Irons showed "Henry's foibles in the heart of a mature male. He's a believer who's never lost that lovin' feeling. There is a fierce longing in the gaze Irons directs ei-ther at Annie or at a blank piece of paper in his typewriter. Where Rees leapt from rapture to desperation, Irons takes small, careful steps" (69). The script accommodates both Irons's view of Henry as emotionally hesitant as well as Rees's interpretation of Henry "as being very Russian—'great swoops of emotion, from the very high to the very low'" (quoted in Ensor). In con-trast, according to Corliss, the portrayal of Annie seemed to be reversed as Felicity Kendal "grounded Annie in roguish common sense" while Glenn Close played the role with "the reckless high spirits of an aging cheerleader" (69). While Corliss believes that Annie "should be the anchor to Henry's fervor" (69), Billington liked the "warmth, ardour, [and] sexual vibrancy" Close brought to the role (*Stoppard* 156).

The play poses the question of what is "the real thing" in love, writing, and politics, and in the process of exploring these realms, many other issues surface, in part debating the values by which people live. In a 1984 lecture at the National Theatre, Stoppard declared, "I'm not a moral relativist; I'm not a political relativist" (Delaney, *Moral Vision*, 1). Similarly, Stoppard's mouthpiece Henry toes a more rigid absolutist line than the other characters, which Stoppard, to his and the play's credit, supplies with some compelling arguments.

The exploration of what is the real thing begins with the opening excerpt of *House of Cards* where with verbal flair and heightened theatricality Max confronts Charlotte with his suspicions of her infidelity. Similar to *Night and Day*'s opening dream sequence, this opening excerpt of a work of fiction violates the basic principles of realism where, unless told otherwise, the audience can assume that what they see is "real." Whether or not this scene "fools" the audience depends on the production's approach. Michael Billington notes that in Peter Wood's London production the "opening scene was played with much the same cool artifice as the rest of the evening. In Mike Nichols's Broadway version the whole scene was played in heavily inverted commas and with a heightened Cowardesque camp so that even the slowest member of the audience would realise he was watching a play-within-a-play" (*Stoppard* 147). Wood's approach might suggest that all is artifice whereas Nichols's approach serves to set up the play's ensuing exploration of different ways of responding to the same situation, and so the "stagey" first scene accents the unreality of conventional, fictional portrayals of adultery. Henry's stage version is tidy, elegant, and quotable, whereas in the second scene Charlotte argues that reality offers no "thinking time" and that Henry would lose his wit: "He'd come apart like a pick-a-sticks. His sentence structure would go to pot, closely followed by his sphincter" (23).

Indeed, the audience gets a chance to see "the real thing" in the third scene when Max confronts Annie over her infidelity. Though not strictly executed in the London production, Stoppard's stage directions ask that the mise-en-scène be "immediately reminiscent of the beginning of Scene One" (40), and Annie's entrance mimics Charlotte's. Likewise, the initial structure, speech patterns, and types of questions ape the fictional interrogation,[11] but when Max produces the circumstantial evidence of Henry's bloody handkerchief, his speech begins to break down. Instead of repartee, Max can only say, "You're filthy. You filthy cow. You rotten filthy — (*He starts to cry, barely audible, immobile*)" (41). Max briefly regains his composure hoping that there was no affair or that it was meaningless, but then he is hit with the full weight of the truth that Annie and Henry are in love. Max breaks down again and the real response of the cuckolded husband is inarticulate and filled with violent emotion as he kicks the radio and *"flings himself upon* ANNIE *in something like an assault which turns immediately into an embrace.* ANNIE *does no more than suffer the embrace, looking over* MAX's *shoulder, her face blank"* (42). The final image captures the way in which Max both physically and emotionally clings to his wife who has let go of him. This "real" confrontation is less than a third as long as the opening staged version as the moment is boiled down to the sheer pain of the betrayed and the calm rationale of the adulterer who is moving on to something better. The gritty realism *is* given an artificial touch as again the play utilizes pop music as Brechtian commentary; when Max kicks the radio, it plays the Righteous Brothers' "You've Lost That Lovin' Feelin'," a song that Henry has described as "possibly the most haunting, the most deeply moving noise ever produced by the human spirit" (27), and here it is all the more ironic because the song is part of Henry's appearance on *Desert Island Discs.*

Sandwiched between the stage confrontation and the real confrontation is a long exposition scene: it is revealed that the first scene was from a play and not real life; Charlotte's acerbic wit is often aimed at Henry, revealing the tension in their marriage; Henry, the intellectual playwright who loves pop music, is worried about what image to project via his appearance on *Desert Island Discs;* the Brodie plot line is introduced; and most importantly, the scene reveals that Henry and Annie are having an affair. Flirtatious when their spouses are present, Henry and Annie openly express their desire as soon as they are alone, with Annie as the aggressor: "Come on, touch me. Help yourself. Touch me anywhere you like" (29). Highlighting Henry's later claim that love is unliterary, the lovers' passion is expressed in short, simple sentences, and Henry himself is completely unquotable, managing only to repeat, "I love you" (29). The exchange proceeds to reveal that Annie is pushing for their respective divorces, while Henry is hesitant:

> ANNIE: You want to give it time . . . time to go wrong, change, spoil. Then you'll know it wasn't the real thing.
> HENRY: I don't steal other men's wives. . . .
> ANNIE: Yes, you mean you love me but you don't want it to get around. (30)

Annie pushes for commitment, arguing that if it is true love, then they need to expose their affair and let the pain happen and not worry about any guilt. Henry is willing to wait until they get caught, while Annie continues to insist that it is better to tell their spouses. Annie's desire for honesty is undercut by her glibness as she rationalizes: "It's only a couple of marriages and a kid" (31). As seen in Max's pain in the ensuing scene, the reality is much harsher than that. At the end of the scene, Annie decides to skip her Justice for Brodie meeting so that she can have a rendezvous with Henry, and it is that encounter that leads to the accidental leaving of the fateful evidence, the bloody handkerchief.[12] The interscene pop music is Herman's Hermits' "I'm into Something Good," a song that captures the joy and excitement of fresh love.

When next the audience sees Henry and Annie together, after the short breakup scene, the new couple is indeed still in a honeymoon high. In most texts, Stoppard's stage directions request another visual parallel as the "disposition of door and furniture makes the scene immediately reminiscent of Scene 2" (1983, 37). Likewise, Annie's entrance wearing some of Henry's clothes that are too big for her mirrors Charlotte's entrance in the second scene. But now instead of a strained relationship, the audience sees a couple in love, with all the vigor and joy it can inspire. Annie revels in her new happiness: "(*Gleefully self-reproachful*) Isn't it awful? Max is so unhappy while I feel so . . . *thrilled*. His misery just seems . . . not in very good taste. . . . He loves me, and he wants to punish me with his pain, but I can't come up with the proper guilt" (44). She complains that authors have written extensively about the misery, but not the tedium, of the unrequited lover. More accurately, Max is a divorced spouse, a rejected lover, and her speech captures her joy and desire to put the past behind her, while it also exhibits her lack of empathy; she and Henry have been living together only two weeks and so Max's feelings of pain and anguish seem reasonable, very human, rather than tiresome.

As a gift to Annie, Henry is trying, unsuccessfully, to write a play for her. The play is about love, but Henry doesn't "know how to write about love"; his efforts are embarrassing, childish, rude, or juvenile (46). He considers putting an artistic touch on love by writing it "completely artificial. Blank verse. Poetic imagery" (46). He concludes: "loving and being loved is unliterary. It's happiness expressed in banality and lust" (46). Annie suggests that in plays, love and passion are best expressed in subtext. Indeed, in *The Real Thing* banality, lust, and subtext are the ways in which real love is presented. In this scene, the peak moment of fresh love, the best Henry can manage is the closing exegesis on the joy of being in love: "You're coming home to me and we don't want anyone else. I love love. I love having a lover and being one. The insularity of passion. I love it. I love the way it blurs the distinction between everyone who isn't one's lover. Only two kinds of presence in the world. There's you and there's them. I love you so" (51). Notably, Henry's speech is about the concept of love and not about Annie in particular; nowhere in the play does Henry ever articulate why he loves her or what about her he loves, and so the bond between them must be enacted by the performers whose physical and vocal interactions play the subtext of lovers in love.

Though they have been living together for only fifteen days, there is already tension in their relationship:

> ANNIE: (*shouting*) You don't love me the way I love you. I'm just a relief after Charlotte and a novelty.
> HENRY: You're a novelty all right. I never *met* anyone so silly. I love you. I don't know why you're behaving like this.
> ANNIE: I'm behaving normally. It's you who's abnormal. You don't care enough to *care*. Jealousy is normal.
> HENRY: I thought you said you *weren't* jealous.
> ANNIE: Well, why aren't *you* ever jealous? (50)

Annie needs continual assurance that she is loved, whereas Henry is almost smugly self-assured over the continued vitality of their relationship. This confidence and refusal to even consider being jealous will carry over into the second act where the issue of fidelity will take center stage in both word and action.

In act 2 Annie does indeed enter into an affair with a fellow actor, and in the course of the act, Stoppard presents four views on fidelity and commitment. At different points Henry discusses the nature of love and relationships with the three women in his life—Annie, Charlotte, and Debbie. Henry is the only one privy to the respective viewpoints, as the emotional arc of the second act concerns Henry's education, his achievement of "self-knowledge through pain," the phrase he had used to describe the theme of *House of Cards.* Discussion of Henry's play spurs his conversation with Debbie, the advocate of free love:

> DEBBIE: As if having it off is infidelity.
> HENRY: Most people think it is.
> DEBBIE: Most people think *not* having it off is *fidelity.*[13] They think all relationships hinge in the middle. Sex or no sex. What a fantastic range of possibilities. (74)

Debbie wisely posits that fidelity involves more than monogamy, but her dismissal of infidelity as inconsequential stems from her limited personal experience in which sex is just "biology after all" (75).

In contrast, Henry offers the play's most passionate pronouncement on the importance of fidelity and on the mystery, transcendence, and sacredness that can be achieved through carnal knowledge:

> It's to do with knowing and being known. I remember how it stopped seeming odd that in biblical Greek knowing was used for making love. . . . Carnal knowledge. It's what lovers trust each other with. Knowledge of each other, not of the flesh but through the flesh, knowledge of self, the real him, the real her, *in extremis,* the mask slipped from the face. Every other version of oneself is on offer to the public. We share our vivacity, grief, sulks, anger, joy . . . we hand it out to anybody who happens to be standing around, to friends and family. . . . But in pairs we insist that we give ourselves to each other. What selves? What's left? What else is there that hasn't been dealt out like a pack of cards? Carnal knowledge. Personal, final, uncompromised. Knowing, being known. I revere that. Having that is being rich, you can be generous about what's shared . . . ; knowledge is something else, the undealt card, and while it's held it makes you free-and-easy and nice to know, and when it's gone everything is pain. Every single thing. (75–76)

This articulation of carnal knowledge as the ultimate, personal knowledge, the value of which, in part, resides in the singularity of the shared expression of the whole self with the lover, is an affirmation of monogamy.[14] Furthermore, just as George in *Jumpers* believes that there is more in humans than meets the microscope, here, as Paul Delaney argues, "Henry asserts that there is more to sex than biology . . . more to human actions than amoral glandular functions" (*Moral Vision* 118). Since Stoppard's own stated belief in moral absolutes still apparently allows for adultery under certain circumstances, and since Henry himself is an adulterer, Delaney may be overstating the case when he insists that Henry's speech is an assertion that intimate human relationships are "inherently, ineluctably moral" (118) and that "Henry's view of relationships is derived from a biblical view of relationships" (119). Henry does indeed offer the strongest affirmation of the belief that a monogamous relationship is to be valued, respected, and revered, and that monogamy is more meaningful and fulfilling than promiscuity, but Henry's moral order is flexible enough to view infidelity as understandable and forgivable.

After Debbie departs, the issue of fidelity is picked up by Charlotte, who wonders why Henry is not curious about or jealous of the men who act opposite Annie, potential romantic threats. When she was married to Henry, Charlotte was bothered by Henry's seeming indifference which she interpreted as a sign of his infidelity, and she herself had a series of affairs before she realized that Henry's lack of jealousy was part of his romantic idealism, his bedrock faith in commitment. Again the play highlights how different expectations and poor communication can cause problems in relationships. Also, Charlotte has a contrasting view of marriage:

> There are no commitments, only bargains. And they have to be made again every day. You think making a commitment is *it*. Finish. You think it sets like a concrete platform and it'll take any strain you want to put on it. You're committed. You don't have to prove anything. In fact you can afford a little neglect, indulge in a little bit of sarcasm here and there, isolate yourself when you want to. (79)

While Charlotte's speech does not justify her nine affairs, it does point to the simple truism that sustaining a relationship takes continual effort by both partners to meet each other's needs. In a speech added to the post-1982 texts, at the end of the scene Henry offers a rebuttal:

> No commitments. Only bargains. The trouble is I don't really believe it. I'd rather be an idiot. It's a kind of idiocy I like. 'I use you because you love me. I love you so use me. Be indulgent, negligent, preoccupied, premenstrual . . . your credit is infinite, I'm yours, I'm committed . . .' It's no trick loving somebody at their *best*. Love is loving them at their worst. Is that romantic? Well, good. Everything should be romantic. (80)

Thus, Henry counters Charlotte's devaluation of commitment with an idealistic affirmation of unconditional love. However, Charlotte warns him that he still has a type of virginity to lose, that he still has something to learn about love and the nature of relationships and commitment.

Whereas Henry *discusses* fidelity and commitment with his ex-wife and daughter, he and Annie must *act* on these issues in real terms, and through their marital discord Henry comes to a greater understanding of what is "the real thing" and what goes into maintaining it. In scene 9, Stoppard engages in his third enactment of a suspicious husband confronting his wife over possible infidelity. As in the previous two instances, the husband has ransacked his wife's belongings looking for evidence, but this time the husband does not find any. Still, Henry latches on to the telltale sign of Annie's frequent mentioning of Billy as a sign of her interest in him. Henry acknowledges that she may not feel the same "exclusive voracity of love" (85) as he does, but he needs to know if she has been unfaithful: "I can manage knowing if you did but I can't manage not knowing if you did or not" (85). Henry articulates how the anxiety of doubt and uncertainty can be even more destructive than the knowledge of infidelity. Annie's response to Henry's questioning harks back to Charlotte and Debbie as she says that she "just learned not to care" whether or not Henry had any affairs, and that though she did not sleep with Billy her extended time spent talking with him "seemed like infidelity" (86). Henry fulfills Debbie's critique of his view of fidelity as he proceeds to press the matter as a simple case of did she or did she not sleep with Billy. In the process Henry loses his romanticism, loses his cool aloofness, and exposes his deeply vulnerable side, the point where lost monogamy equals pain: "I don't believe in behaving well. I don't believe in debonair relationships. . . . I believe in mess, tears, pain, self-abasement, loss of self-respect, nakedness. Not caring doesn't seem much different from not loving" (86). Annie counters that Henry's interrogation is not out of love: "This isn't caring. If I had an affair, it would be out of need. Care about that. You can't play on my guilt or my remorse. I'd have none" (87). In part, Annie is reiterating Charlotte's view of the necessity of continual reinforcement of the relationship as well as arguing/rationalizing that with some affairs some of the responsibility may lie with the cuckolded spouse as well as the two adulterers. Throughout the scene Stoppard's writing captures the tension and emotional dynamics of a marriage in crisis.

While scene 9 offers the tension of a couple on the cusp of infidelity, the last two scenes present a couple in the midst of infidelity and then its cessation. Gordon Davidson, artistic director of the Mark Taper Forum, requested some authorial insight on the play's closing scenes, and so Stoppard offered his own perception of what happens in Henry and Annie's relationship:

> Annie's attachment to Henry gets loosened because he starts to take their relationship for granted, doesn't feel he has to prove anything, at which point she meets Billy. Henry's discovery of Billy is the "virginity" which Charlotte said he still had to lose and his immediate danger is that it will affect him in a way as to make him even less of a rival to

Billy; but he recognizes this and attempts, successfully, to "behave" in the way which would get her back. (Letter)

The pivotal moment in the play occurs in the second-to-last scene when Henry answers the phone, and it is Billy calling for Annie.[15] Knowing they are having an affair, Henry fights to keep his emotions in check, but after the call, in a section that Stoppard repeatedly rewrote, the spouses try to come to terms with the affair:

ANNIE: [Thank you for being like this. I'm sorry it's difficult.][16] I love you. Do you understand?

HENRY: No.

ANNIE: Do you think it's unfair?

HENRY: No. It's as though I've been careless, left a door open somewhere while preoccupied.

ANNIE: I'll stop.

HENRY: Not for me. I won't be the person who stopped you. I can't be that. When I got upset you said you'd stop so I try not to get upset. I don't get pathetic because when I got pathetic I could feel how tedious it was, how unattractive. . . . Dignified cuckoldry is a difficult trick, but it can be done. Think of it as modern marriage. We have to get beyond hypocrisy, you and I. Exclusive rights isn't love, it's colonization.

ANNIE: Stop it—please stop it.

HENRY: (*pause*) The trouble is, I can't *find* a part of myself where you're not important. I write in order to be worth your while and to finance the way I want to live with you. . . . Without you I wouldn't care. . . . I can't cope with more than one moral system at a time. Mine is that what you think is right is right. What you do is right. What you want is right. . . .

ANNIE:[17] So you'll forgive me anything, is that it, Hen? I'm a selfish cow but you love me so you'll overlook it, is that right? Thank you but that's not it. . . . I don't feel selfish. [It was love.] You weren't replaced, or even replaceable. But I liked it. . . . I'm sorry I hurt you. But I meant it. It meant something. And now that it means less than I thought and I feel silly, I won't drop him as if it was nothing, a pick-up, it wasn't that, I'm not that. I just want him to stop needing me so I can stop behaving well. This is me behaving well.[18] I have to choose who I hurt and I choose you because I'm yours. (92–94)

Henry has come to self-knowledge through pain; like other Stoppard characters he has been educated by experience rather than intellect. In part Henry blames himself for her infidelity, and he struggles to respond how she wants him to respond. His adoption of her moral code may be seen as an admirable extension of his unconditional love or negatively as a sign of loss of self-respect. Overall, his response to her affair mixes his own values—his inability to find a part of himself where she does not matter, his refusal to stop caring—with his acceptance of the affair from Annie's perspective, as the fulfillment of some need of hers. He manages to love her in a way that makes her want to return to him.

Annie's response in this scene is also complex. Stoppard's letter to Gordon Davidson provides the playwright's view:

> Annie behaves in a way which the actresses playing Annie, with one exception, found puzzling and "wrong." Briefly, finding herself loved by both men, and the second one turning out to be merely the sort of accident which happens away from home, especially in rehearsal . . . she elects—perhaps unwisely—to ease herself out of the Billy relationship rather than kick him in the head, because she feels responsible for drawing Billy that far in. . . . Anyway, the reason this scene is difficult is that most Annies would have said, "I have to choose who I hurt and I choose Billy because I am Henry's." This one does the opposite, a moral position which makes sense to me. . . . You could say that it's a way of Henry learning that exclusivity isn't love it's colonization.

Stoppard admits his rationale for Annie's actions may be out of sync with other people's moral sensibilities, and it suggests that in the realm of love relationships there are a wide variety of views and experiences that impact one's interpretation of the characters' actions and the play's themes.

The other intriguing aspect of Stoppard's commentary is the closing sentence. Henry and Charlotte's daughter Debbie had offered the epigram that "exclusive rights isn't love, it's colonization" (76), and critics have been divided over the play's stance toward this pronouncement. John Barber and Richard Corballis argue that Debbie's view is the self-knowledge that Henry attains,[19] while Paul Delaney believes that this interpretation is "spectacularly wrong" and that Henry's quoting of the line is said with such "bitter irony" that Annie is compelled to interrupt him (*Moral Vision* 119–20). Indeed, Stoppard's suggestion that Henry has come around to Debbie's way of thinking seems to be at odds with the written text. Henry endures the pain of his unconditional commitment, and while Annie's adultery is forgivable, it cannot continue unabated. There is a point where the relationship must return to exclusivity. Henry asserts that for now his love "will go on or it will flip into its opposite" (95). After Annie promises to return home early, Henry is alone and lets out an agonized plea: "Oh, please, please, please, please, *don't*" (95). Henry's love and pain is expressed not in epigrams but in bald human terms. Henry lives through and learns by the mess and tears he had earlier pronounced as being part of a real relationship.

While Henry stays committed during a period of crisis and matures via the ordeal, Annie also undergoes a transformation. In the closing moments of the play, there is another phone call.

> HENRY: (*suddenly uncomfortable*) Oh, hello. Did you want to speak to Annie?
> ANNIE: No.
> HENRY: (*suddenly relaxes*) Well, that's fantastic, Max! (100).

Stoppard (and Henry) deftly makes the audience (and Annie) believe that it is Billy on the phone, and thus Henry is testing Annie. Delaney asserts that Annie's "No" is "vehement" (*Moral Vision* 122), making it clear to Henry (and if it were Billy) that the affair is over. In the closing moments, the words and movements make it clear that Annie has come around to Henry's view of the importance of fidelity. She "embraces his shoulders from behind," "leans on him tiredly," "kisses him," and declares:

> ANNIE: I've had it. Look after me.
> HENRY: Don't worry. I'm your chap. (100–101)

In these brief, simple sentences, the all-important reconciliation is achieved; again, true love is expressed not in epigrams but in everyday phrases and heartfelt gestures. As Henry wraps up the phone call, Annie turns out all the lights until the only light is coming from the bedroom door, through which she soon exits to wait for Henry. Then amidst the soft, romantic glow, Henry turns on the radio, and the audience hears the last burst of pop music as Brechtian commentary. The song is the Monkees' "I'm a Believer," an upbeat affirmation of love and commitment.

"The Real Thing" in Art and Politics

While the main focus is on love and relationships, Stoppard also explores what is "the real thing" in writing and politics. As a writer, Henry shares many traits with Stoppard. The actors in Henry's play *House of Cards* criticize the playwright for writing intricate, lengthy, but arguably irrelevant speeches (Max's scene 1 digital watch digression); for portraying female characters as fantasy figures who are never fully developed; for creating situations removed from reality; and for crafting stylish, intellectual comedies known for their linguistic craftsmanship: "having all the words is not what life's about" (39). All of these charges leveled against Henry had been voiced against Stoppard's pre–*Real Thing* plays.

In act 2, Henry and Annie get into a heated debate over what constitutes artistic merit, and while Henry is Stoppard's acknowledged surrogate, Annie is given effective arguments. Henry argues for absolute standards, while Annie takes a relativist view: "You're bigoted about what writing is supposed to be like. You judge everything as though everyone starts off from the same place, aiming for the same prize. English Lit. Shakespeare out in front by a mile. . . . You all write for people who would like to write like you if only they could write. . . . Brodie isn't writing to compete like you. He's writing to be heard" (57). She proceeds to argue that people are indoctrinated as to what constitutes good writing and that evaluation often rests on whether or not certain expectations were met. Essentially, Annie argues that in terms of art, different people have different criteria, different desires, and different standards and that if it communicates with people, something as unpolished and technically unskilled as Brodie's script can still be considered art, in part, because it springs from something genuine within him.

Henry counters with the now famous cricket-bat speech: "This thing here, which looks like a wooden club, is actually several pieces of particular wood cunningly put together in a certain way so that the whole thing is sprung; like a dance floor. . . . If you get it right, the cricket ball will travel two hundred yards in four seconds. . . . What we're trying to do is to write cricket bats, so that when we throw up an idea and give it a little knock, it might . . . *travel*" (60). In contrast Brodie's script is compared to a lump of wood that may look like a cricket bat but "if you hit a ball with it, the ball will travel about ten feet and you will drop the bat and dance about shouting 'Ouch!'" (61). Thus, Henry concludes: "This isn't better because someone says it's better. . . . It's better because it's better" (61). While Henry's analogy is clever and compelling, it may not contain the whole picture. While there is danger in complete relativity, one can question the seeming rigidity of Henry's view. Indeed Henry himself, unwittingly, provides a rebuttal. Henry loves superficial, bubblegum music such as "Da Doo Ron Ron" and "Um Um Um Um Um Um," and a musicologist, applying traditional standards, might say that classical music is simply better than the music Henry prefers. However, Henry notes that pop music "*moves* me, the way people are supposed to be moved by *real* music" (27), and so how can one deny the validity of his experience? Likewise, if people respond to Brodie's script and not Henry's more stylish play, how can Henry claim universal superiority? Indeed, Stoppard's personal pronouncements suggest a more flexible view, as the audience is empowered to judge for themselves: "If I say, 'That's what it said to me,' you can't say, 'No it didn't'" (Ickes 38). Likewise, Stoppard notes: "I was an awful critic because I operated on the assumption there was an absolute scale of values against which art could be measured. I did not trust my own subjective responses" (Gussow, *Conversations,* 3).

While Annie argues that it is important to know "who wrote it, why he wrote it, *where* he wrote it" (62), Henry dismisses those things as irrelevant. In contrast to Annie's emphasis on understanding the circumstance of construction, Henry offers a paean to words and the ideal of language as completely objective:

> [Words are] innocent, neutral, precise, standing for this, describing that, meaning the other, so if you look after them you can build bridges across incomprehension and chaos. . . . I don't think writers are sacred, but words are. They deserve respect. If you get the right ones in the right order, you can nudge the world a little or make a poem which children will speak for you when you're dead. (63)

While Henry is justified in objecting to the abuse of language, and while the close of his speech is compelling, in the overall debate on art and writing it is well to acknowledge the validity of both Annie's and Henry's views, that there is a range of valid artistic expressions and responses. The shortcoming of Stoppard's presentation is that he has set up a false binary wherein one is asked to choose between the validity of the apolitical, skilled craftsman who can turn a clever phrase and the opinionated, primitive playwright who is ham-fisted at expressing his ideas. This imaginary binary is further distorted by the later revelation that Brodie's ill-written script, which is supposed to be at least redeemed by the conviction of lived experience, is actually based on lies. In the real world, eloquent expression can mix with impassioned conviction (David Hare's plays, for example), and sometimes the truthfulness of the cause can supersede the inadequacies of the language used to express it.

While Brodie's script inspires the debate on standards of excellence in writing, Brodie himself is the catalyst for the play's examination of political commitment. In scene 2, Max praises Brodie for showing "sheer moral courage" and "pure moral conscience" (35) in demonstrating against the deployment of American missiles on British soil. Henry, in a paraphrase of W. H. Auden, counters with the proposition, "Public postures have the configuration of private derangement" (37), a statement that questions the purity and motivations of people involved in political causes. Indeed, in *The Real Thing* those active in politics all have ulterior motives or can be easily compromised. Henry hypocritically considers joining the Justice for Brodie Committee so that he can spend more time with Annie; Max and Annie protest the missiles because they own a weekend cottage near the base; Max skips a Committee meeting to play a squash match; Annie, the one seemingly most committed to the Justice for Brodie campaign, skips a meeting to have an adulterous rendezvous with Henry; and Billy agrees to act in the Brodie script so that he can be with Annie. Even Brodie himself is shown to be far different than his idealized image. Brodie is a boorish, ungrateful lout who has no moral qualms about stealing a VCR if he wants one. More significantly, Brodie is revealed as a fraud: the image of a morally driven, honorable man protesting the missiles is an illusion. After a fight, Brodie had gone AWOL and knew nothing about the demonstration until he met Annie on the train. His eventual burning of the wreath was an attempt to impress Annie. Thus, the final revelations show a web of motivations that have nothing to do with moral intentions or justice: Brodie's protest was due to infatuation with Annie, who in turn defended Brodie out of a sense of guilt,[20] while Henry acquiesced to "tart up" Brodie's script out of love for Annie.

These revelations seem aimed at "proving" Henry's view that public postures have private, ulterior motivations. While this is no doubt true in some circumstances, the rigid consistency with which the view is expressed in the play distorts the real picture, where, I would argue, some people *are* scrupulously motivated in their political protests. Were Stoppard and the artists and political prisoners who inspired his 1970s political plays motivated by private derangement in their opposition to human rights abuses and suppression of free expression in Eastern Europe? Obviously there is more to the real picture than the play allows. Part of the problem is that Brodie is a straw figure, and an inconsistent one at that. He is a knee-jerk liberal who inexplicably enlisted in the army and who spouts all the cant of the extreme political Left yet is completely unaware of a major anti–nuclear missile demonstration. Extremists from either end of the political spectrum are easy targets, particularly when their views are shown to lack conviction. How much more interesting and complex it would have been if Stoppard had constructed a man whose writing skills and politics were antithetical to Henry's but who had the personal conviction and integrity to offer a formidable rebuttal that would at least merit respect if not agreement.

Overall, *The Real Thing* is indeed the real thing, a romantic comedy that is both emotionally moving and intellectually stimulating. While some of Henry's pronouncements seem too rigid, Stoppard has wisely supplied other characters with compelling arguments that help complete the picture, that move the play toward a both/and view of the world, one that mixes absolute and relative values. More telling is the success with which Stoppard, in conjunction with the actors whose performance of the play's subtext more than the dialogue makes the heart of the love plot incarnate, presents the emotional dynamics of marriage, with its pain and mess, joy and vitality. While *The Real Thing* has its fair share of wit and cleverness, it is simple phrases, gentle touches, commonplace words and deeds that express "the real thing" in love. Also, rare among serious modern plays about marriage, *The Real Thing* ends on an optimistic note as Henry and Annie have overcome infidelity and seem to be on their way to a period of sustained happiness. It is an ending and a play that can rightly proclaim, "I'm a Believer" both in the power of marital love and commitment and in Stoppard's ability to portray them effectively.

Hapgood

AFTER THE HUGE SUCCESS OF *The Real Thing,* STOPPARD, like his fictional playwright Henry, appeared on the BBC radio program *Desert Island Discs.* There Stoppard mentioned that he was interested in writing a play about mathematics. Fans and book publishers soon began sending him suggestions and resources, but Stoppard followed his own path. He explains both his interest in the subject, and why he veered away from his original idea:

> For centuries mathematics was considered the queen of the sciences because it claimed certainty. It was grounded on some fundamental certainties—axioms—which led to others. But then, in a sense, it all started going wrong, with concepts like non-Euclidean geometry. . . . The mathematics of physics turned out to be grounded on *un*certainties, on probability and chance. . . . I started reading about mathematics without finding what I was looking for. . . . So I started reading about [quantum physics]. . . . I was fascinated by the mystery which lies in the foundation of the observable world, of which the most familiar example is the wave/particle duality of light. I thought it was a good metaphor for human personality. (Guppy 179–80)[1]

Stoppard explains his intended metaphor: "[The] central idea is the proposition that in each of our characters . . . the person who gets up in the morning and puts on the clothes is the working majority of a dual personality, part of which is always there in a submerged state. That doesn't seem to me a profound or original idea but I still find it interesting" (Billington, "Secret Agent" 194). He elaborates: "It's not really dual personality. It's just that one chooses to 'be' one part of oneself, and not another part of oneself. One has a public self and a submerged self" (Gussow, *Conversations,* 79). Overall, Stoppard's metaphor is a statement that individuals are comprised of complex, even contradictory, personalities that add up to the whole person. While *Hapgood*'s metaphor is relatively simple, the play itself is often considered Stoppard's most complex and difficult to understand.

Set in the late 1980s, *Hapgood* takes place in the world of espionage and the Cold War battle for scientific knowledge and military secrets. Hapgood, the lone female in the play,[2] runs a British secret service operation that passes false information to the Soviet Union. Kerner, a Russian defector and nuclear physicist working on SDI ("Star Wars") weapons research, is Hapgood's prize double agent (and father of her son), who actually may be working for both sides. Blair is another high-ranking British agent, while Ridley works for Hapgood in helping to pass disinformation to the Soviets. The inciting incident for the play's action is that the Americans and British have learned that one of the above is passing real information to the Russians, and so the plot revolves around trying to discover and prove who the double agent is. Confusion, complexity, and thematic resonances arise from Stoppard's use of multiple twins—Ridley and his brother, the unnamed Russian twins, plus Hapgood and her pseudotwin Celia Newton. Mingled into this spy plot are discussions of quantum theory, including Heisenberg's Uncertainty Principle and the two-slits experiment that proves the duality of light.

The London production of *Hapgood* was Stoppard's first relative failure—no Best Play Awards and a struggling six-month West End run. Likewise, its international success was much more limited than his previous major plays. For example, though premiering in London in 1988, *Hapgood* was not staged in New York until 1994, and then in a limited-run, noncommercial production. Preparing to rewrite the play for that production, Stoppard noted: "It's not the physics that's the problem, it's the story, the plot, the narrative, the mechanism, the twins, all that" (Fleming, "A Talk," 25).

The Science and Spy Background

Stoppard read about a dozen books relating to quantum theory; two of his main resources were Richard Feynman's *Lectures on Physics* (esp. chap. 37,

"Quantum Behavior") and J. C. Polkinghorne's *The Quantum World*.[3] Intent on insuring that his use of science was accurate, Stoppard struck up an acquaintance with Polkinghorne and even had him (plus a scientist at the CERN research center in Switzerland) read the script. Stoppard not only quoted from his correspondence with Polkinghorne in the London program, but he also corrected his script in accordance with both scientists' comments.

Quantum theory includes concepts that run counter to classical, mechanical models of the universe. One of the central axioms of quantum theory is Heisenberg's Uncertainty Principle (a.k.a. the Principle of Indeterminism), which is a statement that when measuring the position and momentum of an electron, one can determine either the position or the momentum but not both. The act of measuring one quality affects the other quality, and thus one gets different results based on which quality is measured first. A ramification of the Heisenberg Uncertainty Principle is that it acts as a limit upon the possibility of exact knowledge, and thus it undermines the idea of a strictly causal universe.

Another implication of the Uncertainty Principle is that the act of observing alters the results, a statement related to the two-slits experiment.[4] When light is shone through one gap in a wall, the result indicates that light is made up of particles. When light is shone through two gaps, the result indicates light is composed of waves.[5] A fascinating part of the experiment is that when one tries to observe the light going through the slits to see how it yields a wave pattern, the result shows a particle pattern. In *Hapgood* Kerner explains: "Every time we don't look, we get wave pattern. Every time we look to see how we get wave pattern we get particle pattern. The act of observing determines the reality. . . . The experimenter makes the choice. You get what you interrogate for" (1988, 12). The experiment suggests that light is both wave and particle, that it is continuous and discontinuous. For Stoppard, this breaking from an either/or to a both/and perspective is part of its metaphoric appeal.

The physics, particularly in the New York version, is explained in a fairly clear and concise manner; however, the spy terminology, clarified and/or eliminated in the New York text, is difficult to decipher when reading, much less when viewing. The terms "joe" and "sleeper" refer to the status or identity of an agent. A "sleeper" is an agent who is sent in years in advance and establishes himself or herself as an ordinary citizen preparing for the moment when he or she will be activated and required to pass on vital pieces of information. A "joe" is an agent who has been turned to work for the other side. Thus the backstory to *Hapgood* is that "Twelve years ago the Russians put Kerner in as a sleeper, i.e., someone who pretends to defect and can be reactivated later" as a spy ("Hapgood Crib" 1). Then Hapgood turned him into a joe—that is, he works for the British. Later in the play, Stoppard further complicates matters by suggesting that Kerner may be working for both sides, but thankfully, Stoppard drops the spy terminology and refers to Kerner as a possible triple, quadruple, or even quintuple agent.

Textual History

Examining Stoppard's notes, drafts, and correspondence, it is clear that *Hapgood* was an extremely difficult script for him to write. He started taking notes in December 1984, but full-time work on the play did not begin until April 1986. Stoppard started with three central conceits: (1) a physicist who loses faith in certainty because of Uncertainty; (2) three aspects of Hapgood—being in charge at work, being a mother to her son, and her dual personality via her pseudotwin; and (3) quantum structural ideas of duality (the double agent), uncertainty (there is no observable reality, and twins as representing momentum and position of an electron), and nonlocality (twins alter each other's state, or Hapgood 1 becomes Hapgood 2) (Notes 27 Apr. 1986).[6] He also considered having a scene where twins are interviewed for a spy position and are mistaken for each other, and experimented with there being Russian triplets, and with Kerner (then known as Ryker) having a twin. Weeks were also spent diagramming the pool scenes, trying to figure out the movements of the characters. Ultimately, the first draft was completed in early January 1987, with plans for a summer production. Stoppard wanted the title role to be played by Felicity Kendal, but since she was pregnant, the production was delayed until March 1988.

The script changed more than usual during rehearsals and during the previews in Wimbledon,[7] but even the final London text was deemed to be too confusing for much of the audience. Part of the problem is revealed in the "Hapgood Crib," which Stoppard supplied to the production team as they struggled to understand the play. In the Crib, he writes: "To be blunt, I don't think that the mechanics of the plot bear scrutiny at all and I don't think they ever will. The trouble is that they don't remotely interest me, they're just a necessary nuisance to provide the opportunity to write about this woman who in Blair's words is 'A sort of double', and the way this bears upon her relationships with Kerner, Blair and Ridley" (6).[8] Intrigued by the physics and the metaphoric possibilities it presented, Stoppard took pains to make the science as accurate as possible, but he neglected to clarify the narrative problems he knew existed, and the result was that he often lost his audience.[9]

Before taking the play to Los Angeles for its 1989 American premiere, the producers urged Stoppard to clarify the narrative. In an attempt to explicate the baffling pool scene that opens the play, Stoppard added a new scene immediately after it. In this new scene 2 the American agent Wates delivers an explanatory monologue—ostensibly to offstage CIA agents. At eighteen minutes, the scene was not only interminably long, but in Stoppard's attempt to mimic the speech patterns of a hard-boiled CIA agent, the explanation itself is somewhat hard to follow. By opening night Stoppard had pared the speech down to seven minutes and the bare essentials that clarified the plot, but Stoppard still disliked the device because he felt it was "A Child's Guide to *Hapgood*" (Delaney, *Conversation,* 225).[10] Delaney reports: "The Los Angeles production played to some appreciative audiences during previews but after opening night it faced completely packed houses of sullenly silent Californians who by subscribing to the entire Ahmanson Theatre season were promised tickets to *The Phantom of the Opera*. Plans for *Hapgood* to have a Broadway run were abandoned" (225–26). The text of this Los Angeles production, preserved at the HRHRC, has never been published.

Hapgood eventually made it to New York in late 1994, where its limited run at Lincoln Center was extended three times.[11] For this production, Stoppard still struggled to clarify and simplify the text, and ultimately he found it helpful to label the play "a new-fashioned melodrama" (Gussow, *Conversations,* 80). He explains: "Once I began to think of *Hapgood* as a melodrama, I felt much more comfortable with it, because it is melodramatic. It's not satiric about the spy business. It operates on a heightened, slightly implausible level of life" (106). For this production, Stoppard made significant revisions to the text, cutting nearly twenty minutes of material, clarifying the spy plot, and paring down some of the physics "lectures." He also trimmed some lines of a sociopolitical nature. While still maintaining the play's complexity and intelligence, this "Broadway Edition" script makes the play easier to follow. This text, with the possible reincorporation of some of the lines cut from the London version, is recommended as the one to use for a production of *Hapgood.*

Textual Construction: Meaning through Form

The structure of *Hapgood,* like that of other Stoppard works, is intimately related to its content: the worlds of espionage and science. In the middle of the play, Kerner discusses the difference between spy stories and scientific writing, and he notes how spy stories "all surprise the same way. Ridley is not very nice: he'll turn out to be all right. Blair will be the traitor: the one you liked" (39).[12] The play is prophetically self-reflexive as indeed Ridley engages in his fateful risk for the sake of Hapgood and her child, whereas Blair breaks his promise and risks Hapgood's son to help insure the success of the mission. This fulfilling of the expectations of the spy genre shows the dual nature of the characters and thus meshes with Stoppard's overall thematic hypothesis of the duality of most people.

While this plot point adheres to the formula, Stoppard explains how in its overall structure *Hapgood* deviates from the conventions of the spy genre: "In a normal spy thriller you contrive to delude the reader until all is revealed in the denouement; this is the exact opposite of a scientific paper in which the denouement—the discovery—is announced at the beginning. *Hapgood* to some extent follows this latter procedure. It is not a whodunit because we are told who has done it near the beginning of the first act, so the story becomes *how* he did it" (Guppy 181). By the third scene, Ridley is identified as the prime suspect, and before the end of the first act (scene 5 in London; scene 4 in New York), it is hypothesized that Ridley carries out his double agent work via a twin brother. Since the play is a spy thriller, one might suspect that these theories cannot be correct, that it is too early for the crime to be solved, but here that is not the case; Ridley and his twin are the correct solution to the problem. In this regard, the play does more clearly resemble a scientific paper, the aesthetics of which are explained by Kerner: "What is interesting is to know what is happening. . . . A science paper is a beautiful thing: first here is what we will find; now here is how we find it" (1988, 47). Again, Kerner's words self-reflexively describe *Hapgood*, a work that embodies the form of a scientific paper: "Act 1 leads to a hypothesis; act 2 carries out the experiment. The denouement leaves to us the interpretation of the results" (Kelly 155). More specifically, the first act might be viewed as the analysis of a failed experiment (the first pool scene) that leads to a hypothesis (Ridley twins), and then the second act is the setting up and playing out of an experiment that tests and proves the hypothesis. Indeed, Kelly's view of the play as a scientific experiment is more accurate than Stoppard's notion of the play as a "howdunit." By the end of the first act, the audience knows that the "how" is twins, and so during the "experiment" portion of the play, the plot mostly becomes an enactment of Stoppard's theme of the duality of people. Blair's double cross, Ridley's redeemable qualities, Hapgood's pseudotwin, and the revelation that Kerner is also working for the Soviets are all central to the second act experiment, and they all embody Stoppard's hypothesis.

The play's structure also engages the theme of duality, as nearly every one of the twelve scenes has a double. There are two pool scenes. The first is an experiment (or trap) that goes awry and that raises the central dramatic question, who is the traitor and how is he or she doing it? The second pool scene is a successful experiment that wraps up the main espionage plot via the successful capture of Ridley and his twin. There are two zoo scenes with Kerner and Blair. The first revolves around Kerner's explication of the dual nature of light, and it provides Kerner's backstory of being a "sleeper" turned "joe." The second elaborates on the theme of duality as it involves Kerner's metaphoric use of square roots to argue that "we're all doubles" (62); it also extends Kerner's personal story into the future by informing the audience of his plan to return to his homeland. The two rugby scenes show Hapgood's personal life, her relationship not only with her son but also with the two men whom she loves (Kerner is the father of her child; Blair the object of her affection, with the specifics of their relationship not revealed). There are two "group meeting" office scenes. The first focuses on the agents explaining/ discovering what happened at the pool, while the second serves as the laying of the trap for the second pool meeting. There are two "personal" scenes with Ridley and Celia. The first not only establishes Celia as Hapgood's "opposite" but also begins the sexual subtext that is consummated in their second "personal" scene. While there is no literal double for the shooting range scene, Ridley's target practice becomes tangibly real in the second pool scene as the original shooter is now the one who is shot. Finally, there is not a double for the third office scene, but it is here that Ridley is "unsettled, somehow thrown by seeing her ["Celia"] in this office, in these clothes . . . She is so obviously Hapgood" (66). Like Ridley, the audience encounters the physical appearance of Hapgood, but the personality of Celia, and thus in this scene the theme of dual personalities is most clearly embodied on the stage. Overall, this doubling structure helps reinforce Stoppard's central thematic concern.

Thematic Analysis of Text and Production

The London and New York productions began with an opening theatrical image that is not in the published text but that gives the audience the vicarious pleasure of spy surveillance. As the audience hears the opening "radio play," a red dot moves about a map of London that is projected onto panels (or the back wall). As the pursuit continues and as the agents home in on their suspect, the map grows in increasing detail, moving from major roads down to side streets and ultimately to the outlines of individual buildings. The scale has grown progressively smaller, probing further into the heart of the matter, and then the dot stops at a municipal swimming-bath, with the set assembling onstage in semidarkness.[13] When the first person walks through the door, the audience assumes (tipped off by the line "You're looking at him" [2]) that he is the man the agents have been tracking. What follows, choreographed to music,[14] is a farcelike series of entrances and exits, done with four entrance/exits, four changing cubicles, identical towels, identical briefcases, Kerner, Merryweather (a minor British agent), and unbeknownst to the audience, two sets of identical twins (the Russian twins and the Ridley twins)—all of whom move in and out of the space swapping (or trying to follow) towels and briefcases. Spywise and plotwise, the audience is thrown into confusion as keeping track of who's who is nearly impossible, especially since no one yet knows that two sets of identical twins are involved.

The opening scene's action serves at least two purposes. First, the tracking of the agent (via the dot on the map and the multiple entrances and exits) parallels the tracking of an electron and helps mimic Heisenberg's Uncertainty Principle. On a much larger scale and at much slower speeds, the actors moving in and out of the space suggest the apparently random motion of electrons as they move about inside atoms while being observed by the experimenter who can never know their position and momentum simultaneously. Polkinghorne notes that when tracking an electron, "[t]he electrons are not only identical, they are also indistinguishable" (38). Similarly, one is not sure which of the twins one is looking at, especially since their identical costuming makes them indistinguishable.[15] Secondly, the opening action hints at the theme of duality as the audience thinks it sees one character, not two, and thus twins physically embody the idea that two personalities are hiding under one exterior. By the end of the confusing first scene, the audience has played the spy tracking the electronic bleep, seen a human depiction of the motion of electrons (and thus implicitly experienced the themes of uncertainty and duality), and are in much the same situation as the characters, left trying to figure out what exactly is happening and who is truly the traitor. But like a good spy story, a significant clue has been planted as to the true culprit: Ridley has revealed his knowledge that twins were used, a trick he could not have known unless he was in on it.

A quantum jump is when an electron passes from one energy level to another without passing in between; it simply jumps from one state to another, and quantum jumps are metaphorically mimicked in many of the act 1 scene changes. At the end of the opening pool scene, Blair stays fixed in place while the pool set dissolves and the zoo set forms around him—he has gone from here to there without passing in between.[16] Blair is a character who "likes to know what's what" (10) and who has an "either/or" view of the world. But this binary worldview and the nature of "truth" (or the difficulty in determining it) are called into question by Kerner, who dominates the second scene by discussing quantum behavior, particularly the two-slits experiment and the dual nature of light, speeches that Stoppard adapted from Feynman.[17] In production, these speeches and their thematic import are accentuated via staging choices. Stoppard's stage directions for the zoo scene read: "The bars make hard-edged shadows. We need one particular and distinct demarcation of light and shadow on the floor, perhaps thrown by the edge of a wall" (8). Thus, when Kerner discusses the dual nature of light, he uses the set and lighting design to illustrate the idea: "Look at the edge of the shadow. It is straight like the edge of the wall that makes it. This means that light is particles" (9). In London, set designer Carl Toms added a backdrop of two giraffes, which were positioned in such a way that from certain angles it looked like two heads were connected to one body.[18] Thus, it is ironic when Kerner chastises Blair: "Objective reality is for zoologists. 'Ah, yes, definitely a giraffe.' But a double agent is not like a giraffe. A double agent is more like a trick of the light" (1988, 10).[19] As with the two-slits experiment, the observer plays a role in determining the reality (where one is sitting affects whether one sees two giraffes or a two-headed giraffe); and metaphorically, the image of two heads on one body suggests the duality of individual identity. Plotwise, the second scene explains how the pool scene was an experiment to see if Kerner was passing secrets, and thus Kerner's explanation of light as both particle and wave suggests that he may be both "sleeper" and "joe," that he may be working for both sides. The scene also reveals that Kerner was not the one who removed the films from the briefcase, and thus someone else is the likely traitor.

The transition to the third scene at the school rugby match is again accompanied by a quantum jump as Blair remains fixed while the set changes.

These "quantum jump" transitions suggest that even the "either/or" Blair has a dual nature. Jenkins, commenting on Nigel Hawthorne's portrayal, argues that at the pool Blair comes across as "brusque, professional, in control" while at the zoo he appears "charming, detached, pragmatic" (*Theatre of Tom Stoppard* 186). While all the characters exhibit a certain degree of duality, the jump to the rugby pitch takes the play to the character who most fully embodies this theme, Hapgood herself.

The pool scene established Hapgood as a take-charge, in-control professional who gave the orders. While she tries to be emotionally detached on the job, with her son she is lovingly maternalistic. She divides her life into that which is "technical" (her job) and that which is "personal" (her son and the men she loves). Her divided loyalties often cause her to break the rules of her job so that she can assuage her guilt over being an often-absent mother. The multiplicity of her identities is reflected by the various ways different people address her. Subordinates such as Ridley and Merryweather call her "Mother"; Blair addresses her by her first name, "Elizabeth"; to her secretary she is "Mrs. Hapgood" (a courtesy title designed to mask the father of her child); Wates calls her "ma'am"; her son Joe says "Mum" or "Mummy"; her pseudotwin Celia refers to her as "Betty"; and Kerner uses the Russian equivalent of her first name, "Yelizaveta," or affectionate diminutives such as "Lilya" and "Lilitchka." The lack of a single, fixed name alludes to the changing, divided nature of her individual identity, and the motif of ambiguous nomenclature runs throughout the play, reinforcing the theme that everyone has multiple identities.[20]

Blair's next quantum jump takes him to Hapgood's office. Here, the plot focuses on Wates's suspicion of Ridley and Hapgood, and (in the New York text) on Blair's closing explanation of how they think Ridley has been passing information. But in the heart of the scene, the audience sees the professional Hapgood, the most complex female role written by Stoppard, in her element. As the head of an espionage unit, she is steady and effectively in control of the men she runs, and though in the rough-and-tumble world of espionage, she is prim and proper and never swears. Her superior, almost superhuman, intellect is also dramatized as she virtually simultaneously reads decrypts, makes decisions on international actions to be taken, carries on a conversation with Wates and Blair about the pool, and plays a game of correspondence chess without a board. Not only is she intellectually superior to Blair and Wates, but she also puts the latter in his place for overstepping his bounds by having her followed. Once Wates backs down, the commanding

Hapgood gives way to the perfect British hostess as she reveals that she made a special trip just to get Wates a lemon for his tea. Overall, Hapgood is a tough, intelligent, effective administrator with a motherly heart and a lingering sense of vulnerability when it comes to personal relationships.

By the end of act 1, the plan to entrap Ridley has been laid out, and so act 2 focuses on getting Ridley to repeat the pool meeting so they can prove the twins' hypothesis and capture their prey. This plot structure helps demonstrate the duality theme; in the second act each of the four principal characters will be shown to be a literal or metaphoric "double agent," with their duality or twinlike state emerging out of their response to the divide caused by "personal" versus "technical" loyalty.

After the first scene of act 2, where Hapgood, Blair, and Kerner effectively bait the trap for Ridley, the dramatization of the duality theme begins in earnest. The opening of scene 2 involves Hapgood "flying out from the other door. We haven't seen her like this. She is as different from her other self as the flat is different from her office; the office being rather cleaner, tidier and better organized" (56). While the reader sees this character identified as "Hapgood," spectators, not yet told that the entrapment plan involves a twin-sister ploy, are in a position similar to Ridley's. They are likely caught off guard and surprised by this character who looks like Hapgood but who goes by the name Celia Newton and whose personality (seemingly rash and scatterbrained), behavior (pot smoking and nonstop talking), speech (frequent swearing), and dress (untidy) are the antithesis of Hapgood. For the ruse to work, the streetwise Ridley must be completely deceived into believing that Celia is truly a different person than Hapgood. The trap's success is due to the duality of both Ridley and Hapgood.

Like the experimenter, Ridley gets what he interrogates for—Celia is "Hapgood without the brains or the taste" (71). Celia is his fantasy made flesh, and through her he fulfills his years-long desire to sleep with (the physical equivalent of) Hapgood. The situation also reveals Ridley's personal-professional divide. Ridley is the "technical" traitor passing secrets, but his personal desire and affection for Hapgood makes him willing to take a perilous risk: "I'll get her kid back for her but it's only personal. If she's set me up I'll kill her" (70). Ridley is willing to place the personal above the professional.

While one reason the pseudotwin ruse works is that Ridley sees only what he wants to see, the other reason is due to the nature of the object under study. For Hapgood to embody Celia so convincingly, Celia must be

Hapgood's own "sleeper" or "double"—Celia is the submerged state hidden beneath the working majority. Only in this altered state can Hapgood come to call Ridley by his first name and realize his redeeming qualities: "You're all right, Ernest. You're just not her type" (71). Also her divided personal and professional loyalties surface as she warns (goads?) Ridley: "If you think she's lying, walk away. If you think bringing back her son will make you her *type*, walk away" (71). Professionally she wants to catch Ridley, while personally, his desire to save her son makes him worthy of being allowed to escape. Faced with this person who looks like Hapgood, but who acts like her opposite, Ridley asks the fundamental, ontological question of the play, "*Who the hell are you?*" (71). Their subsequent sexual consummation, "without the niceties" (71), is Hapgood's acknowledgment of her submerged state, a point accented in the London production where Hapgood "reached up to pull [Ridley] down to her so that she was not so much reciprocating as initiating the kiss" (Delaney, *Moral Vision*, 137). Stoppard elaborates on the duality of Hapgood/Celia:

> What it is inclined to mean is that circumstances lead her to take on what she would initially think of as a false personality, but in doing so she discovers that she is using part of herself she simply hasn't used but has no difficulty in expressing, in assuming. So the woman who wouldn't touch Ridley with a bargepole begins to fancy him in a different set of coordinates. The woman who rather disdains him begins to find him sympathetic. These two arcs intersect at the moment where she kills him, where the working majority of Hapgood pulls the trigger. (Gussow, *Conversations*, 79)

Hapgood discovers that, depending on the circumstances, she can sleep with a man and then later shoot him, and through it she realizes her duality.

Amidst the Celia scenes, Stoppard uses a couple of structural devices that further accent the duality theme. The first Celia-Ridley scene ends with the most dramatic quantum jump: "Ridley stays where he is. The next time he moves, he's somebody else. So we lose the last set without losing Ridley. When the set has gone, Ridley is in some other place. . . . He is a man arriving somewhere. He carries a suitcase. He is a different Ridley" (60).[21] How the audience is made to understand that this is supposed to be Ridley's twin is a task left up to the production team.

The more relevant and accessible device is the inclusion of the second Kerner-Blair zoo scene where Stoppard turns to the world of math for his metaphors—typical of Stoppard, the launching point is a nuance of language. Kerner, the spy novel enthusiast, tries to reconcile spy terminology with the language of math: "Prime suspect: it's in nearly all the books. I don't understand. A prime is a number which won't divide nicely, and all the suspects are prime. It's the last thing to expect with a suspect. You must look for squares. The product of twin roots" (61–62). Square roots have both a positive and negative solution, and Kerner elaborates on this fact in the speech that most clearly expresses the central theme of the play:

> You think everybody has no secret or one big secret, they are what they seem or they are the opposite. You look at me and think: *Which is he?* Plus or minus. If only you could figure it out like looking into me to find my root. And then you still wouldn't know. We're all doubles. Even you. Your cover is Bachelor of Arts first class, with an amusing incomprehension of the sciences, but you insist on laboratory standards for reality, while I insist on its artfulness. So it is with us all, we're not so one-or-the-other. The one who puts on the clothes in the morning is the working majority, but at night—perhaps in the moment before unconsciousness—we meet our sleeper—the priest is visited by the doubter, the Marxist sees the civilizing force of the bourgeoise, the captain of industry admits the justice of common ownership. (62)

Fittingly, the scene also suggests the divides within Kerner and Blair, dualities that affect their individual relationships to Hapgood and that comment on East-West politics.

Earlier Hapgood had told Blair that she "absolutely refuses to live without [him]" (54). But in the second zoo scene, Kerner correctly posits: "*You* would betray [Hapgood] before I would" (63). While Blair is "technically" loyal, on the personal level he is the most traitorous. In the second pool scene, Blair breaks his promise and uses Hapgood's son as part of the trap:

HAPGOOD: I'll never forgive you for that, never ever.
BLAIR: I know that. I knew that. (75)

Blair surrenders his personal relationship with Hapgood and risks her son's safety because for him individual people are sometimes pawns that must be sacrificed to win the "larger" game of international espionage, particularly since it is being waged against the "Evil Empire" (10). But Hapgood no longer sees it in such binary terms:

BLAIR: One has to pick oneself up and carry on. We can't afford to lose. It's them or us, isn't it?

HAPGOOD: What is? What exactly? The game has moved on. Read the signs. It's over.

BLAIR: Try telling that to the opposition.

HAPGOOD: Oh, the KGB! The opposition! Paul, we're just keeping each other in business, we should send each other Christmas cards— oh, f-f-fuck it, Paul! (75) [22]

Hapgood's swearing is indicative that her "sleeper" has awakened, and that she no longer wishes to play the game of international espionage and Cold War politics. In part, her decision is based on a changed perspective— the either/or of "Good West" versus "Evil East" is not so clear-cut, as both sides use lies, deceit, and whatever means necessary to "win" the game: "Both the Soviets and Blair are willing to sacrifice the rights and safety of the individual to secure a political advantage. In a play filled with uncertainties there is no equivocation whatsoever in Hapgood's climactic denunciation of Blair. . . . [She] explicitly indicates her rejection of Blair's impersonal, technical scheme of values as immoral" (Delaney, *Moral Vision,* 144).

In contrast to Blair, Kerner believes that passing scientific secrets is an acceptable exchange for insuring the safety of an individual. In part, Kerner's ethics are based on his being an apolitical scientist who values the idea of pure research. He defected to the West because they had better computers, and though he feels "the West is morally superior" (63), he is preparing to return to his communist homeland. While he believes that democracy is better, he also feels: "It's not my job to change [the political system]" (63). [23] In Kerner's mind, he, not any government, owns his scientific research: "It's mine to give" (47). In the London production, he goes on to say: "What I see at the moment is greed and chauvinism, the appropriation of knowledge for political domination" (1988, 55). Kerner is a theoretical physicist who lives in a real world where, whether he likes it or not, scientific knowledge *does* have political implications. [24] While Kerner generally does not think in terms of ideology, his research *is* part of the multibillion-dollar "Star Wars" defense program, a potentially prime weapon in the ongoing Cold War.

Hinted at in the second zoo scene, and confirmed in the final scene, is that Kerner has indeed been sending the Soviets the results of his research. In the office scene where they bait the trap for Ridley, Kerner says that the Soviets had learned that he is the father of Hapgood's child, and that in order to protect Joe he had been passing them information. When the audience first hears this story, it seems to be a lie, a part of the plan, but in the end, Hapgood observes the paradox of Kerner's story: "You made up the truth" (76). In the "technical" sense, Kerner is a traitor, but in the personal realm, he has remained loyal to Hapgood and their son.

Ironically, Hapgood had broken off the relationship with Kerner because she had placed her joes above her Joes. As Ridley puts it: "When it came to a choice [Hapgood] traded in a daddy for a joe who would have been blown overnight if he was known to be the father" (70). For ten years Hapgood chose the values of the technical over the values of the personal, but now, after killing Ridley and seeing Blair, the man she most wanted, place her son's life in jeopardy, she disavows her profession. In the end, Hapgood chooses her son, and hopes that Kerner will choose them. Indeed, the final moment of the play is ambiguous, but with a subtext of optimism. After a parting embrace, Hapgood says: "How can you go? *How can you?*" (77). Kerner starts to leave, but then Joe's rugby game begins and "Kerner's interest is snagged" (77). When Hapgood glances back, she sees that Kerner is still there (and in the London production, it is a full-stage cross bringing him back right behind her), she "comes alive," and (in production, with tears in her eyes) closes the play shouting, "that's good—that's better!" (77). Whether or not Kerner stays for good is part of the play's uncertainty, and like the two-slits experiment, the audience member makes the choice, with ultimate certainty unattainable.[25]

The closing image of two parents watching their son offers an image of hope, particularly since they are two people whose values now seem to lie on the side of the personal not the technical. In his review of the London production, Michael Billington argues that the play espouses the values "that democracy is better than dictatorship, that love is a possibility and that—a persistent Stoppard theme—children anchor one in the real world" (9 Mar. 1988). In a world of uncertainties and dualities, it may not be possible to determine anything absolutely, but Hapgood's closing words are indicative of the overall stance of the play—some actions might be considered "good" and that in comparison, one action may morally be seen as "better" than another.[26]

While much of Stoppard's play is devoted to the dramatization of the theme of human duality, there is also the hint of a greater mystery. While the worlds of espionage and quantum mechanics offer metaphors for the elusive nature of human identity, on a deeper level, they are also a metaphor for the structure of the universe itself—in a sense, the elusiveness of cosmic identity. In short, Stoppard makes a leap from physics to metaphysics, and "intimates the existence of God not so much *despite* as *because of* the lack of causality and epistemological certainty in the universe" (Delaney, *Moral Vision,* 128). In the last scene of the first act, Kerner says to Hapgood:

> It upset Einstein very much, you know, all that damned quantum jumping, it spoiled his idea of God, which I tell you frankly is the only idea of Einstein's I never understood. He believed in the same God as Newton, causality, nothing without a reason, but now one thing led to another until causality was dead. Quantum mechanics made everything finally random, things can go this way or that way, the mathematics deny certainty, they reveal only probability and chance, and Einstein couldn't believe in a God who threw dice. He should have come to me, I would have told him, 'Listen Albert, He threw *you*—look around, He never stops.' . . . There is a straight ladder from the atom to the grain of sand, and the only real mystery in physics is the missing rung. Below it, particle physics; above it, classical physics; but in between, metaphysics. All the mystery in life turns out to be the same mystery, the join between things which are distinct and yet continuous, body and mind, free will and fate, living cells and life itself; the moment before the foetus. Who needed God when everything worked like billiard balls? (41)

Though faced with a universe riddled with randomness and uncertainties, Stoppard continues to hedge his bet on the side of the existence of God, which is significant because, as espoused in *Jumpers,* for Stoppard a ruling deity is the source of moral values. In his metaphysical examination of ontology and cosmology, Stoppard eschews the reductionism of relying on *either* science *or* theology, but rather sees both as necessary for understanding the mysteries of life.

While quantum theory debunks strict causality and has led some artists and thinkers to accent the uncertainty, indeterminacy, and randomness of human life, for Stoppard this is not the case. In *Hapgood* Stoppard latches on to the quantum mystery of the dual nature of light as both wave and particle for his main metaphor, thus marking an emphasis on a both/and view of the world. Indeed, for his next major play, *Arcadia,* Stoppard would turn to another scientific paradigm, one firmly grounded in the join between order and chaos, two seeming opposites, which have been shown to be interdependent. And it is in *Arcadia,* not *Hapgood,* where the interplay of science, intellect, emotion, dualities, and metaphysics most successfully present Stoppard's vision of the world.

10

Arcadia

IN A 1989 PROFILE PIECE ON STOPPARD, FRIEND AND ACTOR John Wood is quoted as saying: "When I first met [Tom] in the sixties, there was a kind of anarchic joy in him, and it's still there, but it contains its own impossibility now. I can't say that life has disappointed Tom, but I think he once thought there must be a system behind the absurdity, and he found out there isn't" (Schiff 224). The article proceeds to mention that Stoppard had just finished reading James Gleick's *Chaos: The Making of a New Science,* and that he knew that chaos theory could be the seed of a new play. Perhaps what appealed to Stoppard is that chaos theory attempts to systemize that which appears to function outside of any system. It describes a world in which there is chaos in order, but also order in chaos. Stoppard comments: "[Chaos mathematics is] a reconciliation between the idea of things not being random on the one hand and yet unpredictable on the other hand" (Fleming, "A Talk," 19). Elsewhere, he elaborated on the metaphoric appeal of the new science: "[Chaos mathematics] suggested itself as a quite interesting and powerful metaphor for human behavior, not just behavior, but . . . a determined life, a life ruled by determinism, and a life which is subject simply to random causes and effects. Those two ideas about life were not irreconcilable. Chaos mathematics is precisely to do with the unpredictability of determinism" (Gussow, *Conversations,* 84). The nonhierarchical reconciliation of seeming opposites is at the core of chaos theory and its description of the physical world. This combination of apparent randomness yet underlying order epitomizes the structure of many of Stoppard's plays and seems to be congruent with Stoppard's worldview in which there is a high degree of relativity yet also moral absolutes.

Arcadia is set in an airy room in a large, Derbyshire country house. The action occurs in both the early 1800s and the present day, with the scenes alternating between the two time periods. In the final scene characters from both periods share the stage. In the 1800s, a brilliant young girl, Thomasina, her tutor, Septimus, and the guests and members of the Croom household engage in discussions about math, science, art, sex, and landscape gardening. The unseen Lord Byron is a guest at the household as is a minor poet, Ezra Chater, whose wife is involved in numerous extramarital affairs. The nineteenth-century scenes are written in a style reminiscent of the epigrammatic wit of R. B. Sheridan and Oscar Wilde. In the present-day scenes, scholars are investigating the events of the past. Hannah, an emotionally reserved, independent scholar, is studying the history of the family garden. Bernard, an egotistical, fame-seeking professor, is bent on proving his theory that Byron killed the cuckolded Chater in a duel and then fled the country. These scholars' (often inaccurate) sleuthing provides comedic and dramatic enjoyment as the audience gets to see and hear the scholars' interpretation of the past as well as the events they are trying to describe and prove. Rounding out the present-day cast are the descendants of the Coverly household: Valentine, a graduate student chaotician; Chloë, an eighteen-year-old who becomes sexually involved with Bernard; and Gus, a fifteen-year-old who possesses uncanny "natural genius" but who mysteriously never speaks. In both time periods, discussions of chaos theory play a role in the plot. In the past, Thomasina theorizes ideas central to chaos. In the present, Valentine's explanations of the theory educate the other characters as well as the audience.

Deterministic Chaos and the Science Background

"Chaos theory" can be a daunting term, and Stoppard himself did not rely solely on books for his information. He discussed the topic with one of his sons who was studying physics for his doctorate, and he consulted Robert May, a prominent Oxford chaotician in population biology. For the London production, May spent five days teaching the cast the basic concepts of this new science. In New York, Stoppard served that function.

"Chaos theory" is an imprecise and misleading term, and there are at least two different interpretations of the ramifications of the science it describes.[1] It is imprecise because under its umbrella are a diverse range of fields that utilize and concentrate on different aspects and applications of the paradigm. More significantly, the term "chaos" is misleading as it connotatively privileges the unpredictable aspect of the paradigm. Science writer David Porusch states that the "proper name is 'deterministic chaos'" (438), phrasing that more strongly conveys that it is a both/and paradigm in which the terms are interrelated in a nonhierarchical manner. My treatment of "deterministic chaos" is based on Gleick's interpretation of the theory, the account Stoppard used to inform his play.

Deterministic chaos is a hybrid of math and science that describes dynamic systems (any general field of action/behavior). Newton's classical mechanics describes an orderly world. Systems operate via clear-cut cause-and-effect mechanisms, and there is inevitable determinism; given enough information one can predict future events. This traditional view of the natural world has proven to be incomplete. Scientists now believe that the greater part of nature follows the rules of deterministic chaos. Though determined by equations that are understood, natural systems such as the weather, population growth patterns, and heartbeat rhythms behave in ways that cannot be predicted. Thus, simple equations can create complex patterns. Variations are partly due to "the butterfly effect," a term that means dynamic systems have a sensitive dependence on initial conditions; minor changes in input (for example, rounding .506127 to .506, a change of .1 percent) can cause major variations in outcome. The behavior of these systems cannot be strictly predicted; however, the equations that govern such systems follow universal mathematical laws. Gleick asserts that one of the most important aspects of deterministic chaos is that "the laws of complexity hold universally, caring not at all for the details of a system's constituent atoms" (304). Perhaps this paradox of being highly sensitive to local conditions while also participating in a universal pattern was part of the paradigm's metaphoric appeal to Stoppard.

Deterministic chaos deals with systems of unpredictable determinism, but the uncertainty does not result in pure randomness but rather in complex patterns. Traditionally, scientists expected dynamic systems to settle into stable, predictable behavior. However, deterministic chaos has shown that as many of these systems respond to variations in input, the graph of their behavior "bifurcates and creates an oscillation pattern between two 'steady states.' If increases continue, the bifurcated patterns would themselves bifurcate, and then the four would also bifurcate, *ad infinitum,* into a condition of true chaotic randomness" (Demastes, "Re-Inspecting" 246). Surprisingly, within these random states, windows of order reappear: "A new steady state develop[s], a self-similar though downscaled replication of the primary pattern; and within these replications, even further downscaled replications reoccur, again and again. There is order in chaos—an unpredictable order, but a determined order nonetheless and not merely random behavior" (246). As will be discussed, this bifurcation process influenced Stoppard's construction of the script.

Deterministic chaos is only part of the science that informs *Arcadia.* Other concepts include entropy and the Second Law of Thermodynamics, the irreversibility of time, iterated algorithms, fractals, scaling, and population biology. Entropy is a measure of the randomness or disorder of a system. The law of increase of entropy states that as a whole the universe is evolving from order to disorder. This relates to the Second Law of Thermodynamics, which states that heat can flow in only one direction, from hotter to colder. Since these equations, unlike Newton's laws of motion, do not go backward and forward, there is an "arrow of time" that points toward the eventual "heat death" of the universe. (Iteration, fractals, and scaling will be discussed in relation to specific features of *Arcadia.*) Overall, Stoppard covers a shift in the scientific paradigm from the mechanical, predictable universe described by Newton to the unpredictable determinism described by deterministic chaos. Significantly, Stoppard accents those aspects of deterministic chaos that show there is underlying order to seemingly random events.

Textual History and Construction

While Stoppard saw deterministic chaos as a rich metaphor, he felt it was "too abstract and unmanageable" on its own (Hickling 15). The other starting point of *Arcadia* came a couple of years after reading Gleick's book, when Stoppard was "thinking about Romanticism and Classicism as opposites in style, taste, temperament, art. . . . Retrospectively one looks at poetry, painting, gardening and speaks of classical periods and the romantic revolution . . . [and then] one starts dividing people up into classical temperaments and romantic temperaments—and I suppose it's not that far from *Hapgood* in a way. The romantic temperament has a classical person wildly signalling, and vice versa" (Gussow, *Conversations,* 90). Stoppard admits that the final text "says very [little] about these two sides of the human personality or temperament. I don't think it's in the play. It's by no means in the foreground. And yet, it's firing all around the target, making a pattern around the target" (91). The yoking of the differences between classicism and romanticism (as manifested in the evolution of landscape gardening) to deterministic chaos provided a recognizable parallel to describe the shifting scientific paradigm. Once Stoppard latched on to the idea of having scholars investigating past events, the form of *Arcadia* came into shape, and once settled upon, varied very little.

Deterministic chaos is grounded in nonlinear mathematics, and appropriately Stoppard constructs *Arcadia* in a nonlinear manner—the scenes alternate between the early 1800s and the present. Furthermore, the very structure of the play not only embodies the spirit of deterministic chaos, but also, as Stoppard says, "mimics the way an algorithm goes through bifurcations into chaos" (Fleming, "A Talk," 24). He adds: "The play bifurcates two or three times and then goes into the last section which is all mixed up. So, it's very chaos structured" (Demastes and Kelly 5). The nonlinear bouncing between time periods suggests disorder, yet lurking underneath is a tightly ordered dramatic structure. There are seven scenes—three in the past, three in the present, and the chaotic seventh scene where the periods mix. Within that scene there are six subscenes: two of only the past, two of only the present, and two where the different periods share the stage. Thus, as with chaotic systems in the physical world, there are a series of bifurcations and even within the chaotic region there are pockets of order; and so overall, this nonlinear play exhibits a fine, underlying structure.

Benoit Mandelbrot coined the term *fractal,* which from the Latin means "irregular." However, in practice, fractal, above all, means self-similar. Self-similarity is symmetry across scale. It implies recursion, pattern inside of pattern—a trait typical of Stoppard's dramaturgy. As science writer Roger Highfield states, fractal geometry describes the "messy bits and behavior of the real world. Clouds, lungs, mountain ranges, and cauliflowers are fractal objects, ones that reveal similar shapes and motifs at every level of magnification" (13). The self-similarity of fractal construction is abundant in nature and abundant in both the text and in the original London and New York stagings of *Arcadia.* Self-similarity of dialogue, situations, characters, props, costumes, and musical accompaniment are all evident; indeed, it is the aspect of deterministic chaos that Stoppard and the production use most frequently. For example, in Mark Thompson's design the large pattern on the floor appears, in smaller scale, on the backs of the chairs. At one point the present-day characters dress in Regency clothes, creating a costuming similarity to the characters from the past. In one of the most complete forms of self-similarity the same actor plays Gus and Augustus and ends the play wearing the same costume for both characters, as the context reveals which the audience is seeing. All this similarity across scales is significant because in dynamic systems it signifies that some quality is preserved while everything else changes: "some regularity lay beneath the turbulent surface" (Gleick 172). Metaphorically, it suggests that Stoppard is more interested in looking at, or looking for, similarities beneath external differences.

Thematic Analysis of Text and Production

In London, *Arcadia* was performed on a proscenium arch stage, while in New York it was a modified thrust. The downstage apron in New York necessitated some minor variations in blocking, but otherwise the productions were staged and designed the same, in accordance with Stoppard's stage directions for a stately country house whose elegance comes from its large architectural scale.[2] Upon entering the auditorium, the first thing the spectator sees is a front curtain that is based on Nicolas Poussin's classical painting *Spring,* an image of Edenic nature, complete with blue sky, lush green rolling hills, and Eve offering the apple to Adam. It is a pictorial arcadia that also suggests some of the motifs of the play: the conflict between classical and romantic gardening (and ordering of the world), how to describe most accurately the natural world, and the havoc caused by sexual attraction and temptation.

Before introducing the scientific and artistic themes, Stoppard begins with a comical exchange that embodies the human dimensions of the play's intellectual conceits. The precocious thirteen-year-old pupil, Thomasina, queries her twenty-two-year-old Byronesque tutor, Septimus, on the meaning of "carnal embrace" and is told: "Carnal embrace is the practice of throwing one's arms around a side of beef" (1). Thomasina eventually sees through this punning evasion and wants to know "the true meaning of things" (3), and thus is told: "Carnal embrace is sexual congress, which is the insertion of the male genital organ into the female genital organ for purposes of procreation and pleasure" (3). This clinical definition removes the mystery and intimacy of human sexual relations, and in the process seems incomplete. It is a motif that runs throughout the play. Whenever the characters try to fix and understand reality—whether it be through the use of language, the use of narratives designed to control and explain their experiences, or the study of science—they discover that life is not so easily confined and defined.

Science has long been a major way through which humans have sought to understand the world around them, and in the opening scene Thomasina is studying Newtonian science and Euclidean geometry, modes of thought that see the world as linear, stable, and ordered. In human terms, Newton and his classical laws of motion seem to leave no room for unpredictability and free will. In the first scene, Thomasina explains the ramifications of what would happen if everything behaved according to Newton's laws of motion. She says: "If you could stop every atom in its position and direction, and if your mind could comprehend all the actions thus suspended, then if you were really, *really* good at algebra you could write the formula for all the future; and although nobody can be so clever to do it, the formula must exist just as if one could" (5). Newton's laws suggest a deterministic, mechanical universe; it is one of strict order, regularity, and predictability. But Thomasina has already begun to intuit that this view of the universe is incomplete. She tells her tutor: "When you stir your rice pudding, Septimus, the spoonful of jam spreads itself round making red trails like the picture of a meteor in my astronomical atlas. But if you stir backward, the jam will not come together again" (4–5). Her seemingly simple observation points to the Second Law of Thermodynamics, which is a statement about the increasing disorder in the universe.

Since comprehending scientific concepts can sometimes be difficult, Stoppard aids his audience's understanding by paralleling the shift in the scientific paradigm to the analogous transition from classicism to romanticism—that is, classicism metaphorically corresponds to Newtonian science and Romanticism to deterministic chaos. In the play, these artistic movements are embodied in the landscape gardening of the Croom family home. Until the mid-1700s the garden adhered to the classical aesthetics of symmetry, geometrical regularity, and formal simplicity; however, this arrangement was replaced by Capability Brown's asymmetrical style of "natural disorder." Lady Croom describes her garden as having "trees companionably grouped at intervals that show them to their advantage" and "meadows on which the right amount of sheep are tastefully arranged—in short it is nature as God intended" (12). But in the first scene the audience learns that the garden is undergoing yet another alteration as landscape gardener Mr. Noakes is transforming it into a Romantic wilderness, the "picturesque," Gothic style of untamed nature, or what its proponents felt was "nature as it was." Noakes is referred to as "The Emperor of Irregularity" (85) because one of his chief stylistic principles is "irregularity" (12). These gardens, like the scientific paradigms they parallel, offer competing views for what is the "true" nature of the world. Just as the garden moves from regulated order to irregularity, so too has science's view of how nature constructs itself.

In the play, the idea of irregularity as the organizing principle of nature is first laid out in scene 3 when Thomasina declares that she has discovered a "New Geometry of Irregular Forms" (43), a statement that the forms of nature can be written in numbers. Thomasina's words are more metaphoric—the iteration of her equation could produce a picture of a leaf, but not a leaf itself. In the play, Valentine explains iteration and its significance. Iteration is a mathematical process that was invented in the early 1970s, and it is a feedback loop in which one takes the solution of an equation and plugs it back into the equation and solves it again, and then continually repeats the process. Till the twentieth century mathematics was classical, but Valentine explains: "Then maths left the real world behind, just like modern art. Nature was classical, maths was suddenly Picassos. But now nature is having the last laugh. The freaky stuff is the mathematics of the natural world" (45). Deterministic chaos has shown that irregularity is one of the building blocks of life.

Linking the two periods together is the fact that while Thomasina's theory prefigures fractal geometry, Valentine is actually using this iteration process in his study of population changes in biology. He proceeds to explain one of the fascinating features of these algorithms:

> The details change, you can't keep tabs on everything, it's not nature in a box. But it isn't necessary to know the details. When they are all put together it turns out the population is obeying a mathematical rule. . . . It's not about the behavior of fish. It's about the behavior of numbers. The thing works for any phenomenon which eats its own numbers— measles epidemics, rainfall averages, cotton prices, it's a natural phenomenon in itself. Spooky. (45–46)

Here, one sees the paradoxical quality of deterministic chaos—individual dynamic systems are highly sensitive to local conditions, yet they also participate in a universal pattern.

The metaphoric implications of Stoppard's use of the new science are telling. In an article on chaos theory and theatre, Michael Vanden Heuvel argues that some contemporary theorists and artists looking at quantum physics and deterministic chaos, as well as poststructuralist theories of language, have latched on to the idea that since prediction has given way to probability, the defining features of the world are indeterminacy, uncertainty, disorder, and chance (255). In contrast, while acknowledging unpredictability, Stoppard focuses on what is stable and ordered. Science writers Briggs and Peat discuss chaos theory by using a metaphor of a turbulent mirror with one side of the mirror being concerned with the move from order to chaos and the other side the move from chaos to order. In crafting *Arcadia*, Stoppard has emphasized the ideas that correspond to the mirror itself and to those aspects that mark the move from chaos to order. In short, Stoppard stresses the process of recognizing the order within disorder, seeing the fine structure hidden within the seemingly random.

Looking closer at the play, one sees that between the poles of universal laws and indeterminacy, science is offering a new way of looking at the world. In a sublimely passionate speech, Valentine explains:

> The unpredictable and the predetermined unfold together to make everything the way it is. It's how nature creates itself on every scale, the snowflake and the snowstorm. It makes me so happy. To be at the beginning again, knowing almost nothing. Relativity and quantum looked as if they were going to wipe out the whole problem between them. A theory of everything. But they only explained the very big and the very small. The universe, the elementary particles. The ordinary-sized stuff which is our lives, the things people write poetry about . . . these things are full of mystery, as mysterious to us as the heavens were to the Greeks. We're better at predicting events at the edge of the galaxy or inside the nucleus of an atom than whether it'll rain on auntie's garden party three Sundays from now. Because the problem turns out to be different . . . [and] the smallest variation blows prediction apart. . . . The future is disorder. A door like this has cracked open five or six times since we got up on our hind legs. It's the best possible time to be alive, when almost everything you thought you knew is wrong. (47–48)

Hannah challenges him: "The weather is fairly predictable in the Sahara" (48). Valentine responds: "The scale is different but the graph goes up and down the same way. Six thousand years in the Sahara looks like six months in Manchester, I bet you" (48). Two very different phenomena are shown to have an underlying similarity when viewed from an alternative perspective. So perspective does play a role in understanding the world, but order amongst chaos, similarities amidst differences, those are the realms that Stoppard accents in this play.

Characteristic of the both/and nature of deterministic chaos, Stoppard's emphasis on those regions of order and stability is balanced with a healthy celebration of uncertainty. Valentine is genuinely pleased that the old scientific foundation has crumbled and that there are still many mysteries that may never be solved. Indeed, the play as a whole acknowledges the difficulty of truly knowing anything. Hannah offers the sobering perspective: "It can't prove to be true, it can only prove not to be false yet" (74). Hannah proceeds to discuss the fundamental humanness of the search for knowledge:

> It's *all* trivial—your grouse, my hermit, Bernard's Byron. Comparing what we're looking for misses the point. *It's wanting to know that makes us matter.* Otherwise we're going out the way we came in. That's why you can't believe in the afterlife, Valentine. Believe in the after, by all means, but not the life. Believe in God, the soul, the spirit, the infinite, believe in angels if you like, but not in the great celestial get-together for an exchange of views. If the answers are in the back of the book I can wait, but what a drag. Better to struggle on knowing that failure is final. (75–76; second emphasis added)

In its depiction of people striving to understand the past and to find the keys that unlock the mysteries of nature, *Arcadia* is a celebration of the human struggle to obtain knowledge, with meaning arriving as much out of the process as the product. Also, since Hannah ultimately succeeds in proving her theory and since Thomasina's theories are shown to be accurate, the play is an affirmation that despite all the indeterminacy, people can use their intellect and intuition to gain knowledge. It suggests that science often works, that people can lead fulfilling lives, that even without all the answers, people can be happy, and that interacting with uncertainty is part of what makes human life worth living. Or to paraphrase the theory, life can be chaotic, but also stable, and within chaos there are windows of order.

In the play, Stoppard presents five main characters who are engaged in the quest for knowledge. Thomasina, Septimus, and Valentine are pursuing an understanding of the world from a scientific perspective, while Hannah and Bernard represent the arts and humanities. Characteristic of Stoppard's desire to complicate matters, the three "scientists" are the least Newtonian— Thomasina intuits the shortcomings of the Newtonian model; Septimus is perplexed and made skeptical by her theorems; and Valentine is a working chaotician. In contrast, Hannah and Bernard are more "scientific" in their outlook and approach, and through their respective attempts to interpret the past, Stoppard exhibits classical and romantic temperaments at work.

Hannah's dominant personality is "scientific" and classical in that she is a champion of the dispassionate intellect. Her research on the evolution of the gardens at the Coverly estate is aimed at documenting "the decline from thinking to feeling" (27). To her, the Romantic movement was a "sham," while the ordered, classical garden represented "paradise in the age of reason" (27). Hannah, who sees the world in binary terms, privileges thought over emotion, the classical temperament over the romantic. Disliking sentimentality and limiting her emotional expressions to instances of the gains and losses of the intellect, Hannah views emotion as an unwanted irregularity, a potential collapse into disorder. Ironically, to prove her idea that "The Age of Enlightenment [was] banished into the Romantic wilderness" (66), Hannah must rely on instinct and intuition. In short, she embodies Stoppard's notion that classical and romantic temperaments are not mutually exclusive, but rather coexist in people. Again, it is a matter of life being understood via a both/and paradigm as opposed to an either/or model.

In contrast to Hannah, Bernard embodies the romantic temperament in that he is more energetic, more passionate, and more prone to intuition. Dressed with a flamboyant flair (15), Bernard's character is one of style over substance. Characteristic of a romantic, Bernard takes a fervently intuitive approach to his research: "By which I mean a visceral belief in yourself. Gut instinct. The part of you which doesn't reason. The certainty for which there is no back-reference. Because time is reversed. Tock, tick goes the universe and then recovers itself, but it was enough, you were in there and you bloody *know*" (50). While the laws of the universe indicate that time can only go forward, Bernard's declaration suggests that human intuition is an aspect of life that is more mysterious, something that cannot be confined and explained by science. Typical of Stoppard's complicating of perspectives, Bernard's gut instinct is proved dead wrong, while Hannah is ultimately able to prove the validity of her instinctually derived thesis that Septimus was the hermit of Sidley Park. Thus, human intuition is neither completely valorized nor debunked.

While Bernard's dominant temperament is romantic, he, too, exhibits traits of the scientific and classical personality. When he tries to reconstruct the story of Byron's stay at Sidley Park, he thinks in terms of strict linearity and order. He accumulates data from a variety of sources, and then tries to make it fit his preordained cause-and-effect pattern. He makes the mistake of starting with a desired conclusion, and only seeks information that will make his line of reasoning sufficiently logical. Bernard's unerring faith in his theory makes the lack of convincing evidence immaterial; he is determined to prove his theory whether it is true or not. While Bernard's arrogance and lust for fame are obvious character flaws, his more subtle shortcoming is that his sought-after explanation is based on a Newtonian paradigm of complete order; that is, it ignores the complexity and contradiction of real life, such as the fact that Byron took Septimus's book and that one of Byron's letters was burned. Instead of trying to understand how the events actually occurred, he has created an idealized account. His Newtonian narrative is limited, and ultimately is proved false because Bernard has allowed himself to see only what he has wanted to see. Hannah summarizes the problems of Bernard's approach to scholarship: "You've left out everything which doesn't fit. . . . You're arrogant, greedy, and reckless. You've gone from a glint in your eye to a sure thing in a hop, skip, and a jump" (59).

While Bernard is the object of Stoppard's satire on the excesses of academic ambition and competition, he is also an advocate for another type of knowledge—the understanding that comes from the appreciation of art. Possessing a romantic temperament, Bernard provides a passionate defense of art, as he argues that art and artistic genius are mysterious realms of life that cannot be quantified in scientific terms: "Parameters! You can't stick Byron's head in your laptop! Genius isn't like your average grouse" (60). Soon Valentine and Bernard argue over what information is and is not worth knowing:

VALENTINE: But it doesn't *matter*. Personalities. What matters is the calculus. Scientific progress. Knowledge. . . .

BERNARD: Why does scientific progress matter more than personalities? . . . Don't confuse progress with perfectibility. A great poet is always timely. A great philosopher is an urgent need. There's no rush for Isaac Newton. We were quite happy with Aristotle's cosmos. Personally I preferred it. Fifty-five crystal spheres geared to God's crankshaft is my idea of a satisfying universe. I can't think of anything more trivial than the speed of light. Quarks, quasars—big bangs, black holes—who gives a shit? How did you people con us out of all that status? All that money? (61)

Stoppard notes that Bernard's polemic against science is "a kind of performance art" that "does not speak for me" (Hawkes 268).

The exchange does, however, greatly define the characters, and it articulates different approaches and conceptions of knowledge. Valentine takes a traditional scientific approach in valuing knowledge itself, suggesting that knowledge can be separated from the context that produces it, a view antithetical to most contemporary literary theory.[3] Bernard, on the other hand, offers a romantic valorization of art and philosophy. In part, Bernard suggests that great art is timeless, a view that coincides with his desire for a mechanistic universe; that is the laws of the Newtonian universe are insensitive to time. The close of Bernard's speech points to the commercialization of knowledge, a theme that flickers in the background of *Arcadia*. Bernard's paradoxical nature is that he wants to prove his theory of Byron not because of any particular literary value it offers, but rather because of the fame and fortune it will bring him.[4] In contrast to this commercialization of knowledge, Bernard follows up his diatribe by saying: "If knowledge isn't self-knowledge it isn't doing much, mate. Is the universe expanding? Is it contracting? . . . Leave me out. I can expand my universe without you. [Quotes lines of Byron's poetry]" (61). Here, Bernard takes a knowledge-for-knowledge's-sake approach as he stresses how knowledge, particularly that gained from art, has value for its abstract capacity for enriching human life on a personal, nonutilitarian basis.

Bifurcating into Chaos: The Final Scene

In the final scene, which occupies a quarter of the play's three-hour running time and where the ideas of the play are manifested in human terms, the richness and complexity of Stoppard's characters, themes, and dramatic structure coalesce. At the top of this "chaotic" scene, Stoppard employs self-similarity in costuming and dialogue as the contemporary characters are dressed in Regency clothes, and there is a textual echo from the first scene as once again a teenage woman asks a twenty-something male scholar: "Do you think I'm the first person to think of this?" (73). The question again revolves around a deterministic universe, with Chloë positing that the world tries to be deterministic but "the only thing going wrong is people fancying people who aren't supposed to be in that part of the plan" (73). Valentine adds: "Ah. The attraction Newton left out. All the way back to the apple in the garden" (74). The double meaning is later extended when Thomasina explains that Newton's determinism is indeed disproved by "the action of bodies in heat" (84). Lady Croom makes clear the sexual entendre ("[Mrs.] Chater would overthrow the Newtonian system in a weekend" [84]), while Thomasina explains the unidirectional flow of the Second Law of Thermodynamics that undermines the Newtonian worldview.[5] Indeed, the joke that sexual attraction is "the attraction Newton left out" is one of Stoppard's metaphoric conceits for the difficulty in mapping out individual destinies. Newton's laws work very well when they operate in a vacuum—it is the friction of the real world that destroys predictability. Similarly, the multiple variables and contingencies of reality, including love and the heat of sexual passion, preclude predictable, deterministic lives. The richness of deterministic chaos as a metaphor for human life and interactions is its paradoxical quality. There is the sense of determinism, of the inability to control with whom one falls in love, yet the play also shows free will in action as Septimus decides not to consummate the relationship with his pupil. In *Arcadia* the characters experience both determinism and unpredictability, both fate and free will.

As the scene develops, the plot bifurcations move into a chaotic region as the characters from the different periods begin to share the stage. Again Stoppard theatrically utilizes self-similarity as, "doubled by time," Septimus and Hannah turn the pages of Thomasina's iteration (78). In Trevor Nunn's staging, Hannah is positioned over Septimus's shoulder, and they simultaneously turn one page, then another, then back one, and forward one. This temporal recursion is not only aesthetically pleasing but also again suggests the notion that despite external differences some quality is preserved. While Hannah hopes that the science indicates that "the world is saved after all," Valentine clarifies: "No, it is still doomed. But if this is how it started, perhaps it's how the next one will come" (78). Similarly, in the second chaotic region, after the second "doubled-by-time" moment where Septimus and Valentine comprehend Thomasina's diagram for heat exchange, Thomasina "cheerfully" confirms Septimus's conclusion that "we are all doomed" (93). In both instances the characters do not respond pessimistically, but rather remain accepting and hopeful.

The close of the first chaotic region, before it bifurcates back into ordered regions of past and present, is a less obvious moment of interaction of the two periods: at the same time that Lady Croom speaks about the Chaters and the dahlia, the information that disproves Bernard's theory, Hannah silently reads about it. Thus, from a region of disorder comes a new sense of order; Bernard gets his comeuppance. As he colorfully puts it, he is "fucked by a dahlia!" (88),[6] and Hannah gleefully sees to it that the lasting result of Bernard's appearance on "The Breakfast Hour" is egg on his face. The reverse-angle view is that Bernard's life goes from ordered to disordered. His attempt to craft a new high-profile existence has gone dreadfully awry. Again, there is rich interaction between order and disorder, with the two seeming opposites working in conjunction to make things the way they are.

As the last purely ordered region prepares to give way to the final bifurcation into chaos, the play moves toward its intellectual and emotional climax. A full moon glistening through the French windows, candlelight, and the soft strains of a piano create a richly romantic mood as Thomasina, in a soft white nightdress, comes for her late-night waltz lesson. Nunn's staging makes the subtextual sexual tension evident as Thomasina drapes herself over Septimus's chair and shoulder, nestling her face into his hair. He absent-mindedly strokes her hand as he continues reading her essay on thermodynamics. But then his sense of decorum surfaces, and he makes Thomasina sit at the other end of the table while they wait for music to which they can waltz.

The move to chaos is then marked theatrically as the piano music gives way to more modern party music, and the pulsing, red flashes of fireworks appear through the windows. Amidst this romantic setting, there is the second "doubled-by-time" moment, and even though the "universe must cease and grow cold" (93), the characters remain happy, even celebratory—Valentine for the joy of scientific, intellectual understanding, and Thomasina for human contact, embodied in the ensuing waltz and kisses she shares with Septimus. Furthermore, the scientific and the human dimensions of the play are linked in the staging of the waltz. A waltz is emblematic of deterministic chaos in that there is a prescribed series of steps, but that "deterministic equation" can still yield any number of patterns. In the London production, Thomasina and Septimus's waltz takes them on a few different paths through the room, at one point even dancing between Bernard and Chloë, who are in the midst of their hasty and unplanned farewell—one scholar–young female couple is in sync, one out of sync; one coupling is based solely on sex, while the other mixes sexual and intellectual attraction, but ultimately remains a platonic love as they never consummate their affection. Indeed,

Thomasina invites Septimus to spend the night with her, but his final answer, "I will not" (96), is indicative of free will rather than strict determinism. However, the deterministic side of life is also acknowledged in this moment, for it is here that Septimus lights Thomasina's candle, with the audience knowing that her fate is to die that very night in a fire. Her intuition about the heat death of the universe becomes painfully and poignantly personal. The dance of life ends in mortality, but it is still a happy dance.

While Thomasina and Septimus enjoy their final waltz, Gus, identical in appearance to Augustus, enters. This use of self-similar costuming disrupts customary markers of order as for a moment there is no telling which character is on stage. But Gus soon proves to be a bearer of order, for he provides Hannah with the evidence she needs to prove her theory, a theory she instinctively knew was correct, but for which she now has the logical proof. In gratitude for this intellectual assistance, Hannah shows her emotional, human side by agreeing to dance with Gus. Their waltz is clumsy, and nowhere near as fluid as the other dancing couple's, but as music from both periods is heard, the moonlight and candlelight are joined by a lush, purplish glow that bathes the scene. It is a beautifully moving finale as these "bodies in motion" celebrate both the human intellect and the human heart. By the end of the play all the major dichotomies—classical/romantic, Newtonian/chaotic, order/disorder, intuition/logic, heart/mind—have interpenetrated each other, showing that the coexistence and interdependency of these seeming opposites is fundamental to the way the world, life, and humans operate.

Unraveling Another Mystery

Physicist Stephen Hawking closes *A Brief History of Time* by arguing that if humans discover a "unified theory" that describes the workings of the universe, "it would be the ultimate triumph of human reason—for then we would know the mind of God" (175). When I interviewed Stoppard, he acknowledged that Septimus echoes Hawking when he says: "I inspire by reverence for learning and the exaltation of knowledge whereby man may approach God" (80). Explorations of physics (*Hapgood*) and metaphysics (*Jumpers*) have formed central blocks of Stoppard's canon and personal life. Though *Arcadia* derives from Stoppard's fascination with scientific theories, he remains "skeptical of science as the ultimate truth about the world" (Nathan 262). For Stoppard, life is more mysterious, and indeed *Arcadia* is a play filled with mysteries: Did Byron kill Chater? Who was the hermit of

Sidley Park? Who has slept with whom? Does the universe obey the laws of Newton? of entropy? of both? Most of the play's mysteries are solved, but one of the great unanswered mysteries is why doesn't Gus speak? Who is this "natural genius" with psychic-like abilities, but who never utters a word? When I posed this question to Stoppard, he replied:

> [Gus] is about as far as I'm prepared to go into metaphysics, I suppose. By which I mean, intellectually or temperamentally—I don't know which it is—I don't believe in a mechanistic universe. I don't think that's a complete description. So Gus represents, I suppose, my feeling that there is something more mysterious than that. And we don't know how it works, and there's no point in my explaining Gus because that would say I do know how it works. But in the first place, I don't know how it works; in the second place, I don't think anybody does know; in the third place, I don't think it's possible to know; in the fourth place, I don't think it's necessary to know. It's that kind of feeling. (Fleming, "A Talk," 23)[7]

In *Jumpers* Stoppard's moral philosopher declares that "there is more in [humans] than meets the microscope" (68), and Gus seems to be an embodiment of that metaphysical belief—of the "mystery in the clockwork" (72). Knowledge without certainty and knowledge based on intuition are motifs that recur in Stoppard's work, and as a whole, *Arcadia* helps dramatize Stoppard's worldview of life's being comprised of a complex, dynamic interaction of randomness, determinism, and metaphysics.

Indian Ink

JUST AS *Arcadia's* ALTERATION OF PAST AND PRESENT DIS-
rupts a linear narrative, so too does the appearance of *Indian Ink* in the Stop-
pard canon of stage plays. Produced in 1995, *Indian Ink* is a stage version of
Stoppard's 1991 radio play *In the Native State,* and thus the essence of *Indian
Ink* predates *Arcadia.* As such, it is necessary to delve back into the roots of
In the Native State to ascertain the inspiration and origin of the stage play.

In the late 1980s, Stoppard was commissioned by friend John Tydeman,
then head of BBC radio drama, to write a play. Stoppard started working on
the radio play with its genesis being two separate ideas: "I [wanted to] write
a conversation between a poet and a painter. While the poet was having her
portrait painted, she would be writing a poem about having her portrait
painted. There would be this circular situation. That's all I had. And not necessarily in India. . . . I think simultaneously I'd been thinking about a play
about the Raj, or at least India during the time of the British Empire. Things
coalesced" (Gussow, *Conversations,* 120).[1] Stoppard intended the script to
be done by 1990, before he delved into full-time work on directing the film
version of *Rosencrantz and Guildenstern Are Dead,* but the process was not
so simple: "It began as odd pages, dialogue and stuff. I kept trying to find
what play they belonged to. I thought I was going to write a play about [the
poet-painter circle]. Then I found the idea of her poetry so perversely enjoy-

able I went on writing her poetry for far longer than you'd believe" (Reynolds 249).[2]

On the other side was Stoppard's interest in "writing about the ethics of empire" (Allen 240), and so he indulged in extensive reading on India.[3] After completing *In the Native State,* Stoppard acknowledged that he had not sufficiently addressed the issue of the ethos of empire: "I was rather keen not to write a play which was a pair of conflicting polemics or editorials. That's really the problem with writing in any way about historical, political, social movements, oppositions. . . . I don't feel as if I've done it. I think it's terribly hard to balance. In a way, perhaps, the play now isn't actually *enough* about that subject, the subject which really provoked the play in the first place" (243). While Stoppard initially thought that *Indian Ink* might go a little further in exploring colonialism, he has concluded that at its core, "It's much more of an intimate play than a polemical play" (Gussow, *Conversations,* 102).

Instead of engaging the ethical issues of British colonialism, Stoppard, in a rare twist, acknowledges getting "more wrapped up in my characters than in previous plays, particularly Mrs. Swan and her feelings for her elder sister" (Delaney, *Conversation,* 239). At this point in Stoppard's career, *In the Native State* and *Indian Ink* were his most character-driven plays, with a more accurate assessment being that Stoppard got attracted to the character of Flora Crewe. Stoppard dedicated *In the Native State* to Felicity Kendal, and some critics take that dedication even further: "The role of Flora—sharp-witted, strong-willed, sympathetic and doomed—is Stoppard's gift to Felicity Kendal. Perfectly tailored to her unique blend of chipmunk charm and inner steel, it's almost a labour of love" (N. Smith 253). While there are multiple plot lines and diverse thematic strands, most of the play, in one way or another, relates to, or is influenced by, the character of Flora Crewe.

Textual History

In the Native State was written in fragments, different sections at different times, with there being more exploration than the usual strong sense of outline. In August 1988 he wrote scenes between an English poet and an Indian painter. In January 1989 he worked on Flora's poetry, but soon his attention was diverted to revising *Hapgood* for its Los Angeles debut. Stoppard was still stuck on the specific content of the play when he turned to directing the film version of *Rosencrantz and Guildenstern,* but once that was finished Stoppard "got going in September and delivered it in October [1990]" (Reynolds 249).

Broadcast in April 1991, the play received wide acclaim, winning the Giles Cooper Award and Sony Award. Exemplifying the critical reaction, in his review of *Arcadia,* Michael Coveney hailed *Native State* as possibly Stoppard's "finest work to date."

Native State takes place in India in 1930 and in present-day London. The past scenes focus on Flora Crewe, an adventurous, sensual poet who, due to tuberculosis, has left high-society London (and her numerous affairs with major artists of the 1920s) to travel to India, where she can go on the lecture circuit as she tries to regain her health. During her stay in Jummapur (a native state, thus technically ruled by Indian, not British, officials), she befriends Nirad Das, a portrait painter. These past scenes alternate with present-day scenes in London between Flora's sister, Mrs. Swan, and Das's son, Anish. Swan had lived in India much of her life and has undergone a radical (and unexplained) political transformation from an ardent Marxist in her youth to a stout British nationalist who believes India was much better off under British rule. Anish is an Indian who has relocated to London and who challenges Swan's view of history. Gradually, the audience learns that Das painted two portraits of Flora: a European-style oil painting of her seated and clothed, and a nude watercolor that uses traditional Indian techniques and aesthetics. Meanwhile, Flora also has social encounters with Captain Durance, a British army officer, and the ruling Indian Rajah as well as a one-night romance with Das. In many scenes Flora's letters are accompanied by the detailed footnotes of an American academic, Eldon Pike, the object of Stoppard's satire on the excesses of academic research and writing. Overall, the emphasis of the play is more on atmosphere and character than on plot.

Since plots and play ideas come slowly to Stoppard, it is not surprising that he chose to adapt *In the Native State.* He explains: "I had no thought about writing a stage play about Flora Crewe until somewhat later. People kept telling me the radio play was good and I should do something more with it" (Gussow, *Conversations,* 129). Stoppard thought he would either turn it into a small film or else start over and "write a stage play about the same people" (Goreau 259). The stage adaptation began in late 1992, the period when Stoppard was waiting for *Arcadia* rehearsals to begin. Initially Stoppard played with the idea of starting the play in four different time periods, but abandoned it and stayed faithful to the radio play for his first draft completed in January 1993.[4] A second draft followed in May 1993, and sometime later that year it was decided that *Indian Ink* would not be produced until early 1995, with it slated for the National Theatre's black box space, the Cottesloe. Thus, Stoppard set aside the text while he worked on a film script (*Hopeful Monsters*). Then after the huge success of *Arcadia,* Stoppard and Wood decided to bypass the National and take the play straight to the West End, and so he completed another draft in September 1994. Rehearsals were set to begin in December, and so while in New York, tending to the new *Hapgood* text and production, Stoppard revised the text yet again. He noted: "A lot of the time I'm writing in a kind of harassed, interrupted way. I came to the conclusion the other day that the information is being fed in the wrong order in the second act of *Indian Ink*. I came back from *Hapgood* and looked at it for an hour and a half before I fell asleep. It's all done on the space of an hour here, an hour there. That's not how to do these things" (Gussow, *Conversations,* 106). This December 1994 rehearsal text differs significantly from the published text, which itself is different from the produced text as well as from the revised published edition.[5] Thus, as with all of Stoppard's major plays, there is no definitive text for *Indian Ink*.

Indian Ink uses the same plot and most of the dialogue of *In the Native State,* but changes the order of scenes and adds material. The biggest alteration came from Stoppard's desire to integrate Pike into the play as a full character rather than the disembodied voice he is in the original. Thus, as part of the new opening section the audience sees how Pike is dependent on Mrs. Swan for many of his footnotes, and more importantly, throughout the play the audience follows Pike on his journey to construct Flora's biography. The larger presence of Pike is theatrically used to create a fuller integration of the two time periods. In *Arcadia* the two time periods do not dovetail until the final scene, but in *Indian Ink* within minutes the characters share the stage and sometimes they almost seem to interact.[6] Since Pike's journey takes him to modern-day India, there is the theatrical overlap of place in two different time periods. Overall the weaving together of eras is tight and aesthetically effective. On the downside, the shallowness of Pike's character adds easy laughs but does not significantly expand the play's themes.

A significant stylistic change is that both past and present-day plots are told in a linear fashion. The opening section of Flora's arrival in India, her lecture, and meeting Das were part of scene nine in the radio play; the alteration makes the play easier for audiences to follow, but the result of all these changes is that "a near-perfect radio play [has been] transformed into a so-so stage play that lacks the delicacy and mysteriousness of the original" (Edwardes 253). *In the Native State* is like a poem, melding images rather than telling a linear narrative. Felicity Kendal aptly notes that *Native State* "is to do with language rather than action and it lends itself well to radio; it isn't the story that's the thing, it's the spider's web of ideas and circumstances, written very carefully with a lot of loops that loop into something else" (Sarler 22).

One of the reasons the stage play suffers is that Stoppard crafts *Indian Ink* more as a story, yet the narrative line is thin. The use of many intimate, two-person scenes allows for some heartfelt emotional moments, but overall the play lacks the intellectual stimulation and thematic depth characteristic of Stoppard's major plays. The playwright also notes that the play is different from his other work in "its benevolence. . . . There are no villains in it. It's a very cosy play in many ways. I think it's worryingly cosy sometimes. But I really enjoy its lack of radical fierceness. It has its checks and balances. There's no ranting or storming around; there are no long monologues" (Gussow, *Conversations,* 124–25). Indeed, at moments of potential conflict, Stoppard often adds speaker tags such as "unangrily" or "cheerfully."

Coming after *In the Native State* (probably Stoppard's finest radio play) and *Arcadia* (arguably his best stage play), *Indian Ink* inevitably suffers in comparison.[7] Overall, *Indian Ink* is a well-written, albeit lightweight, comedy tinged with sentiment, melancholy, nostalgia, and likable characters. Given a lavish production by Peter Wood, it is an entertaining West End show with nice theatrical effects, but in terms of thematic substance, a less substantial piece of Stoppard's canon.[8]

Thematic Analysis of Text and Production

Indian Ink has three main plot lines: (1) Flora's activities in Jummapur (with those divided primarily among her interactions with the Indian painter Nirad Das, the British army officer Durance, and the Indian Rajah); (2) Mrs. Swan and Anish's conversations in the mid-1980s; and (3) Pike's role as both the supplier of footnotes and the pursuer of biographical material. Likewise, there are three main thematic issues: (1) divergent views surrounding the positive and negative effects of Britain's colonization of India; (2) the nature of cultural identity; and (3) the difficulties and fallibility involved in trying to reconstruct the past. The themes emerge from the characters' activities and interactions.

At the heart of the piece stands Flora Crewe, the free-spirited poet whose one week in Jummapur serves as the touchstone for many of the play's events. The play's opening establishes Flora as the physical representation of British cultural life, which in turn makes her the object of Indian admiration. Flora describes the parade-like atmosphere accompanying her lecture on London literary life: "I felt like a carnival float representing Empire—or depending how you look at it, the Subjugation of the Indian People, and of course you're right, darling, but I never saw anyone less subjugated than Mr. Coomaraswami" (4).[9] Later she describes the Indians at her lecture as being "like children with their faces jammed to the railings of an unattainable park" (6). One of those Indians fixated on British culture is Nirad Das. The seven interactions (six in the first act) between Flora and Das offer some of the most charged scenes of the play as there is a mix of sexual, cultural, and aesthetic tension between them.

In their first personal encounter, the start of the portrait-painting sequence, Flora's poetry establishes her as sensual, while her dialogue, filled with sexual innuendo, marks her as flirtatious. In contrast, Das, "played by Art Malik in my-goodness-gracious-me mode" (Paton),[10] is the shy admirer, enthralled with his subject, and her presence affects how he presents his own identity:

> FLORA: Mr. Das, I have been considering whether to ask you a delicate question, as between friends and artists.
> DAS: Oh, Miss Crewe, I am transported beyond my most fantastical hopes of our fellowship! This is a red-letter day without dispute!
> FLORA: If you are going to be so Indian I shan't ask it.
> DAS: But I cannot be less Indian than I am.
> FLORA: You could if you tried. . . . [W]hat I meant was for you to be *more* Indian, or at any rate *Indian,* not Englished-up. . . . I want you to be with me as you would be if *I* were Indian.
> DAS: An Indian Miss Crewe! Oh dear, that is a mental construction which has no counterpart in the material world.
> FLORA: So is a *unicorn,* but you can imagine it.
> DAS: You can imagine it but you cannot mount it.
> FLORA: Imagining was all I was asking in my case.
> DAS: (*Terribly discomfited*) Oh! Oh, my gracious!—I had no intention—I assure you—(12)

Das is thrilled by Flora's offer to treat him as an equal, but he overreacts in a manner that fulfills a stereotype of how the Indian minority culture might respond to being accepted into the dominant British culture. Furthermore, the dynamics whereby Das can aspire to and be "Englished-up" but where an "Indian Miss Crewe" is unfathomable (except perhaps as a parody) highlight the unequal power relationship in a matrix where a dominant culture rules over a minority culture.

Flora's desire for Das to be himself and to take pride in his Indian heritage persists as a tension. When Flora does not comment on the portrait, which she surreptitiously viewed, Das suffers a crisis of confidence in his artistic abilities. In part, he feels the need to be validated by an artist of the colonizing culture. An ideological discussion ensues:

> FLORA: I said nothing about your painting . . . because I thought you'd be an *Indian* artist. . . . You *are* an Indian artist, aren't you? Stick up for yourself. Why do you like everything English? . . . even painting in oils, that's not Indian. You're trying to paint me from my point of view instead of yours—what you *think* is my point of view. You *deserve* the bloody Empire! . . . .
>
> DAS: (*Passionately*) The bloody Empire finished off Indian painting! . . . Perhaps we have been robbed. (42–43)

Later in the scene Das comes to acknowledge and appreciate his own artistic and cultural roots: "I am Rajasthani. Our art is narrative art, stories from the [Indian] legends and romances" (45). The result of this recognition is that he paints a nude portrait of Flora that is indebted to the traditional style of Rajput miniatures. Flora calls it "the most beautiful thing" (73). Only then can Das confidently assert that he is Indian and an Indian artist. What the audience has previously learned is that the portrait is actually a mixture of Indian and European styles: "He hasn't made her Indian. . . . I mean he hasn't painted her flat. Everything else looks Indian" (58). It is the hybridization that marks it as a personal work of art, one that encapsulates Das's duality (an admirer of English art but also an Indian nationalist) as well as Flora's (an Englishwoman who thinks India should have the right to self-determination).

There is harmony between painter and subject, and there is *rasa*. One of the few moments when Flora feels that Das sounds Indian and not British is when he explains the aesthetic concept of *rasa*: "*Rasa* is juice. Its taste. Its essence. A painting must have its *rasa* . . . which is not *in* the painting exactly. *Rasa* is what you must feel when you see a painting, or hear music; it is the emotion which the artist must arouse in you" (29). There are nine *rasa,* each with its own mood, color, name, and god. The most important *rasa* in the play is "[t]he *rasa* of erotic love. . . . Its god is Vishnu, and its color is *shymana,* which is blue-black. . . . It is aroused by, for example, the moon, the scent of sandalwood, or being in an empty house" (29). One of the plot points of the play's literary detective story is with whom did Flora sleep during her week in Jummapur. While it is never unequivocally stated, both the text and the staging indicate that Flora's romance was with Das. On the night that he presents her the nude portrait, the traits that arouse the *rasa* of erotic love are all present: the house is empty (save for the lovers), Das's handkerchief smells of sandalwood, and Mark Thompson's beautifully, romantic lighting casts the suggestion of both moonlight and a blue-black wash that bathes Das and Flora.[11] After they recount all the traits of the *rasa* of erotic love, the stage goes to black, and the audience hears Flora's poem where "heat collects" and "slides like a tongue-tip down a Modigliani" until it is "lost in the mangroves" and "*nos cedamus amori* [we give way to love]" (74).[12] Based on other parts of the text, one realizes that this poem was written the next morning, presumably as a commentary on her night with Das.

The result of Das's social and sexual encounters with Flora is that he becomes more demonstratively nationalistic. The next morning Das was on the road near Flora's house (another clear textual indication of their affair), and Das saw Durance but showed him disrespect:

> DURANCE: I gave him a wave and he turned his back. I thought—
> "well that's a first!"
> FLORA: Oh! There's hope for him yet.
> DURANCE: They'll be throwing stones next. (76)

Indeed, as revealed in a previous scene, soon thereafter is when Das gets arrested for an Empire Day protest against the Rajah and British rule. The sexual encounter is probably not the main cause of his awakened rebellious spirit; rather his nationalistic feelings seem to be stirred by the same thing that fuels the sexual encounter—the return to his artistic and cultural roots. The beauty of the painting and the invocation of the Indian sense of *rasa* is what excites Flora. In turn her deep admiration of the beauty of his artistic expression aids his confidence and feeling of self-worth as an artist and as an Indian.

For Flora, one result of her relationship with Das is that she is rejuvenated artistically. But Mrs. Swan argues that the specific lover is immaterial: "Men were not really important to Flora. If they had been, they would have been fewer. She used them like batteries. When things went flat, she'd put in a new one" (79). While Das's Indianness may not have mattered to Flora sexually, her interactions with him affected her personally. Her closing letter reveals that the nude portrait assuaged some past regret: "Something good happened here which made me feel halfway better about Modi[gliani] and getting back to Paris too late [for a nude portrait]. That was a sin I'll carry to my grave, but perhaps my soul will stay behind as a smudge of paint on paper, as if I'd always been here, like Radha who was the most beautiful of the herdswomen, undressed for love in an empty house" (82). Flora's identification of herself with a figure from Indian legend helps bridge the cultures, reinforcing on a personal level the play's theme that a legacy of colonialism is a lasting link between British and Indian culture.

Flora's sense that art can leave a permanent mark on the world is one of the traits that unite Das and Flora and that weld the play's aesthetic and political concerns. Das notes that one day the British Empire will be "like the empire of Ozymandias! Entirely forgotten except in a poem by an English poet. You see how privileged we are, Miss Crewe. Only in art can empires cheat oblivion, because only the artist can say, 'look on my works, ye mighty, and despair!' There are Mughal paintings in London, in the Victoria and Albert Museum" (44). The enduring importance of art as personal and cultural expression, as a means of triumphing and imparting beauty to the world, runs as a subcurrent in this play whose pulse is tied to the encounter between a British poetess and an Indian painter.

In colonial affairs, Flora urges Das to take action: "If you don't start learning to *take* you'll never be shot of us. *Who whom.* Nothing else counts. . . . It's your country, and we've got it. Everything else is bosh" (44). However, in her encounters with the ruling British officials, she is more subdued, saving her critiques for her private correspondence to her sister Nell: "It beats me how we're getting away with it, darling, I wouldn't trust some of them to run the *Hackney* Empire" (50).

For the most part the attitudes and practices of the British colonizers are represented by Captain Durance, a man whose job is "to make sure [the Indians] don't get up to mischief" (23). He is presented as an affable, though somewhat stiff, officer who is infatuated with Flora, but who also has an insidious quality. When he first appears, though he's never met them, he greets Flora and Das by name. As the audience learns, one of Durance's main functions is surveillance and writing reports on everyone who is "politically sensitive" (77). While his tone of voice and general disposition are good-natured, there is an intrusive quality to Durance's behavior. For example, in Peter Wood's staging, Durance is already looking at Das's painting when he asks, "May one look?" (21). Likewise, just prior to proposing marriage, he fails to be honest with Flora about his work and the means he employs to obtain personal information. Consistently Durance expresses condescension or outright racial discrimination toward the Indians. Even the British-trained Indian civil servants are not allowed to come into the Club, the place where the British socialize. Durance expresses the possessive attitude of the colonizing officials when he speaks of "India proper, I mean *our* India" (51). And he proceeds: "We've pulled this country together. It's taken a couple of hundred years with a hiccup or two but the place now works" (55).

The paternalistic and racist attitudes of the colonizers who profit immensely from their exploitation of the country's resources stand unchallenged by Flora. When told about the racial segregation of the Club Flora's only response is "Oh" (52). When told that the mistake of the British in India was letting English women into the country, Flora's response is "Oh!" (55).[13] When Das informs her that the Resident knew Flora's personal reasons for being in India because "[a] letter from England to Mr. Coomaraswami would certainly be opened," Flora's response is again, "Oh" (72). The fact that the loquacious and strong-minded Flora, the one who urged Das to take back his country, is so meek and inarticulate when directly confronted with the arrogant, domineering, invasive attitude and practices of the British colonizers is disturbing—offering himself the opportunity to critique the ethos of empire, Stoppard has seemingly passed. In the play, the representatives of the British Empire open private mail, engage in extensive surveillance and documentation of personal and political activities, and suspend an organization that has viewpoints divergent from their own. All these actions are reminiscent of the political practices of the Eastern Bloc totalitarian countries Stoppard justly rebuked in his 1970s political plays; maybe it's because the transgressions are in the past or because the offending country is his beloved England, but now the actions are reported without moral outrage. Indeed, the British perpetrators of these restrictive practices are at best charming and at worst have a rigid sense of duty that stifles their personality, but nowhere, in Peter Wood's production, is there the sense of condemnation of the practices used to maintain the empire.

While Flora is the one the audience sees interacting with the Indians and the colonizers, the issue of colonialism is discussed in the mid-1980s conversations between Mrs. Swan (Flora's sister) and Anish (Das's son). Mrs. Swan exemplifies the way in which many people have assumptions about the impact of a culture on a person's behavior and identity.[14] Meeting Anish for the first time, she is surprised that he does not take sugar with his tea: "Oh. I thought you'd be more Indian" (13). These assumptions about simple activities extend to larger issues. While Mrs. Swan is softly sentimental and filled with warmhearted feelings for her sister, whenever the conversation comes to politics and Britain's colonization of India, she comes across as brusque and rigidly nationalistic, someone who is sure that the British acted properly. Swan applies choplogic to assert that Das was not imprisoned for his beliefs or his opinions, but simply for his actions, and she concludes that whatever he did in protesting British rule, he "obviously deserved what he got" (15). The absolutism of her statement is left unchallenged, in part because Stoppard seems unwilling to engage fully the ethical issues surrounding the means by which the British exerted control in India. Similarly Swan's arrogant (and unchallenged) attitude comes across when she critiques Das by saying, "[Das] took part in actions against the British Raj and loved English literature, which was perfectly consistent of him" (16); left unstated is the rebuttal that there is a large discrepancy between aesthetic tastes and political systems. One can admire the art, while still rejecting the political and economic colonization.

The ensuing acknowledgment that history depends on perspective (Anish's "first war of Independence" versus Swan's "Mutiny" [17]) also shows Swan's own inconsistency. She equates Britain's imperial role in India as similar to the Roman Empire's position in British history, yet then states she would probably have told the Romans, "Go away and take your roads and your baths with you" (17)—an attitude essentially the same as that of Das and the other Indian nationalists. She dismisses her own inconsistency by saying: "It doesn't matter what I would have thought. It's what I think now that matters" (17). In these political discussions, Swan, the defender of colonialism, is somewhat protected by her age and role as hostess, and thus any serious critique of her views is always blunted.[15] When Anish points to the long, rich cultural history of India, she rebuffs him: " (*Angrily*) We made you a proper country! And when we left you fell straight to pieces like Humpty Dumpty! Look at the map! You should feel nothing but shame!" (17). Ultimately, Swan's justification for colonialism is based on pragmatics. Whereas Stoppard typically argues politics in terms of ethics and morality, in this play, all the defenders of colonialism resort to pragmatism, rationalizing that invasive measures are justified as long as, from their perspective, it makes the country work better. As Paul Allen states, the play creates a sense of "India being a kind of English Eden, a place to which you go to have an even more English time than you would actually here in England and of educated Indians feeling much the same way" (241). However, it seems that the conservative Anglophile in Stoppard has trouble overtly criticizing the means it took for the upper class to enjoy that life.[16]

While Mrs. Swan is Stoppard's conservative mouthpiece, she is more enigmatic than she first appears. One of the play's missing pieces is an explanation of how she went from a youthful Marxist (Flora describes her as a radical communist who is opposed to British colonial rule of India) to the reactionary conservative that the audience sees and hears. The only reason given for her polar reversal is a vague statement that "one alters" (78).[17] Based on his 1991 visit to India, Stoppard believes that Swan's transformation is not that uncommon. Talking to older, educated, upper-class Indians, he felt that many of them were nostalgic for British rule. Stoppard explains:

> But not for ideological reasons or for moral reasons, but for very practical reasons—the place worked better for them. I mean one thing about the British Empire was that on the street level it was not corrupt. Empire as an idea might be a very corrupting phenomenon. But on the level of the magistrate, the business man, it was very, very honest. And now India is very corrupt at that level—on the level of the lowest magistrate's court or somebody getting a job or whatever. It's a very corrupt society. And the old generation are troubled by that, because it's just not a practical way of life. (Fleming, "A Talk," 24–25)

Elsewhere Stoppard adds: "I met several people who [felt] that it had all started to go wrong when the British left. . . . One of the Indian actors in the play was telling me that he was brought up in a family to whom everything English was good and the loss and passing of English influence was deeply regretted. I would say that's certainly a minority view among Indians, naturally enough" (Allen 241–42). Within the play itself, Flora and the Rajah acknowledge that the best interests of Britain, India, and the native states are three separate considerations, but overall, in terms of its politics, *Indian Ink* is mostly written from a privileged perspective, one that regrets Britain's leaving India.

The exchanges between Mrs. Swan and Anish also raise questions about what constitutes a person's cultural identity. Part of Swan's anger at how India has been fragmented by racial divisions following independence lies in the paradox that though she is a British nationalist, she refers to India as "home" (79). Now back in England, many of her home furnishings are Indian. In turn, Anish, though born and raised in India, now calls London "home" (18). And though he and his father both are ethnically Indian and are both professional painters, assigning an identifying label is not so simple:

> SWAN: You are a painter like your father.
>
> ANISH: Oh . . . yes. Yes, I am a painter like my father. Though not at all like my father, of course.
>
> SWAN: Your father was an Indian painter, you mean?
>
> ANISH: An Indian painter? Well, I'm as Indian as he was. But yes. I suppose I am not a particularly *Indian* painter . . . not an Indian painter *particularly,* or rather . . .
>
> SWAN: Not particularly an Indian painter.
>
> ANISH: Yes. But then, nor was he. Apart from being Indian.
>
> SWAN: As you are.
>
> ANISH: Yes.
>
> SWAN: Though you are not at all like him.
>
> ANISH: No. Yes. My father was quite a different kind of artist, a portrait painter. (13–14)

This comic exchange highlights the slipperiness of identity, particularly for artists, whose ethnic identity, artistic identity, and chosen identity are not necessarily the same.[18] These distinctions of identity are particularly apt coming from someone whose identity is as denatured and destabilized as the Czech-born Stoppard who has lived in Singapore and India, but who now identifies himself as not only British, but a British playwright who has been bestowed with the honor of Knight of the British Empire.

In adapting his radio play, the biggest challenge facing Stoppard was how to realize the character of Eldon Pike. His solution was to make Pike not only the editor of Flora's letters (and thus still the interpolator of the footnotes) but also her biographer. In part, Pike represents Stoppard's basic mistrust of biographers.[19] As Mrs. Swan says: "*biography* is the worst possible excuse for getting people wrong" (5). As an academic engaged in the detective-like attempt to reconstruct the activities of a dead poet, Pike follows in the footsteps of *Arcadia*'s Bernard—in part, both treat "the past [as] material to be processed and marketed" (Peter, review of *Indian Ink*). However, as a character, Pike pales in comparison. While both scholars have relentless enthusiasm for their quest, Bernard demonstrates his intelligence only to be brought down by his hubris; in contrast, Pike is rather dimwitted, a likable oaf who provides many good laughs, but who is too stoogelike to offer any serious commentary on the difficulty historians have in trying to interpret the past. Stoppard's ironic touch is that Pike is actually correct in his speculation that Das painted a nude portrait.

Unlike previous Stoppard professor characters, Pike is American not British. This is significant because in many ways the satire is not on scholars per se, but rather on the excesses of their endeavors, something that Stoppard believes is more of an American phenomenon.[20] Mrs. Swan says: "Far too much of a good thing, in my opinion, the footnotes; to be constantly interrupted by someone telling you things you already know or don't need to know at that moment. There are pages where Flora can hardly get a word in sideways" (25). She adds that much of the scholarly attention comes "from America" (25). In a passage that Stoppard added during rehearsals, he lampoons Pike's excessive zeal for footnotes and his sense of self-importance:

PIKE: (*gaily*) The notes, the notes! The notes is where the fun is! You can't just *collect* Flora Crewe's letters into a book and call it "The Collected Letters of Flora Crewe", I'm not even sure if it's legal where I come from.

SWAN: America?

PIKE: The Department of English Studies, University of Maryland. Luckily, the correspondence of well-known writers is mostly written without a thought for the general reader. I mean, they don't do their own footnotes. So there's an opportunity here. Which you might call a moral enterprise. No, okay, an opportunity. Edited by E. Cooper Pike. There isn't a page which doesn't need—look—you see here?— "I had a funny dream last night about the Queen's Elm." Which Queen? What elm? Why was she dreaming about a *tree?* So this is where I come in, wearing my editor's hat. To lighten the darkness.

SWAN: It's a pub in the Fulham Road.

PIKE: Thank you. This is why God made writers, so the rest of us can publish. (4)

The satirical subtext to the exchange is Pike's own self-identification of being not from a country, but from an institution, one that grants citizenship and status based on the acceptability of the residents' publications.

While Pike offers another Stoppard satire on academics, his presence serves another function. For Stoppard, Pike's going to India in the present day "justifies the play, a play which would otherwise float between India then and an old lady in a garden in a London suburb now. Just thinking of the theatrical dynamics, it gives the play a big kick when it needs it. Fifty minutes in, suddenly there are a lot of neon signs and traffic noise, and a character who is in one part of the play turns up in another part of the play" (Gussow, *Conversations,* 128). Stoppard's suggestion that the play needs some spectacle hints at the work's lack of significant substance.

The expansion of Pike's role mostly fleshes out the plot and allows for some effective and aesthetically pleasing theatrical doubling of space across time, that is, characters from different eras sharing the same space. The expanded role's thematic contribution is found not in its comments on the world of academe, but rather in what is said about contemporary Indian life. Pike has a speech about the overwhelming, numbing poverty in India, and it closes with a powerful image: "But this one [beggar], she had this baby at the breast, I mean she looked *sixty,* and—well, this is the thing, she had a stump, you see, she had no hand, just this stump, up against the glass, and it was . . . raw . . . so when the light changed, the stump left this . . . smear . . ." (59). This is the play's only reference to the lower class of India, and the beggar's blood leaves its own indelible India ink stamp on living conditions in postcolonial India. Pike's guide—the educated, bilingual, English-language-loving Dilip—cheerfully states:

Yes, it's a disaster for us! Fifty years of Independence and we are still hypnotized! Jackets and ties must be worn! English-model public schools for the children of the elite, and the voice of Bush House is heard in the land. Gandhi would fast again, I think. Only, this time he'd die. It was not for this India, I think, that your Nirad Das and his friends held up their home-made banner at the Empire Day gymkhana. It was not for this that he threw his mango at the Resident's car. What a pity, though, that all his revolutionary spirit went into his life and none into his art. (60–61) [21]

While Dilip's last line is reminiscent of the valorization of the revolutionary artist over the political revolutionary in *Travesties,* the bulk of the speech points to the sad truth that postindependence has not seen an improvement in the standard of living for many Indians.

When I asked Stoppard about how he, as a patriotic, conservative British citizen felt about his play's themes of colonialism and imperialism, he stated: "I tried to complicate the picture. It is the Indian man [Das] who is obsessed with Englishness and elevates it onto a pedestal and all that. And it is the English woman [Flora] who is skeptical about it. Which I think fairly well reflects my own ambivalence about it" (Fleming, "A Talk," 24). I would guess that Stoppard's mixed emotions are due to the conflict between his moral sense that the totalitarian measures used to maintain control violate his ethical views of proper governance and Swan's assertion that from a pragmatic point of view India worked better under British rule. Dilip's suggestion that postcolonial India is not the India dreamed of by those who gained the country's independence seems to be another bone that prevents Stoppard from completely swallowing the idea that India is better off having the right to self-governance.

While much of the play is reactionary and conservative in its politics and bathed in a glow of warm nostalgia and charm, the closing passage of the play stands in sharp contrast. The final words come from Emily Eden, an Englishwoman who, while in India in 1839, wrote: "I sometimes wonder they do not cut all our heads off and say nothing more about it" (83). In a play that "dwells on those areas where Indian and British culture met with fascination if little understanding rather than on the concomitant exploitation and hostility" (Edwardes 253), these closing lines are caustic about the British in India. But the audience knows that the Indians did not take that option, and thus the legacy of the ensuing one hundred–plus years of colonial occupation cannot be erased. Instead, British and Indian cultures are inevitably partially entwined, overlapping like the divergent eras and settings that share the stage of the play itself. While critics are divided as to whether or not *Indian Ink* offers anything new to the field of Anglo-Indian literature, what does emerge from the play is an undercurrent of optimism, one that hopes the two cultures can bridge the gulf between them.

12

The Invention of Love

When actor John Wood heard that Stoppard was writ-ing a play about Alfred E. Housman, he thought: "There's an unpromis-ing subject, a minor poet who lived like a hermit and was staggeringly rude" (Gussow, "So Rude"). By the time Wood read the play and accepted the lead-ing role, he found Stoppard's Housman to be a fascinating character. While Housman has some name recognition in England, he is largely unknown in the United States, and on the surface, he seems an unlikely subject for a ma-jor play, much less one by Stoppard. *The Invention of Love* is a complex play, and to probe its inner workings it is instructive to begin with a consideration of who Housman was and why he interests Stoppard. In particular, there are three main aspects of Housman's life that Stoppard weaves into his play: (1) Housman's unrequited love for Moses Jackson; (2) Housman's work as the foremost Latin textual scholar of his era; and (3) Housman's work as a poet.

Alfred Edward Housman lived from 1859 to 1936. From 1877 to 1881 he attended Oxford, where he studied classics. Already possessing a high degree of proficiency in Latin and Greek, he was able to correct his professors in their pronunciation and translations. While at Oxford, the shy and reserved Housman fell in love with Moses Jackson, an athlete and science student. Though Housman was excellent in classics, he, for reasons that can only be speculated, failed his final exams. For the next ten years he worked in Her

Majesty's Patent Office, a job that kept him near his beloved Jackson; they even roomed together from 1882 to 1885. However, Jackson was heterosexual and did not return Housman's affections. They remained friends, but in 1887 Jackson moved to India. In 1889 Jackson married and he lived abroad, both in India and in Vancouver, until his death in 1923. In the play it appears as if Jackson was Housman's one and only true love, while in real life Housman likely had at least one overseas romance.

After leaving Oxford Housman continued his classical studies as an independent scholar, and within a year published his first article.[1] For the next ten years, while still working in the Patent Office, he continued to publish articles, and by 1892 his reputation was such that he was appointed professor of Latin at University College London. Near the turn of the century he began a thirty-year project that he hoped would be his "monument"; the result was a five-volume definitive Latin edition of *Astronomica* by Marcus Manilius, an obscure first-century Roman poet and astrologist. Regarding his chosen subject, Housman once said: "I adjure you not to waste your time on Manilius. He writes on astronomy and astrology without knowing either. My interest in him is purely technical" (Glover). Though he mostly wrote about minor classical figures, Housman was known for his diabolically witty criticisms of fellow textual scholars whom he castigated for their mistranslations and dubious speculations. Through the years his reputation continued to grow, and in 1911 he was named Kennedy Professor of Latin at Cambridge, a post he held until his death in 1936.

While Housman was making his name as the foremost Latin textual scholar of his era, he also made his mark as a poet. In 1895 Housman wrote most of the poems that comprise *A Shropshire Lad* (1896). This collection, first published at his own expense in a limited edition of five hundred copies, eventually became his most significant artistic work. Melancholic in tone, the sparse poems, reminiscent of English and Classical pastoral poetry, deal mostly with young men looking at lives of promise and desire that go unfulfilled, as they focus on death, guilt, longing, and absence. Some poems suggest a veiled or repressed homosexual desire, while others express a yearning for death as an escape from life's miseries. During the first two decades of the twentieth century Housman's poems enjoyed a fair amount of popularity, but in the ensuing decades his work has cycled in and out of critical favor. The modernist Ezra Pound criticized his poems for being old-fashioned, while W. H. Auden praised the technical mastery of Housman's verses. In his lifetime Housman published only one other collection, *Last Poems* (1922).[2]

He sent a copy to Jackson, who was seriously ill. The accompanying letter noted the book was written and sent by "a fellow who thinks more of you than anything in the world." He added: "You are largely responsible for my writing poetry and you ought to take the consequences" (Glover). The moment makes clear that Housman's idealized love of Jackson never waned, and that the latter exerted an influence on Housman long after their daily spheres no longer coincided.

While this is Housman's background, one might still rightly ask: why Housman as the main focus of a play? Stoppard replies: "What initially attracted me to Housman was the two sides of him. The romantic mind of the poet and the analytical mind of the classical scholar" (T. Hill). Like the metaphor that undergirds both *Hapgood* and *Arcadia,* one sees Stoppard's continuing interest in the duality of the human temperament and the reconciliation of seeming opposites.

Early in 1994 Stoppard approached the National Theatre's Artistic Director, Richard Eyre, proposing to write a play about Housman. At the time Stoppard's interest lay not only in Housman, but also in the literature of antiquity and the process of translation. However, the more Stoppard probed Housman's life, the less the play had to do with translation, and the more it had to do with Housman himself. As Stoppard relates, it took him approximately three years before he latched on to the idea that "the play was really about Housman in the age of Wilde" (T. Hill).[3] Reserved and reclusive, Housman was a repressed, closeted homosexual in an era that initially embraced the flamboyancy of Wilde, but that then destroyed him for his homosexuality. The contrast between how Housman and Wilde both lived and loved is a central thematic point of the play.

Textual Construction[4]

The reviews of the London production suggest the plethora of ideas that percolate through *The Invention of Love*. Georgina Brown says the play is about "poetry, love, aesthetics and attitudes to homosexuality, as well as being a biography of AE Housman." Michael Billington's list of topics includes the nature of memory and the coincidences of history as well as "the quality of passion, the random nature of literary survival, and the idea of life as a route march leading inexorably to the grave." Vincent Canby notes that the play "touches on textual criticism, Britain's notorious 1885 Criminal Law Amendment Bill under which Oscar Wilde was tried, the Esthetic Movement (with its emphasis on 'boy love'), . . . and the nature of love."

The Invention of Love deals with these as well as other issues, and so on the surface it appears as yet another Stoppard juggernaut of intellectual conceits. Indeed, its complexity and learnedness do mark it as a Stoppard play, yet it is also fundamentally different. Stoppard notes how this play's origin and execution differ: "It is character-based, isn't it? I've always started with an idea before, often quite separate from whoever was in the play. This time I've started with whoever is in the play. The idea came exponentially, as the play grew" (T. Hill). Likewise, while the play possesses the typical Stoppard trait of being a predominantly male cast of characters, all of whom speak in witty, quotable language, it exhibits an emotional honesty that critics have often found lacking in Stoppard's plays. Thus, *The Invention of Love* is not only one of Stoppard's most densely intellectual works, it is also one of his most emotionally engaging—a facet strongly evident in the original production where John Wood, as the elder Housman, and Paul Rhys, as the younger Housman, delivered virtuoso performances.

Written in dream-memory form, the play is an impressionistic biography. Stoppard carefully notes: "It's not biographical. Things happen that never happened. The whole thing never happened—it all goes on in Housman's head. In real life Wilde and Housman never met, for example" (T. Hill). While it is not strictly speaking a biography, some of the main character's lines of dialogue are pulled from the writings of the historical Housman.[5] Also, near the end of the play, when commenting on a historical incident, Stoppard's Wilde says: "It's only fact. Truth is another thing and is the work of the imagination" (95–96). Likewise, Stoppard's presentation of Housman may deviate from factual biography, but it conveys a sense of truth.

The Invention of Love uses events from A. E. Housman's life, but the lack of scene divisions and the dream-memory form of the play precludes a simple, concise plot summary. The play begins with the elder Housman (AEH) caught between death and dreaming as he stands on the banks of the Styx waiting for Charon to ferry him to the underworld.[6] However, in Stoppard's multilayered world, the river Styx mingles with the Isis River of Oxford in the Victorian era. Thus, as AEH is ferried to his last resting place, his memories are alive and flow freely through many events, both personal and of the era. Scenes of Housman in his undergraduate days at Oxford with his best friends Jackson and Pollard are juxtaposed with fantasy scenes of a game called Dream Croquet. In the latter, Oxford icons Walter Pater and John Ruskin join administrators Benjamin Jowett and Mark Pattison in a pseudo croquet match that is largely an excuse to discuss matters of art and morality. The heart of the first act, and by far the longest scene in the play, is the poignant meeting between AEH and his younger self where among other things they talk about the joy of knowledge and the nuances of textual criticism. Act I closes with AEH delivering a lecture, to an unseen group of students, on how to translate a passage of a poem by Horace.

The second act focuses on Housman's post-Oxford life and is more regularly constructed as it contains extended scenes that are more clearly divided in time and place. Scenes where Housman expresses his devotion to Jackson are juxtaposed with scenes involving the journalists responsible for getting the Criminal Law Amendment Act passed. This law was initially aimed at raising the age of sexual consent from thirteen to sixteen, but it eventually included an amendment that made homosexual activity illegal.

It is more than halfway through the act before AEH returns to the stage, at which point the play's form reverts to the shorter, more fluid construction of the first act. The central events are Housman's first academic appointment, news of Oscar Wilde's conviction on sodomy charges, and a fantasy meeting between AEH and Wilde where they discuss and reflect on their respective choices and fates. The scene between Wilde and AEH is the thematic crux of the second act. This encounter gives way to one more meeting between AEH and his younger self; now their conversation focuses on the nature of love. Similar to the end of the first act, the play then closes with AEH addressing the audience, a shadowy figure on the banks of the Styx, ready to pass on to the underworld, but leaving behind the palpable emotion of his life and the choices he made.

Thematic Analysis of Text and Production

In the National Theatre's production the preshow setting includes a back cyclorama showing a large curving gray bookcase.[7] The image suggests the world of academics and the books that Housman loved. Then as the preshow lights dim, fog billows in and grand sweeping music rises. Fog covers the stage; suddenly AEH appears in the midst of it. Dark clouds and shadows waft across the cyclorama. The mystical atmosphere evokes the Stygian gloom, and indeed AEH declares: "I'm dead, then. Good" (1). Like the attitude expressed in some of his poems, AEH is glad to have passed on from the world, but in the course of the play, the audience shall get to see AEH reflect back on his life and the events that shaped it.

On a revolve, Charon comes in poling his boat. Apropos of his classics expertise, AEH's afterlife is that of the classical underworld. Charon, played as if he were a cabdriver with a dry, droll sense of humor, believes that he is to pick up two people—a poet and a scholar. The remark is indicative of AEH's duality, that he can not be neatly categorized. As Charon starts to ferry AEH across the Styx, the young Housman, Pollard, and Jackson row into view. Seeing his beloved, AEH exclaims, "Mo!" (4). It is an expression of joy and longing. However, he soon follows this with a plaintive cry: "Mo! I would have died for you but I never had the luck!" (5). In Wood's performance, it is a moment of great poignancy, conveying the depth of his love for Jackson and the anguish that he could never live out the love he felt. At this point AEH references Theseus trapped in the underworld, unable to break the chains that bound his beloved Pirithous. Throughout the play AEH will equate his feelings for Jackson with that of male love found in Greek mythology. Overall, the opening section, spiced by the frequent comedy of Charon, provides exposition on the three realms of Housman's life that shall be explored.

The Oxford scenes that lead up to the meeting between AEH and his younger self are mostly concerned with developing the characterization of the three undergrads and with establishing the milieu of Oxford during this so-called golden age. However, Oxford in the Victorian era faced a central contradiction. The classical worlds of Greece and Rome were looked to as exemplars, but those eras also involved open homosexuality. Thus, while Victorian society thought that a classical education was the ideal way to equip their noble young men to be leaders in society, they also consciously tried to erase the homosexuality that appeared in classical literature. On the other hand, another segment of society, the Aesthetes, co-opted the acceptability of aestheticism so as to validate homosexuality. The Oxford figures whom Stoppard assembles for his game of Dream Croquet express different views on these issues of art, homosexuality, morality, and different historical golden ages.

When aestheticism first came to Oxford in the 1830s from Germany, it was concerned with the study of taste and beauty, with that which was good and beautiful in art and in life. By Housman's time the word *aesthete* had also come into being. Ruskin sees Aesthetes and homosexuality in a negative light. He believes that homosexuality is "unnatural behavior," and he blames the fall of Greece on it. He proceeds to argue: "It was not until the 1860s that moral degeneracy came under the baleful protection of artistic license and advertised itself as aesthetic" (10). Ruskin remains true to the original idea of aesthetics when he declares the meaning of life: "There is nothing beautiful which is not good, and nothing good which has no moral purpose" (15). For

Ruskin, art and morality were inextricably entwined. He believed that art that showed fidelity to nature and that eschewed self-indulgent sensuality was inherently moral. For Ruskin, the golden age of art and life was the medieval era, a period when "the craftsman built the cathedrals which were the great engines of art, morality, and social order" (17). He elaborates: "Conscience, faith, disciplined restraint, fidelity to nature—all the Christian virtues that gave us the cathedral at Chartres, the paintings of Giotto, the poetry of Dante" (19). Whether coincidentally or causally, Ruskin's real-life sexual impotency mirrors the austerity he champions.

Though Pater was Ruskin's pupil, on aesthetic matters he became his polar opposite. For Pater the harmonious ideal of art was achieved in Renaissance Italy with artists such as Raphael and Michelangelo. For Pater the asceticism of the medieval era rightly gave way to the sensuality of the Renaissance:

> The Renaissance teaches us that the book of knowledge is not to be learned by rote but is to be written anew in the ecstasy of living each moment for the moment's sake. Success in life is to maintain this ecstasy, to burn always with this hard gem-like flame. . . . The conventional morality which requires of us the sacrifice of any one of those moments has no real claim on us. The love of art for art's sake seeks nothing in return except the highest quality to the moments of your life, and simply for those moments' sake. (19–20)

Pater argued that people should seek not the fruits of experience, but experience itself. The ideological opposition between Pater and Ruskin mirrors the polarities of the way in which Wilde and Housman lived. Pater's art-for-art's-sake aestheticism was lived to the full by Wilde, while Housman lived similarly to Ruskin's axiom of austerity.

While Ruskin is costumed as a somber, conservative Oxford don, Pater is the quintessential dandy, with accoutrements such as yellow gloves and blue cravat. This flamboyant attire marks Pater as an Aesthete, and by extension, as a man who practices "boy worship." In the play, as in life, Pater is censured for his flirtatious involvement with a student. In theory, Pater lived the conflation of Aesthete and aestheticism. In real life, Pater's writings glorified male eros, but while he entertained thoughts of boy love, he was restrained and largely inactive.

Jowett is the third figure to propose a golden age where art, morality, and social order reach a harmonious ideal. For him the pinnacle of culture is "Greece in the age of the great philosophers . . . buggery apart" (17). Championing homosexuality, Pater calls Jowett on this willful exclusion of part of Greek culture. When Pater tries to dismiss his encounter with the student as being purely platonic, Stoppard offers a minidebate that exposes the irony of the phrase "platonic love" as well as the Victorian era's selective embrace of Greek culture.

> JOWETT: A Platonic enthusiasm as far as Plato was concerned meant an enthusiasm of the kind that would empty the public schools and fill the prisons where it is not nipped in the bud. In my translation of the Phaedrus it required all my ingenuity to rephrase his depiction of paederasta into the affectionate regard as exists between an Englishman and his wife. Plato would have made the transposition himself if he had had the good fortune to be a Balliol man.
>
> PATER: And yet, Master, no amount of ingenuity can dispose of boy-love as the distinguishing feature of a society we venerate as one of the most brilliant in the history of human culture, raised far above its neighbours in moral and mental distinction.
>
> JOWETT: . . . The canker that brought low the glory that was Greece shall not prevail over Balliol! (22)

Like Ruskin, Jowett blames homosexuality for the fall of Greece. Like many people today, Jowett willfully ignores that which he finds distasteful in classical Greek culture.

Jowett is also used to introduce the juxtaposition of Wilde and Housman. Jowett starts to advise Housman that he can achieve great things if only he loses some of his flamboyancy; but seeing how reserved Housman is, Jowett quickly realizes he has the wrong man.[8] However, the audience realizes that the comparison is to Wilde, a figure who has already been referred to in the play. Wilde is known as the wittiest man at Oxford, and Pollard revels in stories about his antics and epigrams. Housman, who often fails to understand or appreciate Wilde's jokes, offers an ironic comment: "It'll be a pity if inversion is all [Wilde] is known for" (15). Here, Stoppard quibbles with the word "inversion." On one hand, it refers to Wilde's characteristic epigrams of inversion, where expectations are put on their head. On the other hand, it also means homosexuality. Indeed, Wilde will ultimately be famous for his inversion—in both senses of the word; one wins him celebrity status, one leads to his social downfall.

The Jowett-Housman scene quickly moves from the comparison of Housman and Wilde to a consideration of the purpose of a university education, particularly a classical education. It is an era when Jowett can seriously say: "If you cannot write Latin and Greek verse how can you hope to be of any use in the world?" (24). While that statement would sound ridiculous in the present era, it is viable in theirs. Still, the noteworthy aspect is Jowett's emphasis on the practical utility of what is learned at school.[9] In contrast, Housman asks, "But isn't it of use to establish what the ancient authors really wrote?" (24). Throughout the play, Housman champions knowledge for its own sake.

Charon and AEH pole into view at the tail end of the Housman-Jowett scene. Charon says they are at Elysium, the abode of the blessed after death. Elysium also refers to a condition of ideal happiness, and indeed, AEH is coming upon Housman during his first year at Oxford. The particular event that AEH keeps returning to is the day that Jackson, Pollard, and Housman had a picnic and took a boat ride.[10] Retrospectively, one realizes that it was that day that Housman fell in love with Jackson—a day of ideal happiness.

The centerpiece of act 1 is the encounter between AEH and Housman. Stoppard himself refers to it as "the heart of the play" (T. Hill), and many critics rank it among Stoppard's finest writing, particularly for the poignancy and emotion it evokes. Initially, AEH does not recognize his younger self. When he does, he wryly remarks: "Well, this is an unexpected development. Where can we sit down before philosophy finds us out. I'm not as young as I was. Whereas you, of course, are" (31). The witty lines also indicate the way in which Stoppard has manipulated the technique of the split time frame in an unusual way. The use of multiple time frames has been employed in a number of plays in the 1990s. Stoppard himself has used it in both *Arcadia* and *Indian Ink,* but there he mostly just alternates between the two periods. Here he intermingles them, allowing the characters to interact, thereby dramatically representing the divided self by having two incarnations of one character simultaneously present.

AEH and Housman pick up on the debate of the purpose of a classical education. With the wisdom of a lived life behind him, AEH challenges the idealized views of Housman. AEH discredits the stated aim of a classical education: "Science for our material improvement, classics for our inner nature. The beautiful and the good. Culture. Virtue. The ideas and moral influence of the ancient philosophers" (31). Empirically there is no evidence to show that classics students are superior in taste or moral sensibilities to science students. Instead, AEH asserts that the ancient philosophers are only useful for settling disputed passages in classical texts.

After AEH examines Housman's books, offering his comments on each scholar's work, they discuss Housman's own poetry, the art begot by experiencing art.[11] The divided self technique is used to reveal a truism often found among artists. Housman likes his poems whereas AEH, like many a writer looking back on his early efforts, denigrates his poems as unspeakable.

These twin topics of art and scholarship soon take on a more personal significance. The young Housman wants to leave his mark, a monument by which he will be remembered. It does not matter to Housman whether he makes his mark as a poet or as a scholar, but AEH offers some worldly wisdom: "I think it helps to mind" (36). To create a legacy one must possess a great passion and a driving desire. Whatever course one chooses, minding or caring, is crucial to succeeding at the goal. Furthermore, in his later Latin lecture, AEH argues: "Life is in the minding" (51). A person's choices, actions, and responses figure prominently in how that person's life develops. Regarding the young Housman, AEH sees a divide between the two pursuits, arguing that one cannot be both a first-rate poet and a first-rate scholar. While the textual scholar must use intuition, the goal is to find fact and the danger is that too often people assume that prior eras' sensibilities are identical to their own. In some significant instances this is not the case. However, this is a moment where AEH does not have the only valid view. Here, Housman is able to educate his older self by arguing that moments of great art endure because they convey an emotional experience that transcends time and place. Typical of Stoppard's dialectical process, AEH concedes that point but also warns:

> Literary enthusiasm never made a scholar, and unmade many. Taste is not knowledge. A scholar's business is to add to what is already known. That is all. But it is capable of giving the greatest satisfaction, because knowledge is good. It does not have to look good or sound good or even do good. It is good just by being knowledge. And the only thing that makes it knowledge is that it is true. You can't have too much of it and there is no little too little to be worth having. There is truth and falsehood in a comma. (37)

This defense of ivory-tower scholarship is the intellectual/academic corollary to art for art's sake. When AEH proceeds to show how moving a misplaced comma changes the meaning of a line of Catullus, he declares it "a small victory over ignorance and error. A scrap of knowledge to add to our stock" (38). AEH refers to textual criticism as a science, and he ultimately lauds "textual criticism [as] the crown and summit of scholarship" (39).[12] In the second act Housman picks up on this idea when he declares: "[Scholarship is] where we're nearest to our humanness. Useless knowledge for its own sake. Useful knowledge is good, too, but it's for the fainthearted, an elaboration of the real thing, which is only to shine some light, it doesn't matter where on what, it's the light itself against the darkness, it's what's left of God's purpose when you take away God" (73–74). As in *Arcadia,* Stoppard valorizes the pursuit of knowledge as one of the defining features of being human. Despite this perspective, AEH aptly notes that most people find textual criticism dry and dull. Indeed the intriguing aspect of their intricate probings of the nuances of obscure Latin texts is the intensity they bring to the task and the joy it evokes in them. In *Poetics,* Aristotle declared: "To learn gives the liveliest of pleasure" (55). Watching AEH and Housman engage these texts, one feels the meaning of Aristotle's words. The excitement of knowledge and the joy of learning emanate from the stage.

While Housman worries about how he will create a legacy, AEH wishes he had lived his life differently: "I wouldn't worry so much about your monument, if I were you. If I had my time again, I would pay more regard to those poems of Horace which tell you you will not have your time again. Life is brief and death kicks at the door impartially" (39). Thus, one of the themes of the play is the dead Housman's advice to live life and enjoy it to the full. In other words, live life more as Wilde did and not as he did. On the other hand, part of the reason that Housman never lived life as fully as he wished is that he was never able to realize the idealized relationship he sought with Jackson. This connection is made explicit in the text by having AEH's advice dovetail into a discussion about male love in Greek mythology.

Housman struggles with the concept of homosexuality. He is enamored of the idea of male love; but influenced by society's standards, he dissociates it from "spooniness" and instead equates it with the friendship and virtue characteristic of Greek heroes (40). Playing off a reference to Theseus and Pirithous, Housman exclaims: "Companions in adventure! *There* is something to stir the soul! Was there ever a love like the love of comrades ready to lay down their lives for each other?" (40). Soon AEH explicates a fascinating example of such love in action:

> If only an army should be made up of lovers and their loves! . . . But there was such an army, a hundred and fifty pairs of lovers, the Sacred Band of Theban youths, and they were never beaten till Greek liberty

died for good at the battle of Chaeronea. At the end of that day, says Plutarch, the victorious Philip of Macedon went forth to view the slain, and when he came to the place where the three hundred fought and lay dead together, he wondered, and understanding that it was the band of lovers, he shed tears and said, whoever suspects baseness in anything these men did, let him perish. (43)

The classical societies accepted homosexuality and judged men by their actions in the social sphere. For the Greeks, virtue was a practical matter, and those who succeeded in war, athletics, or social pursuits were considered virtuous.[13] As Housman progressed into adulthood and came to terms with his sexual inclinations, he likely turned to classical societies for justification. Indeed, throughout the play both AEH and Housman fixate on passages of classical texts that focus on male love.

Housman is disturbed by the way Oxford scholars erase the presence of homosexuality in classical writings. Often they change the pronoun from *he* to *she,* or else simply omit "offending" passages. In contrast, many of Housman's favorite passages and images revolve around moments of male love. Housman's favorite classical poem, Horace's *Diffugere nives,* is the one that closes with the line about Theseus trying to break the chains that bind his beloved Pirithous.[14] Also, in the same book of Horace, the author is in tears over Ligurinus, an athlete whom he chases in his dreams. Stoppard utilizes this passage and Housman's fondness for it by making an explicit connection with Housman and Jackson. The first act ends with AEH lecturing about, and quoting from, this poem, while in a dim spotlight the athlete Jackson is "seen as a runner running towards us from the dark, getting no closer" (51). The classical expert Housman melds with the subject matter under scrutiny, but is left with the empty feeling of not being able to possess the love he seeks.

The conversation between AEH and Housman largely revolves around textual criticism and the classical world. Through their discussion of male love, it also prefigures Housman's personal life, which will be the main focus of the second act. But even in these academic discussions, Stoppard subtly reveals the emotional distance Housman adopted in his personal life. When discussing a love poem by Catullus, AEH says that "*vester* for *tuus* is the point of interest" (42); that is, he takes a clinical, scholarly approach.[15] In a sense, he has bracketed himself off from the practicalities and meaning of life and declared a textual nuance rather than the poem's insights into love as the point of interest. In contrast, the young Housman argues: "The point of interest is—what is virtue?, what is the good and the beautiful really and truly?" (42). This is the idealized goal of a young man interested in exploring and experiencing life. However, this same person at the end of his life, both wiser and more cynical, chides his younger self: "You think there is an answer: the lost autograph copy of life's meaning, which we might recover from the corruptions that have made it nonsense. But if there is no such copy, really and truly there is no answer" (42). While there may not be a knowable ultimate answer to life's mystery, withdrawing from life is also not the answer. In part, the play critiques the historical Housman for being a cold, unfeeling recluse, a man actively engaged in the technicalities of classical texts, but not always in the fundamentals of being human.

The recluse removes himself from life, an attitude related to Housman and AEH's dream of dying for a loved one. Both glorify and virtually revel in the idea of "taking the sword in the breast, the bullet in the brain" (43). While this is a standard of the romantic ideal of love, there is also an element of passive concession in it. Rather than living and experiencing life, with both its highs and its lows, the act of self-sacrifice removes one from the playing field, removes one from having to go through the difficulties of living life. In a sense it is much easier to die in this idealized fashion than it is to actually live a full life. AEH rationalizes the view by dwelling on the fact that everybody's days "are numbered and end with the grave" (44). Appropriately, their desire for an easeful death is a recurrent motif of the poems in *A Shropshire Lad,* poems that will be quoted intermittently in the second act.

Act 2

While the first act emphasizes Housman's love of scholarship, the second focuses more on his love of Jackson. Near the end of act 1, Stoppard introduces the mystery of why Housman, who was obviously an expert in the classics, failed his finals and flunked out of Oxford. How could such a thing occur? This plot point is picked up at the start of act 2 as Housman is talking to his sister, who wonders what happened. Housman is reticent on the point. Historically, there is no official explanation, but Stoppard suggests that Housman deliberately failed and chose a course of action that would allow him to be near Jackson.[16] Rather than be discouraged by his failure, Housman is content to get a civil service job in the same office as Jackson while still doing classical studies in his spare time.

The next scene weds the two developments as it shows Housman and Jackson together, in their office clothes, after a night at the theatre, a night that was a celebration of Housman's first published article. When Jackson questions him as to how he flunked, Housman avoids a direct answer, but instead replies: "I didn't get what I wanted, that's true, but I want what I've got. . . . Here we are, you and I, we eat the same meals in the same digs, catch the same train to work in the same office, and the work is easy, I've got time to do classics. . . . And friendship is all, sometimes I'm so happy, it makes me dizzy" (56). Through meeting Jackson, Housman's desires and expectations have changed. Rather than follow the path that a First degree from Oxford would lead to, he has chosen to live an approximation of the Greek male comrades-in-arms. Housman makes no attempt to consummate the relationship, but rather seems content with a version of the platonic ideal. This repression of physical desire stands in stark contrast to Wilde, whose Aesthetes were the subject of the play they witnessed that night. On the other hand, Housman has no reason to believe a consummated relationship is possible. Jackson has made it clear that he does not like the Aesthetes, that he finds them unmanly, and following Victorian social norms, regards homosexuality as "beastliness."

The next Housman-Jackson scene is three years later. Though not liking sports, Housman is again at an athletic event to watch Jackson.[17] For the first time Housman's homosexuality is brought out into the open. Chamberlain, a gay coworker, equates Housman with a nervous girlfriend, and goes on to say the unspoken, to reveal what Housman really wants:

> Nothing which you'd call indecent, though I don't see what's wrong with it myself. You want to be brothers-in-arms, to have him to yourself . . . to be shipwrecked together, [to] perform valiant deeds to earn his admiration, to save him from certain death, to die for him—to die in his arms, like a Spartan, kissed once on the lips . . . or just run his errands in the meanwhile. You want him to know what cannot be spoken, and to make the perfect reply, in the same language. (67, all ellipses in original)

Chamberlain's speech evokes the Wilde-Douglas idea of "the love that dare not speak its name" as well as the image of Greek male love. Chamberlain also warns Housman that he is doomed to be unhappy because Jackson will "never want what you want" (66).

Later that week Housman and Jackson have their recognition scene, the other emotional linchpin of the play. Characteristic of his unconditional love, Housman is trying to help Jackson deal with a girlfriend problem. The stoutly heterosexual Jackson never suspected that Housman may be "sweet" on him, but his girlfriend noticed it instantly. When Jackson poses the question, neither man can deal with it directly. Tellingly, Housman equates their friendship to that of Theseus and Pirithous, best friends whose story has also been interpreted homosexually:

> Theseus was never so happy as when he was with his friend. They weren't sweet on each other. They loved each other, as men loved each other in the heroic age, in virtue, paired together in legend and poetry as the pattern of comradeship, the chivalric ideal of virtue in the ancient world. . . . It was still virtue in Sophocles to admire a beautiful youth . . . [as it was] for my Roman poets who competed for women and boys as fancy took them; virtue in Horace to shed tears of love over Ligurinus on the athletic field. Well, not anymore, eh, Mo? Virtue is what women have to lose, the rest is vice. (79)

Housman laments the lost days when men could love men, when such feelings, whether sexually consummated or not, were accepted and admired, not reviled.

Jackson, however, still has not caught on, and so, in a nuanced scene that takes on great poignancy in performance, Housman reveals the truth:

> HOUSMAN: Will you mind if I go to live somewhere but close by?
> JACKSON: Why? Oh . . .
> HOUSMAN: We'll still be friends, won't we?
> JACKSON: Oh!
> HOUSMAN: Of *course* Rose knew!—of *course* she'd know!
> JACKSON: Oh!
> HOUSMAN: Did you really not know even for a minute?
> JACKSON: How could I know? [You're normal.] You're not one of those Aesthete types or anything—(*angrily*) how could I know?! . . .
> HOUSMAN: You're half my life. . . . [It was the day of the boat ride picnic] You kissed the dog. After that day, everything else seemed futile and ridiculous. . . . Oh, if only you hadn't said anything! We could have carried on the same! (79–80)

Jackson concludes that it is not Housman's fault, that it is rotten luck, and that they will go on as best friends.[18] However, the truth is out in the open and things will never be the same. The scene closes with Housman isolated in a spotlight, delivering a haunting poem of heartache:

> He would not stay for me; and who can wonder?
> He would not stay for me to stand and gaze.
> I shook his hand and tore my heart asunder.
> And went with half my life about my ways.
> (81)[19]

Now that the central love plot has been brought to a close, Stoppard reintroduces AEH. Ironically, in their first-act meeting Housman had expressed his sympathy that love had made AEH unhappy, and now the audience has just seen why AEH was disappointed in love. Furthermore, Stoppard makes a significant dramaturgical choice here. For the first thirty pages of the second act, there has been Housman but not AEH, and now for the next twenty pages there is AEH but not Housman. Indeed Housman's appearances on the last few pages of the play are actually from earlier points in his life, and so this parting with Jackson is as far as the audience sees Housman go in his life. This choice may be viewed as a symbolic death, the death of half of Housman's life.

While both AEH and Housman contain aspects of the historical Housman's dual loves, for the most part AEH embodies his love of classical learning, while Housman embodies his love of Jackson. Thus as Housman's poem decries the loss of half of his life, AEH's return picks up on the other half of his life, namely the selection process and appointment to his first professorship in classics. Through the scene Stoppard weaves in the caustic wit of A. E. Housman's writing about how classical texts have been edited. He was so good in his field that even one of the scholars he ridiculed remarks: "Mr. Housman is applying for the post at my urging. He is, in my view, very likely the best classical scholar in England" (84). In a discipline rife with egos and personal politics, Housman spared none of his colleagues in his critiques yet still managed to reach the pinnacle of his profession.

Just as the first act interspersed scenes that establish the cultural milieu of Oxford during Housman's undergraduate years, so too Stoppard incorporates scenes that show the social context of London in the late Victorian era, particularly in regard to homosexuality and the Oscar Wilde trials.[20] Stoppard presents the journalists who helped pass the Criminal Law Amendment and the Labouchère Amendment, which made homosexual activity a crime.[21]

In the process, Stoppard offers a view of the power, purpose, and peccadilloes of the popular press, a perspective that is both particular to Victorian-era London but that is also partially applicable today. Labouchère laments that the press helped build Wilde's reputation but cannot bring it down. For him, this "shakes one's faith in the operation of a moral universe by journalism" (60). Stead, the stout moralizer who began the crusade to raise the age of consent, believes that "in the right hands the editor's pen is the sceptre of power" (61). He sees his work as a divine mission to dictate public opinion and standards. In contrast, Harris decides to follow public taste and is simply concerned with printing whatever sells, namely sex, violence, and scandal.

The Oscar Wilde trials provided sex and scandal, and the end result was that Wilde was sentenced to two years hard labor and the Aesthetes' cult was driven underground. At the same time as the Wilde trials, the historical Housman composed most of the poems that make up *A Shropshire Lad.* In the play, Chamberlain quotes some of them to AEH; the excerpts often suggest Housman's continuing love for Jackson and the pain of the unrequited lover. Chamberlain also reveals that the word *homosexual* did not enter the English language until 1897. AEH is outraged by the word because, as he says, "It's half Greek and half Latin!" (94). Besides evoking a good laugh, his response is indicative of how Housman dealt with his sexuality; the men who came up with the word were seeking a form of gay identity, an issue relevant to Housman's life, but he responds academically, rather than personally.

This scene then dovetails into AEH's meeting with Wilde, the era's most famous homosexual, and the man whose life serves as a polar opposite to Housman's. Their encounter stands as one of the major thematic moments in the play. Stoppard himself comments: "Wilde was the one who crashed and burned. Housman the one who died a success. But from our standpoint, from 1997, it's Wilde who is the success, and Housman the failure" (T. Hill). More important than the contrast between their reputations is the contrast between how they chose to live their lives.

When AEH meets Wilde the latter is reading a bleak and angry poem from *A Shropshire Lad,* a poem based on a gay man who shot himself after the Wilde trial so as to escape the shame of his homosexuality. Though Wilde is weathered, overweight, and on the decline from his prison experience, he does not share the poet's cynicism. Wilde's passion for life stands in contrast to Housman's reserve. Wilde had friends, Housman had colleagues (97). Wilde moved with the major figures of the era and "lived at the turning point of the world where everything was waking up new," but while all this was going on, Housman was "at home" (100). In part, their lives reflect the divide between the Dionysian and the Apollonian. Wilde lived the sensual, Dionysian life, while Housman opted for the critical-rational mode of the Apollonian. Each man's tragedy resulted from not balancing the two impulses.

Just as the way they lived was different, so too was how they loved. In act 1, AEH defines love by quoting Sophocles' *The Loves of Achilles:* "Love feels like the ice held in the hand by children" (44). Stoppard omits Sophocles' explanation of the image: "that however much pleasure the ice gives to start with, the children end up being able neither to hold it nor let it go" (Jones). The explanation, from a play about love between two men, aptly summarizes both Housman's and Wilde's experiences with love: Housman could not hold on to Jackson, while Wilde could never let go of Lord Alfred Douglas, his beloved Bosie.

Wilde posits a difference between facts and truth. What happened is "only fact. Truth is quite another thing and is the work of the imagination" (95–96). He then uses this paradigm to analyze his life and his love for Bosie:

> The betrayal of oneself is lifelong regret. Bosie is what became of me. He is spoiled, vindictive, utterly selfish and not very talented, but these are merely the facts. The truth is he was Hyacinth when Apollo loved him, he is ivory and gold, from his red rose-leaf lips comes music that fills me with joy, he is the only one who understands me. [Excerpt of love poem], but before Plato could describe love, the loved one had to be invented. We would never love anybody if we could see past our invention. Bosie is my creation, my poem. In the mirror of invention, love discovered itself. Then we saw what we had wrought, rapture and pain together, the ice that burns who clasps it. (98)

Wilde articulates a tendency to idealize the loved one, a process Housman went through with Jackson, inventing the image of his idealized man. The young Housman believes that the Latin poets were "real people in real love," whose writing showed "love as it really is" (102). While those poems are similar to Wilde's notion of the truth, they are still just words on paper, feelings cast into idealized form. They may contain truth, but they are not the same as love experienced. Since Jackson never reciprocated Housman's love, Housman felt the pain of love rejected, but he never fully lived and experienced his idealized love. To his death, he clung to that idealized invention. In contrast, Wilde experienced his idealized love, and discovered that love sometimes involves contrasting passions, both ecstasy and excruciating pain. Wilde and Housman exemplify extremes of love. Wilde knew his love of Bosie would be his destruction, but he felt helpless to resist. Housman was rejected but still clung to his idealized vision of love. In the process he killed off his inner, emotional life as a practical functioning part of his life. In different ways, each man's passion proved fatal.[22]

AEH feels sorry for Wilde, feels that he was a victim of the times: "Your life is a terrible thing. A chronological error. The choice was not always between renunciation and folly" (99). But Wilde asks for no sympathy: "Better a fallen rocket than never a burst of light. Dante reserved a place in his Inferno for those who willfully live in sadness. . . . Your 'honour' is all shame and timidity and compliance" (99). Rather than see himself as a victim, Wilde suggests that Housman has allowed himself to become a victim of Victorian-era repression. Also, though society may have cut down Wilde in his prime, he will outlive them all: "The blaze of my immolation threw its light into every corner of the land where uncounted men sat each in his own darkness. . . . I made art a philosophy that can look the twentieth century in the eye. I had genius, brilliancy, daring, I took charge of my own myth" (99–100). Wilde lived fully and openly, and though society imprisoned him for that, he left a legacy that outshines that of the cautious, conservative Housman, who made his own life a prison. Through Wilde, Stoppard expresses a carpe diem theme—that one must be willing to take the risk to seize the day.

In contrast to the ever quotable Wilde, AEH says: "My life is marked by long silences" (98). He admits that he chose a life of solitude, and as AEH looks back on his life, he is filled with melancholy not nostalgia. Before he departs, Wilde expresses his puzzlement over Housman's unhappiness: "You didn't mention your poems. How can you be unhappy when you know you wrote them? They are all that will still matter" (100). Wilde valorizes art as the artist's triumph over life and it is art, not scholarship about art, that endures.[23] While Housman spent more time on his edition of Manilius, it is *A Shropshire Lad* that stands as his monument.

Finally, in the play's closing section AEH has an extended monologue. Similar to the end of *Travesties,* Stoppard uses the moment to acknowledge his poetic license, his blending of fact and fiction.[24] Likewise AEH's short final monologue bears a striking structural similarity to Carr's closing monologue: both begin with a summation of the place, the time, and the major ideological types involved, followed by a personal connection of the character remembering the events in these complex pseudomemory plays. Here, AEH closes by saying: "But now I really do have to go. How lucky to find myself standing on this empty shore, with the indifferent waters at my feet" (105–6). The penultimate line, in John Wood's performance, refers both to AEH's death as well as to the recurring "need-to-urinate" motif that marks his suspended state between dreaming and death. It might also be read as indicative of the historical Housman's repression, his holding in of that which yearns to be let out.

Overall, *The Invention of Love* both builds on and diverges from previous Stoppard plays. Unlike earlier works, it is a quiet, relatively static, even somewhat undramatic play that requires some potentially awkward moments of staging; these were, however, deftly handled in Richard Eyre's intimate and efficient production that made clear a sometimes murky text. On the other hand, recurrent Stoppard motifs present in the play include the duality of humans; the need to balance opposite impulses; and the passionate, relentless search for truth and meaning as a defining feature of humanity even as access to ultimate meaning remains elusive. Furthermore, Housman's emphasis on professional integrity and the belief that knowledge is important because it sheds light recall ideas from *Night and Day.* While the focus on homosexual love is somewhat unexpected from Stoppard, the characters are, like those in *The Real Thing,* trying to pin down the true nature of love. Structurally, he melds the use of multiple time periods characteristic of *Arcadia* and *Indian Ink* with the creative-license memory format of *Travesties.* However, here the juxtaposition of time periods is handled more fluidly, with the characters now interacting rather than just sharing the same stage space. Likewise, this cast of historical figures is presented more realistically than those of *Travesties.* In its dense intellectualism, it continues Stoppard's exploration of how our minds apprehend the world, but characteristic of his more recent plays, the ideas and frequent laughs are now coupled with a greater intensity of emotion. Though the historical Housman may have been choleric and curmudgeonly, Stoppard paints his portrait sympathetically. Still, the mood is often somber; this is a dead man looking back on his life and regretting the choices he made.

The London production evoked the atmosphere of a farewell, and appropriately, *The Invention of Love* was the swan song production of the National Theatre's Artistic Director, Sir Richard Eyre. It is only fitting that Eyre's ten-year reign, now seen as a golden age, should be capped by his direction of one of the playwrights who contributed to that excellence. Likewise, Stoppard, now Sir Tom, can look back on his career, though not yet finished, and have no regrets. Though not in his top tier of work, *The Invention of Love* won Stoppard his seventh *Evening Standard* Award (five for Best Play, one for Best Comedy, and one for Most Promising Playwright) and stands as yet another facet in the impressive monument that Stoppard shall leave behind when he exits the stage of the world.

Conclusion

FOR MORE THAN THIRTY YEARS, THROUGH NINE MAJOR PLAYS and one Academy Award, Tom Stoppard has enjoyed widespread respect and admiration.[1] He is one of the few playwrights who can legitimately claim that cornerstones of his canon come from four decades. *Rosencrantz and Guildenstern Are Dead* (1967), *Jumpers* (1972), *Travesties* (1974), *The Real Thing* (1982), and *Arcadia* (1993) have been Stoppard's most lauded works, and they are the plays that seem most likely to endure.

While Stoppard's plays are known for their complexity, their fundamental theses are often rather simple. For example, *Hapgood*'s labyrinthine plot and use of quantum theory can be boiled down to a statement that the duality of light as both wave and particle is a metaphor for the dual nature of human personality. Similarly, at its core, *Jumpers* is an expression of the idea that belief in God is based on intuition rather than logical proof. Indeed, Stoppard has been almost apologetic about how plays are an ill-suited medium for probing issues in depth: "One of the built-in ironies of being a playwright at all is that one is constantly trying to put into dramatic form questions and answers that require perhaps an essay, perhaps a book, but are too important and too subtle, really, to have to account for themselves within the limitations of what's really happening in the theatre, which is that the story is being told in dialogue" (Goreau 260). Compared to books, plays *are* rather brief, and so what is noteworthy is the manner in which Stoppard executes his ideas, the ways in which he uses metaphors to make the complex comprehensible. These intellectual ideas, which are difficult but which also have a more simple level to them, are expressed not only via artful language and complex dramatic structures but also through engaging staging elements that are as theatrically stimulating as they are entertaining.

Not always easy to discern from the written text, and sometimes overlooked in production, are the emotional dynamics of Stoppard's plays. In "Stoppard's Secret Agent" Michael Billington argues that Stoppard's plays "have been analysed as if they were intellectual conceits: I suspect they only work because of their emotional ground-base" (195). Director Trevor Nunn has remarked: "[Tom] writes much more emotionally than he thinks he does" (Billington, "Joker," 3). Feeling that most productions "have played up Stoppard's high comedy at the price of his existential despair and underlying humanism,"[2] Billington suggests that directors should "reveal the sentiment buried underneath the high-grade repartee," and they should "play up the pain and let the comedy . . . look after itself" (3). Stoppard's plays are flexible enough to support multiple interpretations and performance styles, and Billington's suggestions are worth exploring, particularly in light of Trevor Nunn's London production of *Arcadia*, which was emotionally moving as well as thought provoking and funny. Toward this end it is noteworthy that for two of his recent successes, *Arcadia* and *The Invention of Love*, Stoppard branched off from his traditional director, Peter Wood, to work with Nunn and Richard Eyre.[3] Both directors effectively communicated the emotion, as well as the ideas and comedy, of the texts.

The Stoppard Cycle

As a writer, Stoppard has frequently followed a cyclical pattern of creation. Typically, he has found an area of interest, thematically or artistically, which he has then explored over a number of years, often starting with a minor work and culminating in a major work or works. Once he feels he has sufficiently explored that theme or executed that style, he moves on to a new-found interest. This cycle applies to Stoppard's major plays. *Rosencrantz and Guildenstern Are Dead* is a culmination of his presuccess work. Not only does *Rosguil* revise the ur-text *Rosencrantz and Guildenstern Meet King Lear*, it also "perfects" the style and themes of *The Gamblers*. Both plays use Beckettian stichomythic wordplay balanced by philosophical monologue, and both examine issues of fate, role-playing, the nature of identity, theological doubt, and the idea that life is a gamble.[5]

Rosguil's wide success gave Stoppard time to explore new territory, and *Jumpers* and *Travesties* fall into the second cyclical period. Thematically, *Jumpers* has its predecessor in the short television play *Another Moon Called Earth*, while the thematic antecedent of *Travesties* is the radio play *Artist Descending a Staircase*. Artistically, *Jumpers* and *Travesties* are cut from the same cloth: disorienting prologues, dauntingly long but comic monologues, and a series of scenes that mingle highbrow and lowbrow jokes with unexpected bits of music, dance, parody, and the debating of intellectual ideas; in short, both plays have a surface veneer of flashy showmanship and an innovative style that strives to be entertaining, funny, and surprising while also trying to discuss serious ideas. The theatricality and verbal fireworks of these two plays became the trademark Stoppard style. The stylistic similarity of the two plays led Stoppard to conclude that to repeat it a third time "would be a bore" (Hayman, *Tom Stoppard*, 12). Stoppard has frequently expressed his feeling that *Travesties* exemplifies the pinnacle of his stylistic flair, or as he said in 1993: "I've always thought that *Travesties* contained things that were actually better than I can write" (Spencer). Stoppard's criteria are on a linguistic level; for my tastes, *Jumpers* is the better work, for there the breathtaking style and sheer entertainment value is integrated more cohesively with the story and theme.

Having mastered that particular style, that marriage of a play of ideas with an innovative, relentlessly entertaining form, Stoppard turned to explorations of modified realism.[4] *Night and Day*'s emphasis on a narrative throughline, a complex female character, and the exploration of love and sexual relations were then taken to a higher degree of execution in *The Real Thing*. After the success of *The Real Thing*, Stoppard was asked to write other works about love, but again he felt he had reached the end of a particular phase: "For better or worse, that's it—the love play! . . . You've done that. You can't do it again. I think love is the only area that might be private to a writer. . . . I've been aware of the process that's lasted 25 years, of shedding inhibition about self-revelation. I wouldn't have dreamed of writing about it 10 years ago" (Gussow, *Conversations*, 62).[5] Having written his most emotional, most personal play, Stoppard then closed the book on that type of writing.[6]

Stoppard's next cyclical phase involved *Hapgood*, *Arcadia*, and *Indian*

Ink. Since *Indian Ink* is essentially an elaboration of the radio play *In the Native State,* it is an anomaly among the Stoppard canon of major plays in that its core content was not intended for the stage. Though its production post-dates *Arcadia,* its essence does not. Thus, while *Arcadia* is technically the middle play, it is more accurately the culmination of this phase as it mixes *Hapgood*'s interest in the world of science with *In the Native State/Indian Ink*'s satire on academics and narrative alteration between past and present. Audiences had difficulty following *Hapgood*'s intricate plot, and the play had less humor than is expected of a Stoppard work; therefore, when he returned to the realm of science for *Arcadia,* Stoppard addressed these problems, focusing attention on crafting an engaging story line filled with jokes. Furthermore, *Arcadia* represents the joining together of the *Jumpers/Travesties* stylistic display of an intellectual concept with the more emotional, narrative style of *Night and Day* and *The Real Thing.* Stoppard comments: "*Arcadia* is as full of theses as anything I've ever done, but if I hadn't found my way into a kind of detective story, none of it would have been worth a damn dramatically. I think it's the first time I've got both right, the ideas and the plot" (Spencer). In the same interview, Stoppard adds: "I think *Arcadia* is probably where all that was leading. It's lost the comic songs and the parodies, but it's a similar combination of larking about and trying to deliver some kind of thesis." In culminating another cycle of creation and welding two previous phases, Stoppard's writing in *Arcadia* had regained its joie de vivre.

While I included *Indian Ink* in the previous cycle, it might also be joined with *The Invention of Love* to mark a different phase of Stoppard's career. These two works are Stoppard's most character-driven plays. Also, unlike previous efforts, both plays are intimately connected to British culture. Both look back to glory days of England—the Empire in India, and Oxford in the Victorian era. Stoppard plays have traditionally played well in foreign countries for the very fact that their cultural specificity was minimal. In contrast, as of summer 2000 neither *Indian Ink* nor *The Invention of Love* has had a New York production, and their prospects for success in the United States are much less likely.[7]

Though Stoppard has followed this cyclical pattern of creation it remains to be seen in what direction he shall turn next.[8] In his nine major plays Stoppard has explored a variety of subjects and a diversity of styles. He has offered a heady mixture of intellectual inquiry, a liberal dose of comedy, and some palpable human emotion. Through these works Stoppard has articulated a worldview in which life contains a high degree of relativity but in which there is also some sort of absolute truth or metaphysical essence that is beyond our grasp to comprehend fully. Stoppard continually shows a world in which things are simultaneously both this and that, and where there is a dynamic interplay between absolute and relative values.

Stoppard in Theatrical Context

This book has largely looked at Stoppard in isolation, but his plays live in the larger context of society and of the world of theatre—both that of the contemporary British stage and that of the history of drama. From an educational perspective, Stoppard is sometimes passed over because he does not neatly fit into any school of playwriting, is not representative of any particular theatrical movement. In light of this, it is instructive to compare Stoppard to his peers as well as to his historical antecedents.

John Osborne's *Look Back in Anger* (1956) is often cited as launching the renaissance of British playwriting that has continued to the present. Within this generation of British playwrights there is a general division into those who are considered more socially committed and those who are considered more as apolitical stylists.[9] A partial list of the former includes Osborne, John Arden, Arnold Wesker, David Hare, Edward Bond, Howard Brenton, Caryl Churchill, Howard Barker, Peter Barnes, David Edgar, David Storey, Peter Nichols, Trevor Griffiths, Snoo Wilson, Anne Devlin, and Timberlake Wertenbaker. A partial list of the latter includes not only Stoppard but also Harold Pinter, Peter Shaffer, the late Joe Orton, Christopher Hampton, Alan Ayckbourn, Simon Gray, Alan Bennett, Brian Friel, and Michael Frayn. Of course, individual plays by these authors sometimes cross and blur these artificial categories.

Many of the names listed are not well known in the United States. The works of the socially committed playwrights tend to be leftist political dramas that are primarily concerned with social conditions in the United Kingdom, and the immediacy of their politics coupled with the specificity of their concerns often limits their crossing the Atlantic. An illuminating example of this phenomenon is David Hare. One of the best and most prolific of the contemporary British dramatists, Hare began writing for the fringe theatres in the late 1960s, but by the mid-1980s he was a member of the National Theatre. The plays of his 1990s trilogy—*Racing Demon* (1990), *Murmuring*

Judges (1991), and *The Absence of War* (1993)—deal, respectively, with the Church of England, the legal branch of British society, and the state or political (particularly the Labour Party) aspect of British life. These plays premiered at the National Theatre and prompted at least one reviewer to hail Hare as England's most important living playwright. In England, Hare's status as a National Theatre playwright insures him a certain degree of popular acceptance, while his ardent promotion of socialist values also makes him a favorite of many London theatre critics; however, prior to 1995, Hare was rarely produced in the United States.[10] Well written and well produced, Hare's plays were valued in England, but their concerns were apparently too local and/or too political to interest American producers. Then, in the second half of the 1990s, Hare produced a series of works—*Skylight* (1995), *Amy's View* (1997), *The Judas Kiss* (1998), as well as adaptations—that have been critically and commercially successful in New York. Less overtly political, these works focus more on relationships and have won Hare a new following in the United States.[11]

Among the apolitical stylists, Alan Ayckbourn deserves more critical recognition than he has received. In the 1970s Ayckbourn gained a reputation for Neil Simon–like comedies, but in the ensuing decades his plays grew darker and more complex as he balanced comedy and drama to examine human relations and values. Like Stoppard, Ayckbourn loves to explore a variety of dramatic structures. Richard Zoglin summarizes:

> *The Norman Conquest* was a cycle of three plays that recounted the events of a weekend from three different parts of the same house. One Ayckbourn play moves backwards in time. Another conflates all the action in a house, from living room to attic, into a single stage space. His ingenious, nearly unstageable *Intimate Exchanges* has 16 permutations, depending on the choices made by characters at key points in the action.

One of Ayckbourn's most audacious experiments came in 2000 when the National Theatre staged his plays *House* and *Garden*. The two plays are performed in separate theatres by the same cast *at the same time,* the actors shuttling back and forth between the two theatres. With such daring craftsmanship and nearly 60 plays to his credit, Ayckbourn merits more attention from both producers and critics in the United States.

Other contemporary British playwrights have also achieved international recognition.[12] Renowned for plays such as *Cloud Nine* (1979), *Top Girls*

(1982), and *Mad Forest* (1990), Caryl Churchill has profited from the process of collective creation, and by the 1990s may have eclipsed Shaffer in terms of international critical prestige. Since the success of *Amadeus* (1979) Peter Shaffer has suffered a prolonged dry spell as only the lightweight comedy *Lettice and Lovage* (1990) has sustained the reputation gained from his successes of the 1960s and 1970s. From a critical perspective, Shaffer is still primarily known for his spectacular theatricality and carefully constructed extended monologues (traits perhaps only rivaled by Stoppard). Recognition can also come from notoriety, and Edward Bond's work is characterized by "his positive hatred of existing society" (Billington, *Stoppard,* 169). In the United States Bond is probably best known for his role in the removal of England's prior censorship laws.

In comparison to these prominent contemporary British playwrights, the tone, style, and subject matter of Stoppard's theatrical vision is striking. In an environment where socially and politically committed drama has long been valued, Stoppard's cerebral wit, philosophical and scientific inquiry, right-leaning political convictions, and theatrical showmanship set him apart from most of his contemporaries. Indeed, in virtually any list of premier British playwrights of the second half of the twentieth century, two names consistently appear: Tom Stoppard and Harold Pinter. Their standing as the preeminent British playwrights of the last half century seems relatively secure.

Pinter's plays are known for their economy of language and domestic power games whose implicit threats of violence percolate under the subtext and the famous "Pinter pauses." Stoppard himself, while noting that Samuel Beckett "redefined the minima of theatre," points to part of Pinter's lasting influence and impact:

> I think Pinter did something equally important and significant. He changed the ground rules. One thing plays had in common: you were supposed to believe what people said up there. . . . With a Pinter play, you can no longer make that assumption. . . . There are many different possible interpretations for [a] scene. All of them had been discounted until Pinter exploited the off centre possibilities. (Gussow, *Conversations,* 6–7)

The power of Pinter's plays is evident in the frequent London revivals of his work, but since *Betrayal* (1978) Pinter has been more limited in his writing for the stage as his output has focused on screenwriting, stage direction, and the occasional radio play or short one-act play. Even *Moonlight* (1993) and *Ashes to Ashes* (1996) are really only extended one-acts.

Pinter has made an important and lasting contribution to the theatrical world, and the term "Pinteresque" may be taken to mean minimalist dialogue that is packed with menacing subtext. On the other hand, the term "Stoppardian" often connotes an innovatively structured theatrical extravaganza filled with a plethora of jokes and puns, conflicting arguments, intellectual inquiry, elaborate allusions, and cerebral wit. The major playwrights have staked out terrain that helps define their contribution to the world of theatre, and part of what sets Stoppard apart is his continuing contribution of significant new plays. For example, in 1993, Shaffer and Pinter both had new plays, but it was Stoppard's *Arcadia* that captured the Olivier Award and that went on to an extended West End run. Indeed, perhaps what most separates Stoppard from his peers is his ability to play to a wide audience (he is the rare writer who actually makes more money from a hit play than from a screenplay) while also winning approbation from critics and academics alike. Such sustained critical and commercial success has been rare in the volatile artistic and cultural landscape of the last half century.

When Stoppard is viewed in the larger context of the dramatic tradition of European playwriting, his placement is often alongside George Bernard Shaw, Oscar Wilde, and Samuel Beckett. Stoppard's work is akin to Shaw's in that both are known for their verbal dexterity and ability to wed intellectual and moral ideas to high comedy. While both like to debate ideas, Stoppard is known for his theatricality and innovative dramatic structures that deviate from realism whereas Shaw's linear plots are rooted in the well-made play tradition. Stoppard is more of a theatrical showman than Shaw, while Shaw, a committed Socialist and reformer, is more concerned with the social implications of his plays' ideas.

Stoppard's stylistic bravura has invited comparisons to Wilde, a writer whom Stoppard admires. Both artists accent aesthetic concerns, professing a belief that plays should be judged on the basis of how well they are written and not on their social implications. Though Stoppard values craftsmanship in itself, a central difference is that Stoppard's wit and wordplay are also yoked to plays of ideas while Wilde's wit and clever dialogue are aimed more at art for art's sake. Also, as a playwright, Wilde has a much smaller body of work, with much of his reputation resting on the brilliance of *The Importance of Being Earnest*.

The third figure to whom Stoppard has been compared is Samuel Beckett, and much of that comparison stems from the similarities between *Waiting for Godot* and *Rosguil.* However, once other plays are brought into consideration, the similarities between Beckett and Stoppard quickly evaporate. Beckett's minimalism in dialogue, staging, and plotting lies in sharp contrast to Stoppard's extravagant use of these elements. Scholars have sometimes misconstrued the relationship between Beckett and Stoppard by arguing for an affinity in their views of life, but Beckett's absurdist leanings contrast with Stoppard's logical pursuit of answers and his belief in moral absolutes. Stoppard himself has argued that Beckett's influence comes more from his novels and from Beckett's technique of having a character make a firm statement only to refute and unravel his own argument.

Shaw, Wilde, and Beckett have influenced Stoppard's work, but he has gone beyond their contributions to craft a theatrical style uniquely his own. Uniqueness alone guarantees neither quality nor longevity, and by differentiating Stoppard from other playwrights I am only trying to identify the traits that make it more or less likely for a play or playwright to stand the test of time, a process that can only be a guessing game. For different reasons many playwrights have earned their place in history, and Stoppard stands among them. As long as he continues to write, news of a new Stoppard play will be cause for excitement; whatever he creates will be a theatrical event.

The sheer entertainment value of Stoppard's plays coupled with their intelligence, originality, and immense theatricality as well as the timelessness of ideas addressed, of characters employed, and of settings used, all combine to suggest that many of Stoppard's major plays will likely enjoy a long stage life. While it will be up to scholars and practitioners of the future to decide whether Stoppard gains a lasting place in the canon, I believe he will. Toward that end, I hope to have contributed to the current understanding and appreciation of a theatre artist who is one of the twentieth century's most gifted and exceptional playwrights.

Introduction

1. While 1977 is an arbitrary date, it is a year in which Stoppard received much critical acclaim. Though only ten years into his career, the Young Vic was already presenting a Stoppard retrospective, and *Newsweek* hailed him as "the most original and consistently dazzling" of British playwrights: "Without doubt, Stoppard is the most highly praised and widely exported British playwright since Harold Pinter and John Osborne—and he is accessible to a broader audience than Pinter and is less chained to a place in time than Osborne. His plays have been performed by more than 350 companies in nineteen countries" and have been translated into 30 languages (May and Behr 35). In the same article, *New York Times* critic John Leonard says: "There's no better, funnier, more interesting playwright loose in the world today" (35). Likewise, Trevor Nunn asserts: "If one were to ask which plays written by modern British writers will still be performed in 20 or 100 years' time and still be relevant, I would unhesitatingly include Tom Stoppard's work in a very short list" (40). The article boldly concludes: "Even if he never put pen to paper again, his position among the first rank of modern playwrights is solidly established" (40). Since that assessment, Stoppard has only added to his legacy.

2. Categorization is necessarily difficult, arbitrary, and limiting. In particular, the terms modernism and postmodernism mean different things to different people. My use of modernism and postmodernism come from Todd Gitlin's "Postmodern-

ism: Roots and Politics." There Gitlin distinguishes among premodernism (realism), modernism, and postmodernism. Briefly:

The premodernist work seeks unity of vision, continuity, sequence, causality in time or space, and a single narrative voice. In premodernist works, individuals matter.

The modernist work aspires to unity, a unity that is "constructed, assembled from fragments, or shocks, or juxtapositions of difference. It shifts abruptly among a multiplicity of voices, perspectives, materials. Continuity is disrupted, and with enthusiasm. . . . The orders of conventional reality—inside versus outside, subject versus object, self versus other—are called into question. . . . The work composes beauty out of discord" (349). Stoppard's use of multiple perspectives, parodic echoing, and seeming instability (some of the traits that lead critics to label him postmodern) are much more characteristic of the modernist temperament that Gitlin describes. This is especially true when contrasted with Gitlin's vision of postmodernism.

Gitlin asserts that in postmodernism, "the search for unity has apparently been abandoned altogether. Instead we have textuality, a cultivation of surfaces endlessly referring to, ricocheting from, reverberating onto other surfaces. The work calls attention to its arbitrariness, constructedness; it interrupts itself. Instead of a single center, there is pastiche, cultural recombination. . . . Not only has the master voice dissolved. . . . The implied subject is fragmented, unstable, even decomposed; it is finally nothing more than a crosshatch of discourses" (350). While Stoppard's plays are known for stylistic flair, nothing in a Stoppard work is arbitrary; underneath the surface glitter the plays are highly ordered and underpinned with logic and a point of view. Relativity in a Stoppard play is not so much postmodern equivalence, as it is intellectual uncertainty—a hallmark of intellectualism is an open mind, the willingness to see the validity of an alternative perspective. Also as Stoppard's career has progressed, his views have become more hardened, less permeable, while still maintaining a willingness to acknowledge the weaknesses, or comic potentialities, of the things in which he most believes.

Furthermore, Stoppard's emphasis on linguistic matters and rational discourse places him much more firmly in the camp of modernism than it does in the nonintentional visual montages of a postmodern theatre artist such as Robert Wilson. Likewise, other postmodern artists such as The Wooster Group, Spalding Gray, or Laurie Anderson have a markedly different artistic (and often ideological) perspective than Stoppard.

Conversely, perhaps the way in which Stoppard may most be seen as postmodern is if one uses the criteria of how one responds to uncertainty in the world. According to Alan Wilde, modernists exhibit anxiety and a sense of loss whereas postmodernists are characterized by "a willingness to live with uncertainty, to tolerate and, in some cases, to welcome a world seen as random and multiple, even, at times, absurd" (44). Many of Stoppard's plays do show an acceptance of uncertainty and instability as being central components of human life; however, his plays also embrace order, logic, and those things that provide stability in an uncertain world. The both/and quality of Stoppard's work allows him to cut across categories and to attract admirers from different critical, theoretical, and ideological backgrounds.

3. The abbreviation *Rosguil* is taken from Stoppard's letters.

4. After seeing the letters quoted in an article (*Library Chronicle* 26, no. 3 [1996]), Stoppard has refused further permission on grounds that he intended the letters as private correspondence not meant for public consumption. Many of these letters (in HRHRC 37.1 and 37.2) are not only informative, but entertaining as well. The inability to quote directly from these letters hinders the style of the chapter, but I stand by the accuracy of my presentation of this period of Stoppard's life and career.

5. While *Enter a Free Man* (1968) opened on the West End, its appearance there was largely due to Stoppard's selling the option during a time of financial need prior to *Rosguil*'s success. While my definition of "major" play has to do with the intended venue as well as the relative thematic weight of the piece, some of Stoppard's minor works have been among his most commercially successful. For example, *Dirty Linen* (1976), a sex farce set in the British House of Commons, was his longest continuous running show, playing for over four years and more than one thousand performances. Likewise, *The Real Inspector Hound,* a one-act play that parodies Agatha Christie–like mysteries to play with notions of identity, has become part of the international repertoire.

Chapter 1

1. The anecdote is usually told as if Stoppard actually said the line to a reporter, something he may have done later. In 1995, Stoppard said: "I much regret making that remark. It's the only thing I've ever said that refuses to die" (Rees).

2. Stoppard (birth name Tomas Straussler) was born on 3 July 1937 in Czechoslovakia. Being Jewish (a fact Stoppard did not know until 1994; see his September 1999 *Talk* magazine article), the family left the country on the eve of the 1939 Nazi invasion. They went to Singapore but were again dislocated when the Japanese invaded in 1942. While Mrs. Straussler and her two sons went to India, Dr. Straussler remained behind and was killed. After the war Mrs. Straussler married British army officer Kenneth Stoppard. When the family moved to England in early 1946, the children took their stepfather's surname. The family lived in a number of cities before settling in Bristol in 1950. Growing up Stoppard was an avid reader, but had only limited involvement with theatre. Though he was born in Czechoslovakia and did not move to England until he was eight, Stoppard received all of his schooling in English and has never been literate in any other language. Though both Czech and Jewish by birth, Stoppard has always thought of himself as English.

The first Stoppard biography (tentatively titled *The Invention of Tom Stoppard: A Biography,* by Ira Nadel) is due out in 2002. Methuen is the u.k. publisher; St. Martin's the u.s.

3. Being a reporter for the *WDP* also provided Stoppard with one of his rare acting experiences. For an article he played "the seventh Arab" in a production of Shaw's *Captain Brassbound's Conversion,* and his task was to stab actor Emrys James. As he tells it, wearing a "skirt, blouse, kimono, [hooded cloak], and beard" and with his face, hands, and feet "a healthy Moorish brown," Stoppard executed his assignment, but only after he had blanked out and was saved by James who had the great presence of mind to run toward the bewildered walk-on ("Act II").

4. Just before or after writing *The Gamblers,* Stoppard penned a rough draft of a play that was the ur–*Real Inspector Hound.* Stoppard told Gussow that he "wrote a rough draft of the play in 1960, but I abandoned it. It was the second thing I wrote" (*Conversations* 1), while he told the editors of *Theatre Quarterly* that he wrote it "after *The Gamblers*" (Hudson, Itzin, and Trussler 60).

5. In "The Definite Maybe" Stoppard records this development differently when he glibly writes: "Because it was not unlike *Flowering Cherry* it was sent to Ralph Richardson, who declined on grounds that it was not unlike *Flowering Cherry*" (19). Stoppard's published declarations are probably more quotable than accurate, for a year later when the rights were sold to television, Richardson considered playing the lead role. Ironically, Stoppard followed Richardson's suggestion and expanded the play, only to have forty-two minutes cut out of the script that was eventually filmed.

6. In the early plays, Stoppard's other favorite character name is Moon, which comes from his idiosyncratic relationship to an incident in the film *Left-Handed Gun* (see Hudson, Itzin, and Trussler 70–71). The Moon and Boot characters often work in tandem: "Boots are often more ostentatious and outgoing, often in fact more dominant than the submissive Moons. Stoppard himself describes a Moon as 'a person to whom things happen. Boot is rather more aggressive'" (Dean 18). Mel Gussow interprets Moon and Boot as representing "two sides of the author's nature, the philosopher and pragmatist, the intellectual and the entertainer" (*Conversations* x).

7. The three stories are "Reunion," "Life, Times: Fragments," and "The Story." All three were originally published in *Introduction 2: Stories by New Writers* (London: Faber, 1964). For a discussion of these short stories, see Londré's *Tom Stoppard* (91–99) or Rusinko's work of the same name (17–22).

8. As discussed in note 4, the play was started just before or after the first draft of *The Gamblers.* It appears that Stoppard submitted *The Critics* to the Theatre Royal in Bristol in February 1962, but was rejected. In a June 1963 letter to Anthony Smith

he refers to the text as *The Critics;* however, there are multiple manuscript copies, fragments, and notes at the HRHRC. A text entitled *The Critics* is dated 1 January 1962, while there are multiple versions or fragments of *The Stand-Ins* with dates ranging from June 1962 to July 1963. A seemingly later version is titled *Murder at Mousetrap Manor.* After the success of *Rosguil,* the not-yet-completed text of *Mouse-trap Manor,* along with a synopsis of its ending, was sent to Michael Codron, who produced it (i.e., *The Real Inspector Hound*) on the West End in 1968.

9. Uncharacteristically, *Funny Man* exhibits a leftist sense of class consciousness. In contrast, *The Real Thing* is written from the perspective of a reactionary conservative, the personal politics for which Stoppard is known.

10. The short story (four and a half typed pages) was entitled "August." It provided a loose framework, as well as some dialogue, for the radio play (HRHRC 49.6).

11. *"M" is for Moon among Other Things* has been staged. Having seen it off-off-Broadway in 1989, I must agree with Ned Chaillet's review of its first staging in 1977 in Richmond, England: "Stoppard's play does not adjust to the stage very well and looks like a radio play, over-endowed with poignancy" (M. Page 10).

12. Considerations of family life, such as the presence of brothers or sisters or of the parents of adult characters, are extremely rare in the Stoppard canon. In the 1990s this changed a little. *Arcadia* involves some sibling interactions, while in *Indian Ink* the emotional dynamics of sisters is pertinent. In contrast, in previous works, sibling relationships primarily served functional purposes, such as Gwendolyn being Carr's younger sister (*Travesties*) or Ridley having a twin (*Hapgood*).

13. Tynan, with Londré and others following, incorrectly states that Ewing's idea for the King Lear *Rosguil* came after a rejection of *This Way Out with Samuel Boot.*

14. While the BBC enjoyed some of Stoppard's episodes, they declined to hire him for a permanent staff position because his style and treatment were too individual for series writing. Nonetheless, Stoppard received about £90 for his efforts.

15. Curiously, in a January 1964 letter to Anthony Smith Stoppard refers to Rosencrantz and Guildenstern as separate from the stage play.

16. The objects the two men accumulate are similar and include vacuum cleaners, miners' helmets, goggles, and a harpoon gun. Stoppard also reuses dialogue and situations. For example, both Jamie and Jonathan buy a Deaf-Aid even though they hear perfectly well; this leads to Stoppard's joke of having the salesman shout: "There! That's better isn't it?" To which the buyer responds: "You don't have to shout. I'm not deaf" (*Samuel Boot* 19; *ICGYABLB,* sc. 5). Similarly, the dialogue concerning the purchase of the harpoon gun and the scene where the television is repossessed (both discussed in the text) are recycled from *ICGYABLB.*

17. For an extended discussion of the influence of *Next Time I'll Sing to You* on Stoppard and *Rosguil,* see Sammells's *Tom Stoppard* (32–39).

18. A 1966 Vienna production, as well as a German TV play version, used the title *Der Spleen des George Riley.* In English, unproduced drafts of *Enter a Free Man* have been titled *The Preservation of George Riley* and *Home and Dry.*

19. Typifying how Stoppard distances himself from considering *Enter a Free Man* as representative of his writing is the fact that in August 1970 he refused a proposed New York production. He wanted a stronger work to be his second New York offering. *Enter* was eventually produced in New York in December 1974. Likewise, director Nagle Jackson reports that when Stoppard saw *Enter* in San Francisco, he felt the play looked like the work of a complete stranger (Letter to Stoppard).

20. *Rosencrantz and Guildenstern Meet King Lear* was completed by 22 June 1964. However, at the end of the Ford Foundation grant period, Stoppard presented a twenty-five-minute excerpt (entitled *Guildenstern and Rosencrantz*) of what he then projected to be a full-length play in progress. Under Stoppard's direction, this text was presented in Berlin in September and at the Questors Theatre (Ealing, England) on 4 October 1964. Descriptions of that text correspond to an eighteen-page script at the HRHRC (24.1). This Questors text is very similar to the opening section of *Rosguil Lear,* the part that Stoppard most maintained for the third act of *Rosguil.*

21. An expanded version of Rosencrantz and Guildenstern's opening exchange over money appears in *Rosguil* (80–81). All page references to *Rosguil* are from the Samuel French edition.

22. In the original, the Player's lines are spoken by the Captain, and other than switching a couple of speaker tags the exchange going from "Melancholy?" to "And he does both" (*Rosguil Lear* 2; *Rosguil* 52) is almost verbatim. The final dialogue runs close to the original, but in the latter it is shifted to a different context. Likewise Rosencrantz's speech "A compulsion towards philosophical investigation . . ." (*Rosguil Lear* 5, *Rosguil* 91) and Guildenstern's (originally Rosencrantz's) speech "It really boils down to symptoms . . ." (*Rosguil Lear* 6, *Rosguil* 91) are virtually verbatim, but in the original they are separated by a page of dialogue rather than placed following each other.

23. Stoppard's conceit of having the Player's mask resemble Hamlet's face might have come from his reading of Dover Wilson's *What Happens in Hamlet.* In chapter 5 (particularly 170–71) Wilson discusses how Lucianus, by virtue of being the nephew to the king as opposed to the brother of the king, is the Hamlet figure of *The Murder of Gonzago.* Stoppard's inspiration for using an overt visual parallel may have come from Wilson's suggestion that Lucianus might wear the same black doublet as Hamlet.

24. This speech survives nearly verbatim in *Rosguil* (79).

25. The dialogue concerning the letter is fairly similar to the expanded and revised version in *Rosguil* but the sections are reversed. The passage from Rosencrantz's "The letter" through Guildenstern's "No" (*Rosguil* 83, *Rosguil Lear* 15) precedes the passage from Rosencrantz's "We take Hamlet to the English king" through Guildenstern's "That depends on when we get there" (*Rosguil* 82, *Rosguil Lear* 16). Both sections are nearly verbatim.

26. In *Rosguil* it is: "Incidents! All we get is incidents! Dear God, is it too much to ask for a little sustained action?" (91).

27. In *Rosguil* Hamlet reads the letter.

28. Stoppard first wrote *The Gamblers* in 1960 or 1961, and then revised and expanded it before its Bristol production. (Along the way, Ewing tried to sell the play to both radio and television producers.) The HRHRC has multiple versions of *The Gamblers,* none of which are dated by Stoppard. While the literature on Stoppard occasionally includes a brief discussion of *The Gamblers,* most, if not all, accounts seem to be based on Ronald Hayman's description of the play (*Tom Stoppard* 28–31). Unfortunately, Hayman does not provide a source for his information. The excerpts Hayman uses correspond to the partial typescript in Box 67. However, my discussion is based on the longer, complete script in Box 10. More recently the HRHRC has acquired a *Gamblers* script from Gordon Dickerson, an agent of Fraser and Dunlop. That script is similar to the Box 67 version; it is likely the text Hayman used.

29. In the Gordon Dickerson collection there are two undated (likely Apr. or May 1965) synopses for sixty-minute television plays (Box 11.10). *The Waiter* was to be about a guy, Frank, who places ads in the Personals section. He describes himself as a James Bond type, and thus it is ironic that he would be "desperate for a girl." The main action was to revolve around the first meeting between Frank and Daisy, "a squashed little girl." In the course of the play "Daisy's hidden reserves of confidence emerge as Frank's veneer of confidence cracks." By the end of the piece "each of them has gained from the encounter, gained not merely each other's affection, but mainly in their self-awareness." *The Servant Problem* was more developed as an idea and was to focus on a maid, Clara, and a butler, Moon. While the masters are away, the servants role-play seduction scenes between master and servant. Unexpectedly, the Lord and Lady return and each discovers evidence of the servants' playing with their belongings and thus each, unbeknownst to the other, fires a servant. However, at the same time, the Lord begins to lust after Clara and the Lady after Moon. The next day, learning that the desired servant has been given notice, the Lord and Lady feel free to act on their sexual impulses. The Lady sleeps with Moon, and afterward: "Moon treats her as less than an equal, and Lady X enjoys being treated like a tart.

He bullies her. She'll bring him a drink. He treats her like a maid. She joins in. She likes being a maid." Soon Clara and Lord X return and, still teasing him, Clara convinces him to dress as the butler. This leads to the final moment where, dressed as a butler and a maid, the Lord and Lady discover each other while Moon and Clara are seen leaving the manor, dressed to travel.

30. Ironically, the selected play, David Wright's *Strike,* was eventually canceled, partly because, even though the show was in rehearsals, the script had not been finalized.

31. While the novel falls outside the scope of this study, it is worth noting that a main theme of the book is whether there is an underlying order in the world or whether it is all random, a theme that appears in later Stoppard works.

32. Based on a letter Ewing wrote Stoppard, the payment should have been substantially higher—twenty guineas for each script, or approximately £140 every two weeks (29 Oct. 1965).

33. Despite Tynan's claims to the contrary, I have heard that the scripts can be found in the BBC Archives in Reading.

34. At an unspecified point Stoppard submitted the script to the Royal Court Theatre, but they declined (Gollob and Roper 159).

35. The contract, dated 12 July 1966, between the Oxford Theatre Group and Stoppard stipulated he was to deliver the revised script by 31 July and that if they were satisfied with the revisions they would perform it at the Edinburgh Festival from 24 August through 10 September. Stoppard received board and lodging, a first-class round-trip train ticket and up to £15 in expenses. For their part the Oxford Theatre Group was to receive what was to become perhaps the largest windfall in the history of amateur theatre: the contract stipulated that they would get "10% of the gross receipts from the exploitations of the play [including television and film] in the English language for the next 5 years."

36. Despite his last-minute restoration of order, Stoppard relates: "We didn't even attempt to do the very last scene at Edinburgh; it was simply unstageable in those circumstances, the circumstances being a stage the size of a ping pong table and a dozen actors instead of 35" (G. Gordon 17).

37. In 1995 Stoppard clarified that he never had a sincere interest in being a novelist. Regarding the impetus for *Lord Malquist and Mr. Moon,* he told Mel Gussow: "At that age, at that stage of one's career, one doesn't let the opportunity go by. It's hard enough to get a publisher interested in a novel which is completed, let alone having a publisher commission a book, so naturally I wrote a novel. I haven't wanted to write a novel since" (*Conversations* 136). Elsewhere Stoppard told Penelope Mortimer that he wrote *Lord Malquist* for the advance and because he "liked the idea of

having written a novel, and if it was necessary to write one in order to reach that position, I was prepared to make the effort" (31). Depending on when he has been asked about the novel, his retrospective assessment of its quality has ranged from displeasure to satisfaction.

38. Indeed, initially Anthony Blond had seriously considered not even publishing the novel. However, subsequent in-house readers gave the book strong reviews, and so he went ahead with the project (Ewing, Letter to Stoppard, 15 Sept. 1965).

39. This paragraph is based on a letter retrospectively dated late September or early October 1966. In the letter Stoppard says it is a £50 option for six months, but the contract of 1 October is for £250 and nine months. If the National Theatre were to decide to exercise the option, they have one year to put in on. In addition, the National was to receive 33 percent of Stoppard's royalties from subsequent English-language stage and film rights. Thus, due to his agent's fee, the Oxford Theatre Group's 10 percent commission, and the National's share, for the first five years Stoppard only received about 50 percent of *Rosguil*'s stage and film royalties.

40. Stoppard signed the *Rosguil* book contract with Faber on 28 October 1966. Within the week he also signed contracts optioning the rights for productions in Sweden, Holland, and Belgium. Thus, the wheels were in motion even before the National formally decided to stage the play.

41. While John Dexter had claimed to be eager to direct the play, his resignation from the National in March 1967 was in part due to the decision to produce *Rosguil* instead of an all-male *As You Like It* (*London Times*, 23 Mar. 1967).

42. While Stoppard's dissatisfaction reflects his perfectionism, he was not yet accustomed to success and public attention. Now known as a cool, smooth, eminently quotable interviewee, when he was first interviewed after the National's announcement, he remarked: "I am rather neurotic, and this makes me somewhat more neurotic" (Knight).

Chapter 2

1. Though it goes against the lines from *Hamlet,* when the play was revived at the National in 1995 Stoppard claimed that he wanted to call the play "Exit Rosencrantz and Guildenstern" (de Lisle).

2. While the National Theatre production garnered excellent reviews, Stoppard was apparently unnerved by the experience. In 1988 Stoppard told Peter Lewis that he left partway through the premiere performance: "Early in the first act a man sitting in front of me turned to his companion and said, 'I do wish they'd get on with it.' That finished it for me. I went to the pub and never came back" ("Quantum Stoppard" 59).

3. One of Stoppard's favorite metaphors in regard to the nonintentionality of his themes, particularly as they apply to *Rosguil,* is that "of a duped smuggler confronted with a customs officer. I truthfully declare that I am indeed responsible for this piece about two specific individuals in a particular situation. Then he starts ransacking my luggage and comes up with all manner of exotic contraband like truth and illusion, the nature of identity, what I feel about life and death—and I have to admit the stuff is there but I can't for the life of me remember packing it" ("Something to Declare"). While Stoppard denies any specific intent, he was not completely unaware of the potential thematic resonances of *Rosguil.* While writing the play, the playwright agreed with Anthony Smith's assessment that Stoppard was trying too hard to load every line with levels of meaning and that he would be better off humanizing the characters more.

4. For analyses of the similarities and differences between *Rosguil* and *Godot,* see Jenkins (*Theatre of Tom Stoppard* 40–41), Faraone (15–21), Callen (22–30), and Gianakaris (52–58).

5. Examinations of interconnections between *Hamlet* and *Rosguil* can be found in Hunter (emphasis on the travestying of *Hamlet,* 133–40), Huston (emphasis on *Rosguil* as a modern misreading of *Hamlet,* 47–66), and Brassell (emphasis on how Stoppard uses *Hamlet* in his own play to create two levels of dramatic reality—thus giving Rosencrantz and Guildenstern "onstage" selves, through their interaction in *Hamlet* plot, and "offstage" selves, as Stoppard's creation, 35–67).

6. Stoppard has long acknowledged his admiration of *Next Time I'll Sing to You,* and Stoppard's insistence that he knew "very little" about Pirandello is probably accurate, for Stoppard's use of what appear to be Pirandellian notions of the flux between art, life, and reality are central aspects of Saunders's play, a work that is highly Pirandellian in its use of actors, characters, and author (Whitaker 56). In addition to Whitaker's analysis, insightful commentary on the influence of Saunders's play on Stoppard and *Rosguil* can be found in Sammells (32–39) and Faraone (25–28). Incidentally, Saunders strongly encouraged Stoppard to expand *Rosencrantz and Guildenstern Meet King Lear* into a full-length play.

7. In one of the more intriguing interpretations, the Gesher Theatre, an émigré Russian company from Israel, toured *Rosguil* in 1992, presenting it as a parable on totalitarianism: "In such a reading of Stoppard's play, it ceases to have anything to do with alienation and focuses menacingly on the system's way of making spies from citizens" (Franks 10).

8. Stoppard's own stance has been contradictory. His most widely quoted view is: "First I must say that I didn't know what the word existential meant until it was applied to *Rosencrantz.* And even now [1974] existentialism is not a philosophy I find

either attractive or plausible. But it's certainly true that the play can be interpreted in existential terms, as well as in other terms" (Hudson, Itzin, and Trussler 58). In Bryden's review of the Edinburgh production, he called the play an "existentialist fable," and Stoppard himself, in 1967, referred to the protagonists as "existential immortals" ("Definite Maybe"). Also, in 1968, Stoppard aptly noted: "People often seem to mean quite different things by ['existential']. There certainly is a kind of obvious existential element in the situation, taking 'existential' to mean that really one doesn't count and that nothing really makes much difference because things will happen anyway" (Louis). Stoppard's main objection to the existential label seems to be that it connotes a despairing, nihilistic view of life as meaningless; in contrast, Stoppard feels that his characters "make continuous attempts to master the situation and comprehend it with the assumption there is something to comprehend, which would be nearer the position that I would take" (Funke 221).

9. While very interested in *Rosguil,* Jeremy Brooks of the RSC suggested three major revisions: "a) it ought to be in two acts—you'd have to find a bridge that would bring them to Elsinore in the first act; b) that a lot of the double-talk, amusing and stimulating as it is, needs cutting; and c) that the action of the present third act needs to be resolved, somehow, in a more positive way" (Letter to Stoppard). Since Stoppard had written that third act in only two weeks' time, it was greatly rushed, and while Stoppard ignored the first two suggestions, he did ultimately expand and alter the third act, but not necessarily in a more positive way. That original RSC ending is loosely similar to the first published ending discussed in note 11, but with Rosencrantz and Guildenstern playing the roles of the Ambassadors. After counting the corpses, Guildenstern says: "So much for that. And them. Death is so simple it's difficult to credit it. (THEY FOLLOW THE PROCESSION AS IT DISAPPEARS) Once you're off you stay off. That's all there is to say about it." Rosencrantz adds: "Now you see them, now you—" (THEY HAVE GONE. EMPTY STAGE. HOUSE LIGHTS COME UP UNTIL THEY ARE AS BRIGHT AS THE LIGHT ON THE STAGE.) (83). In contrast the Edinburgh ending starts to move closer to the final published ending, but it is still missing major moments such as Guildenstern's stabbing of the Player, the Tragedians enactment of their deaths (in the Edinburgh text, they simply exit because the boat has docked), and Guildenstern's existential ruminations on death (Samuel French ed. 97). However, starting with Rosencrantz's "That's it, then, is it?" (97), many of their lines are present, albeit a number of them are spoken by the other character. That Edinburgh text then ends with the *Hamlet* excerpt, carrying it all the way through Fortinbras's closing speech. Overall, the third acts of the RSC script, Edinburgh script, and National Theatre script are all different enough that it is difficult to note concisely their variances.

10. Edward Petherbridge, Guildenstern in the original London production, reports that one of the endings had the protagonists go into a sort of limbo: "Guil-

denstern had lines [like], 'I don't want to die.' [and] 'No, I don't—not like that, I don't want to fade out, I want a proper death with real blood.' And I personally felt at the time . . . that it wouldn't work if the character of Guildenstern himself was conscious of the fact that there was something totally theatrical and abstract about his death. That it was somehow a playwright's figment . . . it was too literary for the character himself to realize he was a character, that it took the play out of its universality" (Faraone 42).

11. The ending in the first edition of *Rosguil* (Faber and Faber 1967) corresponds to one used during rehearsals of the National Theatre production. After Horatio's speech the text continues through the end of the *Hamlet* text. Then the Ambassadors stychomythically tally the corpses. It closes with the Ambassadors responding to an offstage voice obscurely calling out two names. This summoning is similar to how Rosencrantz and Guildenstern were called to Elsinore.

12. The New York text is preserved at the Billy Rose Theatre Collection at Lincoln Center, the London text at the National Theatre archives, and the Edinburgh text at the HRHRC. Unless otherwise noted all quotations in this chapter are from the Samuel French edition.

13. Stoppard has used this figure in interviews with Sid Smith and Paul Allen, though he told the latter that the estimate came from a friend (245). Though not having done a line-by-line count, my own research suggests that a 40–50 percent cut in the spoken text is a reasonable estimate.

14. Typically the gag works by Rosencrantz's having an intuitive and accidental "discovery" of a scientific principle, which then goes comically awry whenever he tries to show or explain it to Guildenstern: "Newton's apple falls, Archimedes' bath overflows and balls, feathers, and flower baskets scream out the principles of energy and gravity but to no avail. An idly folded piece of paper takes wing as a prototype plane and Rosencrantz munches his way through the first hamburger without knowing it" (Owen 24). There is also a windmill / mobile that is used to prefigure a steam engine as well as their encounter with a pulley and lever system. Stoppard explains that he had long wanted to use this gag: "It just seemed so funny; the thought of someone who almost discovers everything. I tried to make Rosencrantz play the opening bars of Beethoven's Fifth by accidentally rattling broken banisters but the music director said that one was not on" (24).

15. In 1968 Stoppard wrote a film version of *Rosguil* for MGM, with John Boorman to direct. When management at MGM changed, the project was canceled. Among the reasons given by MGM for rejecting the film was their belief that the title

characters were not interesting, sympathetic, or identifiable (Thatcher). Stoppard has retrospectively described the earlier version as "a terrible script" that was "very word-heavy" and that tried to save the play (S. Smith 236). However, that script actually opens out the play quite a bit and is only fractionally more wordy than the 1990 film. When Stoppard started on the new script in the mid- to late 1980s, he began anew, but knowingly or not, he kept some things from the 1968 script. Both screenplays make extensive use of the *Hamlet* text as a throughline, and that earlier script includes the tennis court version of the question game. On the other hand, the 1968 screenplay had additions (such as a debate about the existence of God, including Guildenstern's declaration of atheism [72–73]) that were discarded. One of the most interesting additions to the 1968 script was having two other messengers who were similar to Rosencrantz and Guildenstern. These courtiers were then used in a scene with Rosencrantz and Guildenstern where there was a hall that featured a floor with a chessboard pattern, and so the four courtiers played a game of human chess which the protagonists eventually won (19–20).

16. In a letter to Jon Bradshaw, Stoppard asserts: "The predicament in the case of Rosencrantz and Guildenstern is the same as the predicament of the playwright, namely that they and I had to kill time because we didn't have a story. Until the action of *Hamlet* re-enters my play there's simply no purpose to their existence. So I had to invent ways of passing the time by making them invent ways of passing the time."

17. Guildenstern is the rational one, Rosencrantz the more passive, instinctive one. John Wood (Guildenstern in the original Broadway production) has noted: "The two roles represent the two halves of the same person, one part somewhat cerebral, one part a bit intuitive" (Shepard). Stoppard himself has said: "They both add up to me in many ways in the sense that they're carrying out a dialogue which I carry out with myself" (G. Gordon 19). While working on the RSC draft, Stoppard wrote to Anthony Smith, noting that he needed to make Guildenstern's character less like his own.

18. In Stoppard's self-directed film version, after the Player guesses that the coin has landed "heads," Guildenstern does not even look at it. Rosencrantz does give a quick glance back, but for both it is as if "heads" is a foregone conclusion.

19. Here, the Edinburgh text has an added line for Rosencrantz: "It's the only truth we have" (70).

20. In the Samuel French text, the means of associating the two Spies with Rosencrantz and Guildenstern is that after they deliver the letter and are ordered to death, the Spies "start to spin imaginary coins" (65). In contrast, the Grove Press paperback eliminates the coins in favor of the revelation that the Spies wear coats iden-

tical to those worn by Rosencrantz and Guildenstern. This text also contains extra material (lines that appear in the New York and Edinburgh texts, but not the London text). The added material begins with the Player's fundamental philosophical query: "Traitors hoist by their own petard?—Or victims of the gods?—we shall never know!" (82). While the Player's line is relevant to the theme, Rosencrantz's added speech seems gratuitous, with its main function being to show that despite the visual clue of the identical coats the protagonists still do not understand the connection between the dumb show and their own lives. The use of identical cloaks seems more logical than the use of the Spies' coin-tossing because the coin-tossing suggests that the Player knows the text of *Rosguil* as well as that of *Hamlet*.

21. For those who see *Rosguil* as some form of "theatre of criticism," either of *Hamlet* or of tragedy, I suspect that the play's most tangible "act of criticism" has been its effect on subsequent productions of *Hamlet*, where producers and/or audiences are now more apt to see the courtiers as likable minions whose identity extends beyond the text of *Hamlet*.

22. Stoppard's ensuing stage direction "behind them Hamlet appears from behind the umbrella" (86) can be executed in a manner that implies that Hamlet overhears the content of the letter, a suggestion made in Stoppard's direction of the film version of *Rosguil*.

23. While traditionally the delivery of the fateful letter has been seen as the existential act that defines their existence, Victor Cahn argues that in Guildenstern's desire "not to pass from the earth without somehow mattering" his attack on the Player is "the sheer gratuitous act. If life persists in its senselessness, he will respond accordingly, by behaving without reason and without regard for conventional morality" (62).

24. Philosopher Jonathan Bennett, in an article that examines the play's treatment of reality, identity, memory, activity, and death, argues that Rosencrantz and Guildenstern remain fundamentally unreal: "A person's reality is largely an epistemic matter—how much there is of him is largely to be measured by how much he knows, and that depends on how much recollectable experience has been packed into him. Rosencrantz and Guildenstern, lacking memory, are epistemically empty: they are in touch with no past, and so they can neither construe the present nor direct themselves purposefully towards the future" (87).

25. In an article about the National's 1995 revival, Mel Gussow mentions many different productions and he notes: "Depending on the actors, the balance can shift. When [John] Wood played the Player in an off-Broadway production, he had such comic zest as to share equal billing with the principals. In his hands, the Player became even more of a commentator on the mystery of Hamlet's madness. Wood's ap-

proach was appropriately flamboyant, not histrionic like Alan Howard at the National" ("Wits").

Chapter 3

1. In a letter to Anthony Smith Stoppard indicates that he will start writing the script in January 1970, but the contract preserved at the HRHRC lists the start date as January 1971.

2. The nature of Stoppard's Galileo research is unclear. However, a work he may have consulted, and which directly bears on the historical inaccuracies of Brecht's *Galileo,* is Gerhard Szczesny's 1969 book, *The Case against Bertolt Brecht (with Arguments Drawn from His "Life of Galileo").* This work also offers an excellent condensed biography of Galileo, particularly concerning the events germane to both Brecht's and Stoppard's plays.

3. Through no effort of Stoppard's, the *Galileo* screenplay resurfaced in the early 1990s. In 1993, Disney's Michael Eisner inquired about Stoppard's interest in reviving the project, possibly directing it as well. Stoppard offered Eisner a self-assessment of the screenplay: "In one way my 'Galileo' is a pleasant surprise. It's quite muscular and witty, and well researched. But it does not wear its research lightly and it doesn't really resemble a film script as Disney (or anyone else) would understand the term: long scenes, long speeches, not much movement. It's much more like a free-form play. The level of argument, the language, and the 'dry wit' are obviously influenced by my admiration for 'A Man for All Seasons', but it is much thicker (sluggish) than [Robert] Bolt's play, let alone Bolt's film. I don't think the script is going to be acceptable" (Fax). Stoppard had no interest in directing it, but offered to do a script polish if a director were interested. However, Stoppard figured that to make it commercially viable the script would need a major overhaul, and that was not a script he cared to write, particularly in light of the fact that he was already committed to many other projects.

4. A bulky machine, the Planetarium's projector is a permanent fixture in the center of the intended semicircular playing space. Thus, Stoppard felt that it would sabotage any attempt at illusionism. The props and costumes could be accurate, but the play was written with most effects to be executed theatrically rather than realistically.

5. A curious sidenote is that when I wrote Stoppard in 1996 to ask if he had ever actually written the play version, his secretary wrote back saying he had not (20 May 1996). Also, the HRHRC file has it incorrectly labeled as being a screenplay.

6. Speaking in his own voice, this line about science and theology dancing together as well as time revealing all truths appears in Stoppard's interview with Joseph

McCulloch (41–42). Another major sentiment that Stoppard expresses as being symptomatic of his own view is that all of these scientific discoveries simply show that God has been gravely underestimated.

7. Historically, when Galileo heard about the Dutch telescope, he proceeded to figure out the means of creating a device that could make distant objects appear closer. When successful, he presented his device to the City Council of Venice, claiming it as his invention, and he was financially rewarded. Szczesny provides an account (69–71) of this episode and the controversy it created. Szczesny ultimately defends Galileo by arguing that there were no patent laws and "that the Galilean construction exceeded in its effectiveness the already existing telescopes by a very wide margin" (71). Stoppard ignores the way Galileo profited financially from his deception and instead focuses on Galileo's accomplishment of creating the first telescope capable of astronomical observations.

8. While the main focus of the play is Galileo's scientific career, Stoppard weaves in strands of his domestic life. In the play Galileo has a common-law wife, Marina, with whom he has a daughter, Maria Celeste. The relationship between Galileo and Marina is tempestuous. For example, at the end of the first act when he is teaching both mother and daughter how to read, the scene devolves into a fight where Marina pours a bowl of soup over Galileo. In their final scene together, they get into a struggle that is "short but vicious" and that ends with her scratching his face (2.8). Throughout the play Marina has been urging Galileo to wed her officially, and now Galileo consents to letting Marina go to marry another man. In general, the play shows Galileo as more concerned about his work than his family, but unlike Brecht's Galileo, he never stands in the way of his daughter's happiness.

In his depiction of Galileo's family life, Stoppard does not acknowledge his use of poetic license. From 1599 to 1610, Galileo had a live-in relationship with a Venetian woman, Maria Gamba. Together, they had three children—Virginia, Livia, and Vincenzio. When Galileo and Maria separated in 1610, the daughters went with Galileo and his mother to Florence. When Maria married a few years later, the son also joined the Galilei family (Szczesny 74–75). The play's Maria Celeste corresponds to the eldest child, Virginia. Both Virginia and Livia became nuns, and Galileo wrote of the great love he felt for his children, particularly his close attachment to Virginia. Galileo's only son, Vincenzio, took care of him during the last years of his life when he was under house arrest (Szczesny 105–6).

9. For the reading of the censure Stoppard sought a difficult stage effect: "As the Secretary reads, the eleven theologians are gently lifted into the air in a slow arc, like the arc the earth makes round the run, and at the same time, they gently rotate as the earth does on its journey" (2.16). When the pronouncement is finished "the Theologians pass out of view" (2.17).

10. Periodically, Stoppard shows the tension between science and popular superstition. Most notably there are three scenes where Galileo must provide a horoscope for the Grand Duke Ferdinand. In the first horoscope scene, Galileo pretends that his designs for a pendulum clock are the horoscope he has been figuring. Galileo is clearly improvising as he predicts "general favorability," and the Grand Duke is only reassured when Galileo provides more specific detail as to numbers and colors to avoid. Galileo closes the forecast by promising many years of good health. This proclamation of good health is repeated in the second and third horoscope scenes, but in the third rendition, the words "many years of good health" are followed by "Ferdinand promptly dies" (2.2). Emblematic of the play's theatricality, the death is a black-humored moment rather than a sympathetic one.

11. Szczesny discusses the fateful document (99–102), Galileo's relationship to Pope Urban VIII, and the events surrounding the trial (92–111). Quotations from Galileo's cleverly worded answers during the trial show that he was determined "not to deny his scientific convictions but merely to capitulate before the life-and-limb threatening power of the Inquisition" (103). Notably, in July 1633, less than a month after his conviction, Galileo sent a copy of his banned book to a publisher in Strasbourg "with the request to have a Latin translation of it prepared and published" (106). Throughout the years of his house arrest he corresponded with other scholars and was able to get his work published in Protestant countries (Szczesny 106–11).

12. In 1992, after having a commission study the matter for thirteen years, the Catholic Church finally confirmed Galileo's findings and admitted their error in condemning him.

Chapter 4

1. Though produced after *Rosguil*, *Albert's Bridge* and *Enter a Free Man* were, except for final revisions, written before the National Theatre production of *Rosguil*. The one-act plays include the revisions that led to *The Real Inspector Hound* and the new works *After Magritte* and *Dogg's Our Pet*. Stoppard's correspondence indicates that sections of *Jumpers* were written in 1968, 1969, 1970, and 1971, as well as changes made during rehearsals in early 1972.

2. The television play is set on the day of the parade that celebrates the return of the first man on the moon. Bone, an absentminded historian trying to find a logical pattern to world events, works on his book in the study, while his wife, Penelope, lies sick in the bedroom. For Penelope, like Dotty, the moon landing means "everything we live by is suddenly exposed as nothing more than local customs—nothing more—because he has seen the edges where we stop, and we never stopped anywhere before" (57). Like Dotty, Penelope has taken to bed where she receives visits

from a doctor who may or may not be having an affair with her. A main plot point discovery is that Penelope pushed her old nanny out of the window because the nanny always beat her at games, a killing she can rationalize due to her changed view of morality. (Stoppard began *Jumpers* thinking that Dotty was the murderer of Mc-Fee.) In the television play Stoppard's treatment of its themes are severely condensed, but many of the ideas, much of the situation, and some of the dialogue were used for *Jumpers*.

3. Several critics have offered interpretations antithetical to Stoppard's stated intentions. Gabrielle Robinson has argued that *Jumpers* shows an absurdist universe where rational understanding is impossible ("Plays Without Plot") and that while George clings to a belief in absolute values, the parody of Scott on the moon denies their existence ("Nothing Left but Parody"). In "Stoppard's *Jumpers:* A Mystery Play," Lucinda Gabbard argues that Archie speaks for Stoppard and that the play ridicules morality. In her article "The Universe as Murder Mystery" G. B. Crump provides one of the more cogent and challenging interpretations of *Jumpers* as she argues that though Stoppard may be sympathetic to George's views, the play is not: "Whatever may be Stoppard's personal views about God, *Jumpers* does not endorse George's position at the expense of those of Bones and Archie" (57).

4. In this regard Stoppard is harking back to his original script *And Now the Incredible Archibald Jumpers.* In that text Dotty makes repeated attempts to seek George's help. Early in the play she crosses to the study and says: "George, I want to show you someone. . . . I need a little help" (8). But George can only think about his work. Likewise, on three later occasions, her lines hint at her desire to tell George about the dead jumper, but he never picks up the clue.

5. The 1972 production highlighted the falseness of the charge and gave the scene a comic twist as Peter Wood's blocking had Bones lying on the bed, with Dotty standing over him, hitting him with a large Snoopy doll (National Theatre prompt script 2.13).

6. One could read Bones's transgression as a politically incorrect depiction of black and gay stereotypes, but I doubt that such a critique, though viable, was Stoppard's intent. More likely this charade is offensive to the Neo-fascist police force because it undermines the respectability and image of the police.

7. Unless otherwise noted, all references are to the 1973 text.

8. While Michael Hordern rightly earned rave reviews for his portrayal of George in the 1972–73 and 1976 productions, there is another aspect to the play's success on stage. The role of Dotty involves partial nudity, and part of the play's spectacle is the incredible sex appeal of the actresses who have played Dotty in the major London productions. When she was cast in the 1972–73 production, Diana Rigg

was best known as a sex symbol from the TV show *The Avengers*. Many of the London reviews commented on Rigg's stunning beauty. The 1976 production cast Julie Covington, another TV sex symbol (*Rock Follies*). She offered a harder-edged, less elegant sex appeal, but again some male reviewers duly noted her physical charms. Finally, the 1985 revival featured the glamorous Felicity Kendal, another former TV sex symbol.

9. Astronaut Scott's parting words are Stoppard's macabre parody of the last words of the historical, altruistic Captain Oates who left the Antarctic explorers' camp, saying only: "I am going out now. I may not be back for awhile" (quoted in Faraone 55).

10. Remak Ramsey, who played Archie in Wood's 1974 American production, relates: "The director said, 'You cannot make value judgements about Stoppardian characters. You must never play Archie as a villain.' Archie believes his philosophy is for the best—dispose of Duncan McFee with no fuss. You must play Archie with great charm. It really isn't until the Coda that you can see how evil Archie is in an objective way. Since it is George's dream, there is some question as to whether Archie is Archie, or Archie as George sees him" (quoted in Faraone 71). Thus, Wood's approach is to play the character straight, and let the audience deduce his villainous qualities from his behavior.

11. Dotty references the verification principle when she cites Archie's assertion: "Things and actions, you understand, can have any number of real and verifiable properties. But good and bad, better and worse, these are not real properties of things, they are just expressions of our feelings about them" (41). Notably, the play dramatizes many instances (the dermatograph machine, the blood on the secretary's coat, and others) where observations are ambiguous, untrustworthy, or inconclusive, thus pointing to the limitations of relying solely on the criteria of the verification principle for affirmations of reality.

12. Ayer is expressing the "emotive theory" of ethics. In his later writings Ayer revised his view "conced[ing] that ethical statements are not purely emotive" (Gilson, Langam, and Maurer 541). Ayer continually refined his philosophical positions and by the late 1960s had "abandoned classical logical positivism" (542). Neil Sammells discusses logical positivism in relation to *Jumpers* (98–110) and argues that George's paper is structured "around a protracted critique of A. J. Ayer's *Language, Truth, and Logic*" (98).

13. Near the end of act 2, while talking to Archie, Dotty says: "Well, it wasn't *me*. . . . *I* didn't do it. I thought *you* did it" (74). Likewise the text of *And Now the Incredible Archibald Jumpers* suggests Archie's method of dealing with dissent. While talking about Archie and the Radical Liberal Party's attempts to manipulate the dem-

ocratic process, George asks: "And what about those who won't play?" Dotty then raises her hand like a pistol, points it at George and fires (19–20).

14. Stoppard aptly states: "George's long speeches would of course be much too long, regardless of their content, if it were not that the way in which he talks is itself, to an English audience, a recognizable parody of a philosophical discourse; that the sentence structure has a built-in interest value, basically a humorous value" ("Translators' notes" 1).

15. In the *Incredible Jumpers* text, Stoppard wrote that "it may as well be stated now that a rational explanation of this coda, if such an explanation is required, is that it is George's dream" (77). He emended that to "somebody's" dream. The published text simply says that the coda is done "in bizarre dream form."

16. See Hu (97–100) and Kelly (102–3) for plausible analyses of this complex piece of text. Also, in his "Translators' notes" Stoppard offers a brief, but still cryptic, explanation: "Archie's speech is obviously put together to work in terms of its phonetics, its sounds and so on, as well as its meaning." Thus, the translator should attempt "to combine a sort of fractured meaning which depends on the vocabulary having associations, even if the syntax is fractured." He proceeds to explain some phrases. "Moon mad" refers to the fact that "a full moon is associated with madness." "Herd instinct" is used in "psychology to denote people who have a sort of common instinct like herds of animals might have." He proceeds: " 'Is God dad the inference' means what it seems to mean. 'Nucleic acid testes'—well, 'acid test' is a phrase meaning the hardest proof . . . if something passes the acid test, then it has passed the most important test. Nucleic acid is a substance in physics. Testes is a synonym for testicles. 'Universavice' is vice versa of course. There is a well-known phrase that 'necessity is the mother of invention' and Voltaire said that if God didn't exist it would be necessary to invent him." He closes by noting the allusions to Darwin and Descartes and by writing: "And that is really all the help I can give you. It's a mishmash, and all I can say is good luck" (7). Indicative of the speech's ambiguity, the line "is God dad the inference?" can be interpreted in diametrically opposed ways as it suggests both Nietzsche's assertion "God is dead" as well as the idea of God as the Father, and thus creator, of the universe and moral standards.

17. The original script *And Now the Incredible Archibald Jumpers* included the character Tarzan who rehearsed for the 1972 production but who was cut after two preview performances. Unlike as in the 1986 text, in the original version George conducted the cross-examination of Tarzan and the questioning went on much longer. Indeed, the *Incredible Jumpers* coda text ran fourteen manuscript pages and incorporated a large number of slide projections. By the time the show opened, the coda was down to five manuscript pages. The first published edition is very close to the edition used for the 1972 production, and it includes Captain Scott, who enters to

triumphal band music and a red carpet. In that version Scott actually speaks and Archie has a much longer rationalization of the moon murder as "instinctive" and "rational" (1972, 84). Given an opportunity to question the witness, George desists: "Why should I cross-examine the figures of my dreams. If that is the real Captain Scott, then I am the Archbishop of Canterbury" (85). Once the Archbishop of Canterbury is called, the coda proceeds the same as it does in the 1973 edition. I must agree with Stoppard's original assessment that Scott "added little and delayed much" (1973, 11).

18. Curiously, the 1986 text revises this to "Will no one rid me of this coppers' nark!" (76), a change that dilutes the moral force of the moment. See Thomson (478) for one interpretation of this change.

19. In the 1986 text, after Archie orders the murder, Clegthorpe only has time to shout "George!" (76), who in turn yells "Dotty!"—who then enters on a crescent moon. Stoppard rationalized this excision of George's refusal to help the Archbishop: "[It] merely confirmed, rather than disclosed [his inadequacy] and that it did so at the expense of holding up the momentum which the scene was gaining. It would have been in danger of belabouring the point, I feel" (Jenkins, *Critical Essays*, 6). On the other hand, Stoppard aptly notes: "I should think most directors would be inclined to keep it in" (6). Indeed, the excised section provides much of the moral force of the coda whereas the readdition of Scott and Tarzan only furthers the image of the play as theatrical fluff.

Chapter 5

1. The visual style of the productions were also markedly different. In the original production, the decor of Carr's home gave a sense of domestic realism with elegant leather-padded wooden chairs and bookcases. In contrast, the 1993 production was more surreal with some of the background furniture tilted in unrealistic ways. More strikingly, the walls included "random" splattering of words such as "dada" and "arp" as well as the image of a Bolshevik revolutionary. All these aspects accented the fantasy nature of Carr's reminiscences. Furthermore, the importance of music is a production aspect lost on the reader. Prior to the 1993 revival, Stoppard wrote to that production's director, Adrian Noble: "The overall unity or tension in the play depends surprisingly on the music. For example, apart from the Stripper, we used Maurice Chevalier ["Every Little Breeze Seems to Whisper Louise"] for Tzara's first entrance—i.e., we used a mixture of composed music, rag-time reconstructions and commercial recordings. Looking back . . . I think the wit of the production's music was terribly important to it" (Letter).

2. The RSC Archives at Stratford-on-Avon have the prompt scripts from both productions; these production-specific alterations will not be discussed here. Those

interested in changes made for the 1974 production can see Philip Gaskell's book (245–62) for a comparison of the stage manager's script, the published text, and a tape recording of a performance of the play indicating that the three texts contain a number of differences; while highly informative, Gaskell only covers select first-act excerpts and is nowhere near comprehensive. Further muddling any notion of a definitive text is the fact that *Travesties* was substantially altered both before and during the 1975–76 Broadway run. While that text has never been published, many of the Broadway excisions were carried through, with some modifications, for the 1993 text. The most significant change was the opening of act 2. By early February, Stoppard had supplied a new beginning as the act opened with a condensed version of Lenin's speech on party literature, followed by the last paragraph of Cecily's lecture. That lecture was interrupted by Old Carr, whose comic reminiscence (incorporating part of his speech on page 81 of the 1975 text) set the scene and reinvoked some of the first-act flair. By the third page the text reverted to the point where Cecily translates the prologue dialogue of the Lenins, a scene that, through Cecily's pedantic delivery, is rather comic in performance (Bound script, 2 Feb. 1976). Many of these changes were in response to audience dissatisfaction. Within a week of the play's opening (30 Oct. 1975), producer David Merrick expressed concern over how the general audience would respond to the Lenin section. By 12 December, through his agent, John Wood reported hostile audience backlash, including a considerable number of walkouts at every performance (Lantz, Letter to Ewing). Stoppard therefore made further cuts and changes, such as the new beginning to act 2, but the show, initially projected to run until 26 June, closed on 13 March 1976.

3. This cut goes even further than Stoppard's original assertion that the speech should begin no later than "Karl Marx had taken it as an axiom" (1975, 69). Since the scene is about Lenin, the decision to start the speech one paragraph later makes more sense. On the other hand, Stoppard tells an anecdote about a Paris production that used the entire speech; the difference was that the actress was stark naked ("The Event and the Text" 207).

4. After Carr's speech where he vows Lenin must be stopped (1975, 84), Lenin had a speech culminating with "Tell Pravda" (Draft 71), and then the direct address began. The direct addresses went on for seven pages and were a combination of letter excerpts and exposition. About half of that material remains in the first published text. The scene ended with Lenin's speech about Beethoven's Appassionata. The first draft of *Travesties* is at the HRHRC (Gordon Dickerson Collection 11.8).

5. Why Stoppard now decided to have more fun with the Lenins, to travesty them in places, is unclear. While Stoppard has stated that the fall of communist governments in Eastern Europe did not require any updating of the Lenin plot (Lewis,

"Tom's Gallimaufry"), the fact that the legacy of the Leninist revolution and repression had been largely removed from the day-to-day world may have made him less opposed to treating the Lenins in strictly serious terms.

6. Unless otherwise indicated, all references to *Travesties* are from the 1993 text.

7. At the end of the play the audience learns that Bennett was actually the consular official and that Carr served under him.

8. The excerpts come from "*Julius Caesar, Hamlet, As You Like It, Much Ado About Nothing, Henry V, Henry IV (Part One), Othello, The Merry Wives of Windsor,* and the thirty-second sonnet" (Whitaker 116).

9. The 1993 text alerts the audience to this level by having Gwen announce: "The chapter we are doing next is cast in the form of the Christian Catechism!" (37). When she exits, the play moves into its version of the "Ithaca" catechism episode of *Ulysses.*

10. Stoppard's original ending to the debate was surprisingly anemic:

TZARA: Your art has *failed.* It must begin again. Musicians must break their instruments, galleries should be destroyed and libraries burned! (*He waves the Joycean manuscript.*) And if this is your idea of the high point of English literature, then it's time to return to the magic of the pre-artistic unconscious! (JOYCE *has the door open, unflustered. His final riposte is to take a white rabbit out of his hat and hand it to* TZARA.)
JOYCE: Top o' the morning. (*And goes closing the door.*) (Bound script, May 1974, 54)

Peter Wood's suggestion clearly strengthened the text, and it was probably Wood who had the wisdom to cut half of the speech that Stoppard wrote for Joyce. The excised first half contained biographical information on Joyce and was published in 1980 as "Leftover from *Travesties.*"

11. Tynan objects to Stoppard's presentation of Joyce and Wilde as apolitical, whereas historically both had socialist sympathies (112). However, within the debate as to whether or not art has to be political, Stoppard's presentation seems justified, for both Joyce and Wilde are remembered for their artistic style and for works that emphasized aesthetics, not political engagement.

12. The 1993 revival comically theatricalized Carr's too-late decision to Lenin's departure by having a toy train emerge from the fireplace (thus "quoting" a Magritte painting) and steam across the stage.

13. The 1975 text reads: "*I was uncertain.* What was the right thing? And then there were my feelings for Cecily" (81). The 1993 revision clarifies what is at stake

("the future of the civilized world," an admitted overstatement) and thus further calls into question the normally astute Paul Delaney's assertion that Carr's inaction is justified as the right thing because it is based on his love for Cecily. Delaney concludes: "At least in hindsight we can see that the love between two insignificant individuals just might be more real than ideology" (*Moral Vision* 76). The ramifications of Lenin's ideology in action had very real and harsh effects on many people and so Carr's response might be seen as selfish rather than the "right thing."

14. After the play's revival, Stoppard admitted to some unease: "I felt the play engaged the audience more in 1974 than in 1994. There's always an audience which engages thoroughly with the play. [The majority of the audience seems to enjoy the play], but it doesn't set them alight in the way you'd want. Maybe what was unconventional about *Travesties* then isn't quite as fresh any more. [I also realize that] the play is full of allusions and references to a whole network of cultural background knowledge. And I sense people in their twenties now can't be counted upon to recognize all the allusions. Yet, 20 years ago, one never thought about it. It wasn't an issue" (Gritten). In the same article Stoppard notes that when he saw how well *Arcadia* worked in translation, he realized the importance of storytelling: "It doubly convinced me that story-telling is what separates plays which will always work from plays that may work better in one decade than another." Indeed, the lack of narrative momentum in *Travesties* helps explain why it does not always connect with an audience.

Chapter 6

1. Stoppard has also dealt with Eastern Bloc politics in *Dogg's Hamlet, Cahoot's Macbeth* and *Squaring the Circle*. The former is two interrelated one-act plays written for Ed Berman's theatre company. *Dogg's Hamlet* involves an innovative dramatization of Wittgenstein's language games, while *Cahoot's Macbeth* was inspired by a group of Czech dissident actors who performed a truncated version of *Macbeth* in living rooms. Stoppard's introduction to the acting version provides worthwhile commentary. *Squaring the Circle* is Stoppard's pseudodocumentary (for TV) about Solidarity's struggles in Poland in 1980–81. Epitomizing Stoppard's skepticism of being able to present history as it actually happened, the narrator announces: "Everything is true except the words and pictures" (*Stoppard: The Television Plays* 191–92). Later, Stoppard dramatizes a pivotal meeting between Solidarity's Lech Walesa, the Catholic Church's Archbishop Glemp, and the communist government's General Jaruzelski by playing the scene three different times, showing three different perspectives on what happened and who said what to whom (255–58).

2. On the other hand, in a 1984 article Stoppard said he made a conscious change in his writing in 1977, in part out of a "quiet arrogance about my ability to write any kind of play" (Freedman).

3. As expected, orthodox Soviet press coverage had a different view. According to Reuters (1 Sept. 1978; HRHRC 37.4) the Soviet satirical weekly *Krokodil* "scornfully condemned [*EGBDF*] as inartistic and anti-soviet." In "Cacophony for dissidents and orchestra" the *Krokodil* columnist called the show "monstrously long and gauche. It could have been significantly shorter and above all more honest—it should have been called 'Down with Detente.'" The columnist accused Stoppard and Previn of being "children who do what they are told when the conductor of a military-industrial complex waves his baton."

4. London's National Sound Archive has an audio recording of a televised production of *EGBDF*. One can hear not only the beauty of Previn's composition but also the extensive amount of comedy in the play, humor not always evident in the reading of the text.

5. The lines "But it has to be done right. They don't want to lose ground. They need a formula" were not in the 23 June or 8 July 1976 drafts. They were added in March 1977 as the script was prepared for the start of rehearsals. The change clearly marks how Stoppard wishes to show the final release as an orchestrated plan and not the comic bungling it was often perceived to be.

6. When denied writing materials, Soviet political prisoners often put things they wanted to remember into rhyme.

7. In Stoppard's typescript of 8 July 1976, the passage reads: "We can't change anything by our strength. We can change things by example" (21). He crossed this out and wrote: "And what about the other fathers? And mothers? There are truths to be shown, and our only strength is personal example. I mean important truths—not about prisons and hospitals and legal rights. I'm talking about the difference between good and evil, which even a teen-age boy can understand." Stoppard apparently decided that this speech was too explicit, too preachy, and so he shortened the passage to its suggestive element.

8. Stoppard documents his trip in his newspaper article "The Face at the Window." He also discusses it with Shulman (109–10).

9. A "professional foul" is a soccer term for when a player deliberately commits a foul in an attempt to stop a goal. The England-Czechoslovakia game involves a professional foul, the ethics of which are discussed by McKendrick in scene 10. Anderson later commits his own "professional foul" when he smuggles out Hollar's thesis and when he delivers his unscheduled paper. Both acts violate his previous ethical position that as a guest of the Czech government he has willingly entered into a pseudocontract as to how he will and will not behave.

10. A fourth philosopher at the conference is an American named Stone. He is a linguistic analyst, a school of thought that argues that moral problems are largely

problems of language, and that any statements about morality are expressions of feeling, taste, or vested interest. Prevalent in the 1950s and 1960s, linguistic analysis is here satirized as Stone's paper leads to much comic confusion. Stone's paper does not directly deal with moral issues, but in Anderson's climactic speech, he critiques the linguistic philosophy's view that "justice has no existence outside of the ways in which we choose to employ the word, and indeed consists only of the way in which we employ it. In other words, that ethics are not the inspiration of our behaviour but merely the creation of our utterances" (90). Here, and in *Jumpers*, Stoppard disputes the claims of linguistic analysis.

11. In "Catastrophe Theory in Tom Stoppard's *Professional Foul*" Evelyn Cobley uses E. C. Zeeman's *Scientific American* (vol. 234, Apr. 1976) article "Catastrophe Theory" and Alexander Woodcock and Monte Davis's book *Catastrophe Theory* (New York: E. P. Dutton, 1978) to explicate the theory. Both are layman's guides to the theory and discuss ways in which the mathematical/scientific theory has been applied to the social sciences and other nonmathematical disciplines. Cobley speculates that Stoppard read the Zeeman article, but notably that article does not relate the theory to ethics or moral philosophy and so McKendrick's application appears to be Stoppard's own invention. Interestingly, Thom's catastrophe theory plays a role in deterministic chaos (see Briggs and Peat, *Turbulent Mirror*, 84–87), the mathematical/scientific theory that informs *Arcadia*.

12. Where Stoppard stands on catastrophe theory has been a source of debate. Richard Buhr seems to suggest that McKendrick speaks for Stoppard, but Buhr confuses the issue by mistakenly arguing that Anderson abandons his system of absolute moral principles (328). In contrast, Paul Delaney dismisses the theory because as a Marxist and a pragmatist, McKendrick is the antithesis of a Stoppard hero. My own argument is similar to but different than Cobley's. She discusses the way that Stoppard both embraces and rejects the theory, and she notes how Stoppard evades "fixed positions in favor of 'both-and' solutions" (64).

13. The full explication of Robert Kane's argument can be found in his book *Through the Moral Maze* (New York: Paragon House, 1994).

14. The play's airport search scene has its roots in Stoppard's trip to Russia. In "The Face at the Window" Stoppard discusses the search methods employed on the Cook's Tour members, and many of those details appear in *Professional Foul*. Stoppard and Luff were thoroughly searched twice, and their Amnesty International petition, though legal, was confiscated.

15. While both plays deal with moral philosophers and moral issues, their stylistic difference stems from their medium. For Stoppard, television is inherently a realistic medium, whereas the stage allows for more audacious risks. A key point Stoppard stressed to interviewers when they tried to link his use of realism and political

situations was that their connection was facile: "The equation which I would dis-avow is that any serious, involved, engaging playwriting is equated by this author with naturalism—no" (Gollob and Roper 153).

16. In *Moral Vision,* Delaney elaborates on the similarities and differences be-tween George and Anderson (94–95).

Chapter 7

1. The *Daily Telegraph's* John Barber felt that the play "makes all other Stop-pard plays look like so many nursery games" (15). In contrast, Bernard Levin of the *Sunday Times* found it "a deeply disappointing play" with "some horribly clumsy preaching, stiff with caked earnestness" (37). Likewise, academic critics tend to downgrade *Night and Day.* Neil Sammells argues that Stoppard's move to modi-fied realism (in *Night and Day* and *The Real Thing*) has hardened into a militant political and aesthetic conservatism that "abandons his aesthetics of engagement" and "promote[s] a conservative message by adopting tactics he had previously con-demned and, in so doing, has put his work at the service of a political thesis which is at best self-contradictory and banal and, at worst, cynical and dishonest" (142). On the other hand, Stoppard *is* politically conservative, and though the style is differ-ent than his earlier plays, his thematic/ideological positions have not substantially changed.

2. For the London and New York productions, the text calls for a jeep driv-ing on stage and a mobile set. In the Samuel French acting edition Stoppard has emended the beginning and end of act 1 so the play can be done on a permanent set, sans jeep.

3. While there are many minor changes of individual lines within scenes, there are also some significantly rewritten passages. The major changes include the addi-tion or revision of many lines for "Ruth"; a revision of the section where Ruth tries to tell Carson of her affair (1979, 50–52; 1978, 51–52); an elaboration of the first onstage meeting between Ruth and Wagner (1979, 56–57; 1978, 54); a revision of the second-act Ruth-Wagner press debate (1979, 98–99; 1978, 82–83); the addition of an odd and somewhat momentum-breaking "Ruth" monologue during the Ma-geeba visit that shows how far away Ruth has slipped (94); and a new exit for the President where he further mocks Wagner and notes that he once played Caliban in a production of *The Tempest,* a biographical note that marks Mageeba's bestial side (103–4).

4. Many critics have noted Milne's resemblance to William Boot, the journalist protagonist of Evelyn Waugh's satiric novel *Scoop* (1933), a work Stoppard so admired that he used Boot as one of his journalistic pseudonyms. For the parallels between *Night and Day* and *Scoop,* see Brassell (206), Whitaker (146–48), and Jenkins (*The-*

atre of Tom Stoppard 149–50). Incidentally, when Stoppard was a journalist he was suspended, for unspecified reasons, from the NUJ from mid-December 1959 to mid-February 1960.

5. Stoppard's opposition to the unions was partly due to his view that union corruption had turned them into a "protection racket" and made publishing newspapers almost an "impossible economic proposition"; thus, in the 1970s he saw Rupert Murdoch as "sort of a hero" for breaking the print union. However, in 1994, Stoppard viewed Murdoch as "a very bad influence on English, or indeed global, cultural life" (Gussow, *Conversations,* 96–97).

6. In "But for the Middle Classes", Stoppard's 1977 review of Paul Johnson's *Enemies of Society,* Stoppard asserts his belief in objective truth and absolute morality and his disavowal of Marxist relativists and those who see all facts as theory laden. Stoppard dedicated *Night and Day* to Johnson. Neil Sammells offers an extended discussion of Johnson's book, Stoppard's review, and how the intellectual/ideological content of these pieces affect *Night and Day* and *The Real Thing* (123–32).

7. Stoppard and Wood explain the process that led to the only predenouement scene where Wagner and Ruth are onstage alone:

> Stoppard: I find that I don't actually know what you mean until I've forced you to give the actual dialogue, as though it were written for the worst possible kind of television cops and robbers, and then I find it from that—get a sense of what vaguely he feels should be happening at that moment, what isn't happening.
>
> Wood: A good example—talking over the telephone I say: "This lady goes through this play as a ball-breaker, mowing down everybody before her. Until that man can make her say 'Ouch', there's no play." But Tom's instinct was that Ruth wouldn't say ouch out loud, at least not yet, and not to Wagner. So he wrote the speech for Wagner, and her reply comes out as "If you're waiting for me to say 'Ouch', you're going to get a cramp." So my offer was taken up but turned upside down in a way that refined it. (Hayman, "Double Acts," 148–49)

8. Stoppard comments on the blur between fantasy and reality: "My idea was to stage it as though it was absolutely real, not in half light or anything. And then for the revelation to be retroactive" (Hardin 159). However, after discovering that some people were never clear whether it was a fantasy or not, Stoppard and the production tinkered with the scene for many months after the play opened.

Chapter 8

1. Stoppard's second wife, Miriam, and her first husband, Peter, were part of the Anthony Smith–led cricket circle with which Stoppard played. Stoppard dedi-

cated *The Real Thing* to Miriam, but in 1992, after twenty years of marriage, they were divorced.

2. Delaney lists revised texts as being published in 1986 and 1988. Since there were no major productions of *The Real Thing* in those years, it is unclear what spurred these new imprints.

3. As performed at the Strand Theatre in November 1982, in the second train scene when they are filming Brodie's play, "Billy (playing Brodie) was required to break down, complaining that he could not understand why his character was sitting in a First Class compartment mouthing first class dialogue" (Sammells 139).

4. It is not entirely clear how much the published texts correspond to the productions. Billington, R. Gordon, and Jenkins, the scholars most concerned with the London productions, all cite the 1982 text as the basis of their analysis; this suggests that major changes such as combining scenes 7 and 9 did not occur until partway through the run. Likewise, the pages labeled "last revisions for USA" that Stoppard sent to director Mike Nichols correspond to one of the 1983 texts and not the 1984 Broadway edition, the first American imprint. Other than minor differences in stage directions, the 1984 Samuel French acting edition corresponds to the Broadway edition. Differentiating between the 1983 texts is more difficult. The Bookclub edition includes photos of the forthcoming Broadway production, and that text is fairly close to the 1984 copyright; the other 1983 copyright corresponds to changes made during the London run, and it is that text that will be cited as 1983. The 1982 text will be noted as such; all other citations are to the 1984 Samuel French edition.

5. The 1983 text has additional material. Charlotte laments that because she's the playwright's wife: "All those people out front thinking, that's why she got the job" (20). She also fears that audiences interpret the play autobiographically: "And also thinking that I'm *her,* coming in with my little suitcase and my duty free bag—'it's me!'—ooh, it's her!—so that's what they're like at home—he's scintillating, and she's scintillated. (*Henry starts to speak.*) Look out, he's going to scintillate" (20).

6. The 1983 text keeps the bickering (21), but is intermediate in length on the Brodie story (32–35).

7. Debbie is a problematic character. After seeing the Brussels production Stoppard wrote to the director regarding Debbie's character: "I don't think that she ought to be a sort of hostile punk. After all, she was a punk before intermission. Just a phase. I think Debbie works better if she appears to be very young and virginal. And the other thing about her is that she and Henry have a close and sympathetic relationship" (20 Dec. 1983). While Debbie does not have to be a hostile punk and while she and Henry can have a close relationship, the text works against Stoppard's other views. Debbie, now seventeen, has been obsessed with sex since age twelve, is a believer in free love, has slept with her riding instructor and Latin instructor, and is

on at least her third lover; the 1982 text suggests that she occasionally sleeps around on her current lover who lives with her in the squat, while in the post-1982 texts she is traveling around the country with her current lover. Overall, she seems far from virginal.

8. Stoppard's directors have never been fully satisfied with the Brodie play scene. Peter Wood had Stoppard acknowledge the artifice of Brodie sitting in first class, while Mike Nichols requested clarification of the closing stage direction that indicates tension in Billy and Annie's relationship. Stoppard grudgingly added a lengthy section designed to show: "Look, look, all is not well with Annie and Billy—*she's* full of self-doubt, *he* is in love with her, she feels guilty and responsible, and isn't sure what to do" (Letter to Mike Nichols, n.d.). The revision is not in the Broadway version, but does appear in the 1983 text.

9. The choice of Nichols was a combination of artistic, economic, and practical concerns. He offered to direct it if Wood wasn't interested, and Stoppard liked the idea because once the show opens, now there was someone to watch over it. Also, despite Maggie Smith's appearance, *Night and Day* was a relative failure on Broadway, and Stoppard realized that "the same production that works in Britain doesn't always work here" (Gorfinkle).

10. Holly Hill herself preferred Roger Rees's portrayal: "Rees was more convincing as an intellectual who could reel off Mr. Stoppard's lines and Henry's plays. Because he had that stature, his personal pain was more harrowing . . . and his ascent to self-knowledge more moving." Benedict Nightingale argues: "[Rees] is a bravura performer, refreshingly unafraid of bold, volatile, un-English emotions, yet there was something external about his acting. He shaped and pointed Stoppard's many witty lines more adroitly than Irons, who lets several escape, but Irons does something more important—[he opens] himself to the possibility of pain and, without ado or pretension, shows this pain when it strikes. Early on, one senses a vulnerability, a yearning behind the banter; later something melancholy, even somber; and at the end that long, willowy figure has drooped, blanched, and vocally crumbled into what, were a chain attached to its legs, one might almost suppose to be Marley's Ghost. Much more than Rees, he shows us that the play is centrally about Henry's emotional education, his evolution from a man who could write that opening scene to one who knows how thin and cold it is, and in this endeavor he's greatly helped by Glenn Close, a more vibrant, magnetic, and sexually formidable Annie" ("January" 139).

11. The 1982 text (cf. 36) does not include the parallel use of ambiguous questions where Max asks about "Julie"—that is, Strindberg's *Miss Julie,* the play Annie is rehearsing. This addition appears in the 1983 text (36) and the 1984 text (40).

12. Sammells posits that besides the overt quoting of *Miss Julie* and *'Tis a Pity She's a Whore*, this handkerchief recalls *Othello*, while the door slam that ends scene 1 echoes *A Doll House*. He argues: "In doing so, *The Real Thing* ranges itself alongside 'fine writing': touchstones of literary excellence shared by author and audience alike, which help to measure and confirm the distance between 'good stuff and rubbish'" (140).

13. The 1982 text illustrates Debbie's argument that fidelity and infidelity involve more than sex: "We had this fellow come round from the Council to look at the fire escape. He spent ten minutes looking at the fire escape and an hour and a half betraying his wife. Little jokes about her ways, her relatives, her cooking, who she fancied on TV. It was his way of flirting. Finally, after two cups of tea and maddened by torn denim everywhere he looked, he started telling how often she liked it, how she liked it, getting off on telling, working up to it, and he might have got some too since there's fourteen more people in the house than there's supposed to be and at least three of them would've given him one just to keep him quiet, but at the last moment he panicked, denied himself, went away. Faithful, you see?" (67).

14. Similar to Henry, while married to Miriam, Stoppard said: "I haven't really considered revealing my other side to more than one person at a time" (Billington, "Secret Agent," 195). On the other hand, critics have noted that ten years after *The Real Thing*, Stoppard's own life would mirror his play as he eventually left his wife for a relationship with Felicity Kendal, the actress who originated the role of Annie.

15. Henry cannot get himself to say Billy's name and so he simply says, "It's your friend" (92), a line that can take on a wide variety of emotional resonances. In the London production Henry was shown as significantly upset by Billy's call (Corballis 144).

16. The bracketed section is from the 1983 text (76).

17. Here, the 1982 text has a different speech: "Billy's not a threat. But I didn't start it casually, and I can't stop it casually. I can't and I don't want to go. I go around all the time saying 'Thank you' like a child because I can't behave well towards you both, and you allow me to behave well towards him without having to be furtive, so I'm grateful and I say thank you. I need you" (79).

18. The 1983 text has added dialogue here, the most significant lines being Annie's: "This is the me who loves you, this me who won't tell Billy to go and rot, and I know I'm yours so I'm not afraid for you—I have to choose who I hurt and I choose you because I'm yours. I'm only sorry for your pain but even your pain is the pain of letting go of something, some idea of me which was never true, an Annie who was complete in loving you and being loved back. (*With sad disdain*) Some Annie" (78).

19. Corballis's argument is based on viewing Debbie as a child-as-natural-moral-guide figure like that Stoppard uses in *Professional Foul* and *Every Good Boy Deserves Favor* (146). However, Debbie is not so innocent (see note 7), and thus seems to be cast from a different mold than other children in the Stoppard canon.

20. In his April 1986 letter to Gordon Davidson, Stoppard notes that he was trying to draw a parallel between Annie's easing out of her affair with Billy and her response to Brodie's legal problems: "There's supposed to be an analogy here with the responsibility she feels for drawing Brodie into *his* false position (as I told you I originally considered Billy and Brodie being played by the same actor mainly for this reason)."

Chapter 9

1. Elsewhere Stoppard has stated that the play's impetus stemmed from his desire to "write about ultimate uncertainty. Quantum mechanics is about probability and the lack of absolutes. In investigating matter, the deeper they go, the smaller the particles, the less certainty they find. That seemed to me to be an exploitable idea" (Lewis, "Quantum Stoppard," 58).

2. The male secretary Maggs was originally written as Madge, but due to understudy considerations a male was cast. Stoppard notes: "It turned out to be better for the play, because then Hapgood is the only woman surrounded by all these men" (Guppy 185).

3. Feynman's book has also been published in three volumes; chapter 37 corresponds to the first chapter of volume 3, which deals specifically with quantum mechanics. A more accessible introduction to the world of quantum theory is Fred Alan Wolf's *Taking the Quantum Leap: The New Physics for Non-Scientists*.

4. The 1988 London *Hapgood* text (scene 2) contains a long description of this experiment, but the 1994 New York *Hapgood* cuts this explanation down to its essence.

5. To get wave pattern means that "the indivisible electron came through both slits," an explanation that is "classically inconceivable [but] quantum mechanically inescapable" (Polkinghorne 37). In rewriting *Hapgood* for New York, Stoppard cut the specific reference to this particular quantum mystery.

6. In quantum theory, nonlocality refers to "the property of permitting a cause at one place to produce immediate effects at distant places" (Polkinghorne 94). For example, protons often appear in pairs in which one proton has an "up" spin and the other a "down" spin so that combined they cancel each other out to give a spin of zero. The curious feature of nonlocality is that even though the protons (say, A

and B) are separated in space, if when measuring a property of proton A a change occurs in that property, then instantaneously an opposite change occurs in proton B. Though separated by space, the protons are somehow linked and each is influenced by what happens to its "partner."

7. Typifying Stoppard's tendency to write dialogue that is non–character specific, he transferred a large section of dialogue from Hapgood in scene 3 to Blair in scene 2. It was not so important who said it as it was that the information needed to come sooner. Similarly, at one point the Königsberg Bridge problem material was between Kerner and Blair, but restructuring the play led to its being between Kerner and Hapgood.

8. In another memo Stoppard wrote: "Spare me a critique of this plot. The play is about dualities and uncertainties and about two people pretending to be one person and one person pretending to be two people, and a cartload of such things, and was perforce written in the hope that we would keep our eye on the cart rather than on the tottering five-legged horse behind it" ("Hapgood says").

9. Defensive about the worst reviews he had ever received, Stoppard argued that the ordinary theatergoer "has less trouble [understanding *Hapgood*] than some of our critics" (Billington, "Secret Agent," 194). Beyond the intricacies of the plot, actor Nigel Hawthorne (Blair), in a private letter to Stoppard, suggests another possible reason for *Hapgood*'s relative failure in London. Near the end of the run, Stoppard gave a note to Hawthorne and Roger Rees (Kerner) about their first zoo scene, which Stoppard felt in that night's performance had become too much about the human reactions and not enough about the physics. In his reply, Hawthorne mentions uncharacteristic friction between the cast and the Stoppard-Wood team during the rehearsal process. More importantly Hawthorne offers specific comments on how he as an actor saw the play differently from how it was directed:

> [Tonight's note] ties up many of the notes you have given both during rehearsal and the run so far. Those to Felicity affect me the most—by reflection. She is, I understand, frequently instructed to make Hapgood I less approachable. Stricter and colder. Any thought of the four of us working as a "team" went out the window years ago. . . . [In the first rugby scene there isn't] a flicker of recognition between the two. No indication of past affection, perhaps even a love. If there was, she would never give him the particle meeting the antiparticle explanation without a glimmer of FUN. You seem to be advocating the sacrifice of relationships to theories by telling us that the 'characters' are 'getting in the way of' the physics. . . . I was advised by both you and Peter that Blair needed to be harder and more ruthless. I still believed that the relationship with Hapgood I was one of sharing and gentle teasing. No. Wrong. . . . We could all see the way it was going back at [the Wimbledon previews]. That

there was to be no clarification for the audience and that time was to be taken up with getting the text right and, only now and then discussing things like attitudes and moments of human contact.

Since the play is grounded in a concern for showing the duality of human identity, Hawthorne's advice to accent the human emotions and relationships suggested by the text should be strongly considered by would-be producers of *Hapgood*. (While Hawthorne and Stoppard had this professional disagreement, they have remained friends and mutual admirers of each other's work.)

10. A result of this added scene was that Stoppard reversed the ensuing zoo and rugby scenes, perhaps so that this lecture was not followed by Kerner's physics lecture.

11. The New York production of *Hapgood* took place in the 300-seat Mitzi E. Newhouse Theatre, Lincoln Center's second stage. The original run of 11 November to 5 February sold out before the first preview. The first extension, through 19 February, sold out in ninety minutes. Subsequent extensions took the play into March where it overlapped with Lincoln Center's production of *Arcadia* in its main house, thereby making Stoppard the first playwright with simultaneous Lincoln Center productions. Stoppard explains his choice of a not-for-profit theatre venue: "I just wanted *Hapgood* to be done well for a few weeks and finished. I didn't want to get into this kind of Broadway scene where it's either jackpot city or you go home with your tail between your legs. At Lincoln Center you can have a five-month success; on Broadway, you can have a ten-month failure" (Ickes 38). Indeed, while New York audiences and critics were still often confused by the play, the number of extensions suggests the play could be classified as a success. Ironically, the London production was considered a relative failure, but based on length of run and size of theatre, probably more tickets were sold for that production than for the New York one. While the difficulty of the plot and the density of the science make the play less popular than Stoppard's other works, I suspect another reason for the play's not being as successful is that it is not as funny. While *Hapgood* plays more comically than it reads, it does not have as many laughs as audiences might expect and/or desire from a Stoppard play.

12. Unless otherwise noted, all page references are to the 1994 Broadway Edition of *Hapgood*.

13. Stoppard describes the opening of the London production: "Onto a shadowy, empty stage, while short-wave radio voices are occupied in keeping tabs on a car somewhere in the streets of London, a swimming-pool's diving tower descends soundlessly from the flies. . . . The tower comes to earth as lightly as a leaf, and thus with perfect elegance and economy makes the first clear statement of the evening:

'We are at the pool.' The point is that you can't *write* anything that good" ("The Text's the Thing").

14. Zeifman reports that the London production used Bach's *Brandenburg Concerto* (182), while Jenkins characterizes the music as "a whistled tune and jaunty drum beats" (*Theatre of Tom Stoppard* 183). At the HRHRC, in what appears to be a rehearsal script, there are pasted-in stage directions meant to clue the audience in to the fact that there are two Ridleys. The convention was that Ridley wears a Walkman, and the audience hears the faint sounds of the tape to which he is listening. Ridley listens to the saxophone music of Johnny Hodges, while his twin listens to Vivaldi. This convention was to be used throughout the production, and thus in the first scene, the use of Hodges or Vivaldi was meant to cue the audience to a different person being onstage. Subsequently the Walkman and Johnny Hodges device was used for the beginning and ending appearances of Ridley in the shooting range (act 1, sc. 5), and it was used at the start of the act 2 (sc. 1) office scene where "the music that starts the Act does not fade with the lights but becomes what [Ridley] hears through [his] headphones" (Jenkins, *Theatre of Tom Stoppard,* 184). The inter-scene (between 2.2 and 2.3) used Vivaldi to suggest that this Ridley was not the same Ridley. Furthermore, when Ridley and Celia get sexually involved, the passion is accompanied by the sax music. Finally, in the last pool scene when both Ridleys are present, both Vivaldi and Hodges are heard (Undated printout, Box 13.1). While this device may not have been completely successful in indicating twins, something like it may be worth trying.

15. Jenkins explains how one actor portrays both twins: "Coming from the pool, he re-enters his cubicle: his wet hair identifies him, and we know his position. But we cannot trace his movements when (presumably) he exits through the back of that cubicle, appears again from the lobby dressed, as his 'brother' had been, in a blue tracksuit and fur hat, crosses the stage to another cubicle, leaves through the back of that, and emerges from the first cubicle as the wet-haired twin who, carrying the fur hat, now leaves the building, 'in two places at once'" (*Theatre of Tom Stoppard* 183–84).

16. In New York, these quantum jumps were accompanied by map projections that spilled onto the floor. Thus, as Blair stayed rooted, the projection moved to show to where he had "jumped."

17. In addition to Feynman's book, Hersh Zeifeman (200) notes that much of Kerner's "lecture" is based on Feynman's article "Probability and Uncertainty: The Quantum Mechanical View of Nature" in *The Character of Physical Law* (Cambridge: MIT Press, 1967). When Stoppard severely condensed these speeches for the Broadway Edition the dialogue became less indebted to Feynman.

18. This arrangement was used on the proscenium arch stages of London and Los Angeles, but in New York, on the thrust stage of the Mitzi E. Newhouse Theatre, the giraffes were separated and placed in the vomitoriums, thereby losing the visual metaphor.

19. In the Broadway text Kerner's doubt about a fixed, either/or reality is more explicit: "Oh, you think there's a what-what? Your joe. Their sleeper. Paul, what's what is for zoologists" (9).

20. All the principal characters are called by more than one name. The American agent is both "Ben" and "Wates"; there is "Blair" and "Paul," "Ridley" and "Ernest," "Kerner" and "Joseph," and "Josef" and "Joe" as well as "a joe." Ridley even gives the pseudotwin "Celia" the nickname "Auntie."

21. Jenkins notes that early in the London run Stoppard moved the interscene to between I.3 and I.4, and both Ridleys were "shown together" onstage (*Theatre of Tom Stoppard* 199). The New York text and production kept the interscene in act 2 and only used one actor.

22. In the London text, Blair's first line here is preceded by: "Why am I supposed to feel sorry for Joe? There's worse things. I'd feel a damn sight sorrier for anyone who didn't know there was an either-or and we can't afford to lose" (87). While this line accents Blair's coldheartedness, that it was cut for the New York production is rather surprising in light of a statement Stoppard makes in his "Hapgood Crib." There he states that one of the things that "matters most to me in the play" is "Blair's final insistence that there *is* an either-or, and that even a child knows the difference, is something which has to be said, because we don't live in the particle world, we live in the macro world of giraffes and gulags" (9). On the other hand, the historical positions of the London and New York audiences were vastly different; namely, by the time Stoppard rewrote the play in 1994, the Communist Bloc had fallen.

23. In the 1994 text, Stoppard added a speech for Blair: "No, [the system] can't [change]. Come on, Joseph, *you know them*—Budapest in '56—Prague in '68—Poland in '81—we've been there!—and it's not going to be different in East Berlin in '89. They can't afford to lose" (63). Blair pinpoints historical instances of Eastern Bloc repression of democracy, but he is also undercut by the audience's knowledge that he is wrong about East Berlin.

24. Kerner's idealistic goal of apolitical knowledge is a sentiment shared by Stoppard. In his "Hapgood Crib," Stoppard writes that Kerner's speech is "the remnant of a longer passage which laid out the absurdity of Kerner's research being a 'military secret'—it belonged to the realm of human knowledge just as it would have been absurd for Einstein's theory of relativity to be guarded by a particular country" (9).

25. In his "Hapgood Crib," Stoppard writes: "I'm not quite sure what to make of the end of the play—the idea that Hapgood would rebound from Blair to Kerner is too simplistic, and yet Kerner remains the truest character and perhaps the one most likely to appeal to her, quite apart from the emotional tie of their parenthood" (9). In his notes from 27 February 1988, Stoppard comments on why there is no "The End" notation to the text: "The play doesn't 'end' because her 'rugby [cheers]' should be in accelerated rhythm—like a liftoff."

26. For a discussion of the moral values of the play, see Paul Delaney's *Tom Stoppard: The Moral Vision of the Major Plays* (125–48). For analysis of how *Hapgood* exemplifies postabsurdist theatre, see Zeifman (175–201).

Chapter 10

1. As discussed in the text, Gleick stresses the hidden order within chaotic systems. The other main form of chaos theory comes from Nobel Prize–winning scientist Ilya Prigogine. He emphasizes the idea that disorder is the necessary precursor and partner to order. Michael Vanden Heuvel summarizes: "[Prigogine's theory] states that entropy-rich systems (i.e., disorganized or far from equilibrium) facilitate rather than impede an evolution toward 'dissipative systems', which exhibit higher self-organization and which maximize information" (260). In addition to Gleick's book, another introductory text is John Briggs and F. David Peat's *Turbulent Mirror*. Briggs and Peat include aspects of both Gleick's and Prigogine's interpretations.

2. While the London and New York productions (both directed by Trevor Nunn and designed by Mark Thompson) used Stoppard's suggested staging, the playwright describes a Zurich production (done by his usual director-designer team of Peter Wood and Carl Toms) that completely ignored his stage directions, but that created an effective result: "The set was very different, but not only in its angles and planes. But what I mean is it was a completely different kind of room and atmosphere. It was shabby and beat up. And the designer had a very good idea, he put a mural of an idealized, sort of [Nicolas] Poussin/Claude [Lorrain] landscape on the big wall facing the audience. It was like a mural on the wall. And so one of the main subject matters of the play was in your face the whole night, which was a terrifically good idea. And the mural was on a scrim, so you can light through it. Sometimes this mural disappears and you can see the terrace of the garden outside, and the people would walk into the room, and then the wall would go solid again, and then you'd have this picture of the landscape in front of you again. It was a very brilliant notion" (Fleming, "A Talk," 22).

3. In a related matter, there is a noticeable difference in the attitudes of Thomasina and Septimus versus those of the present-day scholars. The past scenes are im-

bued with a romantic notion of research for the sake of intellectual progress. Thomasina desires "the advancement of knowledge" (37) whereas Bernard seeks "*fame*" (31). Indeed, in the present day, Hannah, Bernard, and Valentine almost always couch their discoveries in terms of what is and is not publishable. Stoppard satirizes how publication authorizes worth, and the excessive importance placed on publication, as opposed to teaching, as the means by which professors procure advancement. An added satire on contemporary academe can be found in Bernard's insistence to Hannah: "No, no, look at me, not at the book" (30). This moment might suggest the shift in literary criticism from emphasizing the work of the artist to the work of the interpreter, or it might simply satirize the ego of a scholar who sees himself as more important than the evidence.

4. I suspect there is a personal subtext for Stoppard in Bernard's getting his comeuppance. Stoppard's personal life, in regard to his relationship with Felicity Kendal, became the source of extensive coverage by the tabloids, which defended their reporting under the claim of the public's right to know. Since *Arcadia* was Stoppard's first major play after the news, many of the preview articles and interviews either touched on Stoppard and Kendal's relationship or on Stoppard's views on recent biographies that revealed the secrets of writers' personal lives. Stoppard's cynicism about artistic or journalistic rationale for printing "the whole truth" shines through: "Nobody ever speaks about the commercial imperative and I think that's the one which is fuelling the more respectable gloss on the intellectual rights or wrongs. It really is whoopee time at the publishing house if you find out something really scandalous" (Edwardes 15). Thus, that Bernard's commercially driven enterprise results in great personal embarrassment is sort of Stoppardian poetic justice.

5. Sound effects help suggest these ideas. The steady, droning beat of the Newcomen steam engine and the flirtatious piano music of Lady Croom and Count Zelinsky accompany Thomasina's realization of the ramifications of the action of bodies in heat.

6. In *Arcadia,* the swearing typically works better when the words are treated as "throwaway lines." An exception is this moment of discovery and dread.

7. Stoppard reports on the Zurich production: "Gus was treated slightly differently, but in a way which I liked very much; it took a while before you realized he didn't speak. He didn't say anything, but it didn't seem important. It's a while into the play before you think, 'That boy, he hasn't said anything yet,' but there's nothing spooky about it. He files. A lot of time he just hangs out. And I liked it" (Fleming, "A Talk," 23). Some 1993 editions of *Arcadia* do not include the Peter Wood-inspired decision to have Gus present throughout most of scene 5. He exits after Chloë, and Hannah tells Bernard to "give Plautus a kick" (62).

Chapter 11

1. From 1942 to 1946 Stoppard (then still Tomas Straussler) lived in India. He states: "[*In the Native State* contains] almost nothing of my own experiences, not even indirectly. On the other hand, India is the only Empire country I would want to write about in any way. I was there between the age of four and eight and the country has always fascinated me" (Allen 240–41). Despite some nostalgia, Stoppard did not return to India until early 1991, after the radio play was already written.

2. Stoppard's poet-painter idea originally had more narrative and framing levels as the painter was to be in conversation with someone, while a filmmaker filmed the poet, painter, and speaker. (Undated notes, HRHRC 67.7).

3. Stoppard acknowledges admiring E. M. Forster's novel *A Passage to India* but says he has not read Paul Scott's *The Jewel in the Crown,* the other work to which Stoppard's play is often compared. Stoppard told Gussow that he read parts of fifty or sixty books, most of them being autobiographies, biographies, and histories. Some of his sources include *Autobiography of an Unknown Indian* by Chaudhuri, *No Full Stops in India* by Mark Tully, two books by V. S. Naipaul, and the two volumes of Emily Eden's letters. He adds: "Charles Allen's *Scrapbooks of the Raj* are wonderful source material: picture books of old photographs and advertisements from the time" (*Conversations* 126). The latter may be useful for designers.

4. *Arcadia*'s satire on academics and alternating past/present plot structure are somewhat indebted to *In the Native State.* Thus, when Stoppard turned *Native State* into *Indian Ink* he ran the risk of seeming to repeat himself (and less successfully), and so he may have tried to take the alternating-time-periods device through another bifurcation. The four time periods were to revolve around the Emily Eden book: Spotlights would show Emily writing in 1839, Flora reading in 1930, Nell [the young Mrs. Swan] getting the book in 1931, and Swan showing it to Anish in the present. This initial concept also had the play circling back to the opening as it was to end with all four periods involved with the book ("Notes," 6 Dec. 1992).

5. The ending of the production text is not included in either published version. For the Nell-Eric cemetery scene, Mrs. Swan remains center stage and watches the scene as it is played on an elevated level behind an upstage scrim. When Nell says "bye-bye, darling" (80) to Flora, Mrs. Swan also says it, a device further emphasizing the loving feelings she has for her sister. Also, at the very end, Pike enters with a copy of the Emily Eden book, saying a passage has been underlined, and so he reads the closing passage of the play. The revised published edition, like the production text, moves the scene where Anish shows Mrs. Swan the nude portrait of Flora (34–35) back to its original placement in the midst of the long Flora-Das scene (35–45).

The scene is placed after Flora says that she prefers to be painted in the nude because it has more *rasa* (41).

6. One of Stoppard's favorite moments is when he tries to create the illusion that when Pike's footnotes start to get excessive, Flora tells him to "shut up!" (33); the real-time justification for Flora's outburst is a barking dog. While this theatrical device serves a thematic point of the subject getting to speak back to the scholar, other uses serve an aesthetic if not thematic function. For example, in act 2 when Pike is in India, there is theatrical doubling of space across time as there are scenes where both Pike and Flora are at the Club, and scenes where they both wait for the Rajah, and thus the same stage setting simultaneously represents two different eras. Also, in Peter Wood's staging the characters freely moved through each period's space. For example, when Anish enters Mrs. Swan's garden, he crosses between Das and the portrait he is painting. Furthermore, since the characters do not always exit at the end of their scene, sometimes they would freeze or silently continue what they are doing, with Wood sometimes opting for a parallel action such as Das silently giving Flora a signed pencil sketch (started on page 16) at the same moment Anish asks Mrs. Swan "May I draw you?" (18).

7. This sentiment, as well as those of the rest of the paragraph, is shared by many of the London critics. See *London Theatre Record* 15, no. 5 (1995): 245–53.

8. Lost on the reader are the atmospheric effects of the London production: evocative Indian music; flexible, moving sets by Carl Toms; and Mark Henderson's beautiful, richly colored lighting, which involved projections onto a back scrim, creating a *rasa* for each scene. The production also accented the text's romantic sentiment. For example, when Flora and Durance are on the horses, a light fog glided along the ground while their bodies were lit by "moonlight." Also, as the transition for the cemetery scene, during Mrs. Swan's description of the graveyard, flower blossoms fell like a gentle snow.

9. In Peter Wood's staging, Flora's description "[Coomaraswami] holding a yellow parasol over me while the committee bicycled alongside, sometimes two to a bike, and children ran before me and behind" (4) was partially realized onstage. Throughout the play Wood often tried to represent Flora's descriptions so that the audience saw and heard the atmosphere of her Indian visit.

10. When asked about the difficulty of writing Indian characters, particularly since he is perceived as being from the colonizing culture, Stoppard noted an obstacle that he had not sufficiently overcome: "There is this slight embarrassment about actually not really knowing much about how to write an Indian character and really merely mimicking the Indian characters in other people's work. Because my own memory of living in India really hasn't been that much help because my conscious

knowledge of how Indians speak and behave has actually been derived from other people's fictions (Allen 242–43). In the play the present-day Indian characters Anish and Dilip seem to escape more successfully this pitfall of being indebted to other fictional creations.

11. The first published text has the line "Your handkerchief smells faintly of . . . something nice" (72). In previews Stoppard added the phrase "Is it cinnamon?" (the phrase used in *Native State*), but Peter Wood, rightly believing most audiences would not get the connection between cinnamon and sandalwood, persuaded Stoppard to add the phrase "Is it sandalwood?" (Gussow, *Conversations*, 123). Similarly, Wood and Stoppard debated over how to suggest the romance without verbally stating it. One of their solutions was: "She woke up in bed wearing his [brown-orange] shawl" (122). But this device was seemingly not used throughout the run; in some performances Flora appeared the morning after in a black shawl and in possession of Das's handkerchief.

12. To understand the poem's climax, the audience must either know Latin or recall the earlier Club scene where the Resident provides a translation of the Latin phrase (46). Also, Stoppard has pointed out, in a note he gave to Felicity Kendal on the reading of the poem, "The word 'mangrove' is not there entirely accidentally. It has a gender connotation too" (Twisk 253).

13. This inarticulate response to Durance's sexist remark contrasts with her reaction to the Rajah's mention of the long history and serious purpose of Indian erotic art: "(*Unangrily*) But only for men, your highness?" (65). (In *In the Native State* Flora argues that the response to erotic art is more likely "a matter of culture than gender" [67].) Around Indian men Flora freely speaks her mind, but with British men, on matters of politics and gender, she is restrained to the point of submissiveness. The staging can help alleviate some of this, as for example, in Peter Wood's blocking, when Durance tells Flora, "Sit down, that's an order" (53), she was already almost seated, and she jokingly chastised him: "Oh dear, you're not going to be masterful, are you?" (53). Overall, textually, there is a seemingly unconscious pecking order of supremacy from British male to British female to Indian male to the completely absent and unmentioned Indian female. All of this is glossed over, hidden beneath the warm veneer of the nostalgia for the English Eden of India under the Empire.

14. Assumptions about race were expressed more explicitly in the early drafts of the play. After Anish says he is married, there is the following exchange:

SWAN: An English girl?
ANISH: Yes. Australian.
SWAN: Oh . . . How disappointing.
ANISH: Why?

SWAN: You thought I meant colour.

ANISH: I'm sorry. It is what people usually mean.

SWAN: My prejudices are quite different.

(Jan. 1993 printout, 15)

15. My point is twofold: first, I would guess that an elderly British woman nostalgic for the empire is more sympathetic to a West End audience than a young, Indian deconstructive painter, and second, Swan's role as a hostess is a structural device that limits debate. For example, Swan's statement that Das "deserved what he got" (15) is immediately followed by the offering of cake and a switching of topics. Later, Stoppard makes a joke of it by having Anish state: "You advance a preposterous argument and try to fill my mouth with cake so I cannot answer you" (17). But Anish's ensuing argument is followed by an outburst by Swan, who rejects Anish's view, and thus Anish apologizes; his disagreeing with her is a violation of hostess-guest etiquette. Thus, while Stoppard allows for brief counterarguments to Swan's political perspective, she is always allowed the last and most forceful word on the justification of British colonial rule.

16. Playwright James Saunders once remarked: "[Tom] feels grateful to Britain, because he sees himself as a guest here, and that makes it hard for him to criticize Britain" (Tynan 71).

17. It takes a while before one realizes that in her youth Mrs. Swan was a Marxist. In Stoppard's earlier drafts (Jan. and May 1993), the opening dialogue between Pike and Swan revealed the political sympathies of her youth. Stoppard makes clear his own distaste for Marxism by having Mrs. Swan call herself stupid for memorializing Lenin. Likewise, while she clearly recalls Lenin's death, she only remembers her father's death as an afterthought. Indeed, Stoppard's omission of any explanation for Swan's political transformation might suggest an attitude that any adult in their right mind would disavow Marxism.

18. Swan characterizes Das's nonnude portrait as "fairly ghastly, like an Indian cinema poster" (10). When Anish weeps at the vibrancy of his father's work, Swan changes her view: "It just goes to show, you need an eye. And your father, after all, was, like you, an Indian painter. . . . No, I should not have been disparaging. I'm sorry" (34). It is a moment where Swan loses some of her cultural superiority, and the *rasa* felt by Anish in viewing the work makes him, in her eyes, an Indian painter.

19. The subject of biography is a personal touchstone for Stoppard. He loves to read them but, in a statement made at the time that his relationship with Felicity Kendal was a leading tabloid story, he admitted to "a sense of doom" (Lawson 22) at the thought of a biography being written of him.

20. Regarding academic scholarship, Stoppard has said: "I think the only thing which has certainly bothered me and I think it's more of an American phenomenon,

is just the sheer disproportionate scale of the enterprise, there's just so much writing about writing, it's just a major industry and there's something wrong about the scale of it all" (Kuurman 50).

21. In the May 1993 draft, Dilip's speech included a statement about the importance of a common language in shaping the culture of a people: "Yes, it's a disaster for us! It is why we have no Indian language. Without a language for everyone, how can we have an Indian India?" (65). In the September 1994 draft, Dilip notes: "There are seventeen recognized Indian languages, and many many more which are the mother tongues of the Indian people" (75). The final version's only statement about language as a unifying element is Das's nicely ironic observation that Lord Macaulay's decision to educate Indians in English resulted in "English [being] the only language the nationalists can communicate in!" (19).

Chapter 12

1. In the play AEH says that he did not even get a pass degree (46), but in real life, Housman returned the following fall to successfully take his pass degree examination. But it was not until ten years later, when he applied for an academic position, that he formally received the degree (N. Page 48).

2. Posthumously, *More Poems* and *Additional Poems* were published. Both are collections of earlier works, often of a more personal nature. Notably, the majority of Housman's poems were written in two concentrated periods—one near the Oscar Wilde trials, the other when Jackson was seriously ill and near death.

3. In his review of *The Invention of Love* John Peter argues that Plato is also a looming presence:

> One question Stoppard is asking, with a learned but friendly smile, is: what is Platonic? Is it what is unsensual, unfulfilled? The idea would have made Plato himself smile a learned but perhaps less friendly smile. Is it not, rather, that which fulfills, both sensually and beyond sensuality? Love, for example: is it real in itself, or did it need, as Housman ponders, Catullus to invent love poetry and so make it real? Perhaps love is not true but it is a truth about people. If so, which is more real: the poem or the feeling? Which is the real thing?

4. For the other major plays I have discussed multiple drafts or versions. However, when writing this chapter Stoppard's papers for *The Invention of Love* were not yet available at the HRHRC. The production text does vary in small ways from the published text, mostly in the trimming of a few speeches. The changes appear in the Grove Press edition.

5. Stoppard marks his characters as AEH (the elder Housman) and Housman (the younger Housman). I am using "the historical Housman" or "A. E. Housman" to clarify when I am referring to the actual person as opposed to his stage incarna-

tion. Often these identities overlap, but this nomenclature should make clear which character (Wood's or Rhys's) is onstage at a given moment.

6. I refer to the play as "dream-memory" and "caught between death and dreaming" because Stoppard mingles together these different aspects. AEH begins the play announcing that he is dead (1), only later to say: "Not dead, only dreaming!" (5). Likewise, he follows it up with repeated references to the fact that he may be sleeping/dreaming in the Evelyn Nursing Home, the place where the historical Housman lapsed into unconsciousness and died. Overall, the character seems to be in a border zone just before or after death. While the play relives memories and events of Housman's life, there are also scenes and conversations to which he could not have been privy. Most of these are social-context scenes where Stoppard "illustrates huge intellectual movements by gathering representative figures together to have highly unlikely representative conversations" (Clanchy).

7. The cyclorama was pivotal to the National Theatre's staging. The play is written with cinematic-like fluidity between scenes, and so to clarify the changing time and place, Anthony Ward's back projections helped indicate the new location.

8. Housman's first year at Oxford was Wilde's last.

9. Historically, Jowett was a passionate Platonist who "deplored the utilitarian trend of industrialised Victorian life" (Jones).

10. For the Oxford boat scenes Stoppard is loosely "quoting" Jerome K. Jerome's comic novel *Three Men in a Boat (To Say Nothing of the Dog)* (1889). Stoppard has long admired the book, and he has written both a screenplay (1975) and a radio play (1997) of it. Jerome later appears as a character, as again three men are in a boat, only now they are paddling down the Thames to get a view of the imprisoned Oscar Wilde. In the play Stoppard notes how Jerome wrote a newspaper editorial that was a catalyst for Wilde's downfall (104).

11. The lines AEH speaks about the quality, or lack thereof, of each scholar's work are taken from the historical Housman's writings. Dramaturgically, this quick sampling of commentary by AEH serves to telescope Housman's work as a textual scholar.

12. Stoppard makes a distinction between textual criticism and literary criticism. Textual criticism is important because it establishes what was and was not actually written. On the other hand, AEH and Stoppard have little regard for literary criticism, the much less scientific endeavor of trying to determine meaning.

13. In his monologue-lecture at the end of act 1, AEH's imagery suggests that as long as he lives he will wage war against the corruption of Latin texts. From a classical perspective, A. E. Housman's relentless pursuit of knowledge is good and virtuous, a moral endeavor, one way he can achieve a classical ideal.

14. The poem is about the inevitability and permanence of death.

15. *Vester* is the plural form of "your"; *tuus,* the singular form. Earlier in the play, Housman says: "*Basium* is a point of interest. A kiss was always *osculum* until Catullus" (13). *Basium* simply means kiss, whereas *osculum,* being a diminutive of *os,* technically means small mouth. Notably, Pollard follows Housman by saying: "Now, Hous, concentrate—is that the point of interest in the kiss?" (13). For Housman, it is. The moment shows Housman's perpetual emphasis on the technical over the human, on the academic over the emotional. (Latin translations/explanations courtesy of Paul Fleming.)

16. In his Housman biography Norman Page discusses a number of factors that may have come into play (43–46). The historical Pollard "blamed the [Jackson] friendship for Housman's failure" (43), but mostly because Housman spent idle time with Jackson when he should have been reading and studying. Others believed that "over-confidence bred of contempt for the Oxford establishment may have also contributed. . . . Housman had pursued a course of studies of his own devising rather than that laid down by authority" (43). Also figuring into the picture was his father's serious illness.

17. The events in act 1 were a scene where Housman watches one of Jackson's rowing races and a scene where Housman times Jackson in the half mile. In the latter Housman does not pay attention to the timing because he is preoccupied with admiring Jackson as he runs; the image recalls Horace and Ligurinus.

18. Jackson offers an ambiguous response to the nature of homosexuality in that on one hand his words suggest a modern sensibility that there is a biological cause for Housman's homosexuality—that it is not his fault that he is in love with Jackson. On the other hand, he also adheres to the traditional societal notion that Housman just needs to meet the right girl.

19. This is one of the personal poems that was published posthumously. It is also notable that, in this play about love, handshakes are the extent of physical contact/ expression. Besides the two handshakes Jackson offers in this scene, in act 1, AEH and Housman part with a handshake (44).

20. The National Theatre production used the three actors that played Ruskin, Pater, and Jowett to play Labouchère, Harris, and Stead. They function as a pseudo-Greek chorus, filling in the social context. Also, whereas in the first act they play croquet, here they play billiards, both games associated with upper-class, English gentility. In production the balls for both games were mimed, with sound effects indicating when balls were struck.

21. Why Labouchère added the antihomosexual amendment has been a source of dispute. The conventional view is that he did it for moral reasons, but the play

presents the conjectural view, advocated by the historical Harris, that Labouchère "intended to make the Bill absurd to any sensible person" (64) but it went astray. After Wilde's conviction, the play presents Labouchère's public position that he not only intended the amendment but had originally wanted the penalty to be seven years, not two. The National Theatre program, based on a 1976 F. B. Smith article in *Historical Studies,* presents both sides of the controversy. The incident highlights the difficulty of writing history and of sorting out fact from fiction, truth from conjecture.

22. In *The Real Thing* Stoppard championed carnal knowledge as a fundamental component of love. However, in *Invention* he has assembled an unusual group for a discussion about love. Besides the severely repressed A. E. Housman, there are the undergraduates, of whom only Jackson has kissed a girl. Likewise, as detailed in the National Theatre program, of the four historical Oxford figures, Ruskin was impotent, Pater terrified, Jowett celibate, and Pattison a cuckolded married celibate.

23. Wilde has a number of observations on art. He argues: "Art deals with exceptions, not types. Facts deal only with types" (96); "Art cannot be subordinate to its subject, otherwise it is not art but biography, and biography is the mesh through which our real life escapes" (96); "Sincerity is the enemy of art" (96). All of these statements apply to how Stoppard has crafted this play about Housman, making a piece of art that evokes a sense of truth as opposed to a biography just filled with facts.

24. AEH's monologue offers self-reflexive commentary on the play and is stylistically reminiscent of Carr's opening monologue in *Travesties* as it includes extended stream-of-consciousness sentences filled with wordplay. Both plays were written with John Wood in mind, and this monologue exemplifies Wood's "ability to deliver with tremendous clarity and pace quite complicated sentences and quite complicated thoughts" (Stoppard, quoted in Gussow, "So Rude").

Conclusion

1. Stoppard has often mentioned his desire to write an original screenplay, but never has. However, in 1984 he produced a formal outline for a proposed film entitled *A.O.P.* The acronym stands for "Assault on the Principal," the Secret Service code word for an assassination attempt on the President. The film was to be about a bodyguard in his late thirties, a man born at the end of World War II, whose "boyhood coincided with the peak years of American prosperity and self-confidence during the 50s . . . ; [and whose] young manhood coincided with the decade, the 60s, when so many things in America began to break loose and [who] had entered his maturity as America entered a sober period of conservatism and recession" (2). As events

unfold, the bodyguard was to become disillusioned with the values he is supposed to protect, questioning the lengths to which they go to prevent demonstrations at the President's public appearances. Thus, he leaves the Secret Service and becomes a bodyguard for a rock star the magnitude of Mick Jagger or Bob Dylan. "The circle closes when the Rock Star performs for the President, and thus the bodyguard's old and new lives come together" (2). Stoppard did not know the film's resolution, but knew he did not want to use a "melodramatic assassination attempt on either the President or the Rock Star" (2). Stoppard's interest sprang from two fascinations. The first was the sight of a Secret Service agent jumping in front of President Reagan and "stopping" the bullet, an action that goes against our "natural" reflex (4). To pursue this aspect, Stoppard interviewed the head of the Washington Field Office of the Secret Service, talked to several agents, and even observed an antiassassination training exercise. The other impulse stemmed from his oft-expressed desire to write about America and "Americanness" in a political and cultural sense: "To my generation there is and always will be a residual sense of [fascination] with Americanism" (5). The HRHRC has Stoppard's notes from 1981, 1983, and the 1984 outline. While Stoppard seemed deeply interested in the project, apparently he was unable to interest a producer.

2. Billington clarifies these terms when he asserts that Stoppard's plays often exhibit a "terror of cosmic disorder and a hunger for some kind of post-Christian value system" ("Joker" 3).

3. Peter Wood has an impressive résumé and has been instrumental in Stoppard's success. While it would be erroneous to blame Wood, the last two Stoppard plays he directed, *Hapgood* and *Indian Ink,* are the only two major plays that did not win Stoppard an *Evening Standard* Award. Also, continuing Stoppard's recent trend of working with other renowned directors, in 1997, Peter Hall staged Stoppard's adaptation of Chekhov's play *The Seagull.*

4. While Stoppard's major stage plays experimented with modified realism, his shorter plays and television work went through a thematic cycle. *Professional Foul* (1977), *Every Good Boy Deserves Favor* (1977), *Dogg's Hamlet, Cahoot's Macbeth* (1979), and *Squaring the Circle* (1984) all address aspects of the ethics and politics of pre-perestroika Eastern Bloc totalitarian repression.

5. In an interview for *The Invention of Love,* Stoppard was reminded of this quotation, and so he explained: "*The Real Thing* was different—that was a world understood. This—the world of 19th-century scholasticism and homosexuality—is a world I can't approach except as a well-read anthropologist" (T. Hill).

6. Notably, Stoppard's most successful screenplay, *Shakespeare in Love,* is a romantic comedy revolving around love and art. The basic plot was provided by

cowriter Marc Norman while virtually all the dialogue is Stoppard's. The popularity of the film and the accolades given to Stoppard may help introduce his stage work to an even wider audience.

7. Both plays had their U.S. premiere in San Francisco (American Conservatory Theater). Also, it should be noted that "success" is a relative term. *Indian Ink* played for ten months on London's West End whereas *Jumpers* had only forty-eight performances on Broadway.

8. After *The Invention of Love* Stoppard said that he will think twice before doing another biographically based play (T. Hill).

9. Because I am focusing on writers with a body of work, my list is composed mostly of playwrights who began their careers in the 1960s and 1970s. Since the mid-1990s the London stage has been energized by an exciting new wave of young playwrights, including Martin McDonagh, Patrick Marber, and Mark Ravenhill.

10. To be fair, the 1995 Lincoln Center production of *Racing Demon* was nominated for a Tony Award. Hare's previous Broadway productions were *Plenty* (1978) and *The Secret Rapture* (1988).

11. Ironically, as Hare began writing less specifically British plays, Stoppard penned his most British-based works—*Indian Ink* and *The Invention of Love.*

12. Trying to assess international stature is a precarious venture, and my admittedly Eurocentric assessment is artificially skewed in favor of how British playwrights have fared in the United States, an assumption that is not always an accurate barometer of international standards. For example, Marxist playwright Dario Fo is widely produced in Europe, much less so in the United States. Thus, it is reasonable to assume that the work of the leftist political playwrights would find more receptive audiences in Europe than they would in America. That said, I am reasonably sure that none of them have been translated into at least thirty languages, as Stoppard has. Likewise, Stoppard's success in the United States and on the Continent is verifiable.

BIBLIOGRAPHY

Published Works by Tom Stoppard

Rosencrantz and Guildenstern Are Dead. London: Faber and Faber, 1967; New York: Grove Press, 1967; New York: Samuel French, 1967.

Jumpers. London: Faber and Faber, 1972, revised 1986; New York: Grove Press, 1973.

Travesties. New York: Grove Press, 1975; London: Faber and Faber, 1993.

Every Good Boy Deserves Favor and Professional Foul. New York: Grove Press, 1978.

Night and Day. London: Faber and Faber, 1978; New York: Grove Press, 1979; London: Samuel French, 1979.

Dogg's Hamlet, Cahoot's Macbeth. New York: Samuel French, 1980.

The Real Thing. London: Faber and Faber, 1982, revised 1983; Broadway Edition 1984; New York: Samuel French, 1984.

Lord Malquist and Mr. Moon. London: Faber and Faber, 1985. (First published 1966.)

Artist Descending a Staircase. London: Faber and Faber, 1988. (First published 1973.)

Hapgood. London: Faber and Faber, 1988; Broadway Edition 1994.

Stoppard: The Plays for Radio, 1964–1983. London: Faber and Faber, 1990. (Contains *The Dissolution of Dominic Boot,* "M" *is for Moon Among Other Things, If You're Glad I'll Be Frank, Albert's Bridge, Where Are They Now?, Artist Descending a Staircase,* and *The Dog It Was That Died.*)

In the Native State. London: Faber and Faber, 1991.

Arcadia. London: Faber and Faber, 1993, reprinted with corrections 1993.

Stoppard: The Television Plays, 1965–1984. London: Faber and Faber, 1993. (Contains *A Separate Peace, Teeth, Another Moon Called Earth, Neutral Ground, Professional Foul,* and *Squaring the Circle.*)

Indian Ink. London: Faber and Faber, 1995, reprinted with corrections 1995.

The Invention of Love. London: Faber and Faber, 1997; New York: Grove Press, 1998.

Articles by Tom Stoppard

"Act II . . . In Which Tom Stoppard Tries Another Profession." *Western Daily Press and Bristol Mirror,* 13 Sept. 1958, 8.

"Tom Stoppard on a Dazzling New Writer Who Leaves No Stone Unturned to Find Out What They Look Like the Wrong Way Up." Review of *Next Time I'll Sing to You,* by James Saunders. *Scene,* 9 Feb. 1963, 46–47.

"The Definite Maybe." *Author* 78 (spring 1967): 18–20.

"Something to Declare." *Sunday Times,* 25 Feb. 1968, 47.

"Playwrights and Professors." *Times Literary Supplement,* 13 Oct. 1972, 1219.

"Dirty Linen in Prague." *New York Times,* 11 Feb. 1977, 27.

"The Face at the Window." *Sunday Times,* 27 Feb. 1977, 33.

"But for the Middle Classes." Review of *Enemies of Society,* by Paul Johnson. *Times Literary Supplement,* 3 June 1977, 677.

"Journalists' Closed Shop." Letter to the editor. *Times* (London), 11 Aug. 1977, 13.

"Leftover from *Travesties.*" *Adam International Review* 42, nos. 431–33 (1980): 11–12.

"The Text's The Thing." *Weekend Telegraph,* 23 Apr. 1988. [Source: Gordon Dickerson Collection 18.6]

"The Event and the Text." The Whidden Lectures, McMaster University, Hamilton, Ontario, 24 Oct. 1988. In *Tom Stoppard in Conversation,* edited by Paul Delaney, 199–211. Ann Arbor: University of Michigan Press, 1993.

"On Turning Out To Be Jewish." *Talk,* Sept. 1999, 190–94, 241–43.

From the Tom Stoppard Archive at the University of Texas's Harry Ransom Humanities Research Center

I. Scripts and Related Material by Tom Stoppard

AUTHOR'S NOTE: The early scripts are undated. Bracketed material is my own approximation or editorial comment. The number after the box number refers to the specific folder where the item can be found.

Items from the HRHRC's Gordon Dickerson Collection of Modern British Playwrights are labeled G.D.

The Gamblers. Synopsis. Typescript (hereafter Ts.). [n.d.] Box 10.11.

The Gamblers. Ms. [n.d.] Box 10.13; Ts. Box 10.14; Ms. Box 67.5.

I Can't Give You Anything but Love, Baby. Unproduced teleplay. Ts. [1963] Box 14.10.

Funny Man. Unproduced teleplay. Ts. [1963] Box 67.4.

This Way Out with Samuel Boot. Unproduced teleplay. Ts. [1964] Box 68.5.

Rosencrantz and Guildenstern Meet King Lear. Ms. [1964] Box 23.10.

Guildenstern and Rosencrantz. Ts. [Questors text, 1964] Box 24.1.

Higg and Cogg. Ts. [1965] Box 13.11.

The Explorers. Ts. [1965] G.D. 8.7.

Synopsis of *The Waiter.* Proposed teleplay. Ts. [1965] G.D. 11.10.

Synopsis of *The Servant Problem.* Proposed teleplay. Ts. [1965] G.D. 11.10.

How Sir Dudley Lost the Empire. Unproduced teleplay. Ts. [1965] Box 67.6.

Doctor Masopust, I Presume. Pilot for radio serial, cowritten with Gordon M. Williams. Ts. [1966] G.D. 8.1.

Rosencrantz and Guildenstern Are Dead. Ts. [RSC text, 1965] Box 24.2.

Rosencrantz and Guildenstern Are Dead. Ts. [Edinburgh text, 1966] Box 68.2.

Rosencrantz and Guildenstern Are Dead. Unproduced screenplay. Ts. [1968] Box 8.3.

Galileo. Unproduced screenplay. Ts. [1970 or 1971, 1st draft] Box 43.5; [1971, 2nd draft] Box 43.6.

Galileo. Unproduced stage play. Ts. [1972 or 1973] Box 43.4.

And Now the Incredible Archibald Jumpers. Bound script. [1st draft, n.d.] G.D. 7.3.

"Jumpers—Translators' notes." Ts. Mar. 1972. G.D. 19.6.

Travesties. Unbound script. [1st draft, n.d.] G.D. 11.8.

Travesties. Bound script. May 1974. Box 30.5.

Travesties. Bound script. 2 Feb. 1976. Box 30.7.

"Notes for Translators [of *Travesties*]." Ts. [n.d.] Box 30.6.

Every Good Boy Deserves Favor. Ts. 23 June 1976, Box 9.6; Ts. 8 July 1976, Box 9.6; Ts. Mar. 1977, Box 9.7.

Professional Foul. [Adapted for radio] Ts. June 1978, Box 20.11.

A.O.P. Proposed screenplay, never produced. "Film Outline." Ts. May 1984. Box 1.1.

The Real Thing. "Last revision pages for USA." Ts. [n.d.] Box 23.10.

"Notes [for *Hapgood*], 27 Apr. 1986." Ms. Box 11.2.

Hapgood. Undated printout. Box 13.1.

"Hapgood Crib." Ts. [n.d.] Box 13.6.

"Hapgood says." Ts. [n.d.] Box 13.6.

Hapgood. Bound script. [1989 Los Angeles production] Box 12.7.

"Notes for *In the Native State.*" [n.d.] Box 61.7.

"Notes for *Indian Ink.*" 6 Dec. 1992. Box 47.1.

Indian Ink. Jan. 1993 printout, Box 47.1; bound script. May 1993, Box 62.1; bound script. Sept. 1994, Box 62.7.

II. Correspondence

Boorman, John. Letter to Stoppard, 7 Dec. 1967. Box 36.2.

Brooks, Jeremy. Letter to Stoppard, 22 July 1965. Box 36.2.

Ebdon, John. Letter to Stoppard, 12 Dec. 1972. Box 36.1.

Ewing, Kenneth. Letter to Stoppard, 15 Sept. 1965. Box 36.2.

———. Letter to Stoppard, 29 Oct. 1965. Box 36.2

Fainberg, Victor. Letter to Stoppard, 17 Dec. 1976. Box 38.2.

Hawthorne, Nigel. Letter to Stoppard, 1 Aug. 1988. Box 13.6.

Jackson, Nagle. Letter to Stoppard, 24 Sept. 1984. Box 35.2.

Lantz, Robert [John Wood's agent]. Letter to Kenneth Ewing, 12 Dec. 1975. Box 31.6.

Oxford Theatre Group. Letter/contract to Stoppard, 12 July 1966. G.D. 19.4.

Stoppard, Tom. Letter to John Boorman, 17 Apr. 1968. Box 36.2.

———. Letter to Peter Bart [Paramount Pictures], 28 May 1971. Box 36.1.

———. Letter to David Merrick, 3 Nov. 1975. Box 31.6.

———. Letter to Frances Cuka and Harry Towb, 6 Nov. 1975. Box 31.6.

———. Letter to Jon Bradshaw, 8 Dec. 1976. Box 34.4.

———. Letter to Mike Nichols, n.d. Box 23.10.

———. Letter to Adrian [surname not listed], 20 Dec. 1983. Box 23.10.

———. Letter to Gordon Davidson. 17 Apr. 1986. Box 22.9.

———. Fax to Michael Eisner. 13 June 1993. Box 59.8.

———. Letter to Adrian Noble, 12 July 1993. Box 52.8.

Thatcher, Russell [MGM Films]. Letter to Robert Chartoof [Caribury Films], 15 Jan. 1969. Box 36.2.

General Bibliography

Books

Andretta, Richard A. *Tom Stoppard: An Analytical Study of His Plays.* New Delhi: Vikas Publishing House Pvt. Ltd., 1992.

Aristotle. *Poetics.* Translated by S. H. Butcher. New York: Hill and Wang, 1961.

Ayer, A. J. *Language, Truth, and Logic.* 17th ed. London: Victor Gollancz, 1967.

Bigsby, C. W. E. *Tom Stoppard.* London: Longman, 1976, revised 1979.

Billington, Michael. *Stoppard: The Playwright.* London: Methuen, 1987.

Bloom, Harold, ed. *Tom Stoppard.* New York: Chelsea House, 1986.

Brassell, Tim. *Tom Stoppard: An Assessment.* New York: St. Martin's Press, 1985.

Bratt, David. *Tom Stoppard: A Reference Guide.* Boston: G. K. Hall, 1982.

Briggs, John, and F. David Peat. *Turbulent Mirror.* New York: Harper and Row, 1989.

Bürger, Peter. *Theory of the Avant-garde.* Translated by Michael Shaw. Minneapolis: University of Minnesota Press, 1984.

Cahn, Victor L. *Beyond Absurdity: The Plays of Tom Stoppard.* Rutherford, N.J.: Fairleigh Dickinson University Press, 1979.

Corballis, Richard. *Stoppard: The Mystery and the Clockwork.* New York: Methuen, 1984.

Dean, Joan Fitzpatrick. *Tom Stoppard: Comedy as a Moral Matrix.* Columbia: University of Missouri Press, 1981.

Delaney, Paul. *Tom Stoppard: The Moral Vision of the Major Plays.* New York: St. Martin's Press, 1990.

————, ed. *Tom Stoppard in Conversation.* Ann Arbor: University of Michigan Press, 1994.

Ellman, Richard. *James Joyce.* Oxford: Oxford University Press, 1965.

Faraone, Cheryl. *An Analysis of Tom Stoppard's Plays and Their Productions, (1964 – 1975).* Ann Arbor: UMI, 1980.

Feynman, Richard. *The Feynman Lectures on Physics: Quantum Mechanics.* Reading, Mass.: Addison-Wesley, 1966.

Gilson, Etienne, Thomas Langam, and Armand A. Maurer. *Recent Philosophy: Hegel to the Present.* New York: Random House, 1966.

Gleick, James. *Chaos: Making a New Science.* New York: Penguin, 1987.

Gordon, Robert. *Rosencrantz and Guildenstern Are Dead, Jumpers, The Real Thing.* Text and Performance Series. New York: Macmillan, 1991.

Gussow, Mel. *Conversations with Stoppard.* London: Nick Hern Books, 1995.

Harty, John, III, ed. *Tom Stoppard: A Casebook.* New York: Garland, 1988.

Hawking, Stephen W. *A Brief History of Time.* New York: Bantam, 1988.

Hayman, Ronald. *Tom Stoppard.* 4th ed. London: Heinemann, 1982.

Hu, Stephen. *Tom Stoppard's Stagecraft.* New York: Peter Lang, 1988.

Hunter, Jim. *Tom Stoppard's Plays.* London: Faber and Faber, 1982.

Jenkins, Anthony. *The Theatre of Tom Stoppard.* 2nd ed. Cambridge: Cambridge University Press, 1989.

————, ed. *Critical Essays on Tom Stoppard.* Boston: G. K. Hall, 1990.

Kelly, Katherine E. *Tom Stoppard and the Craft of Comedy: Medium and Genre at Play.* Ann Arbor: University of Michigan Press, 1991.

Londré, Felicia Hardison. *Tom Stoppard.* New York: Frederick Ungar, 1981.

Marowitz, Charles. *Confessions of a Counterfeit Critic.* London: Eyre Methuen, 1973.

Page, Malcolm. *File on Stoppard.* London: Methuen, 1986.

Page, Norman. *A. E. Housman: A Critical Biography.* New York: Schocken Books, 1983.

Polkinghorne, J. C. *The Quantum World.* Princeton: Princeton University Press, 1985.

Prigogine, Ilya, and Isabelle Stengers. *Order Out of Chaos: Man's New Dialogue with Nature.* New York: Bantam, 1984.

Richter, Hans. *Dada: Art and Anti-Art.* London: Thames and Hudson, 1965.

Rusinko, Susan. *Tom Stoppard.* Boston: Twayne Publishers, 1986.

Sammells, Neil. *Tom Stoppard: The Artist as Critic.* New York: St. Martin's Press, 1988.

Shakespeare, William. *Hamlet.* New York: New American Library, 1963.

————. *King Lear.* New York: New American Library, 1963.

Szczesny, Gerhard. *The Case against Bertolt Brecht.* Translated by Alexander Gode. New York: Frederick Ungar, 1969.

Whitaker, Thomas R. *Tom Stoppard.* New York: Grove Press, 1983.

Wilde, Alan. *Horizons of Assent: Modernism, Postmodernism, and the Ironic Imagination.* Philadelphia: University of Pennsylvania Press, 1987.

Wilson, John Dover. *What Happens in Hamlet.* 2nd ed. Cambridge: Cambridge University Press, 1937.

Articles and Interviews

Allen, Paul. "Third Ear." BBC Radio Three, 16 Apr. 1991. In *Tom Stoppard in Conversation,* edited by Paul Delaney, 239–47. Ann Arbor: University of Michigan Press, 1993.

Amory, Mark. "The Joke's the Thing." *Sunday Times Magazine,* 9 June 1974, 65–73.

Anonymous. "Dexter Dispute over *As You Like It.*" *Times* (London), 23 Mar. 1967, 10.

Barber, John. "Comedy as Erudite as It Is Dotty." *Daily Telegraph,* 3 Feb. 1972, 11.

————. "Newspaper Drama is Year's Best New Play." *Daily Telegraph,* 10 Nov. 1978, 15.

Barker, Felix. "First Night: Theatre: *Jumpers.*" *Evening News,* 3 Feb. 1972, 3.

Barnes, Clive. "Theater: 'Rosenkrantz [*sic*] and Guildenstern are Dead.'" *New York Times,* 17 Oct. 1967, 53.

Bennett, Jonathan. "Philosophy and Mr. Stoppard." *Philosophy,* 50 (Jan. 1975). In *Critical Essays on Tom Stoppard,* edited by Anthony Jenkins, 73–87. Boston: G. K. Hall, 1990.

Berkvist, Robert. "This Time, Stoppard Plays It (Almost) Straight." *New York Times,* 25 Nov. 1979. In *Tom Stoppard in Conversation,* edited by Paul Delaney, 135–40. Ann Arbor: University of Michigan Press, 1993.

Berlin, Normand. "Death in *Rosencrantz and Guildenstern.*" *The Secret Cause: A Discussion of Tragedy.* Amherst: University of Massachusetts Press, 1981. In *Critical Essays on Tom Stoppard,* edited by Anthony Jenkins, 43–50. Boston: G. K. Hall, 1990.

Billington, Michael. "Joker above the Abyss." *Guardian,* 2 Apr. 1993, sec. 2, 2–3.

————. Review of *Hapgood. Guardian,* 9 Mar. 1988. In *London Theatre Record* 8, no. 5 (1988): 288.

————. Review of *The Invention of Love. Guardian,* 2 Oct. 1997. In *London Theatre Record* 17, no. 20 (1997): 1261.

————. Review of *Night and Day. Guardian,* 9 Nov. 1978, 12. In *London Theatre Record* 8, no. 5 (1988): 288.

————. "Stoppard's Secret Agent." *Guardian,* 18 Mar. 1988. In *Tom Stoppard in*

Conversation, edited by Paul Delaney, 193–98. Ann Arbor: University of Michigan Press, 1993.

Bradshaw, Jon. "Tom Stoppard, Nonstop: Word Games with a Hit Playwright." *New York,* 10 Jan. 1977. In *Tom Stoppard in Conversation,* edited by Paul Delaney, 89–99. Ann Arbor: University of Michigan Press, 1993.

Bragg, Melvyn. "The South Bank Show." Transcript of show transmitted on London Weekend Television, 26 Nov. 1978 (recorded 22 Nov. 1978). In *Tom Stoppard in Conversation,* edited by Paul Delaney, 115–28. Ann Arbor: University of Michigan Press, 1993.

Brecht, Bertolt. "Praise or Condemnation of Galileo?" *Brecht: Collected Plays* 5:224–25. Translated and edited by Ralph Mannheim and John Willet. New York: Vintage Books, 1972.

Brown, Georgina. Review of *The Invention of Love. Mail on Sunday,* 12 Oct. 1997. In *London Theatre Record* 17, no. 20 (1997): 1256.

Brustein, Robert. "Waiting for Hamlet." *New Republic,* 4 Nov. 1967, 25–26.

Bryden, Ronald. "Theatre: Wyndy Excitement." *Observer,* 28 Aug. 1966, 15.

Buck, Joan Juliet. "Tom Stoppard: Kind Heart and Prickly Mind." *Vogue* 174 (Mar. 1984). In *Tom Stoppard in Conversation,* edited by Paul Delaney, 167–71. Ann Arbor: University of Michigan Press, 1993.

Buhr, Richard J. "Epistemology and Ethics in Tom Stoppard's *Professional Foul.*" *Comparative Drama* 12 (winter 1979–80): 320–29.

Callen, Anthony. "Stoppard's *Godot:* Some French influences on Post-War English Drama." *New Theatre Magazine* 10 (winter 1969): 22–30.

Canby, Vincent. "An Abundance of Wit on the London Stage." *New York Times,* 14 Dec. 1997, sec. 2, p. 4.

Clanchy, Kate. Review of *The Invention of Love. Scotsman,* 7 Oct. 1997, 15.

Cobley, Evelyn. "Catastrophe Theory in Tom Stoppard's *Professional Foul.*" *Contemporary Literature* 25 (spring 1984): 53–65.

Coe, Richard. "*Jumpers:* Further Elaboration on Its Meaning." *Washington Post,* 24 Mar. 1974, L6.

Cohn, Ruby. "Tom Stoppard: Light Drama and Dirges in Marriage." In *Contemporary English Drama,* edited by C. W. E. Bigsby, 109–20. New York: Holmes & Meier, 1981.

Corliss, Richard. "Stoppard in the Name of Love." *Time,* 16 Jan. 1984, 68–69.

Coveney, Michael. Review of *Arcadia. Observer,* 18 Apr. 1993. In *London Theatre Record* 13, no. 8 (1993): 410.

Crump, G. B. "The Universe as Murder Mystery: *Jumpers.*" *Contemporary Literature* 20, no. 3 (summer 1979). In *Tom Stoppard,* edited by Harold Bloom, 45–57. New York: Chelsea House, 1986.

de Lisle, Tim. "Re-Enter Stoppard." *Sunday Telegraph,* 3 Dec. 1995. [Source: G.D. 18.3.]

Demastes, William. "Re-inspecting the Crack in the Chimney: Chaos Theory from Ibsen to Stoppard." *New Theatre Quarterly* 10, no. 39 (Aug. 1994): 242–54.

———, and Katherine E. Kelly. "The Playwright and the Professors: An Interview with Tom Stoppard." *South Central Review* 11, no. 4 (winter 1994): 1–14.

Edwardes, Jane. "Head Case." *Time Out*, 31 Mar.–7 Apr. 1993, 14–15.

———. Review of *Indian Ink*. *Time Out*, 8 Mar. 1995. In *London Theatre Record* 15, no. 5 (1995): 253.

Eichelbaum, Stanley. "So Often Produced, He Ranks with Shaw." *San Francisco Examiner*, 28 Mar. 1977. In *Tom Stoppard in Conversation*, edited by Paul Delaney, 103–6. Ann Arbor: University of Michigan Press, 1993.

Emmet, Alfred. "Followthrough: *Rosencrantz* in Embryo." *Theatre Quarterly* 5 (Mar.–May 1975): 95–96.

Ensor, Patrick. "An Actor at the Sheepdog Trials." *Guardian*, 12 Nov. 1982, 9.

Fleming, John. "A Talk with Tom Stoppard." *Theatre Insight* 10 (Dec. 1993): 19–27.

———."Tom Stoppard: His life and Career before *Rosencrantz and Guildenstern*." *Library Chronicle* 26, no. 3 (fall 1996): 111–61.

Franks, Alan. "Unstoppered." *Times Magazine*, 16 Apr. 1994, 8–10.

Freedman, Samuel G. "Stoppard Debates the Role of the Writer." *New York Times*, 20 Feb. 1984, C13.

Funke, Lewis. "Tom Stoppard." In *Playwrights Talk About Writing: 12 Interviews with Lewis Funke*, 217–32. Chicago: Dramatic Publishing, 1975. (Interview conducted in 1968.)

Gabbard, Lucinda. "Stoppard's *Jumpers*: A Mystery Play." *Modern Drama* 20 (Mar. 1977). In *Tom Stoppard: A Casebook*, edited by John Harty III, 139–52. New York: Garland, 1988.

Gaskell, Philip. "Stoppard, *Travesties*, 1974." *From Writer to Reader: Studies in Editorial Method*, 245–62. Oxford: Clarendon Press, 1978.

Gianakaris, C. J. "Absurdism Altered: *Rosencrantz and Guildenstern Are Dead*." *Drama Survey* 7 (winter 1968): 52–58.

Gitlin, Todd. "Postmodernism: Roots and Politics." In *Cultural Politics in America*, edited by Ian Angus and Sut Jhally, 347–60. New York: Routledge, 1989.

Glover, Michael. "Theatre: Housman." *Independent*, 27 Sept. 1997, 30.

Gollob, David, and David Roper. "Trad Tom Pops In." *Gambit* 10, no. 37 (summer 1981). In *Tom Stoppard in Conversation*, edited by Paul Delaney, 150–66. Ann Arbor: University of Michigan Press, 1993.

Gordon, Giles. "Tom Stoppard." *Transatlantic Review* 29 (summer 1968). In *Tom Stoppard in Conversation*, edited by Paul Delaney, 15–23. Ann Arbor: University of Michigan Press, 1993.

Goreau, Angeline. "Is *The Real Inspector Hound* a Shaggy Dog Story?" *New York Times*, 9 Aug. 1992. In *Tom Stoppard in Conversation*, edited by Paul Delaney, 256–60. Ann Arbor: University of Michigan Press, 1993.

Gorfinkle, Constance. "Stoppard: A Gamesman Turns to Human Concerns." *Patriot Ledger* (Boston), 29 Nov. 1983, 13.

Gritten, David. "Damned Allusive Pimpernel." *Evening Standard,* 19 May 1984, 29.

Gruber, William. "Artistic Design in *Rosencrantz and Guildenstern Are Dead.*" *Comparative Drama* 15, no. 4 (winter 1981–82). In *Tom Stoppard,* edited by Harold Bloom, 101–17. New York: Chelsea House, 1986.

Guppy, Shusha. "Tom Stoppard: The Art of Theater VII." *Paris Review* 109 (winter 1988). In *Tom Stoppard in Conversation,* edited by Paul Delaney, 177–92. Ann Arbor: University of Michigan Press, 1993.

Gussow, Mel. "So Rude, So Complex, So Like Oneself." *New York Times,* 13 Jan. 1998, sec. E, p. 1.

———. "Wits in Hamlet's Wings." 23 Dec. 1995. [Source: G.D. 18.1]

Halton, Kathleen. "Tom Stoppard." *Vogue,* 15 Oct. 1967, 112.

Hardin, Nancy Shields. "An Interview with Tom Stoppard." *Contemporary Literature* 2 (spring 1981): 153–66. (Interview conducted in Apr. 1979.)

Hawkes, Nigel. "Plotting the Course of a Playwright." *Times* (London), 13 Apr. 1993. In *Tom Stoppard in Conversation,* edited by Paul Delaney, 265–69. Ann Arbor: University of Michigan Press, 1993.

Hayman, Ronald. "Double Acts: Tom Stoppard and Peter Wood." *Sunday Times Magazine,* 2 Mar. 1980. In *Tom Stoppard in Conversation,* edited by Paul Delaney, 145–49. Ann Arbor: University of Michigan Press, 1993.

———. "Peter Wood: A Partnership." *Times* (London), 8 June 1974, 9.

Hebert, Hugh. "A Playwright in Undiscovered Country." *Guardian,* 7 July 1979. In *Tom Stoppard in Conversation,* edited by Paul Delaney, 125–28. Ann Arbor: University of Michigan Press, 1993.

Hedgepeth, William. "Playwright Tom Stoppard: 'Go Home, British Boy Genius!'" *Look* 31 (26 Dec. 1967): 92–96.

Hickling, Alfred. "A Clever Play on Words." *Yorkshire Post,* 26 Nov. 1993, 15.

Highfield, Roger. "Stoppard Solves the Problem." *Daily Telegraph,* 15 Apr. 1993, 11.

Hill, Holly. "Stoppard Still Accelerating." *Times* (London), 16 Feb. 1984, 9.

Hill, Tobias. "The Arts." *Sunday Telegraph,* 28 Sept. 1997, 11.

Hobson, Harold. "A Fearful Summons." *Sunday Times,* 16 Apr. 1967, 49.

———. "*Jumpers.*" *Sunday Times,* 28 Feb. 1974, 25.

Huckerby, Martin. "KGB to Blame in the End." *Times* (London), 17 Aug. 1978. In *Tom Stoppard in Conversation,* edited by Paul Delaney, 113–14. Ann Arbor: University of Michigan Press, 1993.

Hudson, Roger, Catherine Itzin, and Simon Trussler. "Ambushes for the Audience: Towards a High Comedy of Ideas." *Theatre Quarterly* 4, no. 14 (May 1974). In *Tom Stoppard in Conversation,* edited by Paul Delaney, 51–72. Ann Arbor: University of Michigan Press, 1993.

Huston, J. Dennis. "'Misreading' *Hamlet:* Problems of Perspective in *Rosencrantz and Guildenstern Are Dead.*" In *Tom Stoppard: A Casebook,* edited by John Harty III, 47–66. New York: Garland, 1988.

Ickes, Bob. "Surely You're Joking, Mr. Stoppard." *New York,* 9 Jan. 1995, 36–39.

James, Clive. "Count Zero Splits the Infinite." *Encounter* 45 (Nov. 1975). In *Critical Essays on Tom Stoppard,* edited by Anthony Jenkins, 27–34. Boston: G. K. Hall, 1990.

Jones, Peter. "Aphrodite in All Her Guises." *Daily Telegraph,* 8 Oct. 1997, 24.

Kane, Robert. "What Is Worth Believing?" *Texas Alcalde,* Sept./Oct. 1997, 20–24.

Kerensky, Oleg. "Tom Stoppard." *The New British Drama: Fourteen Playwrights since Osborne and Pinter.* New York: Taplinger, 1977. In *Tom Stoppard in Conversation,* edited by Paul Delaney, 85–88. Ann Arbor: University of Michigan Press, 1993.

Knight, John. "Saturday Night, Sunday Morning." *Sunday Mirror,* 18 Dec. 1966, 13.

Kuurman, Joost. "An Interview with Tom Stoppard." *Dutch Quarterly Review of Anglo-American Letters* 10 (1980–81): 41–57.

Lawson, Mark. "Tomcat's New Tale." *Independent Magazine.* 10 Apr. 1993, 20–24.

Levin, Bernard, "Theatre: Tom Stoppard's African Journey." *Sunday Times,* 12 Nov. 1978, 37.

Lewis, Peter. "How Tom Went to Work on an Absent Mind and Picked Up £20,000." *London Daily Mail,* 24 May 1967, 6.

———. "Quantum Stoppard." *Observer Magazine,* 6 Mar. 1988, 58–59.

———. "Tom's Gallimaufry." *Sunday Times,* 12 Sept. 1993, 14.

Louis, Patricia. "See the Father. See the Baby." *New York Times,* 24 Mar. 1968, D3.

McCulloch, Joseph. "Dialogue with Tom Stoppard" [20 Mar. 1973]. In *Under Bow Bells: Dialogues with Joseph McCulloch.* London: Sheldon Press, 1974. In *Tom Stoppard in Conversation,* edited by Paul Delaney, 38–45. Ann Arbor: University of Michigan Press, 1993.

Marowitz, Charles. "Tom Stoppard—the Theater's Intellectual P. T. Barnum." *New York Times,* 19 Oct. 1975, sec. 2, 1, 5.

Maves, C. E. "A Playwright on the Side of Rationality." *Palo Alto Times,* 25 Mar. 1977. In *Tom Stoppard in Conversation,* edited by Paul Delaney, 100–102. Ann Arbor: University of Michigan Press, 1993.

May, Clifford D., and Edward Behr. "Master of the Stage." *Newsweek,* 15 Aug. 1977, 35–40.

Mayne, Richard. "Arts Commentary." Transcript of interview broadcast on BBC Radio Three, 10 Nov. 1972. In *Tom Stoppard in Conversation,* edited by Paul Delaney, 33–37. Ann Arbor: University of Michigan Press, 1993.

Mortimer, Penelope. "Tom Stoppard: Funny, Fast Talking and Our First Playwright." [British] *Cosmopolitan.* Jan. 1978, 30–31, 39.

Nathan, David. "In a Country Garden (If It Is a Garden)." *Sunday Telegraph,* 28

Mar. 1993. In *Tom Stoppard in Conversation,* edited by Paul Delaney, 261–64. Ann Arbor: University of Michigan Press, 1993.

Nightingale, Benedict. "Arts & Entertainment: Debriefing." *New Statesman* 96 (17 Nov. 1978): 671–72.

———. "January." *Fifth Row Center* (n.d.): 136–43. [Source: G.D. 18.1]

Owen, Michael. "Stoppard and the Nearly Man." *Evening Standard,* 17 May 1991, 24–25.

Paton, Maureen. Review of *Indian Ink. Daily Express,* 28 Feb. 1995. In *London Theatre Record* 15, no. 5 (1995): 248.

Peter, John. Review of *Indian Ink. Sunday Times,* 5 Mar. 1995. In *London Theatre Record* 15, no. 5 (1995): 249.

———. Review of *The Invention of Love. Sunday Times,* 5 Oct. 1997. In *London Theatre Record* 17, no. 20 (1997): 1257.

Porusch, David. "Making Chaos: Two Views of a New Science." *New England Review and Bread Loaf Quarterly* 12, no. 4 (summer 1990): 427–42.

Rees, Jaspar. "R and G Are Alive and Well: TS Is Rather More Guarded." *Independent Weekend,* 2 Dec. 1995, 3.

Reynolds, Gillian. "Tom's Sound Affects." *Daily Telegraph,* 20 Apr. 1991. In *Tom Stoppard in Conversation,* edited by Paul Delaney, 248–51. Ann Arbor: University of Michigan Press, 1993.

Robinson, Gabrielle Scott. "Nothing Left but Parody: Friedrich Durrenmatt and Tom Stoppard." *Theatre Journal* 32 (Mar. 1980). In *Tom Stoppard: A Casebook,* edited by John Harty III, 121–38. New York: Garland, 1988.

———. "Plays without Plot: The Theatre of Tom Stoppard." *Educational Theatre Journal* 29 (Mar. 1977). In *Tom Stoppard: A Casebook,* edited by John Harty III, 67–87. New York: Garland, 1988.

Sarler, Carol. "Thoroughly Modern Memsahib." *Radio Times,* 20–26 Apr. 1991, 19, 22.

Scaffidi, Richard. "Tom Stoppard: Playwright Turns Movie Director." *Drama-Logue,* 28 Feb.–6 Mar. 1991, 4.

Schiff, Stephen. "Full Stoppard." *Vanity Fair* 52, no. 5 (May 1989). In *Tom Stoppard in Conversation,* edited by Paul Delaney, 212–24. Ann Arbor: University of Michigan Press, 1993.

Schlueter, June. "Moon and Birdboot, Rosencrantz and Guildenstern." *Metafictional Characters in Modern Drama.* New York: Columbia University Press, 1977. In *Tom Stoppard,* edited by Harold Bloom, 75–86. New York: Chelsea House, 1986.

Shepard, Richard. "Hamlet's Chums Develop a Certain Affinity." *New York Times,* 23 Oct. 1967, 55.

Shulman, Martin. "The Politicizing of Tom Stoppard." *New York Times,* 23 Apr.

1978. In *Tom Stoppard in Conversation*, edited by Paul Delaney, 107–12. Ann Arbor: University of Michigan Press, 1993.

Smith, Neil. Review of *Indian Ink*. *What's On*, 3 Mar. 1995. In *London Theatre Record* 15, no. 5 (1995): 253.

Smith, Sid. "Script Jockey: The Flickering Images of Theatre." *Theatre Magazine*, no. 1 (Apr. 1991). In *Tom Stoppard in Conversation*, edited by Paul Delaney, 235–38. Ann Arbor: University of Michigan Press, 1993.

Spencer, Charles. "Stoppard, Master of the Play on Words." *Daily Telegraph*, 8 Sept. 1993, "Arts" section.

Sullivan, Dan. "Young British Playwright Here for Rehearsal of *Rosencrantz*." *New York Times*, 29 Aug. 1967, 27.

Tallmer, Jerry. "Tom Stoppard Pops In on the Cast." *New York Post*, 26 Aug. 1972, 15.

Taylor, John Russell. "Our Changing Theatre, No. 3: Changes in Writing." Recorded 12 Oct. 1970. Broadcast on BBC Radio Four, 23 Nov. 1970. In *Tom Stoppard in Conversation*, edited by Paul Delaney, 24–29. Ann Arbor: University of Michigan Press, 1993.

Thomson, Leslie. "'The Curve Itself' in *Jumpers*." *Modern Drama* 33, no. 4 (Dec. 1990): 470–85.

Twisk, Russell. "Stoppard Basks in a Late Indian Summer." *Observer*, 21 Apr. 1991. In *Tom Stoppard in Conversation*, edited by Paul Delaney, 252–55. Ann Arbor: University of Michigan Press, 1993.

Tynan, Kenneth. "Withdrawing with Style from the Chaos." *Show People: Profiles in Entertainment*, 44–123. New York: Simon and Schuster, 1979.

Vanden Heuvel, Michael. "The Politics of the Paradigm: A Case Study in Chaos Theory." *New Theatre Quarterly*, 9, no. 35 (Aug. 1993): 255–66.

Wandor, Michelene. "Travesties." *Spare Rib* 38 (Aug. 1975): 42

Wardle, Irving. "Shakespeare as Folklore." In National Theatre program for *Rosencrantz and Guildenstern Are Dead*, 11 Apr. 1967.

———. "An Essay in Intellectual Impotence." *Times* (London), 22 Sept. 1976, 15.

Watts, Janet. "Stoppard's Half-Century." *Observer*, 28 June 1987, 17.

———. "Tom Stoppard." *Guardian*, 21 Mar. 1973. In *Tom Stoppard in Conversation*, edited by Paul Delaney, 46–50. Ann Arbor: University of Michigan Press, 1993.

Weightman, John. "Theatre: Art versus Life." *Encounter* 43 (Sept. 1974): 57–59.

Weiner, Bernard. "A Puzzling, 'Traditional' Stoppard." *San Francisco Chronicle*, 29 Mar. 1977, 40.

Wetzsteon, Ross. "Tom Stoppard Eats Steak Tartare with Chocolate Sauce." *Village Voice*, 10 Nov. 1975. In *Tom Stoppard in Conversation*, edited by Paul Delaney, 80–84. Ann Arbor: University of Michigan Press, 1993.

Zeifman, Hersh. "A Trick of the Light: Tom Stoppard's *Hapgood* and Postabsurdist Theatre." In *Around the Absurd: Essays on Modern and Postmodern Drama*, ed-

ited by Enoch Brater and Ruby Cohn, 175–201. Ann Arbor: University of
Michigan Press, 1990.

Zoglin, Richard. "Ayckbourn's Conquest." *Time,* 28 Aug. 2000, 60.

Other Sources

Stoppard, Tom. Letter to the author. 20 May 1996.

———. National Theatre prompt script for *Rosencrantz and Guildenstern Are
Dead,* 1967 production. National Theatre Archives, London.

———. *Rosencrantz and Guildenstern Are Dead.* Text for 1967 Broadway production at Alvin Theatre. Billy Rose Theater Collection at Lincoln Center Library,
New York.

———. National Theatre prompt scripts for *Jumpers,* 1972 production and 1976
production. National Theatre Archives, London.

———. Royal Shakespeare Company prompt scripts for *Travesties,* 1974 production and 1993 production. Royal Shakespeare Company Archives, Stratford-
on-Avon.